Tear Off the Masks!

Tear Off the Masks!

IDENTITY AND IMPOSTURE
IN TWENTIETH-CENTURY RUSSIA

Sheila Fitzpatrick

PRINCETON UNIVERSITY PRESS
PRINCETON AND OXFORD

Copyright © 2005 by Princeton University Press
Published by Princeton University Press, 41 William Street,
Princeton, New Jersey 08540
In the United Kingdom: Princeton University Press,
3 Market Place, Woodstock, Oxfordshire OX20 1SY

LIBRARY OF CONGRESS CATALOGING-IN-PUBLICATION DATA

Fitzpatrick, Sheila.
Tear off the masks! : identity and imposture in twentieth-century Russia /
by Shelia Fitzpatrick.
    p.   cm.
Includes bibliographical references and index.
ISBN 0-691-11353-X (alk. paper)—ISBN 0-691-12245-8 (pbk. : alk. paper)
1. Group identity—Soviet Union. 2. Social classes—Soviet Union. 3. Group
identity—Russia (Federation) 4. Social classes—Russia (Federation) I. Title.
HN523.F58 2005
305′.0947′0904—dc22   2004058652

British Library Cataloging-in-Publication Data is available.

This book has been composed in Sabon

Printed on acid-free paper. ∞

pup.princeton.edu

Printed in the United States of America

10 9 8 7 6 5 4 3 2 1

In memory of Michael Danos

Table of Contents

Illustrations

Preface and Acknowledgments

Many of the essays in this book have been published before in some form. The exceptions are chapter 1 ("Introduction: Becoming Soviet"), chapter 12 ("Wives' Tales"), and chapter 15 ("Afterword: Becoming Post-Soviet"), which are published here for the first time. The original versions of some chapters go back to the early 1990s, since which time a fair amount of relevant publication has appeared. In the newly written chapters, I have addressed and cited recent publications. In editing chapters written earlier, however, I have generally not added citations of work that appeared after the original writing or was unknown to me at the time of writing, since this might compromise the integrity of the argument. Exceptions to this rule are citations of dissertations that subsequently appeared as books and unpublished articles and papers that now exist in published form.

Like most books written over time, this one contains some evolution of perspective, interpretation, and data base; readers may therefore find it interesting to note the dates of the articles and papers that formed the basis of various chapters. Information on the publication history of earlier versions and parts of chapters is given at the beginning of each chapter.

Permission to republish articles is gratefully acknowledged from the following: Oxford University Press for "The Bolshevik Invention of Class: Marxist Theory and the Making of 'Class Consciousness' in Soviet Society," in Ronald Suny, ed., *The Structure of Soviet History* (New York, 2002).

Indiana University Press for "The Problem of Class Identity in NEP Society," in *Russia in the Era of NEP*, eds. Sheila Fitzpatrick, Alexander Rabinowitch, and Richard Stites (Bloomington, Ind., 1991).

University of Chicago Press for "Ascribing Class: The Construction of Social Identity in Soviet Russia," *Journal of Modern History* 65:4 (1993), and "Signals from Below: Soviet Letters of Denunciation of the 1930s," from *Journal of Modern History* 68:4 (1996).

Institut d'études slaves, Paris, for "Lives under Fire: Autobiographical Narratives and their Challenges in Stalin's Russia," published in *De Russie et d'ailleurs. Mélanges Marc Ferro* (Paris, 1995).

Fondation Maison des Sciences de l'Homme for "The Two Faces of Anastasia: Narratives and Counter-Narratives of Identity in Stalinist Everyday Life," in Berthold Unfried, Irene Herrman, and Brigitte Studer, eds., *Parler de soi sous Staline. La construction identitaire dans le communisme des années trentes* (Paris, 2002).

Charles Schlacks Jr., publisher, for introduction to publication in "From *Krest'ianskaia gazeta*'s Files: Life Story of a Peasant Striver," *Russian History* 24: 1–2 (1997).

Princeton University Press for revised version of introduction ("Lives and Times") to *In the Shadow of Revolution: Life Stories of Russian Women from 1917 to the Second World War*, eds. Sheila Fitzpatrick and Yuri Slezkine (Princeton, N.J., 2000), pp. 3–17—chapter 8.

Slavic Review for revised version of "Supplicants and Citizens: Public Letter-Writing in Soviet Russia in the 1930s," *Slavic Review* 55:1 (Spring 1996), and for "The World of Ostap Bender: Soviet Confidence Men in the Stalin Period," *Slavic Review* 61:3 (2002), an expanded and divided version of which appears as chapters 13 and 14.

Historisches Kolleg and R. Oldenbourg Verlag (Munich) for "Intelligentsia and Power: Client-Patron Relations in Stalin's Russia," in Manfred Hildermeier, ed., *Stalinismus vor dem Zweiten Weltkrieg. Neue Ansätze der Forschung/Stalinism before World War II. New Lines of Research* (Munich, 1998).

• • •

Many people have helped in the thinking that went into this book, but as it occurred over a fairly long period it is more difficult than usual to single out particular individuals for mention. In the first stage of the book's preparation, my husband Michael Danos, who died in August 1999, was my main and irreplaceable interlocutor. Throughout the process, I bounced many of the ideas off my graduate students at Chicago. Katerina Clark, Ron Suny, Leora Auslander, and Catriona Kelly provided encouragement, both personal and intellectual, and stimulating criticism. It was a pleasure to work with my editor at Princeton University Press, Brigitta van Rheinberg. In the final stage of writing, the unexpected bonus of a Distinguished Achievement Award from the Mellon Foundation released me from some teaching obligations and thus facilitated the work. I am grateful to Benjamin Zajicek and Heidy Berthoud for research assistance on the new chapters, and to June Farris, Bibliographer for Slavic and East European Studies at the University of Chicago, for her unfailing help in locating materials.

Note on Transliteration

To make it easier for the reader, I have used standard anglicizations of familiar names like Trotsky and Gorky and dropped the extra "i" that strict transliteration would require in names like Maria and Evgenia. Otherwise I have followed the Library of Congress's transliteration rules, except that in the text (though not the footnotes) I have not used diacritical marks for proper names and place names.

Introduction

Figure 1. Cartoon by Osbert Lancaster, *Daily Express*, 18 July 1941, p. 4.

CHAPTER ONE

Becoming Soviet

Tear off the masks! is a slogan with only limited appeal in most societies, since they operate on the assumption that civilization requires a certain amount of masking. In revolutions, however, that assumption is suspended. Successful revolutions tear off masks: that is, they invalidate the conventions of self-presentation and social interaction that obtained in pre-revolutionary society. This happened in Russia after the October 1917 revolution which laid the foundations for the Soviet state. It happened again in 1991, when that state collapsed. In such upheavals, people have to reinvent themselves, to create or find within themselves personae that fit the new postrevolutionary society. The process of reinvention is at once a process of reconfiguration (a new arrangement of data about oneself) and one of discovery (a new interpretation of their significance). It always involves strategic decisions (how should I present myself in this new world?) and may also prompt ontological reflection (who am I really?). Those who are engaged in self-reinvention generally prefer not to discuss what they are doing, claiming instead that in their hearts they were always the new Soviet (post-Soviet) persons that they are now trying to become.

Yet in revolution, even as the millions of people that comprise the society are necessarily engaged in self-reinvention, the revolutionary militants tend to be obsessed with authenticity and transparency. They hunt for "double-dealers" who are trying to hide their true identity, for "careerists" and "accomodators" who have assumed a revolutionary persona for purposes of gain, in order to "unmask" them. In the first two decades after 1917, "vigilance" in identifying and exposing such enemies of the revolutionary was one of the cardinal virtues of a Communist. Purges (*chistki*) periodically conducted in the Communist Party and government and educational institutions served the same purpose of rooting out hidden enemies in the 1920s and '30s. Half a century later, post-Soviet Russia eschewed the path of purging and loyalty checks. Yet, as political scientist

Sections of this chapter draw on my article "Making a Self for the Times: Impersonation and Imposture in Twentieth-Century Russia," *Kritika* 2:3 (Summer 2001). I am grateful to Leora Auslander, Katerina Clark, Ronald Suny, Yuri Slezkine, Catriona Kelly, and members of the University of Chicago's Russian Studies Workshop for perceptive critiques of earlier versions of the chapter.

Michael Urban observed, the first phase of the transition in post-Soviet Russia—when almost everyone in politics had formerly been a Communist–was riven by constant accusations that some politician or other was still "really" a Communist, or unreconstructed Soviet man at heart. Urban interpreted this as a way for the accusers to give credibility to their own new personae as post-Soviet democrats,[1] which, *mutatis mutandis*, may have some validity for the earlier revolutionary period as well.

This is a book about the remaking of identities in a society cast into turmoil by revolution. What I am investigating is how individuals who find themselves in such situations deal with the question of identity—basically, how they construct new personae to suit the new circumstances of life, and how those new personae are for some considerable time uncertain, vulnerable to challenge. I am also interested in the social consequences: what social practices (purging, self-criticism, denunciation) and mentalites (suspicion, identity anxieties) develop in a situation where the individuals are busy reinventing themselves and defending their newly invented selves, and moreover are aware that their neighbors are similarly engaged. My inquiry differs from many of the "identity" studies published in recent years in that it is primarily concerned with identity at the individual, not national or group, level. Once the focus is on individuals, it is immediately clear that imposture is a necessary part of the study of identity. The impostor is one who has assumed or claimed an identity to which he or she is not entitled. In a revolutionary situation, it is extremely important to unmask the impostors who are falsely claiming revolutionary identity. Yet at the same time, imposture as a practice is uncomfortably close to the more benign practices of self-fashioning or impersonation that the revolution demands of all citizens.[2] How this difficulty was handled, and how the two were distinguished in everyday life, is one of the subjects of this book.

The identity issue in early Soviet Russia focussed strongly on social class. The Bolsheviks had taken power in the name of the proletariat, and they assumed that proletarians were the people likely to support Soviet power and the "bourgeois" (which in the usage of the 1920s often encompassed membership of any privileged group under the old regime, including the service and landowning nobility) to oppose it. This led to a certain amount of circular thinking, whereby those who supported the revolution tended to be regarded as "proletarian" and those who opposed it to be labeled "bourgeois." Nevertheless, the new rulers were sufficiently serious about class to undertake major statistical analyses of the class structure

---

[1] Michael Urban, "The Politics of Identity in Russia's Postcommunist Transition: The Nation against Itself," *Slavic Review* 53:3 (1994), p. 747.

[2] For more discussion and definition of "impersonation," see below, pp. 18–19.

of the population and of various institutions in the 1920s, and also to put in place policies discriminating against "class enemies" (that is, people who were by definition enemies because of their membership of a particular social class) and providing affirmative action (the Russian term was *vydvizhenie*, which literally means promotion) for those whose class position made them natural allies of the revolution.

"Class," alas, turned out to be an ambiguous category. It was less easily identifiable to the eye than race or gender and less readily assessed on the basis of native language and last name than ethnicity (*national'nost'* or "nationality" in Soviet terminology). Class was, of course, associated with social position—but in the Revolution, and indeed as a result of it, many people's social position and occupation had changed. That left manners—that is, forms of self-presentation that had been learned and could be unlearned—and biography as possible markers of class identity. The last turned out to be key in Soviet determination of an individual's class. Recounting of one's autobiography, challenges to the account from others, and defense of it became standard Soviet practice in a variety of situations, including purging and "self-criticism" sessions; moreover, all personal files contained a narrative autobiography and a questionnaire designed to elicit both an individual's political and occupational history and (in detail) the nature of his or her class position, including changes over time. Given the existence of legal and administrative structures that discriminated on the basis of class, it was obviously in the interest of individuals to compose an autobiography that concealed "bad" class backgrounds and presented backgrounds that were ambiguous in class terms in the most favorable possible light. Such practices of concealment and editing—inextricably linked with the broader self-reinvention required by the Revolution—became second nature to Soviet citizens, as did the counterpractices of unmasking and denunciation.

This book is a study of individual practices of identity in Soviet Russia. It does not deal with state practices of identity-molding via propaganda, the media, and educational institutions, or with peer-group socialization in schools and Pioneer and Komsomol organizations, though these are topics of interest in their own right. Nor does it say much about intellectual debates about identity or individual soul-searching of a philosophical kind. I would have been happy to include debates and soul-searching had I found them, but in fact both are surprisingly rare. The Communist Party and Soviet government made policies on such matters as class discrimination but did so almost without debate (where it existed, I have noted it) or theoretical exegesis. This silence of the Russian Revolution on key issues of social practice may be contrasted with the passionate debates and deeply felt theorizing of the French Revolution on such topics as denunciation. With regard to individual philosophical soul-searching about identity, here, too, we encounter a notable silence. Judging by diaries and memoirs, Soviet citizens worried pragmatically about presentation of identity and might also work conscientiously on developing a "Soviet" persona, but they rarely seem to have asked metaphysical questions about essences (who am I in this boundless universe?). This may be related to the unusual stresses of living in the Soviet Union in the 1920s and '30s, which tended to produce the kinds of behavior seen in societies in wartime. Living under a political regime that was constantly directing and often punishing its citizens, people developed a sense of fatalism that may, paradoxically, have freed them of some of the neuroses and anxieties that flourished in the capitalist West at the same period.[3]

HISTORIOGRAPHICAL NOTE

This book is written by a social historian who began publishing in the 1970s. Its subject matter, however, has been associated more with cultural than with social historians in the Soviet field, particularly with the young cohort of mainly Foucauldian cultural historians that arrived on the scene in the second half of the 1990s and pioneered the study of "Soviet subjectivity."[4] This combination of author and subject matter may initially be confusing for some readers—not (for once) the readers who are ignorant of the field, but rather those who know it well. It is important, therefore, to make clear from the outset that this is neither an attack on the Foucauldian "Soviet subjectivity" school nor a contribution to it, but something different. The best way I can explain what that "something different" is and how I came to engage in it is to offer a brief excursion into intellectual autobiography. Readers who are not Soviet historians are welcome to skip this section.

As a social historian, I have a long history of dissatisfaction with class as an analytical category for Soviet society and of impatience with Soviet and Western Marxist discussions of "class consciousness," particularly proletarian consciousness, in a Soviet context.[5] The Russian workers

---

[3] On Soviet fatalism, see Sheila Fitzpatrick, *Everyday Stalinism: Ordinary Life in Extraordinary Times: Soviet Russia in the 1930s* (New York, 1999), pp. 218–22.

[4] For an introduction to this field, see the "Soviet Subjectivity" issue of *Russian Review* 60:3 (2001), pp. 307–59, containing articles by Eric Naiman ("On Soviet Subjects and the Scholars Who Make Them"), Igal Halfin ("Looking into Oppositionists' Souls: Inquisition Communist Style"), and Jochen Hellbeck ("Working, Struggling, Becoming: Stalin-Era Autobiographical Texts").

[5] See, for example, my "The Bolsheviks' Dilemma: Class, Culture and Politics in the Early Soviet Years," originally published in *Slavic Review* 47:4 (1988), and "Reply to Suny and Orlovsky" (commentators on "The Bolsheviks' Dilemma") in *ibid.*

whose story I knew best, though lauded as "conscious" by Soviet commentators, were primarily interested in getting themselves and their children out of the working class, something that Soviet affirmative action policies on behalf of proletarians and poor peasants made easy to accomplish in the first fifteen years after the Revolution.[6] Social historians in the Soviet Union were, of course, required to use Marxist class categories in their analysis and did so in an exceptionally static, reified manner. As Western social history of the Soviet Union emerged in the 1970s, I argued against the tendency to take class at face value and focus on what I saw as Marxist scholastic questions (whether Russian workers *really* had proletarian class consciousness; whether the peasants whom the Bolsheviks called "kulaks," meaning rural exploiters, were *really* kulaks or just "middle peasants").[7]

In the late 1980s, however, I began to take class seriously myself. This was not because I had become converted to the Marxist analytical framework but rather because I had suddenly realized what may seem obvious: that class was a matter of classification.[8] The reason to take class seriously was because *class classification* was a very serious activity in Soviet society. This had nothing to do with the actual social structure but everything to do with individual fate and opportunity. To me, debates about whether peasants were "really kulaks" or urban dwellers "really proletarian" might seem scholastic, but to millions of individuals the real-life outcome of such deliberations was crucial. To be labeled a kulak meant ruin: you were liable to expropriation and deportation. To be labeled a proletarian meant you could become one of the bosses instead of being a mere hired hand, and the road was open for your children—and even yourself—to get higher education and rise into the white-collar professional class.

That revelation lay at the root of a series of articles published in the early 1990s in which I explored the Bolshevik practices of class labeling and class discrimination and the social practices of masking and unmasking of class identities to which they gave rise. These were the years in which hitherto closed Soviet archives opened. Of all the archival discov-

---

[6] See my *Education and Social Mobility* and "Stalin and Making of New Elite," in *The Cultural Front*.

[7] See, for example, Fitzpatrick, "New Perspectives on Stalinism" and "Afterword: Revisionism Revisited," in *Russian Review* 45:4 (1986), pp. 357–73 and 409–13; and commentaries on "New Perspectives, in *Russian Review*, 45:4 (1986), pp. 375–408, and *Russian Review* 46:4 (1987), pp. 379–431.

[8] This may have been, as Ron Suny has suggested to me, a response, albeit from afar, to the famous "linguistic turn" among Marxist social historians, stimulated by the new attention paid to language and perception in works like Gareth Stedman Jones's *Languages of Class: Studies in English Working Class History, 1832–1982* (Cambridge, 1983). Certainly I found more in common with Marxist historians after the turn than before.

eries of those years, the one that most interested me was the huge mounds of letters to the authorities from individual citizens. Initially, I was particularly interested in denunciations, which in the 1920s and 1930s were often attempts to discredit the class self-presentation of others. Later, my interest broadened to petitions and appeals, which involve authorial self-presentation (in the 1920s and '30s, often including a claim to a "good" class identity). Such identity claims necessarily involved the telling of life-stories, so I became interested in them as well.

As it happened, my social historian's trajectory had landed me in territory that was simultaneously being colonized by the young cultural historians of the "Soviet subjectivity" school.[9] The dissimilarities between us are obvious. They are interested in discourse and ideology and have a strong theoretical orientation; I am interested in social practice and the everyday and have a low tolerance for totalizing theory, including Marxist and Foucauldian (though sharing with Marx an ingrained suspicion of ideology as false consciousness). Their focus is on the self and subjecthood;[10] mine on identity and identification. For me, however, differ-

---

[9] Important works in this genre include Jochen Hellbeck, "Fashioning the Stalinist Soul: The Diary of Stepan Podlubnyi, 1931–39," in Sheila Fitzpatrick, ed., *Stalinism: New Directions* (London: 2000) and idem., "Self-Realization in the Stalinist System: Two Soviet Diaries of the 1930s," in David L. Hoffmann and Yanni Kotsonis, eds., *Russian Modernity: Politics, Knowledge, Practices* (Basingstoke, Hampshire, U.K., 2000); Igal Halfin, *From Darkness to Light: Class Consciousness and Salvation in Revolutionary Russia* (Pittsburgh, 2000), and *Terror in My Soul: Communist Autobiographies on Trial* (Cambridge, Mass., 2003); Oleg V. Kharkhordin, *The Collective and the Individual in Russia: A Study of Practices* (Berkeley, 1999); Amir Weiner, *Making Sense of War: The Second World War and the Fate of the Bolshevik Revolution* (Princeton, 2001); Anna Krylova, "Soviet Modernity in Life and Fiction: The Generation of the 'New Soviet People' in the 1930s," PhD. diss., Johns Hopkins University, 2000. A seminal work for all these authors was Stephen Kotkin's *Magnetic Mountain: Stalinism as Civilization* (Berkeley, 1995), though Halfin and Hellbeck have respectfully criticized Kotkin for leaving "the Stalinist *subject* unproblematized" (Igal Halfin and Jochen Hellbeck, "Rethinking the Stalinist Subject: Stephen Kotkin's 'Magnetic Mountain' and the State of Soviet Historical Studies," *Jahrbücher für Geschichte Osteuropas* 44:3 [1996], p. 458).

[10] The argument made by Jochen Hellbeck and others of the "Soviet subjectivity" school that the Revolution was not, as previously thought, primarily repressive of individuals' sense of self but rather productive of it (Hellbeck, "Working, Struggling," p. 341) makes intuitive sense. But, as noted by the *Oxford English Dictionary* in its definition of self as "that which is really and intrinsically he (in contradistinction to what is adventitious)," the concept is "chiefly *Philos[ophical]*," and philosophy is a realm that my kind of historian approaches with caution. In this book, I have tried as much as possible to avoid the term "self" (except in its pronominal and compound usages) in order to avoid invoking either its Foucauldian implications (the "technologies" involved in the "care of the self," which is the subject of vol. 3 of Foucault's *A History of Sexuality*) or the philosopher Charles Taylor's understanding of self as, above all, a moral or ethical orientation, an "orientation to the good" (Charles Taylor, *Sources of the Self: The Making of Modern Identity* [Cambridge, Mass., 1989], pp. 27–33).

ences in historical approach are what makes scholarship interesting. The new cohort's arrival on the scene was a major part of the revitalization of Soviet history in the 1990s. If I were to isolate two aspects of this revitalization that I particularly appreciate, one would be the shift of attention toward experience, and the other the definitive end of the Cold War in Soviet history (the new cohort, unlike its "revisionist" predecessor, did not attack Cold War frameworks directly, but its indifference to them proved more deadly than frontal attack). Fifteen years ago, there was still a lingering sense that "Soviet ideology" was something that the regime force-fed to a population whose atomized members were merely passive consumers. It is a great step forward to have the Stalinist subject emerge as "an ideological agent in its own right."[11]

IDENTITY: DEFINITION AND THEORETICAL FRAMEWORKS

Before proceeding further, we need to address the concept of "identity." This has become a catchword in social science in recent years, much overused and invoked in a confusing multiplicity of meanings.[12] I am interested in social rather than personal identity, by which I mean the way people locate themselves in a social or group context rather than the way they think about themselves as individuals.[13] I use "identity" to mean a self-identification and/or self-understanding constructed with reference to currently accepted categories of social being. There is, of course, a difference between self-identification (a labeling process that may carry only an instrumental purpose) and self-understanding (implying belief that the self is as one understands it). My definition intentionally elides this distinction, since my assumption is that the self-understanding of subjects is accessible to historians only through practices like self-identification. In this book, "identity" is shorthand for the complex revisions of self-identification that were associated with the Russian Revolution.[14]

---

[11] Halfin and Hellbeck, "Rethinking," p. 457.

[12] For a recent critique on these lines, see Rogers Brubaker and Fred Cooper, "Beyond 'identity,'" *Theory and Society* 29 (2000).

[13] This is close to David Laitin's definition of social identities as "labels that people assign to themselves (or that others assign to them) when they claim membership (or are assigned membership) in a social category that they (and others, whether members of that category or not) see as plausibly connected to their history and present set of behaviors": David D. Laitin, *Identity in Formation: The Russian-Speaking Populations in the Near Abroad* (Ithaca, 1998), p. 16. For Rom Harré's definition, see below, p. 11.

[14] Note that I use an expansive definition of "the Russian Revolution" (see Sheila Fitzpatrick, *The Russian Revolution*, 2nd ed. [Oxford and New York, 1994], pp. 2–4): not 1917 alone, but the two decades of upheaval that began in October (or, to be pedantic, November, according to our Western calendar) 1917.

In early Soviet discourse, the closest equivalent of the term "identity" was *litso* (literally, *face*). In its "identity" meaning, however, the term was used almost entirely with two qualifiers: *klassovoe* (class) and *politicheskoe* (political). The class identity (as well as the closely related political identity) had to be made manifest (*vyiavleno*, defined in Ushakov as "exposed, shown in its true colors.")[15] Discussion of identity was closely linked with questions of disguise and concealment, since the Revolution had made certain social and political identities dangerous handicaps and thus fostered concealment. A disguised identity must be "unmasked" (*razoblacheno*),[16] a very common term in early Soviet discourse. Double identity or duplicity (*dvulichie, dvurushnichestvo*), the latter defined as "behavior of a person ostensibly belonging to one group but acting on behalf of the opposing side," was regularly excoriated in the Soviet press.[17]

In the Soviet context, the notion of double identity presupposes misrepresentation of one's real position on a particular axis of identity, the class/political one. But there are actually many possible axes of identity: for example, ethnic/national, familial, confessional, and gender, in addition to social and political. Individuals always have multiple identities, that is, self-identifications that mark their location in the world and relationship to other people. Assuming identities to be the classifications that a person accepts as applicable to him/herself and expects the outside world to recognize in him/her, a single person may simultaneously embrace the identities of, for example, man, worker, Communist, husband/father, Russian.

While self-identifications are grounded in real-life phenomena such as native language, parentage, and occupation, they are also fluid and subject to modification. Modification may be a product of circumstance: for example, when the Soviet Union disappeared as a state at the beginning of the 1990s, "Soviet" suddenly ceased to be a viable identity. It may also be a product of a combination of circumstance and personal choice, as in

---

[15] *Vyiavit'* = "(3) Razoblachit', pokazat' v podlinnom vide": *Tolkovyi slovar' russkogo iazyka*, 4 vols., ed. D. N. Ushakov (Moscow, 1935–40), vol. 1, and see also A. M. Selishchev, *Iazyk revoliutsionnoi epokhi: Iz nabliudenii nad russkim iazykom poslednikh let (1917–1926)* (Moscow, 1928, 2nd ed.), p. 48. For a useful discussion of terms associated with revelation of a true self, see Kharkhordin, *The Collective and the Individual in Russia*, pp. 175–81. With regard to the word *proiavit'*, it seems to me that Kharkhordin exaggerates the frequency of its usage in the 1920s and '30s. Ushakov characterized it in the late 1930s as "bookish" (*knizh.*), in contrast to his description of *vyiavit'* as "new newspaper" language; and the examples he gives of revelation all involve positive qualities ("*Proiavit' geroism, khrabrost'*," etc.). In the discourse of unmasking, *vyiavit'*, not *proiavit'*, played the central role.

[16] See definition in *Tolkovyi slovar' russkogo iazyka*, vol. 3.

[17] *Tolkovyi slovar' russkogo iazyka*, vol. 1: "*Povedenie cheloveka, naruzhno prinadlezhashchego k odnoi gruppe, no deistvuiushchego v pol'zu vrazhdebnoi ei storony (gaz. prezrit.).*"

the case of "noble" (*dvorianin*), a disadvantageous and even disgraceful identity in Soviet times that made a comeback in the 1990s after decades of nonviability. The real-life data upon which identities are constructed can yield very different results according to circumstance and choice: consider, for example, the multiple possibilities of ethnic self-identification available to a Russian-speaker born in Russia with one Jewish and one Ukrainian grandparent. Moreover, the comparative importance to an individual of different types of self-identification (for example: wife, woman, Communist, *intelligentka*, Jew) may change radically in different external circumstances and stages of life.

Most present-day social scientists and philosophers see identities—social, national, confessional, and so on—as "constructed," that is, learned from the surrounding culture rather than innate. Personal identities are the exception: as political scientist David Laitin notes, they are "firmly entrenched in a primordial or generic discourse," so that anyone constructing himself a new name or credit history is generally seen as perpetrating a fraud.[18] All the same, there is no real consensus among scholars on this question: in his work on social psychology, Oxford philosopher Rom Harré argues that personal identities, too, are essentially fashioned by individuals on the basis of cultural norms.[19]

Of course, common sense requires some degree of qualification of the "constructed" view of social identity. As Laitin points out, "social solidarities are built on real foundations" and "people are limited by, [though] they are not prisoners of, their genes, their physiognomies, and their histories in settling on their own identities."[20] If we think of likely Soviet identity projects, it would generally be scarcely feasible for an educated urbanite without rural connections to construct himself an identity as a "poor peasant," but this was a perfectly plausible project for a rural resident whose family, though poor, belonged to the clerical estate or had at one time (though not the present) prospered to the point of being labeled by their enemies as kulaks.

Harré sees two kinds of identity projects: the one dedicated to constructing social identity, which involves identification with a group or category, and the one dedicated to constructing personal identity, whose purpose is to establish a degree of uniqueness within one's category. The first, he argues, is the "primary task" for all "marginal people" who initially lack a clear social location and need to "blend . . . into a background, . . .

---

[18] Laitin, *Identity*, p. 14.

[19] "Our personal being is created by our coming to believe a theory of self based on our society's working conception of a person": Rom Harré, *Personal Being: A Theory for Individual Psychology* (Cambridge, Mass., 1984), p. 26.

[20] Laitin, *Identity*, pp. 20–21.

acquir[e] camouflage," the other for firmly located people—"those who have too much social identity, who have have born into families, classes or nations which provide them with a very detailed mode of social being," whose "problem is to stand out from the crowd," develop a sense of uniqueness.[21] Psychologists, Harré remarks mischievously, have been particularly interested in social identity projects because they are "themselves in one way or another marginal people." But what about revolutionary upheavals, in which destabilization of social identity occurs on a mass scale? Harré's approach seems to me particularly applicable to such conditions. Indeed, it could be argued more broadly that social constructionist approaches to history yield greatest dividends when the largest number of people feel themselves socially unmoored (as in revolution) and experience the greatest need to find a social category to which they can anchor themselves.

Another way of approaching the same issues is to look at the behaviors whereby people project—like actors to an audience—the roles and characters (social and personal identities) they have assumed.[22] This is the leitmotif of Erving Goffman's work, beginning with *The Presentation of Self in Everyday Life* and continuing with *Frame Analysis*, *Stigma*, and other works; and it was Goffman's great contribution to show that such role-playing is not fraudulent but universal, that is, to elaborate Shakespeare's insight that "all the world's a stage."[23] In the words of Robert Ezra Park, quoted by Goffman: "It is probably no mere historical accident that the word person, in its first meaning, is a mask. It is rather a recognition of the fact that everyone is always and everywhere, more or less consciously, playing a role. . . . It is in these roles that we know each other; it is in these roles that we know ourselves. In a sense, and in so far as this mask represents the conception we have formed of ourselves—the roles we are striving to live up to—this mask is our truer self, the self we would like to be. In the end, our conception of our role becomes second nature and an integral part of our personality."[24] Thus, as Goffman stresses, there is no clear line between "cynical" performances—those in which "the individual

[21] Harré, *Personal Being*, p. 23.

[22] Note that the discussion of performance that follows does not draw on notions of performativity, either as formulated in the 1960s by the linguistic philosopher J. L. Austen (which focus on the speech act that does something, as when a priest pronounces a couple man and wife) or as later developed with respect to gender in queer studies, for example, in Andrew Parker and Eve Kosofsky Sedgwick, eds., *Performativity and Performance* (London, 1995).

[23] But note the qualification in Erving Goffman, *The Presentation of Self in Everyday Life* (New York, 1959), p. 254.

[24] Robert Ezra Park, *Race and Culture* (Glencoe, Ill., 1950), p. 249, quoted in Goffman, *Presentation*, pp. 19–20.

has no belief in his own act and no ultimate concern with the beliefs of his audience"—and "sincere" ones, in which the actors "believes in the impression fostered by their own performance."[25] In fact, a performance may start off "cynical" and end up "sincere" (as Park suggests) or vice versa (if something happens to shake the performer's sense that the persona he is projecting is "real").

To be sure, one might add to Goffman's sense of the ubiquity of dramatic self-presentation Harré's qualification: that it is, so to speak, *more* universal for some people, and in some societies, than others; that marginal people do it more (and no doubt are also more interested in it).[26] Revolutionary Russian (Soviet) society, with its pervasive anxiety about class and political identity and rich array of practices of masking and unmasking, is surely a case in point. Self-consciousness about performance was not only widespread among the population but also strayed into official discourse. The theatrical metaphor of masks was ubiquitous in the 1920s and '30s, and the same period saw a flowering of that peculiar form of political theater: the show trial.[27] Theatrical and performance imagery shows up even in such unexpected contexts as the Aesopian discussion of the 1932–33 famine (whose existence was officially denied): in newspapers and bureaucratic documents, peasants were said to be "staging" a famine and "turning on" a hunger strike; beggars to be "passing themselves off as ruined kolkhozniks."[28]

Nor were the performance metaphors always negative. Stalin was interested in the concept of impersonation, the actors's ability to "become" the character he plays.[29] This notion of *becoming* was central to the discourse of socialist realism in the 1930s.[30] If it was the society's task to become socialist, a matter of essential transformation, the individual's task of becoming a cultured man (*kul'turnyi chelovek*) was more a matter of behavior than essence—that is, it was akin to learning a role. It would not be an overstatement to suggest that the ubiquitous exhortations of

[25] Goffman, *Presentation*, p. 18.

[26] Note in this connection that the most interesting recent work on performance in the Soviet field concerns a quintessentially marginal group: Alaina Lemon's *Between Two Fires: Gypsy Performance and Romani Memory from Pushkin to Postsocialism* (Durham, N.C., 2000).

[27] See Julie A. Cassiday, *The Enemy on Trial: Early Soviet Courts on Stage and Screen* (De Kalb, Ill., 2000); Elizabeth A. Wood, "The Trial of Lenin: Legitimizing the Revolution through Political Theater, 1920–23," *Russian Review* 61:2 (2002), pp. 235–48.

[28] See Sheila Fitzpatrick, *Stalin's Peasants: Resistance and Survival in the Russian Village after Collectivization* (New York, 1994), p. 75.

[29] G. Mariamov, *Kremlevskii tsenzor: Stalin smotrit kino* (Moscow, 1992), p. 87. The context is a discussion of theatrical performance with the actor Cherkasov and director Sergei Eisenstein in 1947; the word used was *perevoploshchat'sia*.

[30] See Fitzpatrick, "Becoming Cultured," in *The Cultural Front*.

the 1930s to "study," "learn," and "master culture" were part of a discourse of performance central to prewar Stalinism.

Fashioning of "File-Selves" in Soviet Life[31]

Harré proposes a notion of "file-selves"—that is, the selves or accounts and histories of selves that are documented in bureaucratic files labeled with the person's name—that may help in thinking about Soviet identity issues.[32] Such documents may include curricula vitae, applications for jobs, credit ratings, copies of birth and marriage certificates, and information on criminal records. "Since most file encounters involve some sort of assessment of a person relative to a moral order, the fate of one's file can play an enormously important part in one's life," Harré writes. "Though a person has only one real-self, he or she will be accompanied through life by a flock of file-selves of unknown extent, each member of the flock representing an aspect of a person as defined by the appropriate file-master."[33] This notion applies particularly well to Soviet (and Soviet-type) societies, where, in the words of a Romanian political prisoner, Herbert Zilber, "the first great socialist industry was that of the production of files. . . . In the socialist bloc, people and things exist only through their files. All our existence is in the hands of him who possesses files and is constituted by him who constructs them. Real people are but the reflection of their files."[34]

The making of files was a basic project of the Soviet state from its early years. Social statistics were eagerly collected throughout the 1920s, particularly those illuminating the "social composition" or "class composition" of various institutions and populations. These statistics were in effect a collective portrait of file-selves: what they measured, strictly speaking, was not how many party members were former workers but how many party members' files identified them as such. The purpose of such intensive statistical work may be broadly defined as surveillance and population control, though the overtones of these anachronistic terms can

---

[31] Note that, although the phenomena and processes outlined here are discussed extensively in the chapters that follow, I do not use the concept of "file-selves" in other chapters because I had not encountered it when they were written.

[32] Harré, *Personal Being*, pp. 69–71. Harré's category has recently been vastly broadened by the emergence of Internet "file-selves": that is, the collection of documents—growing vaster by the day—that one obtains by typing in one's name and initiating a search.

[33] Harré, *Personal Being*, p. 70.

[34] Quoted Katherine Verdery, *What was Socialism, and What comes Next?* (Princeton, 1996), p. 24.

sometimes be misleading.[35] The statisticians who collected the data in the 1920s (many of them non-Bolshevik Marxists) thought of themselves as being engaged in a scientific enterprise. Making the population legible to government through the creation and aggregation of file-selves was understood as a deeply progressive endeavor.[36] When in the 1930s the regime largely ceased to aggregate and analyze the data, while continuing to collect it for purposes of individual surveillance and internal security, this was undoubtedly seen by the party's intellectuals as a regressive move.

Soviet file-selves resided in the personnel files (*lichnye dela*) kept on all wage and salary earners, trade union members, party and Komsomol members; in the questionnaires (*ankety*), filled in in a variety of circumstances and including questions on key classifications like "social position"; in the narrative curriculum vitae (*avtobiografiia*) submitted along with the *anketa* for the personnel file; in the internal passport (introduced in 1933), which included an entry for nationality and an entry for social position; as well as in the files of "compromising material" on party members obtained from denunciations and the extensive files on individuals under surveillance kept by the secret police. In the Soviet Union in Stalin's time, the almost inevitable "black spots" or gray shadows in any individual's personnel file might lie unnoticed for years, or even forever, but were always liable to be discovered and brandished as damning evidence against him.

In the comment quoted above, Zilber assumes that the file-self (being constituted by the bureaucratic possessor of the files) is inaccessible to its subject. According to Harré, similarly, "file-self memory" (unlike "real-self memory") is "normally impervious to self-reconstruction,"[37] meaning that it cannot be revised and edited by the subject. This is undoubtedly true in a general sense. We shall see, however, that with respect to Soviet file selves in the 1920s and '30s, some qualifications are in order. The content of file-selves was not static and could change as a result of changes of state policy: for example, when whole categories of criminal—actually, criminal-political—convictions imposed by courts in the early 1930s were annulled by law a few years later, leading to a new entry of annulment (*sniatie sudimosti*) in individual files.[38] A file on one individual could be changed if another individual sent compromising information on him or her in a denunciation to the bureauratic institution holding the file. Fi-

[35] See Peter Holquist, "To Count, to Extract, and to Exterminate: Population Statistics and Population Politics in Late Imperial and Soviet Russia," in Ronald G. Suny and Terry Martin, eds., *A State of Nations: Empire and Nation-Making in the Age of Lenin and Stalin* (New York, 2001).

[36] See James C. Scott, *Seeing like a State* (New Haven, 1998), pp. 76–83.

[37] Harré, *Personal Being*, p. 70.

[38] See Fitzpatrick, *Stalin's Peasants*, pp. 178, 180.

nally, individuals had some possibilities to manipulate their own files. Thus, file-making was not only a state project but also an individual one, and "self-fashioning" in the sense of fashioning a *file*-self must be part of the discussion on Soviet identity.[39]

How could Soviet citizens fashion their file-selves? At the crudest level, they could and did manufacture false data and false identity documents. In a cartoon of the late 1930s (see figure 2), the humorous journal *Krokodil* implied that such practices were widespread—the cartoon showed an *anketa* from a personnel file filled in with two sets of answers: "true" answers that would get the author in trouble (bourgeois origins, service with White Armies, and so on) overwritten with "false" answers that would help his self-advancement (worker, fought with the Red Army in Civil War).[40] It was possible to buy false passports on the black market, thus creating a set of basic personal data (for example, place and date of birth, nationality, social position) that would subsequently be entered in the individual's various personal files. In the days before passports were introduced, it was possible for peasants leaving the village for outside wage work to bribe local officials to provide an identification document (*spravka*) that gave them a "good" social position ("poor peasant," not "prosperous peasant" or "kulak").[41]

Short of outright falsification, there were many ways in which Soviet citizens could manipulate their file-selves. It was possible to act in certain ways in order to change the file-self. For example, a woman from a privileged background might marry a worker (marrying down being the postrevolutionary equivalent of marrying up in "normal" societies) with the object of discarding her own family background and assuming his "class position." A child of intelligentsia parents might go to work in a factory for a year or so after school in order to enter college as a "proletarian"; a child of kulaks with aspirations to higher education might try to get into *rabfak* (workers' preparatory faculty) or get accepted for the army (formally closed to kulaks' sons) to acquire a quasi-proletarian entitlement. Rural priests might send their children away to live with relatives of better social standing who would become their guardians or adoptive parents.

Fashioning of the file-self regularly occurred in the process of composition of two of its basic components: the narrative *avtobiografiia*, which the subject composed, and the *anketa*, which he or she filled in. The auto-

---

[39] In contrast to Jochen Hellbeck's quite legitimate usage of the term to describe fashioning of the soul.

[40] *Krokodil*, 1935 no. 10, back page: captioned "The Resumé (*anketa*) and Life: How One Should Sometimes Read the Resumé."

[41] Many examples of the "self-fashioning" of file selves are to be found in the essays on Class Identities in part I of this book, as well as in chapters 5 and 6 in Part II.

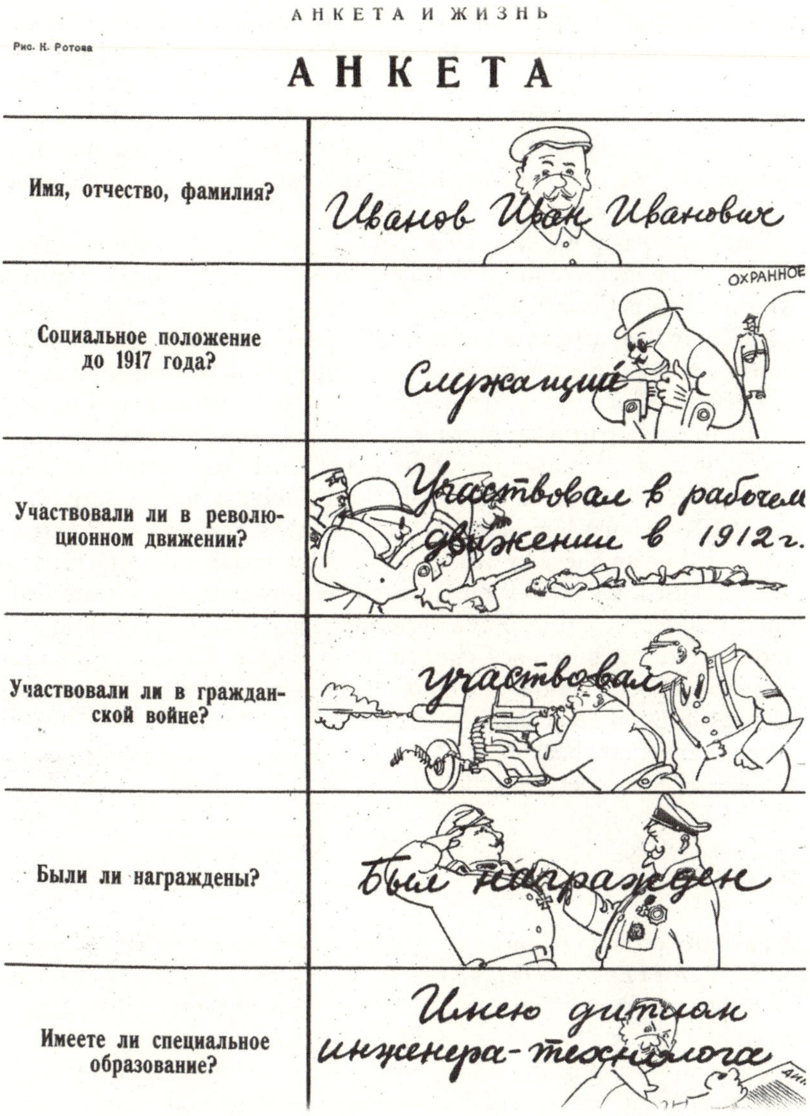

АНКЕТА И ЖИЗНЬ

АНКЕТА

Рис. К. Ротова

Figure 2. "The Questionnaire (*Anketa*)." Typed text reads: "First name, patronymic, last name? Social position before 1917? Did you participate in the revolutionary movement? Did you participate in the Civil War? Were you decorated? Do you have specialized education?" Drawing by K. Rotov from *Krokodil*, 1935 no. 10, back page.

biography could simply omit awkward aspects of the life, such as residence in territory occupied by the White Army during the Civil War. In a life that included different occupations, it could stress one and play down the others. In ambiguous social situations—for example, when a poor relative had lived with and worked for a richer relative—one interpretation (in this case, the "exploited labor" one) could be preferred to another ("member of the family").[42]

Finally, it was possible in some circumstances to challenge or appeal against an undesirable social classification of a file-self. While the citizens who tried to petition the courts for a formal change of "estate" were mistaken in their assessment of what Soviet law could do, it was certainly possible to appeal against various discriminatory measures, arguing that one's class position had been wrongly evaluated.[43] Such actions—in effect, efforts to edit a particular bureaucratic file-self—might be taken, for example, in cases of refusal of voting rights,[44] a student's expulsion from higher education, a peasant's classification as a kulak for tax purposes in the 1920s (making him liable to extra taxes), a harsh judicial sentence predicated on an allegedly mistaken understanding of the social position of the accused, the level of ration card issued by a rationing board, eviction from one's apartment as a class alien, or refusal by a local housing authority to recognize one's entitlement, by virtue of social position, to extra space.[45] The petitioner would explain why he or she deserved a social classification other than the one given by the institution he was petitioning, sometimes backing up the claim with documentation taken from his file-self in another institution.

IMPOSTURE

All identity projects require impersonation, in both of the senses offered by the *Oxford English Dictionary*: (1) "to assume the person or character of; to play the part of"; and (2) "to invest with an actual personality, to embody." But at a certain point, or in certain circumstances, impersonation becomes imposture, defined by the *OED* as "the action or practice of imposing on others; wilful and fraudulent deception." Or, to put it

---

[42] For two cases of this kind, see below, chapters 6 (pp. 108, 111) and 8 (p. 132).

[43] For examples, see below, chapters 2 (p. 37) and 4 (p. 76).

[44] See Golfo Alexopoulos, *Stalin's Outcasts: Aliens, Citizens, and the Soviet State, 1926–1936* (Ithaca, 2003) for discussion of the multitudes of petitions for reinstatement in voting rights of lishentsy.

[45] In the 1920s, "specialists" were entitled to extra living space for a study, a decision strongly supported by the education authorities, but generally uncongenial to housing authorities. See *Education and Social Mobility*, p. 80.

another way, impersonation is always trembling on the brink of imposture, and societies in which large numbers of citizens are actively engaged in impersonation may well turn out to be societies in which imposture and the fear of imposture are widespread. In the Soviet case, at any rate, it is impossible to discuss identity adequately without dealing with the question of imposture.

Two different types of imposture can be identified in Soviet prewar discourses. One may be called political imposture: the attempt to "deceive the party" as to one's true social or political face, to hide one's true identity from the authorities and claim a false one, but not for criminal purposes. There were regularized and institutionalized procedures for unmasking "wolves in sheep's clothing," and regular exhortations to party members not to relax their "vigilance." Periodic purges were conducted in government institutions and party organizations of the 1920s and early '30s to remove social aliens and impostors as well as other categories of undesirables like former members of political opposition groups. Among the most frequent allegations made in such contexts were concealment of clerical, bourgeois, or noble origins, misrepresentation of behavior during the Civil War, and, in the case of recent migrants from countryside to town, misrepresentation of status in the village.

There were always serious consequences to an unmasking: depending on the context, the victim was in danger of losing his/her job, status as a student, party or Komsomol membership, etc. But at periods of high political tension, the possible consequences could be much graver. At such times, the unmaskers often lost sight of what in ordinary life they knew perfectly well, namely that all sorts of comparatively harmless circumstances could lead people into impersonation. Harmless impersonation was then reconstrued as imposture, and the motives for even a trivial manipulation of biographical data suddenly became sinister. Thus, in the case of Stanislav Rataichak, an official in the chemical industry, a formerly trivial ambiguity in his *avtobiografiia* as to whether his nationality of origin was German or Polish, became virtually a capital crime in Vyshinsky's indictment when Rataichak found himself among the defendants in the 1937 Moscow show trial:

> Whether [Rataichak] is a German or a Polish spy is not clear, but that he is a spy there cannot be any doubt; and as is appropriate to his profession, a liar, a swindler and a rascal. *A man who, on his own confession, has an old autobiography and a new autobiography. A man who, according to circumstances, forges and re-shuffles these autobiographies.*[46]

[46] *Report*, p. 474. Emphasis mine.

When such abrupt category switches from impersonator to impostor occurred, it is possible that those in the environment—or even the subject himself—understood them as revelations of essential evil.[47] But this is hard to prove one way or the other. What can be said with confidence is that watchers and the subject themselves understood that a disastrous amendment of the file-self had occurred, a fundamental reclassification as dangerous to state security that made any attempts to edit or amend it pointless, as well as putting other individuals peripherally mentioned in it at risk. This sense of a disastrous file-self change is well conveyed in the comment of one Great Purge victim (who considered herself innocent and was reporting only a reclassification): "I turned out to be an enemy of the people."[48] Victims of such file-self changes and their close relatives were rarely willing to accept their reclassification: Vyshinsky's archive, for example, is full of petitions for removal of the "enemy" classification.[49] When, after Stalin's death, a mechanism of rehabilitation was officially set in place, almost all the survivors from the "enemy of the people" category of the late 1930s seem to have petitioned for rehabilitation—that is to say, for formal removal of the "enemy" label from the file-self.

The second type of imposture, criminal imposture, whereby an individual claimed a false identity for the purposes of gain, was very common in postrevolutionary Russia but provoked very different reactions from political imposture. Common confidence men (often called *moshenniki* [swindlers] or *obmanshchiki* [deceivers]) were a noticeable presence, not just in everyday life but also in contemporary journalism and literature.[50] A common form of such imposture in prewar Soviet times, as in the days of Nikolai Gogol's *Inspector General* (1836), was to present oneself in the provinces as an emissary of a central government institutions, taking advantage of the tradition that such emissaries should be hospitably welcomed with food, drink, and other perquisites—even money—to encourage them to make a favorable report back to the authorities that had sent them. Ostap Bender, the lovable swindler of Ilf and Petrov's novels, was an adept of such impostures, using his mastery of Soviet jargon and official mores to pass himself off in a variety of quintessentially Soviet roles, even including that of Soviet journalist.

---

[47] As suggested in Halfin, *Terror in My Soul*, esp. chapters 1 and 5.

[48] See Sheila Fitzpatrick and Yuri Slezkine, eds., *In the Shadow of Revolution: Russian Women's Life-Stories from 1917 to the Second World War* (Princeton, 2000).

[49] Gosudarstvennyi arkhiv Rossiiskoi Federatsii (GARF), f. 5446, op. 81a. Only some of these petitions directly requested release from imprisonment, but virtually all of them made the argument that the victim (usually the writer's husband or son) was *not* an enemy of the people.

[50] This is described in detail in chapter 13.

Despite the fact that the officials were often the dupes of Ostap Bender–type confidence men, this kind of imposture was treated comparatively benignly in Soviet discourse. Newspapers in the 1930s (particularly *Izvestiia* under Bukharin's editorship) delighted in reporting ingenious confidence tricks. The Ostap Bender stories—related in a similar vein to the journalistic articles—were wildly popular with Soviet readers and generally tolerated by the authorities,[51] despite the fact that Bender was never properly punished, nor did the authors spend much time holding forth on the antisocial nature of his crimes. In real life, of course, confidence men who were caught were punished by the courts, sometimes severely. But, like other criminals, criminal impostors had one great advantage over political, namely that they could be redeemed or, in the terminology of the 1930s, "reforged" as new Soviet men.

The project of remaking adult and juvenile delinquents was very popular in the Soviet official world in the 1930s. Lev Sheinin, a fascinating character who was both a writer/journalist, member of the Soviet Union of Writers, and a senior NKVD criminal investigator, devoted particular attention to such reclamation projects, stimulating a short-lived but highly publicized movement whereby criminals renounced their professions, in return for which the state forgave them their offenses and helped them make a new start. Among the beneficiaries was the notorious con-man "Count Kostia," who was trained as a topographer and sent off on an expedition to the Arctic, and "dark-eyed, well-built Avesian," whose recitation of a monologue from Othello so impressed Sheinin that he arranged for him to be retrained as an actor.[52] All the more remarkable was the fact that all this was occurring in the early months of 1937, almost the same time as another enterprise in which Sheinin was deeply involved: the great show trial of Piatakov, Rataichak, and other "enemies of the people." For people like Count Kostia, the road back into Soviet society was open at any time; they were, in effect, prodigal sons whose return to the fold caused particular joy. For people like Rataichak, by contrast, the way back was closed forever—or at least for the period that the file remained in the "dangerous to state security" category. As long as a file-self retained the classification of "enemy," the subject was not available for reforging.[53]

---

[51] They were briefly out of favor in the postwar period: see below, pp. 285–86.

[52] For more on this episode, see Fitzpatrick, *Everyday Stalinism*, pp. 78–79; on Avesian, see Lev Sheinin, *Zapiski sledovatelia* (Moscow, 1965), pp. 108–109.

[53] Intellectually, this was a really untenable position for Soviet ideologists, so it is unusual to find an explicit statement, despite the unmistakable evidence of a taboo on such reclamation in practice. At the height of the Great Purges, Anton Makarenko, the educationist who more than anyone else was associated with reclamation projects, conceded (in an uneasy, embarrassed fashion) that some people were "vermin by nature" and thus beyond reach. See Fitzpatrick, *Everyday Stalinism*, pp. 79 and 242 (n. 57).

OVERVIEW

The book begins with an investigation of the question that first drew me to this topic, namely class and its meaning in early Soviet Russia. These first three chapters (a reworking of several essays written in the late 1980s and early '90s, of which the best known is "Ascribing Class") investigates why the Bolsheviks thought it so important to know what social class individuals belonged to, how they tried to find this out (which brings us into the realm of the collection and interpretation of social statistics), the practical and legal forms of class discrimination that became so crucial a determinant of individual fates in the 1920s and first half of the 1930s, and the evasive and contestatory responses they provoked. I introduce here the theme of masking and unmasking that will run throughout the book. In chapter 3, I argue that, for all that many of the Bolshevik leaders were intellectuals well versed in Marxism and derived their interest in class from this source, we misread the term "class" in prewar Soviet usage if we assume that it means class in a Marxist sense. In its practical meaning in early Soviet Russia, class was only secondarily about one's place in a system of social relationships generated by a regime of production. It was primarily about the place ascribed to an individual in a system of entitlements and obligations—in short, about a relationship to the state, similar to that implied in membership of a social estate (*soslovie*) such as the nobility or clergy before the revolution.

In part 2, I turn to the impact of practices of class ascription on individual lives starting with two vignettes ("Lives under Fire" and "Two Faces of Anastasia," both written in the early 1990s) about challenges to the class identity that an individual claimed. One challenge occurred in public, in the course of an election for trade-union office held at a time of high political tension during the Great Purges; the other in private, initiated by a denunciation and subsequent investigation to which the subject of investigation responded with a vigorous attempt to ensure that her file-self corresponded to her version of her life, not her accuser's. The theme of editing and presenting lives runs through this section. "A Peasant Truthteller" examines a rare example of a peasant life story (related in the course of a long denunciation of abuses by local bosses sent to a peasant newspaper), showing the different ways in which one enterprising and intelligent man tried to define himself against a changing background of tumultous times. In "Women's Lives," a whole array of women's first-person narratives (both Soviet and émigré) is under examination, with emphasis on the women's sense of their autobiographical task as testimony rather than confession, their slighting of private life, and their experience of class and class identity problems in the Soviet period.

Parts 3 and 4 deal with mainly with different epistolary genres—the letters of appeal, complaint, and denunciation that individuals sent in vast numbers to the authorities in the Stalin period. Here the central theme is self-presentation: how the writers represented themselves and their lives to the authorities in their effort to win "justice" and "pity," and more concretely to gain benefits and favors from the state, settle scores with other individuals, and so on. "Supplicants and Citizens" provides a typology of citizens' letters to the authorities; "Patrons and Clients" examines the practice of patronage, using letters as a major source. Denunciation is the focus of "Signals from Below" (written in tandem with "Supplicants and Citizens" in the mid 1990s) and "Wives' Tales." Denunciations were often challenges to the identity of their subjects, involving accusations of false claims about class identity or—the ultimate reclassification attempt—assertions that someone who was passing as a good Soviet citizen was actually an "enemy of the people." In the 1930s, spousal denunciation seems to have been rare, but in the postwar period, denunciation of husbands by wives became common. "Wives' Tales" investigates this phenomenon, relating it to postwar tensions between the sexes and the 1944 law restricting divorce.

Part 5, on imposture, deals with criminal imposture in real life and fiction in the interwar period ("The World of Ostap Bender") and the impact of the postwar upsurge of anti-Semitism and "anti-cosmopolitan" campaign ("The Con Man as Jew"). Underlying the discussion of imposture is the suggestion that in a society collectively involved in a revolutionary transformation project, where individual practices of impersonation are unavoidable, imposture—that close but criminal relative of impersonation—becomes a focus of societal attention. That attention may be alarmed and hostile, as in the case of political imposture, but it may also be sympathetic and even admiring, as in the case of criminal impostors like Ostap Bender who display enviable skill at performing new social roles. When Ostap Bender and his ilk (who had always tended to be read by Russian readers as non-Russian and probably Jewish) started to look unmistakably Jewish in the postwar climate of rising antisemitism, that sympathetic tolerance was temporarily suspended and the conceptual separation of the two types of imposture blurred.

While most of this book deals with identity issues and practices in the prewar period, 1917–1941, two chapters ("Wives' Tales" and "The Con Man as Jew") deal with the 1940s and '50s, and the last chapter, "Afterword: Inventing a Post-Soviet Self," moves forward to the 1990s. That means that we need to consider briefly what changes occurred in the postwar and post-Stalin periods. In the realm of identity, the most important postwar development was that class, the great focus of identity concerns in the 1920s and 1930s, became less central. The Soviet Constitution of 1936 started the move away from the revolutionary rulers' former preoccupation with class as a way of "reading" the population (in James C. Scott's phrase). Most class discriminatory policies were dropped (except for the newly incorporated territories of the Baltics and Eastern Poland, as well as in Sovietized Eastern Europe, where they were introduced for the first time in the 1940s and '50s as part of the Soviet "transformation" package). It took time for the shift away from class discrimination to take root in local administrative practice. Local authorities in the Russian provinces in the late 1940s were still entering class data in personal dossiers, including parents' class and soslovie status and whether anyone in the family had ever been deprived of voting rights on class grounds (a practice officially discontinued in 1936).[54] In Moscow, however, the Central Committee had ceased to note the social origins of prospective appointees by 1952,[55] and the party had become markedly less responsive to class denunciations (kulak uncles, capitalist grandfathers, and so on) than it had been before the war. In 1951, after investigating a denunciation that a physician and his associates had concealed the fact that they came from families of priests, the Party Control Commission concluded that the allegations were true but irrelevant: "there are no grounds to show distrust of them."[56] The conclusion would surely have been different fifteen years earlier.

Distrust, however, had not disappeared; rather, it had shifted its focus. With regard to the large proportion of the Soviet population that had lived under German occupation during the war, suspicions of collaboration (with all the familiar panoply of denunciations, rebuttals, and counteraccusations) took over from the earlier suspicions that "bourgeois" origins translated into sympathy with the old regime, the Whites, or non-Bolshevik political parties. Whole ethnic groups were deported in the 1940s as alleged collaborators with the occupying forces. All contacts with foreigners were regarded with deep suspicion, and were sometimes severely punished, in the postwar years. In the late 1940s and early '50s, rising state and popular anti-Semitism gave rise to rumors (never substantiated but pervasive in the era of the "Doctors' Plot" allegations of 1953) that Jews would be next on the list for group deportation.

[54] Gosudarstvennyi arkhiv Riazanskoi oblasti (GARO), f. R-6, op. 1, d. 1800, ll. 13, 28 (attestations from oblast soviet, 1946); Tsentral'noe khranilishche dokumentatsii noveishei istorii Samarskoi oblasti (TSKhDNISI), f. 1683, op. 16, d. 268, l. 100 (*lichnyi listok po uchetu kadrov* for Komsomol members, 1949).

[55] Rossiiskoi gosudarstvennyi arkhiv sotsial'no-politicheskoi informatsii (RGASPI), f. 17, op. 119. d. 1090 (appointments memoranda, 1952). These memoranda still included a space for social position (*sotsial'noe polozhenie*), but this was usually filled in with a standard answer "Sluzhashchii" (employee).

[56] Tsentral'noe khranilishche sotsial'noi dokumentatsii (TsKhSD), f. 6, op. 6, d. 1574.

The other important postwar change in the identity realm—impossible to date precisely, but certainly well established by the mid 1960s—was naturalization of Soviet identity. At a certain point, the Revolution and its destabilizing consequences for social and political became history. By the 1960s, what it meant to be "Soviet" was no longer problematic. This is not to say that a monolithic model of Soviet identity held sway: on the contrary, this was a period when the range of choices available to Soviet citizens expanded greatly and public debate about lifestyles and mores proliferated.[57] But the society was no longer composed of individuals learning to "speak Bolshevik," in Kotkin's phrase: the older generation had already learned the language, while the younger—the majority of the population—were native speakers.[58] Indeed, "Bolshevik" was spoken with such fluency that the whole Soviet idiom and persona was becoming a cliché. Foreigners made jokes about it; internal critics wrote disparagingly of "Homo Sovieticus"; and by the late 1980s, the contemptuous "*sovok*" had gained broad currency as a term for right-thinking Soviet citizens. Nobody talked any more about the lineaments of a future New Soviet Man: instead, there was a "really existing" Soviet Man to go along with the "really existing socialism" of the Brezhnev era.

The establishment status of the Soviet persona is indicated by its capacity to generate both parody and rejection. As long as Soviet identity was still insecure, as it was in the prewar period, articulated countercultures that played off and challenged the dominant culture were virtually unknown. The first recognizable counterculture was that of the *stiliagi*—style-conscious young men appropriating Western fashions and challenging the prevailing drabness of Soviet dress—of the 1940s and '50s.[59] The stiliagi were followed by the dissidents of the 1960s and '70s, who moved the arena of challenge from fashion to politics. In the 1970s, Western political scientists started to talk about the ossification of the Soviet political system, implying something that was both stable and increasingly inflexible. An analogous process surely existed in the realm of Soviet identity, though that is a story that has yet to be told.

And then came the collapse of 1991, an event no less dramatic in its consequences for individual identity than the 1917 Revolution had been. The afterword examines the process of identity change and self-reinvention in the 1990s, the discrediting of "Homo Sovieticus" and Soviet values, the embrace of capitalism, and the attempt to recover Russianness

[57] See Catriona Kelly, *Refining Russia: Advice Literature, Polite Culture, and Gender from Catherine to Yeltsin* (Oxford, 2001), pp. 312–38.

[58] Kotkin, *Magnetic Mountain*, chapter 5.

[59] See Mark Edele, "Strange Young Men in Stalin's Moscow: The Birth and Life of the Stiliagi, 1945–1953," *Jahrbücher für Geschichte Osteuropas* 50 (2002), pp. 37–61.

and/or entrepreneurial democracy (which Russians, unfortunately, tended to define as polar opposites) as a basis for post-Soviet identity. In terms of the imperative of self-reinvention, the wheel seemed to have come full circle back to the last great transition after 1917. This time, however, it was not a matter of becoming Soviet but of rooting out the Sovietness in oneself. Then came the new puzzle: what did "post-Soviet" mean, apart from something dialectically opposed to Sovietism? What were the behaviors and codes appropriate to New Post-Soviet Man, and how could Old Soviet Man remake himself? The book ends with a story of identity reconstruction that is still in progress.

PART I

Class Identities

CHAPTER TWO

The Bolshevik Invention Of Class

The "imagined communities" for which revolutionaries fight are often nations.[1] But the Bolshevik revolutionaries who took power in Petrograd in October 1917 were exceptions to the rule. They did not at first "imagine" a new Russian or even Soviet nation. Instead, being Marxist internationalists, they imagined a *class*—the international proletariat—whose revolution, begun in Russia, would soon sweep Europe. The international revolution failed to materialize, however, and the Bolsheviks were left with the unexpected task of building a previously unimagined socialist nation. Their commitment to the international proletariat became increasingly tenuous, finally disappearing, perhaps, with the formal dissolution of the Comintern during the "Great Patriotic War" against Nazi Germany.

Much of this is common knowledge, yet the nature and consequences for Soviet society of the Bolsheviks' imagination of class remains largely unexplored. In this chapter, I will argue that the Bolsheviks, cherishing an imagined class community yet inheriting a shattered and fragmented class structure in Russia after the Revolution, found themselves obliged to invent the classes that their Marxist theoretical commitments told them must exist.[2] This provides a striking confirmation of Bourdieu's proposition that classes in the real world are at least partly a product of the Marxist theory that purports to describe them.[3]

This chapter is a revised version of "L'Usage Bolchévique de la 'Classe': Marxisme et Construction de l'Identité Individuelle," *Actes de la Recherche en Sciences Sociales* 85 (November 1990), first published in English as "The Bolshevik Invention of Class: Marxist Theory and the Making of 'Class Consciousness' in Soviet Society," in Ronald Suny, ed., *The Structure of Soviet History* (New York, 2002). Some material has been incorporated from "The Problem of Class Identity in NEP Society," in *Russia in the Era of NEP*, eds. Sheila Fitzpatrick, Alexander Rabinowitch, and Richard Stites, (Bloomington, Ind., 1991); and my "Ascribing Class. The Construction of Social Identity in Soviet Russia," *Journal of Modern History* 65:4 (1993).

[1] The term is from Benedict Anderson, *Imagined Communities: Reflections on the Origin and Spread of Nationalism* (London, 1983).

[2] This phrase is used with acknowledgements to Eric Hobsbawm, whose "invention of tradition" suggested some of the present lines of enquiry. Eric J. Hobsbawm, ed., *The Invention of Tradition* (Cambridge, 1983).

[3] "*J'en viens de plus en plus à me demander si les structures sociales d'aujourd'hui ne sont pas les structures symboliques d'hier et si par exemple la classe telle qu'on la constate*

CLASS AND THE BOLSHEVIK REVOLUTION

Marxism, a Western import of the late nineteenth century, quickly won great popularity among Russian intellectuals, particularly but not exclusively those on the revolutionary left. The industrial proletariat and capitalist bourgeoisie were important concepts in political discourse some time before they became actual socioeconomic entities in Russia. By the first decades of the twentieth century, however, thanks to an energetic program of state-sponsored industrialization initiated in the 1890s, reality was catching up with Marxist imagination. The industrial working class of Russia in the immediate prewar years was small but highly concentrated and politically active. Petersburg and Moscow workers created the first soviets in 1905, and played a crucial role in bringing down the Tsarist regime in February 1917.

Though intelligentsia-led (like all other revolutionary groups), the Bolsheviks became a mass party with broad working-class support in 1917. They profited from the progressive radicalization of workers and conscript soldiers and sailors in the months after the February Revolution, having distinguished themselves from other socialist parties by their intransigent stand against the war and the politics of coalition and compromise. By the fall of 1917, the Bolsheviks' claim to be "the party of the proletariat" seemed justified by a run of electoral successes, and it is at least arguable that they had a popular mandate in October for their seizure of power in the name of the workers' soviets.

One of the great strengths of Marxism in Russia had been its success in predicting the future. In the 1880s, Marxists and Populists had argued about the inevitability of capitalist industrialization in Russia—and in less than a decade, the Marxist prediction had come to pass. Marxism had accurately identified the urban working class as a revolutionary force in Russia. It had asserted that class conflict was the basis of politics—thus in effect predicting the collapse of the February coalition between "bourgeois liberalism" (the Provisional Government) and "proletarian socialism" (the Petrograd Soviet). To the Bolsheviks, and even to many of their political opponents, the October victory seemed only the latest proof that in Russia, at least, history was on the Marxist side.

But, as it turned out, this was to be not just the latest but also the last Russian proof of Marxist axioms. No sooner had the proletarian revolution occurred than, by a spectacular irony, history abruptly dis-

---

n'est pas pour une part le produit de l'effet de théorie exercé par l'oeuvre de Marx . . . Dans certaines limites, les structures symboliques ont un pouvoir tout à fait extraordinaire de constitution (au sens de la philosophie et de la théorie politique) qu'on a beaucoup sous-estimé." Pierre Bourdieu, Choses Dites (Paris, 1987), p. 29.

owned the Russian Marxists, mocking their theories by destroying the class structure of Russian society and the class basis of revolutionary politics.[4] War, revolution, civil war, and famine in the years 1914–23 were the main causes of this debacle. The landowning nobility and capitalist bourgeoisie had been annihilated as classes by revolutionary expropriation and emigration. The old bureaucratic elite had suffered a similar eclipse as a result of the fall of the Tsarist regime. In the countryside, the emerging class differentiation of the peasantry that Stolypin's agrarian reforms had sought to stimulate had been wiped out, at least temporarily, by the spontaneous "Black Repartition" of 1917–18 and the revival of the peasant commune.

Worst of all, from the Bolshevik point of view, the industrial working class, battered by hunger in the towns and the closure of industrial plants and mines, had fragmented and dispersed during the Civil War. A million or more workers had left the towns for the villages and were now, to all appearances, peasant cultivators of the land.[5] In addition, hundreds of thousands of workers had gone into the Red Army, or left the factory to take up managerial and administrative positions in the new governing institutions of Soviet power, and other factory workers had become artisans and small traders on the black market. The proletarian coach that had brought Cinderella to the revolution had turned into a pumpkin.

The phenomenon of "declassing" was not restricted to industrial workers. In the tumult of revolution, millions of citizens of the former Russian Empire were in process of moving—from one occupation to another, from one place to another, from one social status to another, from an old life to (perhaps) a new one. Men conscripted to the Imperial Army returned home, and then in many cases departed again to serve as volunteers or conscripts in the Red Army or the White Army (some served sequentially on both sides). Inhabitants of Northern cities fled to the South and East, but often returned as the White Armies retreated. Former nobles became bookkeepers and black marketeers. Volga residents fled West from famine, or dispatched their children from the stricken areas. With the demobilization of the Red Army at the end of the Civil War, almost five million young men were released to go home to their former lives in villages or towns—or, perhaps, to go seek their fortune elsewhere. The railway stations were full of soldiers, homeless children (*besprizornye*) and citizens in transit to destinations that often proved illusory.

---

[4] This is the theme of my essay "The Bolsheviks' Dilemma: Class, Culture and Politics in the Early Soviet Years," in Sheila Fitzpatrick, *The Cultural Front: Power and Culture in Revolutionary Russia* (Ithaca, 1992).

[5] This was an intellectual as well as political blow to the Bolsheviks, since they had acted on the premise that, despite the presence of many recent arrivals from the village and peasant

The result was that in 1921, when the Bolsheviks emerged victorious from the Civil War, they found themselves in a truly new world—one in which class and class conflict had become irrelevant. The class that had made the revolution was dispersed and fragmented, and the classes that had opposed it no longer existed. There were no further guidelines for political action in Marxist theory, and no Marxist basis for understanding an amorphous and essentially classless (but not yet, alas, socialist) society. The Bolsheviks' revolutionary imagination of class had reached an impasse. At this point, the Bolsheviks had the choice of repudiating Marxist theory and the legitimacy of their own revolution, or soldiering on regardless. Not surprisingly, they chose the latter. But that choice led them inexorably to reinvent the class base of Russian politics and society that history had so capriciously denied them.

THE REINVENTION OF CLASS IN THE 1920S

For the Bolsheviks, society was divided into two antithetical class camps. The two camps revolved around the proletariat, on the one side, and the bourgeoisie, on the other. The "proletariat" consisted of the industrial working class (very small at the beginning of the 1920s, but growing with the revival of industry under the New Economic Policy, or NEP) and its landless and poor peasant allies in the villages (although poor peasants were unfortunately difficult to distinguish as a stable socioeconomic group). Cast as symbolic leader of the proletariat was the Bolshevik Party, self-identified as the vanguard of the dictator class.

The "bourgeoisie" was an amalgam of pre- and postrevolutionary social groups, including the remnants of the old nobility and capitalist classes, urban Nepmen (private traders and entrepreneurs, whose activity was legalized with the advent of NEP in 1921), and kulaks (the more prosperous peasants, whom the Bolsheviks regarded as potential capitalists). This composite class had, in fact, little coherence and no leadership. But the Bolsheviks were inclined to cast the old Russian intelligentsia—now collectively labeled the "bourgeois" intelligentsia, in contrast to its miniscule Communist counterpart, and individually known as "bourgeois specialists"—as its symbolic leader. This conveyed recognition that the intelligentsia had been one of the prerevolutionary elites (a proposition many of its members vehemently denied), was the only such group to survive the Revolution more or less intact, and constituted the Bolsheviks' main potential rival for authority and leadership.

---

otkhodniki in the industrial labor force, Russia had a "mature" working class, essentially separate from the peasantry.

Large segments of the society were neither clearly proletarian nor clearly bourgeois. But they nevertheless had to be associated with one or the other camp and given a precise social location and class analysis. The Bolsheviks devoted much energy and ingenuity to the task of identifying the class tendencies of such groups as "middle peasants" (those who were neither exceptionally poor nor exceptionally prosperous—that is, the great majority of the peasantry), artisans, and white-collar state employees (*sluzhashchie*). A whole Soviet statistical industry sprang up in the 1920s around the problem of identifying classes and strata, quantifying them, and determining the exact "class composition" of particular demographic and institutional groups, ranging from members of peasant cooperative organizations to Red Army inductees, Communists, and senior civil servants. Even the 1926 national population census made a valiant attempt to classify respondents by class as well as occupation.

But the Bolshevik reinvention of class involved more than passive record keeping and data collection. They actively developed the concept of class by creating legislative and bureaucratic structures that were class sensitive—that is, they discriminated in favor of the proletariat and against the bourgeoisie. This list of such structures in the 1920s included schools, universities, the Communist Party, the Komsomol, the Red Army (which discriminated in favor of proletarians and against kulaks and other "bourgeois elements" in admissions and recruitment), taxation departments, law courts, municipal housing bodies, rationing boards (which gave preference to proletarians and penalized the bourgeoisie), and local electoral committees (which kept lists of residents who were ineligible to vote in soviet elections because they were "class aliens"[6]). The Bolsheviks' class-discriminatory policies had both a social justice and a social engineering aspect. In the cause of social justice, they aimed to redistribute resources and opportunities, giving preferential treatment to those who had been excluded from privilege under the old regime and denying it to those who came from the old privileged classes. In the cause of social engineering, they aimed to "proletarianize" recruitment to key institutions and elites in order to consolidate the position of the new regime and secure the gains of the Revolution.

In addition, Bolshevik policies and perceptions created entirely new "classes"—that is, collective social entities whose members had not previously had a common identity, status, or consciousness but acquired them through their experience as Soviet citizens. One such group con-

---

[6] The 1918 Constitution of the RSFSR withheld the right to vote from persons who were not "toilers," that is, kulaks, rentiers, priests, former Tsarist gendarmes, and White officers. This remained in force for almost two decades, until the introduction of the Stalin Constitution (see below, p. 42).

sisted of *byvshie*, "former people", who had once held high position and privilege in society, but lost it as a result of the Revolution. An overlapping group, more of a juridical entity, was that of *lishentsy*, that is, persons deprived of voting rights because of their class background and affiliation with the old regime. Deprivation of voting rights carried with it other civil disabilities such as lack of entitlement to housing, rations, and higher education. At the end of the 1920s, the total number of *lishentsy* increased sharply, and so did the authorities' thoroughness in imposing other civil disabilities on *lishentsy* and their immediate families.

So far, our discussion has assumed that the Bolsheviks were rational actors whose reinvention of class served specific and definable purposes. But, of course, this is an expository convention that conveys only a partial truth. In fact, the Bolsheviks were generally irrational on the question of class in the 1920s because it was their collective obsession. Class was the universal referent, the touchstone of political and personal identity. Intuitive perceptions of class were valued and cultivated: for example, that village blacksmiths were proletarians, that women in all social strata tended to be petty bourgeois, that Jews were "a bourgeois nation." Elaborating such class cosmologies was a favorite pastime of Bolshevik autodidacts in the 1920s.

However, it was the question of class *enemies* that was central for most Bolsheviks. The idea of class could not be separated from the idea of struggle. Bolshevik "class consciousness" was above all an awareness of the need for vigilance and ruthlessness in the face of the threat of bourgeois counterrevolution. Working-class Bolsheviks kept a keen watch for signs of "bourgeois liberalism" and faintheartedness on the part of the party's intellectuals. Bolsheviks of intelligentsia background abased themselves before the toughminded "proletarian instincts" of their lower-class confrères. Although it was the party leadership's policy during NEP not to "fan the flames of class war," the party's rank and file accepted this message only unwillingly and imperfectly. Uncompromising intolerance of Nepmen, kulaks, and "bourgeois" intellectuals was always considered to be a sign of Bolshevik principle.

A second premise of our argument so far has been that the Bolsheviks were sole authors of the Soviet discourse of class. But this too needs to be qualified. The imagination of class became a societal and individual preoccupation as well as a Bolshevik one after the Revolution. Indeed, it may be said that the Bolsheviks' invention of class produced in all strata of Soviet society a degree and intensity of class consciousness—in the literal sense of consciousness of class as an issue and a problem—that has rarely been equaled.

Citizens of the new revolutionary state struggled to assimilate and improve the class identities available to them. They learned the new public language of class. This language was not simply, as is sometimes suggested, an Orwellian "ClassSpeak" that existed in Soviet newspapers but was shunned by ordinary people. On the contrary, ordinary people —not to mention intellectuals—were often fascinated by it. By the mid 1920s, the use of class language was *de rigueur* for many groups of young city-dwellers: Komsomols, high-school pupils, and young industrial workers.[7] It was as alluring and chic as *blatnoi iazyk*, the jargon of the criminal world, which came into fashion at the same time, and it was, indeed, part of urban youth's popular culture as well as Communist political culture in the 1920s.

In other circles, class discourse might be used ironically, like the new acronyms (Sovnarkom, Cheka) by which Soviet institutions were known. But even this was a form of societal acceptance. The centrality of the discourse can be gauged by its suddenly dominant position in Russian humor and satire: from the time of the revolution (and for many decades thereafter), the wittiest jokes and funniest anecdotes in circulation revolved around class. The use and misuse of class language in everyday life was a stock-in-trade of satirical journalists, caricaturists, and writers in the 1920s and 1930s, from Zoshchenko and Ilf and Petrov to Platonov. A somewhat different response to class discourse is recorded in peasant milieux in the 1920s. Peasants were more puzzled than city-dwellers by the new class jargon, and therefore generally less amused. But they appreciated its potential for invective, and the word "burzhui", virtually unknown in the villages before the Revolution though well established in urban slang, reportedly became popular as a term of abuse in village arguments in the early 1920s.[8]

Individual Soviet citizens were deeply involved in the invention of class because they had to have personal class identities. Obviously, there were fortunate individuals whose class identity was clear and unambiguous, but there were also large numbers who were not in that position. Because of the chaotic and amorphous condition of the society and the high degree of social and occupational mobility in the revolutionary period, the social position of a great many citizens was ambiguous. Such people had to "invent" social and class identities—not in the sense of wholly making them up but in the sense of selecting and interpreting their own biographical data in such a way as to produce an optimal (in terms of personal security and career opportunities) result.

[7] See A. M. Selishchev, *Iazyk revoliutsionnoi epokhi: Iz nabliudenii nad russkim iazykom poslednikh let (1917–1926)*, 2nd ed. (Moscow, 1928).

[8] See *Derevnia pri NEP'e. Kogo schitat' kulakom, kto—truzhenikom. Chto govoriat ob etom krest'iane?* (Moscow, 1924), p. 19.

The necessity of creativity in the definition of individual class identity was all the greater because of the lack of clarity about the rules. It was generally accepted that both class origin and current social (occupational) position were or might be relevant to an individual's class status. But there were no hard-and-fast guidelines about the relative importance of the two criteria. Additional complications were introduced by the prevalent opinion that an individual's social position *in October 1917* was of particular importance in determing his or her "real" or essential class. As a result of these complexities of classification, no class identification could be regarded as ironclad. Even apparently solid social identities could crumble when challenged, and in such cases the individual was said to have been "unmasked." Thus, from the standpoint of individual citizens, especially those of ambiguous background and circumstances, it was necessary not only to create a class identity but also to put some effort into maintaining and protecting it.

It has already been pointed out that the class position officially ascribed to individuals had important practical implications in the society of the 1920s. A "good" class identity could get you into higher education, or into the Komsomol and the Communist Party, with all the career advantages that these implied. A "bad" class identity could result in loss of an apartment or compulsory *uplotnenie* (when the local soviet settled another family in your living space), special taxes, refusal of unemployment benefits or other social services, and, if you found yourself before a court, increased likelihood of conviction and a heavy sentence. Thus, persons with "bad" social origins were under considerable temptation to disguise them, for example, to invent a class identity in the literal sense, especially if they had career or educational ambitions.

A whole range of Soviet strategies emerged for avoiding penalties (i.e., disadvantageous class labels) by modifying behavior in such a way as to suit the letter but not the spirit of the prevailing codes, much as U.S. citizens behave in response to the IRS and tax laws. The best examples relate to kulaks, since Soviet legal and taxation authorities and statisticians published many guidelines in the 1920s on the signs by which kulaks might be recognized, and the kulaks read them. Thus, if the hiring of labor was a sign of kulak status, prosperous (and literate) peasants might decide not to increase cultivation by hiring labor, but rather to hire themselves out—with horses—to plough land for horseless poor peasants.

The attitude of individuals to their own manipulated or fraudulent class identities is often hard to determine. It certainly cannot be taken for granted that they regarded the invented identities as false. In autobiographies written by postwar refugees from the Soviet Union, for example, the authors often report their conscious misrepresentation of class origins in almost the same breath as they recall how sincerely they identified with the assumed "Soviet" persona and how devastated they were when it was challenged.[9] There are many instances, moreover, where the question of sincerity seems beside the point: the individual was aware of two available class identities and used the one that was most advantageous. Take the case of the peasant woman Sarbunova of Sviiazhsk village, for example. After the dekulakization of her husband and the confiscation of their household property, Sarbunova appealed unsuccessfully to the courts for the return of the property. Then, having divorced her husband, she

> submitted a petition to the Procurator of the [Tatar]/ Republic stating that her husband really was a kulak, and deprived of voting rights, but for the whole period of their marriage, about twenty years, she had been nothing but a hired female laborer (*batrachka*).[10]

The court regarded the divorce as fictitious, but who can tell? No doubt Sarbunova mainly blamed Soviet power for the disaster that had befallen her and her husband. But sometimes she probably blamed her husband as well—using for that purpose the "Soviet" language of class exploitation with which she addressed the court.

IMAGINING CLASS WAR: THE PROLETARIAT'S BID FOR HEGEMONY

Parallel to the "invention of class," which is our subject in this chapter, there were undoubtedly some processes in the 1920s that might be described as "real" class formation in the Marxist sense. But these will not concern us here, particularly since they were abruptly halted at the end of the decade by the new social upheaval associated with Stalin's "revolution from above": collectivization of peasant agriculture, the First Five-Year Plan industrialization drive, and cultural revolution. In this period of radical social engineering by the state, whole classes were "liquidated" and millions of individuals changed their social position either voluntarily or involuntarily.

In an atmosphere of extreme social and political tension at the end of the 1920s, the Communist Party called for an intensification of class war, motivating this by the external challenge of an allegedly imminent danger of military attack by the encircling capitalist powers and the internal challenges of collectivization and the First Five-Year Plan. The proletariat, it was said, was now ready to settle once and for all with its class enemies. This "proletariat" was clearly virtually synonymous with the state and Communist Party.

[9] See *Soviet Youth: Twelve Komsomol Histories* (Munich, 1959), series 1, no. 51.
[10] *Sovetskaia iustitsiia*, 1933 no. 1, p. 18.

In the new phase of imagined class war and actual state aggression against segments of the society, an important symbolic role was played by the cultural revolution of the late 1920s. Cultural Revolution was a process through which the proletariat allegedly cast off bourgeois hegemony in culture and claimed hegemony for itself.[11] It may be understood as a symbolic expropriation of the old intelligentsia—which was collectively brought under suspicion through the show trials of some leading "bourgeois specialists" on charges of treason and sabotage—and its renewal as a class by an infusion of new proletarian and Communist cadres. Other class enemies, notably kulaks and Nepmen, were less fortunate, since their "liquidation as a class" was more than symbolic. The unmasking of class enemies rose to a pitch of hysteria and became a real witch-hunt. The most remarkable episode of "class war" in this period was the dekulakization campaign whose purpose was to "liquidate kulaks as a class." This involved not only the expropriation of all those ascribed to the kulak class and their "hirelings" (*podkulachniki*) but also the deportation of a substantial part of the group to distant regions of the country. Priests, victims of mass arrests that accompanied the closing of churches, were also liable to "dekulakization" in rural areas. Urban Nepmen were being forced out of business and in many cases arrested at the same period, as the entire urban economy was nationalized.

The "heightened class vigilance" of the Cultural Revolution meant that the situation of *lishentsy* became ever more precarious even as the lists of officially disenfranchised persons grew longer. *Lishentsy* were liable to be fired from their jobs, evicted from housing, and declared ineligible for rations, while their children were unable to enter university and join the Komsomol or even the Young Pioneers (for ages 10 to 14). A wave of social purging swept through government offices, schools, universities, Komsomol and party organizations, and even factories in 1929–30. Rural schoolteachers lost their jobs because they were sons of priests; kulaks who had fled the village and found work in industry were denounced; elderly widows of Tsarist generals were "unmasked" and subjected to various indignities. Neighbors and professional colleagues accused each other of hiding class stigmas. Persons from stigmatized classes sometimes publicly repudiated their parents in a vain effort to wipe out the stain.[12]

To complete the picture of social upheaval at the end of the 1920s and beginning of the 1930s, two other important social processes must be introduced. The first was rapid industrialization under the First Five-Year

---

[11] On this phenomenon, see my essay "Cultural Revolution as Class War," in Sheila Fitzpatrick, ed., *Cultural Revolution in Russia, 1928–1931* (Bloomington, Ind., 1978).

[12] See Sheila Fitzpatrick, "Cultural Revolution as Class War," in *The Cultural Front*, pp. 115–48.

Plan (1929–32), which radically expanded the labor force and urban population and prompted the move of millions of peasants from countryside to town. The second was large-scale recruitment of young workers and peasants into the administrative and specialist elite, via affirmative action programs in higher education, on the one hand, and direct promotion from manual to white-collar jobs, on the other.[13] This was, in its way, as dramatic an example of social engineering as the "liquidation of kulaks as a class." Stalin described its aims as the creation of a new "worker-peasant intelligentsia," which, as I have argued elsewhere, meant essentially elite formation, the making of Djilas's "New Class."[14] With simultaneous programs of class liquidation and class creation, Stalin's "revolution from above" may be regarded as going beyond the general "invention of class" of the 1920s into a new realm of the invention (and annulment) of *classes*.

In rhetorical terms, the outcome of the grand confrontation of proletariat and bourgeoisie at the end of the 1920s was, needless to say, a victory for the proletariat. Proletarian hegemony was firmly established. The bourgeoisie as a class was annihilated. From the standpoint of Marxist theory, even the possibility of its resurgence was precluded by the changes in the underlying economic structure and modes of production, namely from traditional-cum-small-capitalist peasant farming to collective farming and from partially private trading and manufacturing in the towns to complete state ownership and control of urban production, distribution, and exchange. The proletarian state was strengthened, the proletariat grew vastly in size as a result of industrialization, and workers were freed forever from the danger of being held to ransom by hoarding peasants or economically exploited by Nepmen.

But which proletariat was the victor? As we have already seen, the term "proletarian" was applied both to the industrial working class and to the Communist Party in the early Soviet period. In the early 1930s, however, the two aspects of the concept started to diverge. Increasingly, the word "proletarian" (*proletarii, proletarskii*) was kept for formal and ceremonial purposes, and the words "worker" and "working-class" (*rabochii*) were preferred in other contexts.

One reason for the shift in usage was that the Soviet working class had changed as a result of Stalin's revolution. During the rapid industrial

[13] On the affirmative action program, see Sheila Fitzpatrick, *Education and Social Mobility in the Soviet Union, 1921–1934* (Cambridge, 1979), pp. 184–205. On direct promotion, see Fitzpatrick, "The Russian Revolution and Social Mobility: A Reexamination of the Question of Social Support for the Soviet Regime in the 1920s and 1930s," *Politics and Society* (fall 1984), pp. 119–41.

[14] For more discussion of this, see "Stalin and the Making of a New Elite" in Fitzpatrick, *The Cultural Front*, pp. 149–82.

expansion of the First Five-Year Plan, it had been flooded by new peasant recruits, who constituted a majority of all workers in many branches of the economy in the early 1930s. It was hard to see these peasants—fresh from the farm, many of them fleeing collectivization and dekulakization, inexperienced, aggrieved—as proletarian in consciousness or class essence. Furthermore, the industrial working class had simultaneously lost many of its most capable and "conscious" young cadres via "proletarian promotion," which took them away from the factory bench and launched them on new administrative and professional careers. This trajectory raised all kinds of theoretical problems. Could the proletariat still be the center of the Communist cosmos if it was possible and desirable to "promote" workers outwards and upwards?[15] Indeed, the whole concept of "proletarian promotion" was difficult to square with the bipolar or dialectical class structure of early Soviet imagination, since its implications were all hierarchical.

THE RETREAT FROM CLASS WAR IN THE 1930S

The phase of intensified imagination of class war lasted only a few years. This was not because Communist cadres lacked enthusiasm: all the evidence suggests that hunting class enemies was an extremely popular activity in the Communist Party and the Komsomol, and that low-level cadres and activists much preferred it to more mundane administrative and organizational tasks. It was the party leadership that backed off in the second quarter of the 1930s, evidently satisfied that major objectives like dekulakization and collectivization had been achieved, and perhaps also worried by the degree of disruption, the rapidly expanding size of the Gulag and prison population,[16] and the economic and social costs incurred.

By the mid 1930s, the party leadership had firmly put on the brakes, and a series of initiatives had been taken to redress the balance and move away from class discrimination. New rules on educational admissions, designed to move away from a class basis of selection to either an academic or egalitarian one, began to be introduced as early as 1931, but it took several years fully to implement and codify them. At the end of 1935, rules on entry to higher and secondary technical educational institutions were changed to allow admission of "all citizens of both sexes who pass

[15] The Russian terms used for proletarian promotion—"vydvizhenie" or, with reference to a specific policy objective, "vydvizhenchestvo"—literally convey only movement outward, but their usage in practice had strong connotations of upward movement as well.

[16] For a vivid statement of the leadership's concern at the out-of-control mushroooming of arrests, petitions for deportation of kulaks, etc., see the secret Central Committee instruction dated 8 May 1933, signed by Stalin and Molotov, in *Smolensk Archive*, WKP 178, p. 135.

the examinations."[17] This removed all trace of proletarian priority and lifted the earlier ban on admission of "social aliens" and children of kulaks and other disenfranchised persons.

In general, kulaks' children (though not kulaks themselves) had recovered most of their civil rights, including the right to vote, by the middle of the 1930s. The new stance towards kulaks' children was publicized in dramatic form at the end of 1935 at a conference of Stakhanovite tractor and combine drivers. One of the delegates, combine driver Tilba, described his travails as the son of a dekulakized kulak, complaining that, despite his fine record as a Stakhanovite, local party officials had tried to prevent him attending the conference because of the disgrace of his class background. At this point, Stalin interjected the momentous words: "A son does not answer for his father."[18]

The previous rule that sons *did* answer for their fathers had been enforced with particular zeal by the Komsomol, whose successive leaders in the 1920s and early '30s cherished its reputation for proletarian vigilance. The Komsomol had always used class criteria in admitting new members to the organization. These criteria were routinely incorporated in the draft of a new Komsomol constitution prepared for the Tenth All-Union Congress of the Komsomol, which was to meet in the spring of 1936. Stalin, however, amended the draft to eliminate class discrimination in admissions, recommending that the Komsomol should no longer consider itself "primarily a proletarian organization" but rather as "an organization of all progressive Soviet youth—workers, kolkhozniki, employees, and students."[19]

The Communist Party's admission procedures were amended not long after the Komsomol's. After several years of intensive (and intensively class-biased) recruitment that had greatly increased the numbers and proportional weight of worker and peasant members, the party had imposed a temporary moratorium on admission of new members in 1933. In 1936 it announced new rules on admissions which would come into force in 1937. In future the emphasis would be on recruitment of "the best people" in Soviet society rather than, as before, proletarian recruitment. "The best people" was a new concept in Soviet discourse. It implied a status hierarchy along a continuum (though without defining the axis), and it clearly represented a departure from the two-camp, Manichean approach to class that had been characteristic of the 1920s. In practice the new

---

[17] Resolution of TsIK and Sovnarkom on enrollment in higher educational institutions and technicums, *Trud*, 30 December 1935, p. 3.

[18] Reported *Komsomol'skaia pravda*, 2 December 1935, p. 2.

[19] Reported by Central Committee secretary Andreev in his keynote speech to the Tenth Komsomol Congress, *Pravda*, 21 April 1936, p. 2.

admissions rules opened the way to intensified recruitment from the white-collar, professional, and administrative group whose new collective name was "the Soviet intelligentsia."

The culmination of the retreat from class war came with the adoption of a new Constitution of the USSR, known as "the Stalin Constitution." This was promulgated in 1937, after extensive preparation and public debate, and it provided for juridical equality, including voting rights and the right to be elected as soviet deputies, for all citizens. This restored voting rights to former *lishentsy*, kulaks,[20] priests, and others formerly in the category of "class aliens."

It was in connection with the forthcoming Constitution that Stalin articulated a new theory of class in Soviet society, appropriate to circumstances in which proletarian dictatorship was giving way to the "building of socialism." In a speech on the draft constitution in November 1936, Stalin said that Soviet society had grown beyond the initial revolutionary phase of class war. It still contained classes, but these were nonantagonistic—that is, not liable to class conflict among themselves.[21] Stalin subsequently developed this concept:

> The distinctive thing about Soviet society at the present time, in contrast to any capitalist society, is that there are no longer antagonistic, hostile classes. The exploiting classes have been liquidated, and workers, peasants and intelligentsia, which comprise Soviet society, live and work on a basis of friendly cooperation . . . Soviet society . . . does not know [class] contradictions; it is free of class conflicts . . .[22]

According to Stalin's famous "two-and-a-half" formula, Soviet society in the current phase of the building of socialism consisted of two main classes, the working class and the kolkhoz peasantry, together with a "stratum" (*prosloika*), the intelligentsia. This "new" or "Soviet" intelligentsia subsumed both the old bourgeois intelligentsia (a term that was no longer used) and the new group of working-class and peasant *vydvizhentsy* promoted since the late 1920s.[23] For most purposes, it also included white-collar employees (*sluzhashchie*). By calling the intelligentsia a "stratum," Stalin evidently wanted to detach it from a class context and minimize any connotations of hierarchy. Nevertheless, a sense of social hierarchy—peasants, workers, and intelligentsia, in an ascending se-

---

[20] But note that kulaks did not recover all civil rights, since those that had been deported were not allowed to move out of the areas in which they had been resettled.

. [21] Stalin, "O proekte konstitutsii Soiuza SSR," 25 November 1936, in I. V. Stalin, *Sochineniia*, vol. 1 (14), ed. Robert H. McNeal (Stanford, 1967), pp. 142–46, 168–70.

[22] "Otchetnyi doklad na XVIII s"ezde partii—10.III.1939," in Stalin, *Sochineniia*, vol. 1 (14), pp. 366–67.

[23] Beneficiaries of "proletarian promotion."

quence—was definitely creeping in to the Communist discussions of the second half of the 1930s. In his speech to the Eighteenth Party Congress, for example, Stalin rebuked those comrades who were still in the grip of the "old theory" that workers or peasants who moved up into the intelligentsia were "second-rate people" compared with those who remained in the proletariat.[24] How could they be second-rate people, Stalin asked, when they belonged to that still, alas, relatively small proportion of the population that was "cultured and educated"? In time, culture and education would be accessible to all workers and peasants, but until then, he implied, members of the "new Soviet intelligentsia" were first-rate people, superior in social worth to the less-cultured workers and peasants.

CLASS TRAJECTORIES: "THEN" AND "NOW"

In the 1930s, as in the 1920s, the Soviet approach to class involved an important retrospective dimension. Even more significant than an individual's current social position was his class origin. A true class identification required that both situations ("then" and "now") be considered. It was not enough to know that an individual was a worker: was he a "cadre" (*kadrovyi*) or "hereditary" (*potomstvennyi*) worker or a worker "from the peasantry"? Similarly was a member of the intelligentsia "from the old intelligentsia" or "from the workers"? Was a kolkhoznik a former poor peasant or a former kulak?

This preoccupation was reflected in the statistical surveys of various groups taken in the 1930s. There were fewer in the Stalin period than earlier, but almost all of them focused on a "then and now" question. The 1932–33 Trade Union Census, for example, had a special category of trade union members who had recently arrived from the village, and even provided a more detailed breakdown on their pre-collectivization class status as peasants (whether they were kulaks, middle peasants, or poor peasants).[25] The 1935 Census of Soviet Trading Personnel distinguished employees and managers in state and cooperative trade who had formerly been Nepmen or employed in private enterprises.[26] A survey of senior cadres published in 1936 identified those who were of working-class background, as well as a narrower group that had still been "workers at the bench" in 1928.[27]

---

[24] "Otchetnyi doklad," in Stalin, *Sochineniia*, vol. 1 (14), p. 399.

[25] *Profsoiuznaia perepis' 1932–1933 g.* (Moscow, 1934).

[26] *Itogi torgovoi perepisi 1935 g.*, part 2: *Kadry sovetskoi torgovli* (Moscow, 1936).

[27] *Sostav rukovodiashchikh rabotnikov i spetsialistov Soiuza SSR* (Moscow, 1936).

The importance of "then and now" identification is illustrated by the standard questionnaire used in dossiers on Soviet wage- and salary-earners in the second half of the 1930s. Judging by the number of questions allocated to different subjects in the standard questionnaire, an individual's class definition was still considered more important than his educational history, criminal record, family status and responsibilities, and so on. The only subject that matched it in prominence was party and political record. Moreover, we have Malenkov's assurance (speaking retrospectively and critically about the situation in the 1930s) that the social data in the dossiers were taken extremely seriously.[28]

The following questions were asked on social position:[29]

Q.5. Social origin (*sotsial'noe proiskhozhdenie*):
   (a) former *soslovie* (title, rank),
   (b) basic occupation of parents.
Q.6. Basic occupation (for party members, occupation when you joined the party; for others, [occupation] when you began work in Soviet institutions)
Q.7. How many years did you work in that occupation?
Q.8. Year of moving out of production or quitting agriculture (*God ukhoda s proizvodstva ili ostavleniia sel'skogo khoziaistva*).[30]
Q.9. Social position (*sotsial'noe polozhenie*).

There are a number of "then and now" comparisons implicit in these questions. First, how does the respondent stand in social terms compared to his parents? Second, what is his position now compared with his position at the beginning of his working life? Perhaps the most remarkable of the questions is Question 8, which simply takes for granted that some basic change in social status (moving from a manual to a white-collar occupation or leaving the peasantry to become an urban worker) was

[28] In February 1941, Malenkov told the XVIII party conference that "We must put an end to the biological approach in the selection of cadres and judge cadres on performance, evaluating them on their work, and not just going on what is in their personal dossiers. Up to the present, despite the Party's instructions, when an official is appointed in many party and economic organs, people spend more time establishing his genealogy, finding out who his grandfather and grandmother were, than studying his personal managerial and political qualities [and] his abilities." G. Malenkov, "O zadachakh partiinykh organizatsii v oblasti promyshlennosti i transporta," *Pravda*, 16 February 1941, p. 3.

[29] Gosudarstvennyi arkhiv Rossiiskoi Federatsii (GARF), f. 5457, op. 22, ed. khr. 48: Union of Knitting Workers, 1935: *lichnyi listok po uchetu kadrov*. A 1938 dossier in the archive contains the same questions. In both cases, the respondents (or the officials who filled in the questionnaires for them) answered all the questions on social position in detail, although some questions on other subjects were left blank.

[30] "God ukhoda s proizvodstva" refers to the year when the individual moved from blue-collar work into white-collar.

likely to have occurred in the life of the average Soviet citizen, and asks when it was. Taken as a whole, the point of these questions is not so much to identify an individual's *location* in social space but to establish his *trajectory*.

There was no specific term for social mobility in Stalinist discourse, but the idea was very familiar to Soviet citizens of the 1930s. One trajectory in particular was often described and offered for emulation. This was the Soviet version of the Horatio Alger story, in which a young man rises from the working class or peasantry by dint of hard work and commitment to the Revolution, is helped by the party to acquire an education, and becomes a member of the "new Soviet intelligentsia"—that is, the professional and administrative elite.[31] A typical example is the short autobiographical sketch offered by the rising young politician P. S. Popkov when he ran as a candidate in the 1938 elections for the Russian Supreme Soviet:

> My life is the life of an ordinary warrior of the party of Lenin and Stalin. The son of a landless poor peasant, I worked as a shepherd from nine years of age. Then I was a laborer, a carpenter, a rabfak student, a university student. In 1937, I became an engineer . . .[32]

Popkov, a peasant's son who had worked for a few years as a young man in various blue-collar occupations before receiving his "proletarian promotion," was of lower-class origin, but clearly his actual working-class affiliations were marginal. His proletarian roots were in the invented class of the 1920s, and that class was in process of conceptual evolution in the latter part of the 1930s. It was becoming an imagined community that existed *only in the past tense*—a place people came from, but not a place they currently inhabited.

In the spectrum of "then and now" trajectories, not all were as benign as Popkov's. A second trajectory that frequently attracted attention in the 1930s was that of the apparently harmless Soviet citizen, usually a *sluzhashchii* or worker, who had successfully concealed his "alien" origins. In legal terms, such people always had the right to employment, and from 1936 even had the right to vote. In practice, however, their presence in the workforce, when discovered, was almost invariably regarded as undesirable, and a sinister interpretation was put on their attempts to "pass" as normal citizens.

The common "alien" origin of such persons was, of course, the invented bourgeoisie of the 1920s. Like its antithesis, the invented proletariat, this class underwent evolution. But its evolution was different: instead

---

[31] The myth and the substance behind it are discussed in my article "Stalin and the Making of a New Elite," in Fitzpatrick, *The Cultural Front.*

[32] *Pravda,* 2 June 1938, p. 3.

of being reimagined in a new form, it had actually made the transition from imagination to substance. Part of the original invented bourgeoisie split off and assumed concrete form in the 1920s as *byvshie* (people who had lost their former privileged status because of the Revolution) and *lishentsy* (people who were disenfranchised as social aliens). In the 1930s, the same process occurred with peasants expropriated as kulaks during collectivization, who formed a new social class of the dekulakized (*rasku-lachennye*).

This is one of the most interesting examples of Soviet invention of class, since it can be seen as a second attempt to invent a kulak class after the first attempt had failed to win universal acceptance. The concept of a kulak class of peasants, defined by its exploitative relationship to other peasants, was very attractive to Communists in the 1920s. But peasants were not readily convinced that such a class existed in their midst, and Communist officials often found it difficult to define the criteria for kulaks or to say exactly which peasants in a given community they fitted. This ambiguity was completed resolved by dekulakization. There might previously have been room for argument about whether peasant X—with his two cows, an orchard, and an uncle in trade in a nearby town—was or was not a kulak. Once he had been formally dekulakized, however, there was no room for further argument about his status: he was a *raskulachen-nyi*—that is, by definition a former (dekulakized) kulak. Thus, the Soviet liquidation of the kulak class could even be regarded as the final, definitive step in its invention.

Shadows of Old Class Enemies

> *The time has been,*
> *That, when the brains were out, the man would die,*
> *And there an end; but now they rise again,*
> *With twenty mortal murders on their crowns,*
> *And push us from our stools: this is more strange*
> *Than such a murder is.*
>
> William Shakespeare, Macbeth

Soviet Communists of the 1930s had the same trouble with the class enemy as Macbeth with Banquo. The liquidation was carried out, but the ghost returned to taunt them at the feast. According to Marxist theory, transformation of the Soviet Union's economic base and the relations of production had not only removed the last remnants of capitalism but also guaranteed against the possibility of resurrection. Yet Communists could still sense the presence of those class enemies that had been consigned to the dustheap of history and it turned out to be almost more terrible to fight them as ghosts.

This had been sombrely predicted by Stalin in 1929 when he first formulated the theory that that the more certain the defeat of the class enemy, the more desperate and uncompromising would be his resistance.[33] The theory had then seemed implausible and un-Marxist to many Communist intellectuals. Five years later, however, after practical experience of the "liquidation as a class" of kulaks and Nepmen, the paradox may have acquired broader resonance. Stalin, in any case, had developed his thought more fully. His remarks on the subject in 1934 were paraphrased thus by State Prosecutor Krylenko:

> How does the question [of class enemies] stand today? Is the landowning class in existence or not? No, it has been annihilated, destroyed. The capitalists? No, destroyed, annihilated. Merchants? . . . annihilated. Where are the [old exploiting] classes? It seems there are none! Wrong! Thrice wrong! Th[os]e people exist . . . We did not physically destroy them, and they have remained with all their class sympathies, antipathies, traditions, habits, opinions, world views and so on . . . The class enemy, despite the annihilation of the class of landlords, has remained in the person of living representatives of those former classes.[34]

An entrenched Communist *mentalité* of suspicion of class enemies meant that the policies of class conciliation introduced in the mid 1930s (see above) were neither wholeheartedly recommended by party leaders nor systematically implemented by lower-level party officials. There was a basic ambivalence on the class issue in the 1930s that swung over toward genuine relaxation only at the end of the decade, in the period of exhaustion and hungover sobriety that followed the bacchanalia of the Great Purges. Before that time, it was always likely that a Communist's head and his heart (including, no doubt, Stalin's) would be at odds on questions of class and the class enemy. The rational man might accept that class-discriminatory policies had outlived their day and the class enemy was no longer a real threat, but the intuitive man remained dubious and fearful.

We see examples of this at every level, not only within the party but also outside it. The Smolensk Archive contains large numbers of party investigations based on the denunciations of persons "linked with the class enemy" that continued to pour in from all sides—villages as well as

---

[33] See "O pravom uklone v VKP(b)" (April 1929), in Stalin, *Sochineniia*, vol. 12 (Moscow, 1952), pp. 34–39.

[34] Speech by Krylenko to judicial officers in Ufa, March 1934, from *Sovetskaia iustitsiia*, 1934 no. 9, p. 2.

towns, nonparty citizens as well as party activists.[35] It is striking that not only were citizens inclined to inform on hidden "class enemies" in their midst but Communist officials continued to dignify these accusations by investigating them seriously and conscientiously. Huge numbers of bureaucratic man-hours were spent on careful on-site investigations of whether kolkhoz brigade leader Y was really married to the daughter of a former priest, or Komsomol Z had tried to conceal the fact that his uncle had been dekulakized.

The party leadership was sometimes, but not always, more relaxed on the question of class enemies than rank-and-file Communists. With regard to deported kulaks, for example, local activists objected strongly when a proposal to allow them to return from exile after three years was floated at the Second Congress of Kolkhoz Shockworkers in 1935, presumably by Iakovlev, the Central Committee secretary in charge of agriculture.[36] (The proposal was subsequently dropped, and the deported kulaks remained subject to restriction on mobility until after the Second World War—despite the fact that they were called up for wartime military service along with everybody else.)[37]

A sense of similar indecisiveness is associated with Stalin's interjection at the Stakhanovite Congress of 1935 that "A son does not answer for his father" (see above, p. 41). Uncharacteristically, this remark was left almost without commentary in the Soviet press of 1935. Several newspapers even published editorials and articles shortly afterward that reaffirmed the party's commitment to vigilance against class enemies, as if to mitigate its impact. Moreover, Stalin himself did not repeat the thought in any more formal context or include it in any of his published works, and, in a departure from normal practice, it was only rarely cited by his colleagues.[38] As a result, although the remark seems instantly to have entered Soviet folklore and was firmly attributed to Stalin, a certain mystery surrounded it. Was it Stalin's opinion, but not that of others in the leadership, that "A son does not answer for his father"? Had Stalin really said it? Or was the persistent rumor that he had said it spread by enemies for the confusion of Communists?

---

[35] Among the large number of files in this category are *Smolensk Archive*, WKP 190 (1935), 195 (1936), 355 (1936), and 362 (1937).

[36] *Vtoroi Vsesoiuznyi s"ezd kolkhoznikov-udarnikov. 11–17 fevralia 1935 g. Stenograficheskii otchet* (Moscow, 1935), pp. 60, 81, 130.

[37] I. Ia Trifonov, *Likvidatsiia ekspluatatorskikh klassov v SSSR* (Moscow, 1975), pp. 390–91.

[38] The only two citations I have located are by S. Kaftanov, chairman of the All-Union Committee on the Higher School, in 1938 (*Vysshaia shkola*, 1938 no. 3, p. 16), and by Politburo member Andrei Zhdanov in his speech to the Eighteenth Party Congress in 1939 (*Vosemnadtsatyi s"ezd VKP[b]. Stenograficheskii otchet* [Moscow, 1939], p. 523).

In each successive political crisis of the 1930s, Communists hastened to round up "the usual suspects," knowing instinctively that the class enemy must be somehow to blame. This happened during the 1932–33 famine, when the NKVD expelled hundreds of thousands of "class aliens" and *lishentsy* from Moscow, Leningrad, and other cities at the time of the introduction of passports.[39] There were similar mass expulsions from Leningrad in 1935 after Kirov's murder, and a local newspaper reporting them scarcely even bothered to explain why a connection might be suspected between Kirov's assassin and *byvshie* such as "former Baron Tipolt [who had] got himself a job in an industrial meal-service as an accountant, General Tiufiasev [who] was a teacher of geography, former *politsmeister* Komendantov [who] was a technician at a factory, [and] General Spasskii, [who] was a cigarette seller in a kiosk."[40]

The pattern was repeated even in the Great Purges, despite the fact that "class enemies" were no longer (as in the First Five-Year Plan) the primary target of victimization and that the official rhetoric against "enemies of the people" did not stress the theme of origins.[41] In the autumn of 1937, the head of the Leningrad NKVD identified university students who were sons of kulaks and Nepmen as a particular category of "enemies of the people" who should be exposed and rooted out.[42] At the same period, the Smolensk Komsomol expelled dozens and probably hundreds of its members on grounds of alien social origin, connection by marriage with class aliens, concealment of such origins and connections, and so on. (A large number of these victims were formally reinstated in the Komsomol in 1938 after appealing their expulsions.)[43] In Cheliabinsk, former class enemies were among those executed as counterrevolutionaries in 1937–38.[44]

• • •

The Bolshevik "invention of class" in the 1920s probably served at least some useful organizational and restructuring functions, but there was a price to be paid. In the first place, individual class identities that had to be "invented" were liable to contain elements of deception. That in-

---

[39] See reports in *Sotsialisticheskii vestnik*, 1933 no. 3 (13 February), p. 16, and 1933 no. 8 (25 May), p. 16.

[40] *Krest'ianskaia pravda* (Leningrad), 24 March 1935, p. 3.

[41] In fact, in an unreported speech in the Defense Commissariat on 2 June 1937, Stalin explicitly dismissed class origins as an automatic indicator of disloyalty: *Istochnik* 3 (1994), p. 73.

[42] Reported in *Komsomol'skaia pravda*, 5 October 1937, p. 2.

[43] The rehabilitations are in *Smolensk Archive*, WKP 416.

[44] See data from local NKVD files cited in G. Izhbuldin, "Nazvat' vse imena," *Ogonek*, 7 (February 1989), p. 30.

creased the regime's distrust of its citizens and citizens' distrust of each other. In the second place, the notion of *enemies* became inseparable from the idea of class. That introduced a corrosive chemical into the Bolsheviks' social cement whose virulence was demonstrated in the Great Purges.

The bewildering vagueness of the accusations against "enemies of the people" becomes fully comprehensible only if we remember the light in which Bolshevik imagination cast their precursors, the "class enemies." A class enemy was potentially harmful to society regardless of his specific actions or individual intentions, and often wore a mask concealing his true identity. He was a member, whether he knew it or not, of an imagined community of class whose interests were inimical to those of Soviet power. It was only a small conceptual step from being part of an imagined class community to being part of an imagined conspiracy. One step further, and the imagined *class* basis of the conspiracy would fall away.

CHAPTER THREE

Class Identities In NEP Society

> CLASS RELATIONS are considered very important by Communist leaders, in accordance with their program. The **class principle** is applied in many contexts. It is also often necessary to speak of **declassing** and of **declassed** groups: "the de-**classed** petty-bourgeois intelligentsia" . . . "the mass of de-**classed** persons, the unemployed, the mass that has lost its sharply defined class profile, the mass of social fragments." [1]

The 1920s were the great age of Marxist analysis of Soviet society. The statisticians collected data on the class composition of every conceivable social institution and organization, including the Commmunist Party. The peasantry was diligently analyzed to identify the breakdown into class categories of "poor peasant," "middle peasant," and "kulak." The social origin of state officials and university students was repeatedly investigated and tabulated. The statistical department party's Central Committee issued guidelines on occupations and class classification: gravediggers and chauffeurs, it turned out, were "proletarian," but domestic servants, porters, and shop assistants belonged to the class of "junior service personnel" (*mladshii obsluzhiaviushchii personal*).[2]

It was not just intellectual curiosity that led the Bolsheviks to collect these sociological data on such a large scale. As discussed in the previous chapter, they needed the information in order to carry out their own class-discriminatory legislation, which affected people's everyday life as well as social status in the new society. But it quickly became obvious that identification of individuals by class was no easy matter in a society that had just been through a revolutionary upheaval. In 1924 officials conducting a purge of Perm University found it extraordinarily difficult to identify the class position of individual students, despite intensive interviewing:

This is a slightly edited version of my article "Problems of Class Identity in NEP Society," in *Russia in the Era of NEP*, eds. Sheila Fitzpatrick, Alexander Rabinowitch, and Richard Stites.

[1] A. M. Selishchev, *Iazyk revoliutsionnoi epokhi: Iz nabliudenii nad russkim iazykom poslednikh let (1917–1926)* (Moscow, 1928, 2nd ed.,), p. 105.

[2] *Slovar' zaniatii lits naemnogo truda: Posobie dlia rabotnikov iacheek i komitetov VKP(b) pri opredelenii roda zaniatii kommunistov i prinimaevykh v partiiu* (Moscow: Statisticheskii otdel TsK, 1928), passim.

"What did your parents do before [the Revolution]?"

"My father is a worker, here is the document."

In the document, which is twenty years old, it says: "Metalworker in depot of the Singer Company."

"And what did he do in 1918?"

"He worked here as a baker, he was in a baker's artel . . ."

"Hm, a metalworker and a baker," says the registrar in bewilderment. "And then, in 1919 and 1920, where did he work?"

"The A[merican] R[elief] A[ssociation] offered Papa a place as an inspector . . . He worked as an ARA inspector until 1923. . . . And then he was unemployed for a year."

"What does he do now?"

"Now he has got a job. Here is the document from the Labor Exchange."

It reads: "Sent at the request of a private entrepreneur to 'manage the Office.' "[3]

If this degree of occupational and social mobility was baffling to the Bolsheviks, it was also bewildering and frightening for the individuals concerned. Was that Perm student's father, in his own eyes, a temporarily declassed proletarian or a new recruit to the ranks of the white-collar petty bourgeoisie? Was his social self-identification shared by his daughter, who needed to qualify as a proletarian in order to stay in college? If she satisfied the examining registrar, would she feel herself to be proletarian? If she failed, would she accept a petty bourgeois identity?

THE BOLSHEVIKS AND PROLETARIAN IDENTITY

The most desirable class identity in NEP Russia—proletarian—was, for that reason, the most problematical. The Bolshevik Party defined itself as the party of the proletariat and the events of October as the proletarian revolution. The industrial working class had, for the most part, supported the Bolsheviks in October. The Bolsheviks assumed that this class would also provide the necessary social support for the new revolutionary regime, the "dictatorship of the proletariat."

But what if this turned out not to be so?

In 1920 and 1921 the Bolsheviks confronted a double disaster. In the first place, the industrial working class had largely disintegrated. In the second place, many of the remaining workers had become alienated from

[3] V.Sh-rin, "Chistiat (s natury i po ofitsial'nym dokumentam)," *Krasnaia molodezh'*, 1924 no. 2, p. 126.

the Bolshevik party, as was evident in the strikes in Petrograd in early 1921 and the Kronstadt revolt. Within the party, the Workers' Opposition had mounted a significant, though ultimately unsuccessful, challenge to the Bolshevik leadership. All this produced a brief crisis of faith in which leading party members (including Lenin) hovered on the brink of disillusionment with the Russian working class.[4] But it proved impossible for the party to abandon the proletarian connection. A majority of all party members in 1921 had been workers before the Revolution and defined themselves as proletarian. The party's intellectuals, who often saw themselves as having adopted "proletarian" identity when they became revolutionaries, were also emotionally committed. The intellectuals, moreover, felt caught on the horns of a Marxist dilemma. If the proletariat was no longer the base of support, on what class did the party and the new Soviet depend? To that question, there was no acceptable answer.[5]

The party remained proletarian by self-definition, and at the beginning of 1924, with the announcement of the mass recruitment of workers known as the "Lenin levy," the party leaders did their best to turn this premise into reality. For the Bolsheviks, however, the word "proletarian" was not simply a synonym for "working-class." Real proletarians had to have proletarian consciousness, which from the Bolshevik standpoint implied commitment to the Revolution and the Bolshevik Party. There were many actual workers at the beginning of the 1920's who failed this test and were therefore shown to be "accidental elements" in the working class, people whose *mentalité* was essentially peasant or petty bourgeois.

There were also increasing numbers of "proletarians," often but not invariably members of the Bolshevik Party, who had once been workers by occupation and social position but were now, in the aftermath of the Revolution, Red Army commissars and commanders or cadres in the new soviet and party bureaucracies. It was necessary for the Bolsheviks to distinguish them from "workers at the bench," while at the same time emphasizing their continuing proletarian identity.[6]

By the early 1920s, therefore, analyses of the class composition of institutions, including the Bolshevik Party itself, used two categories for class

[4] See discussion in "The Bolsheviks' Dilemma," in Fitzpatrick, *The Cultural Front*, pp. 16–36.

[5] "An awful situation has been created," said Iurii Milonov at the Tenth Party Congress. "We find ourselves above an abyss, between the working class, which is infected with petty bourgeois prejudices, and the peasantry, which is petty bourgeois in essence. It is impossible to depend solely on the soviet and party bureaucracy." *Desiatyi syezd RKP(b). Mart 1921 g. Stenograficheskii otchet* (Moscow, 1963), p. 74.

[6] According to Selishchev, the terms "rabochie ot stanka" and "krest'ianin ot sokha" were new coinages in Russian, introduced by the Bolsheviks on the semantic pattern of the German "Arbeiter von Erde." Selishchev, *Iazyk revoliutsionnoi epokhi*, pp. 36–37.

identification: "before" and "after" the Revolution. The first category, social position, was based on social origin and occupation in 1917, or in some cases occupation at the moment of joining the Bolshevik Party. The second category was current occupation. Thus, a working-class party cadre would be listed as working-class by social position and white-collar (*sluzhashchii*) by current occupation. A Bolshevik worker who had been a peasant at the time of joining the party would be listed as peasant by social position and worker by current occupation.[7]

For Bolshevik purposes in the 1920s, the "before" category was usually the crucial one. What really mattered about class, from the Bolshevik standpoint, was its implication for political attitude. If someone had been a member of the exploiting classes on the eve of the Revolution, he was likely to regret the passing of the old regime and dislike the Bolsheviks. But if someone had belonged to the exploited masses, he was probably on the side of the Bolsheviks and the revolution.

There remained a residual problem about the "before" category, namely that social origin (*proiskhozhdenie*) and prerevolutionary occupation did not always coincide. For example, it was common for a worker to have been born and spent his early years in the village. For purposes of party entry and the like, his social position was defined as proletarian. But what was the right category for a *former* worker, village-born, and now a cadre? The answer was still proletarian, even though the individual in question might have spent less than ten of his thirty years actually working as a worker in a factory.

Since there were many such cases, the Bolsheviks instinctively moved toward a concept of *formative proletarian experience* as a determinant of class position. There were no formal guidelines, but as a rule of thumb, seven or more years experience as a worker in a factory before the Revolution (or before joining the prerevolutionary Bolshevik Party and becoming a professional revolutionary) was assumed to make a man proletarian.

In addition, it became widely accepted that Red Army service as a volunteer during the Civil War also constituted formative proletarian experience, at least for persons of lower-class urban or peasant background. Thus, a young man of provincial, probably peasant, origin could legitimately claim that he qualified for the rabfak (the workers' preparatory school that was a stepping stone to higher education in the 1920s): "Why don't they take me? I served in the Red Army as a volunteer, I am worthy, I have earned the Rabfak."[8]

---

[7] See *Sotsial'nyi i natsional'nyi sostav VKP(b). Itogi vsesoiuznoi partiinoi perepisi 1927 g.* (Moscow, 1928).

[8] Rostovskii, "Khozhdenie po mukam odnogo rabfakovtsa," *Molodaia gvardiia*, 5 (1924), p. 212. But note that, when the young Communists who headed RAPP (the militant

PROLETARIAN AND WORKING-CLASS IDENTITIES

When workers of the older (prerevolutionary) generation described themselves as "proletarian," this was a sign that their consciousness had been raised by contact with the Bolsheviks or other revolutionary intellectuals: the word would not otherwise have been a part of their vocabulary. "Proletarian" was sometimes used interchangeably with "worker" (*rabochii*), but it was most often used to denote a particular type of worker—one who had participated in labor organizations and protests, identified with the workers' factory (or shop) collective, and was aware of capitalists as the class enemy and the Tsarist state as the capitalists' ally.

When the Bolsheviks spoke of the proletariat in the 1920s, they still thought above all of the type of worker "tempered in the revolutionary struggle." But the revolutionary struggle was over, and this kind of proletarian consciousness probably could not be reproduced in future generations.[9] As the Bolsheviks gradually redefined the concept of proletarian consciousness into a notion of revolutionary and ultimately civic responsibility, the distance between the ideal proletarian and the actual worker grew larger.

With the revival of industry and re-formation of the working class in the 1920s, new working-class *mentalités* emerged and old ones revived in new forms. Among the recognizable working-class (but not completely "proletarian") identities of NEP was that of the skilled worker with ties to the land. Although Marxist sociologists of the 1920s often tried to minimize or explain away these ties, they seem to have been strengthened in the Civil War years, when many workers (including skilled workers) went back to the villages. Perhaps the most interesting feature of workers' "ties to the land" during NEP is that they were in many cases ties to the improving farmer—sometimes the worker-peasant himself, sometimes a close family member.[10] In some industries, like textiles in the Ivanovo region, whole communities of workers were involved in profitable farm-

---

proletarian writers' organization of the 1920s) made similar claims, these were often regarded sceptically, despite their credentials of Civil War experience, because they came from upper-class, intelligentsia families.

[9] See Diane P. Koenker, "Class and Consciousness in a Socialist Society: Workers in the Printing Trades during NEP," in *Russia in the Era of NEP*, eds. Fitzpatrick et al., pp. 34–57.

[10] See, for example, the interesting biography of I. E. Kniazev, a worker whose participation in the revolutionary movement from 1905 led him to return periodically to his village in Moscow gubernia to escape the police. In 1917, impressed by the agricultural techniques of German colonists, he returned permanently to the countryside to put them into practice, becoming a prosperous peasant farmer and Soviet official by the mid 1920s: S. Leningradskii, *Ot zemli na zavod i s zavoda na zemliu* (Moscow-Leningrad, 1927).

ing.[11] The scale of this phenomenon was recognized only at the end of the 1920s (and then only semipublicly), when many skilled workers and their families were threatened with dekulakization.[12]

Another emerging working-class *mentalité* might be described, with apologies to Lenin, as "trade-union consciousness." The trade unions of NEP, whose tone seems to have been set by male, middle-aged, firmly urban workers who had been in the factories before the Revolution, were committed to working within the system but also to defending labor's (or the unions') interests against Soviet management. Since unemployment was high, the unions did their best to enforce closed-shop rules and limit the influx of nonunionized peasants. Their bias was not only antipeasant but to some degree antiwomen and antiadolescent as well, because it was assumed by most trade unionists that adult, urban males needed the jobs most.

Young workers of the postrevolutionary cohort often had prickly relations with their elders in the factory. They were said to be disrespectful, overconfident and not amenable to collective discipline.

> The lads do not always want to obey the administration or the foreman or anyone else. If, for the good of production, they get transferred to worse work in another shop, they make objections and threaten to give both the foreman and the administration a thrashing. Boys still wet behind the ears beat their chests and declaim: 'What did we fight for!'[13]

Youth unemployment was high, and it was hard for young people to get a factory job. Those who did were an educated and ambitious group, little different in sociocultural profile[14] and political culture[15] from their white-collar and student peers, whose sights were often set (consciously or unconsciously) beyond the factory. Young proletarians were an elect group in NEP society. They were the *smena*, the coming generation, the future builders of socialism. The Komsomol and party wanted them as members, and every educational institution in the country wanted them as students to meet its proletarian quotas. To be a young, skilled male worker in the

---

[11] See N. Semenov, *Litso fabrichnykh rabochikh prozhivaiushchikh v derevniakh i polit-prosvetrabota sredi nikh* (Moscow-Leningrad, 1929).

[12] See, for example, the anxious discussion of this problem in *Ianvarskii obyedinennyi plenum M[oskovskogo] K[omiteta VKP(b)] i M[oskovskoi] K[ontrol'noi] K[omissi]. 6–10 ianvaria 1930 g.* (Moscow, 1930), p. 34, and *Sessiia TsIK Soiuza SSSR 6 sozyva. Stenograficheskii otchet i postanovleniia. 22–28 dekabria 1931 g.* (Moscow, 1931), Bulletin 10, p. 13.

[13] A. Bordadyn, "Rabochaia molodezh' kak ona est'," *Molodaia gvardiia* 3 (1926), p. 102. For an interesting discussion of the attitudes of working-class youth, see N. B. Lebina, *Rabochaia molodezh' Leningrada: Trud i sotsial'nyi oblik 1921–1925 gody* (Leningrad, 1982).

[14] For a description of a young Moscow worker's recreational and cultural habits, see S. A. Antonov, *Svet n v okne*, (Moscow, 1977), pp. 19–24, 69–70.

[15] On the new political culture of young workers, see Selishchev, *Iazyk*, pp. 198–200.

1920s was to have a new kind of proletarian consciousness—that of a potentially upwardly mobile proletarian *vydvizhenets*.

THE BOURGEOIS OTHER

> *In the revolutionary years, . . . many words changed their meaning in connection with the circumstances of the time and with the moods and sufferings of social groups . . .*
> **Bourgeois** *and* **petty-bourgeois** *[now] have a pejorative meaning.*[16]

The bourgeoisie was, of course, the antithesis of the proletariat in Marxist analysis. Its old elite social role was one the Bolsheviks particularly disliked, yet in some respects could be seen as inheriting. In Soviet usage of the 1920s, the term "bourgeois" was applied to the class enemy in general, as well as to three distinct social groups in NEP society: "byvshie" (members of the old privileged classes, including the landowning and bureaucratic nobility), Nepmen, and the non-Communist intelligentsia.

Although Russia had lost a large part of its prerevolutionary elites during the years of war, revolution, and civil war, as a result of expropriation and emigration, the old "bourgeoisie" was still seem as a threat by Bolsheviks. This was because of the possibility of a capitalist *revanche* staged from abroad. Lenin explained:

> They [Russian bourgeoisie] have retained their class organization abroad, as an emigration which probably numbers one and a half to two million persons and possesses more than fifty daily newspapers of all the bourgeois and "socialist" (that is, petty bourgeois) parties, the remnants of an army and many links with the international bourgeoisie. This emigration devotes all its strength and resources to the destruction of Soviet power and the restoration of capitalism in Russia.[17]

The *byvshie*—those of the former privileged classes who had remained in Russia—were assumed to be potential allies of the Russian and foreign capitalists abroad. Bolsheviks feared their influence in Soviet society, even when (as was generally the case) they occupied humble positions, steered clear of politics, and tried to conceal their past. Their children, also seen as a possible source of corruption, were barred from the Pioneers, the Komsomol, and, as far as possible, higher educational institutions.[18]

---

[16] Selishchev, *Iazyk*, pp. 192–93.

[17] V. I. Lenin, *Polnoe sobranie sochinenii v 55-i tomakh*, vol. 44 (Moscow, 1964), p. 5.

[18] See, for example, the case of young Lidia Tolstaia, who was refused entry to the Pioneers on the grounds that her grandmother, widow of an Admiral in the Imperial Fleet,

Nepmen—the "new bourgeoisie" of private entrepreneurs engendered by NEP—were also regarded with great distrust and suspicion. While Nepmen, like *byvshie*, showed few signs of political activism or aspiration, the Bolsheviks still thought of them as potential challengers and future leaders of a return to capitalism, and regarded their reticence as a sign of cunning. Although their activities were no longer illegal, as they had been when they operated on the black market under War Communism, this did not convey any marked increase in social tolerance on the Bolshevik side. Nepmen were caricature figures, depicted as bloated and rapacious exploiters, "stroll[ing] along the alleys with self-important expressions in the company of their overfed, incredibly well-groomed wives, dressed up to kill."[19]

The majority of Nepmen seem to have been parvenus, not descendants of the old merchant and capitalist business classes.[20] Nevertheless, the possibility of links forged between Nepmen and members of the old elites was anxiously monitored, and one observer (a contemporary criminal investigator) claimed that "Leningrad Nepmen eagerly married brides with princely and ducal titles and in the way of life and manners imitated the old Petersburg 'high society' in every way."[21] Still more alarming, and more plausible, was the danger of *rapprochement* between Nepmen and the new Soviet elite. Under NEP conditions, the most profitable entrepreneurial activities were across the boundary of the public and private sectors, and the Nepmen's function as a *tolkach* made him a valuable contact for Bolshevik managers and industrial officials.[22]

In Soviet discourse of the 1920s, educated professionals (members of the intelligentsia) were also "bourgeois," unless they had proved otherwise by joining the Bolshevik Party before the Revolution. The term Bolsheviks used for the intelligentsia was "bourgeois specialists." This had an ironic ring, since historically the Russian intelligentsia had supported radical causes, prided itself on being above class, and despised the commercial bourgeoisie as philistine. Nevertheless, the intelligentsia had been one of the elites of prerevolutionary society, and, unlike other prerevolutionary elites, it had emerged from the upheaval of revolution and civil war more or less intact, unsympathetic to Bolshevism, and strongly con-

---

spoke French and was "from the byvshie," and that her parents knew the poets Khlebnikov and Viacheslav Ivanov. Lidiia Libedinskaia, *Zelenaia lampa. Vospominaniia* (Moscow, 1966), pp. 48–60.

[19] Lev Sheinin, *Zapiski sledovatelia* (Moscow, 1965), pp. 32–33.

[20] *Izmeneniia sotsial'noi struktury sovetskogo obshchestva 1921—seredina 30-kh godov* (Moscow, 1979), pp. 116–17; I. Ia. Trifonov, *Klassy i klassovaia bor'ba v SSSR v nachale NEPa (1921–1925 gg.)* (Leningrad, 1969), part 2, pp. 70–71.

[21] Trifonov, *Klassy*, pp. 268–69.

[22] Fixer, procurer of goods, expeditor of deliveries.

scious of its identity as a group. The Bolsheviks had some reason to fear the intelligentsia as a viable competing elite with pretensions to moral if not political leadership.

"Bourgeois specialists" remained a relatively privileged group in the 1920s, because the Bolshevik leaders concluded that their skills were irreplaceable. But this policy was not popular with the rank and file of the party or its urban lower-class sympathizers. "Whatever privileges you give them, it's like the proverb—'No matter how much you feed the wolf, he still looks to the forest'. . . ," one soviet deputy from the provinces complained.[23]

"The word 'intelligent' is becoming a term of abuse," an Old Bolshevik intellectual commented with alarm in the mid 1920s.[24] Intelligentshchina, an unambiguous pejorative, was widely used during NEP, especially in Komsomol circles, to describe attitudes that were liberal, vacillating, weak, and lacking the necessary Bolshevik quality of tverdost' (tough-mindedness). The disgust with which many lower-class Bolsheviks viewed the intelligentsia is well conveyed in a report by a Workers' Control official on the Stanislavsky Theater in Moscow. The theater people mocked the Bolsheviks' slogans and sneered that their red banners were "aesthetically displeasing," and the general manager was

> a repellent manifestation of a class that has had its day, a sycophant . . . Today he shakes our party member's hand and tries to bow low to him, but in fact hates that Communist to the depths of his soul, hates everything Communist, every value that the working class and the party inculcates."[25]

BOURGEOIS AND PETTY BOURGEOIS TENDENCIES

Rank-and-file Bolsheviks often used a "genealogical" approach to class in the 1920s, although this upset the Party's Marxist intellectuals.[26] "Once a bourgeois always a bourgeois" was what the genealogical approach

---

[23] Tret'ia sessia Tsentral'nogo Ispolnitel'nogo Komiteta SSSR 5-go sozyva. Steno-graficheskii otchet, (Moscow, 1931), Bulletin 10, p. 13.

[24] Skrypnik, in Biulleten' VIII-i vseukrainskoi konferentsii Kommunisticheskoi partii (bol'shevikov) Ukrainy. (Stenogramma). 12–16 maia 1924 g. (Kharkov, [1924]), pp. 64–65.

[25] Karaseva (Moscow Control Commission), speaking at III-ia moskovskaia oblastnaia i II-ia gorodskaia konferentsiia VKP(b), (Moscow, January 1932), Bulletin 10, p. 11.

[26] Emelian Iaroslavskii complained that the Bolsheviks were doing (in reverse) "almost what the Whiteguards do when they take a prisoner: they look to see if there are callouses on his hand, and if there are, that means he's a real criminal, a Bolshevik." XI syezd RKP(b). Mart—aprel' 1922 g. Stenograficheskii otchet (Moscow, 1961), p. 105.

meant in practice, but that did not mean that members of other classes were safe from the siren song of the bourgeoisie. The Bolsheviks believed that their revolution had interfered with the society's natural progression to capitalism, and they were constantly on guard against a spontaneous reversion. "Bourgeois" and "petty bourgeois" influences were everywhere, and persons of any social class were liable to succumb to them.

Discussion of "bourgeois" and "petty bourgeois" tendencies could sometimes be taken more or less literally. For example, a worker whose wife was in trade might be said to be under petty bourgeois entrepreneurial influence, and a worker-peasant who clung to his plot of land in the village might be thought to show petty bourgeois proprietorial instincts. In other cases, however, the accusations had a more tenuous connection to social reality. For example, Bolshevik Oppositionists and persons who had once belonged to other political parties were identifiable ipso facto as bourgeois or petty bourgeois.

There were serious reasons for the party to fear embourgeoisement of its cadres. In taking power from the old ruling classes, the Bolsheviks risked inheriting materialist bourgeois values and style of life as well. This was described in the 1920s as the danger of "degeneration"—that is, loss of the Party's revolutionary dedication. Such degeneration might occur, Bolsheviks feared, if party cadres were corrupted by *byvshie*, Nepmen, and bourgeois intellectuals, or by contact with the foreign capitalist world.[27]

Nepmen might corrupt the Soviet officials with whom they did business by arousing "aspirations towards the 'easy life' " and using "bribery and all kinds of small services, entertainments and 'gifts'."[28] As noted above, this was not an idle fear. In Moscow, at least, Nepmen, members of the old intelligentsia, and party leaders mingled in the cafe society of NEP, and it is reasonable to suppose that in this milieu "bourgeois" values were more likely to influence Communists than vice versa. Bolsheviks also feared degeneration of cadres through contact with the bourgeois specialists with whom they worked. It was assumed that the cadres would feel themselves at a social and cultural disadvantage, since the *spetsy* were likely to know more about the business at hand than their Communist superiors, and they might react by imitating and assimilating the values of the *spetsy*.

---

[27] In the early Soviet years, the masking of "proletarian" identity involved in international diplomacy caused Bolsheviks great anxiety. One memoirist, for example, recalls that in 1922, ordinary party members could not refrain from making uneasy jokes about the fact that Soviet diplomats at the Lausanne Conference had to wear tails, the formal garb of "the bourgeoisie." A. G. Zverev, *Zapiski ministra* (Moscow, 1973), p. 43.

[28] Sheinin, *Zapiski sledovatelia*, p. 268.

There were dangers on the domestic front, too, if cadres of lower-class origin married wives who came from the old privileged and educated classes. Such marriages were not uncommon and often had a visible effect on the Communist husband's lifestyle: a growing taste for luxury, christening of children, and social interaction with "alien class elements," including the wives' relatives, were noted as consequences of such *mésalliances*. The Party's Central Control Commission received many complaints from rank and file Communists about cadres who had married out of their class. For example:

> Is it permissible for an old party man to indulge in a personal life that is often philistine and petty bourgeois (with an aristocratic wife and so on)?
>
> How does the Central Control Commission react when our party members, especially those holding responsible positions, throw over their peasant or working-class wives and families and go off with priests' daughters and the former wives of White officers?[29]

Solts, chairman of the Central Control Commission, sympathized with the concerns expressed in these notes. He told young Communists that

> We are the governing class, and that's how we ought to think of ourselves. Rapprochement with a person of the camp hostile to us ought to provoke such public criticism that a person would think thirty times before making such a decision . . . People ought to think many times before deciding to marry a wife from an alien class.[30]

In addition to the fears about bourgeois influences in Communists' private lives, young Communists and Komsomols, in particular, were concerned about petty bourgeois influences, namely the danger of succumbing to *meshchanstvo*, petty bourgeois philistinism and vulgarity. The term "meshchanstvo," derived from the prerevolutionary urban *soslovie* (social estate), *meshchane*, was always used pejoratively. This usage had its roots in the discourse of the prerevolutionary Russian intelligentsia, for whom the values associated with *meshchanstvo* constituted the antithesis of the values of the intelligentsia.

For Communist youth, *meshchanstvo* was the antithesis of proletarian, revolutionary values, but it also had a more specific meaning. In the young Communist milieu of NEP, *meshchanstvo* meant oppressive, patriarchal, narrowly conventional views about sex, marriage, and the family. The implication (rejected by many older party members, including Lenin) was

---

[29] *Biulleten' TsKK i RKI SSSR i RSFSR*, 1927 nos. 2–3, p. 55.
[30] In I. Razin, compiler, *Komsomol'skii byt. Sbornik* (Moscow-Leningrad, 1927), p. 66.

that proletarians and Communists should liberate themselves from any such conventional restraints on their personal lives:

> Don't think that your family—husband, child and so on—should constitute an obstacle to you or me if our feelings for each other are deep and sincere [wrote the young "proletarian" writer Aleksandr Fadeev in 1924]. We live in the Land of Soviets, and it would be shameful for us to behave like petty bourgeois Philistines (*pokhodit' na meshchan*).[31]

Rural Identities

> *Nobody is trying to work his way into the prosperous peasantry (lezt' v zazhitochnykh) now. Everyone is trying to work his way into the poor peasantry, because that has become more advantageous in the village.*[32]

The Bolsheviks and other Russian Marxists believed that the peasantry was divided (or at least in process of dividing) into classes, with "kulaks" exploiting the "poor peasant" class, while "middle peasants," as yet undifferentiated, occupied the social terrain between the two extremes. This view of the peasantry and its development was disputed in the 1920s by neo-Populists like Chaianov, and has since been contested by many historians and sociologists.[33] It was certainly problematical in its application to the Russian peasantry of the NEP period, if only because of the equalizing effect of the redistribution of land in 1917—18.

Nevertheless, forms of economic and sociocultural differentiation did exist in the Russian peasantry in the 1920s. Some peasants were wholly dependent upon cultivation of their allotments for survival, while others had important secondary occupations (trade, crafts, seasonal departure [*otkhod*] to wage-earning jobs in mines, factories, and commercial agriculture), many of which brought them in contact with the town. *Otkhodniki*, in particular, had long been associated with the introduction of urban artifacts and mores into village society.[34]

---

[31] Letter to A. A. Ilina, 4 October 1924, in *Aleksandr Fadeev: Materialy i issledovaniia* (Moscow, 1984), vol. 2, p. 121.

[32] Delegate from Western oblast, speaking at *Tret'ia sessiia Tsentral'nogo Ispolnitel'nogo Komiteta*, Bulletin 10, p. 13.

[33] For example, Moshe Lewin, *Russian Peasants and Soviet Power* (London, 1968) and Teodor Shanin, *The Awkward Class: Political Sociology of Peasantry in a Developing Society: Russia 1910–1925* (Oxford, 1972).

[34] See, for example, the data on Viriatino (Tambov gubernia) at the turn of the century cited in Sula Benet, ed. and trans., *The Village of Viriatino* (New York, 1970).

The Bolsheviks were inclined to interpret all conflict within the peasantry as class conflict between exploited poor peasants and exploiting kulaks. While the existence of a class basis might be disputed, conflict of various kinds existed. During the Civil War, when otkhodniki and worker-peasants were forced to return to the villages and make a living on the land, often without the animals and equipment to render this feasible, many conflicts arose between the new arrivals and the old inhabitants.[35] Probably the new arrivals, with their urban experience, skills, and literacy, were disinclined to defer to the elders of the commune. When otkhod and opportunity for outside earnings diminished in Saratov province in the mid 1920s, the former otkhodniki, "poor peasants" in terms of their capacity to support themselves by agriculture alone, "were forced to stay in the village, and entered into sharp conflict with the kulak bosses (*verkhushka*)."[36]

Conflict also arose on the basis of generational differences, often in connection with otkhod, which was particularly common among younger male peasants, or the return of young men from military service. In Tver, for example, where out-migration and otkhod had long been a major fact of peasant life, there were major generational conflicts over culture. The fashion of the 1920s for the young male peasants of Tver was "Civil War" dress (Red Army uniforms or homemade imitations, worn with wide leather belts and *budennovki*). Young peasant women in the region were similarly attracted to styles of modern, urban dress that their elders deplored.[37]

It is reasonable to assume that peasants who were young and had had contact with modern, urban mores through wage work in the towns or military service were more likely than other peasants to sympathize with Soviet power.[38] The Komsomol, whose constituency was youth, proved

---

[35] See, for example, A. Gagarin, *Khoziaistvo, zhizn' i nastroeniia derevni* (Moscow-Leningrad, 1925).

[36] V. A. Kozlov, *Kul'turnaia revoliutsiia i krest'ianstvo 1921–1927* (Moscow, 1983), p. 105.

[37] L. A. Anokhina and M. N. Shmeleva, *Kul'tura i byt kolkhoznikov Kalininskoi oblasti* (Moscow, 1964), p. 145.

[38] This is not to suggest an absolute correlation between "modern" attitudes in the peasantry and Soviet values. One of the main Soviet values offered to the peasantry was scepticism about religion, and in many villages a sharp decline in Orthodox religious observance was reported in the NEP period. Part of this decline, however, may be attributed to the rise of Christian sectarian influence in the countryside: the sects claimed an almost fourfold increase in membership in the decade from 1917 (A. Angarov, *Klassovaia bor'ba v sovetskoi derevne* [Moscow, 1929], p. 32). Their appeal was at least partly to the same "modern" constituency in the peasantry, and indeed they often mimicked Soviet forms: for example, in Saratov the Baptists organized a "Day of Classless Solidarity with Brothers-in-Christ" on 1 May 1929, and in the North Caucasus they ran a "campaign against biblical illiteracy"

one of the most effective purveyors of Soviet values in the countryside. Young peasants who had served in the Red Army probably played a similarly important role. In 1927 more than half the chairmen of Russian rural soviets were Red Army veterans.[39]

If the Bolsheviks' description of their rural sympathizers as poor peasants and their opponents as kulaks was simplistic, this is not to say that the class categories they applied to the peasantry were meaningless. The terms "poor peasant" and "kulak" had long had meaning in the village. Moreover, they acquired additional meaning in the 1920s, because the Bolsheviks gave them practical significance. A new "poor peasant" role was created after the Revolution as a result of the fact that the Bolsheviks rewarded people identified as poor peasants. Similarly, a new "kulak" role came into existence because the Bolsheviks punished people identified as kulaks.

The basis of "poor peasant" identity was the possession of an allotment too small for its cultivation to support the peasant family. Poor peasants were therefore peasants who were in danger of being forced off the land and who often had to seek outside income as otkhodniki. The basis of "kulak" identity was officially the exploitation of poorer peasants, as manifest, for example, in hiring of nonfamily labor. In practice, however, "kulak" was often almost synonymous with "prosperous peasant." In many areas, kulaks often had nonagricultural earnings (from trade, milling, and so on) as well as a comparatively large area under cultivation. Both poor peasants (with below-average sown area) and prosperous peasants (with above-average sown area) tended to be more literate than other ("middle") peasants.[40]

During NEP, peasants often denied the existence of any special group of poor peasants in the village ("We have no poor peasants; we are all poor peasants").[41] This should be taken with a large grain of salt, since it was surely aimed primarily at the tax collector. Later, during the collectivization and dekulakization campaign at the beginning of the 1930s, peasants also often denied the existence of kulaks. But such denials were not characteristic of the NEP period, when the term seems to have been used fairly freely by peasants as well as Soviet officials.

The main benefit available for "poor peasants" in the 1920s was release from the agricultural tax. Poor peasants also had preference in educa-

---

(imitating the contemporary Soviet anti-illiteracy campaign) and even issued a Soviet-style challenge to Siberian Baptists to compete with them. *Kommunisticheskii put'* (Saratov), 1929 no. 19, p. 41; V. A. Kumanev, *Sotsializm i vsenarodnaia gramotnost'* (Moscow, 1967), pp. 226–27.

[39] Kozlov, *Kul'turnaia revoliutsiia*, p. 154.

[40] See table in Kozlov, *Kul'turnaia revoliutsiia*, p. 94.

[41] Kozlov, *Kul'turnaia revoliutsiia*, p. 147.

tional, Komsomol, and party admissions, at least in principle, and were supposed to have first rights to jobs in industry, clerical, and administrative jobs in the rural soviets. Kulaks were penalized by being deprived of the right to vote, and they had last priority of access in all situations where poor peasants had first priority. The existence of such penalties and rewards presumably meant that the original premise—that poor peasants were Soviet sympathizers, and kulaks were hostile—became, at least to some degree, a self-fulfilling prophecy.

In some contexts, notably taxation, poor peasants were recognizable by their marginal status as cultivators. But in other contexts (education, Komsomol membership, jobs) it was probably their literacy and status as past or present otkhodniki that enabled officials to identify them as candidates for advancement (*vydvizhenie*). Potential kulaks were well aware of their position during NEP, and often took care to avoid behavior likely to earn the label. In Siberia a survey of peasant reading habits disclosed that kulaks bought "mainly juridical books" and knew more about the Soviet Land Code and the Criminal Code than most local lawyers.[42]

Since it was advantageous for a peasant to "work his way into the poor peasantry," this group undoubtedly contained many persons who were essentially imposters in the category—particularly prosperous peasants and rural priests and their children, who were officially disadvantaged but tended, like the poor peasants, to have above-average literacy. The disadvantages of kulak status had the reverse effect. Prosperous peasants in danger of being labeled kulaks often took evasive action: for example, hiring out their own labor (and horse) to a horseless peasant in order to create the image of a "poor peasant."

MASKING AND UNMASKING OF CLASS IDENTITY

Tear off each and every mask from reality.[43]

The NEP structure of rewards and penalties based on class created the temptation for anyone with a "alien" class identity to conceal it or invent a new one. This sometimes involved outright falsification. However, given

---

[42] *Plenum Sibirskogo Kraevogo Komiteta VKP(b) 3–7 marta 1928 goda. Stenograficheskii otchet* (Novosibirsk, 1928), vypusk 1, p. 21.

[43] Slogan of the proletarian writers' association RAPP in the 1920s, cited S. Sheshukov, *Neistovye revniteli: Iz istorii literaturnoi bor'by 20-kh godov* (Moscow, 1970), pp. 153, 276–77. The RAPP leader, Leopold Averbakh, took the slogan from Lenin's comment that the "realism of [Lev] Tolstoy was the tearing off of each and every mask (*sryvanie vsekh i vsiacheskikh masok*)."

the fluidity of Russian society in the 1920s, it was often not so much a question of falsification as of making selective use of different elements of one's personal and family history. The former noble, now working as a *spets* or an accountant in some government institution, might reasonably describe himself simply as a white-collar worker. The child of a village priest whose peasant wife cultivated the family allotment might well feel that "peasant" identity was appropriate as well as advantageous.

Class identity was generally determined on the basis of an individual's statements about himself, although the authorities might ask for documentation from local soviets and employers, and a claim that was not congruous with the individual's appearance and manner might be immediately challenged. Since persons from "alien" classes did not have the right to vote, local soviets were supposed to identify them and exclude them from the electoral register. However, rigorous investigation of an individual's class position usually occurred only when he sought admission to the Komsomol, the Party, secondary school or university; or in the course of one of the periodic purges of party and Komsomol membership, the student body in universities and secondary schools, and white-collar employees in the bureaucracies.

The conscious creation of desirable class identities took various forms. One way of creating a new identity was to change occupation or choose a different occupation from one's parents. It was common, for example, for the child of an urban white-collar or professional family to try to establish proletarian identity by working in a factory for a few years before college. This was usually done for practical reasons—sometimes for urgent reasons of self-preservation—but not usually done entirely cynically.[44] For many adolescents of the NEP period, there was romantic appeal to the idea of the factory and proletarian toil.

For young people with "alien" class background, another way of creating a new class identity was adoption by a friend or relative with better social credentials than the parents. For example, a priest arranged for his son to be adopted by an uncle who was a village teacher in order that the child should not be barred from further education on grounds of his social position.[45] The son of another priest tried to persuade a relative who was a Soviet official to adopt him, partly for career reasons, but partly because

---

[44] For example, the son of a Ukrainian bourgeois family, son of a former Tsarist officer who served in Petliura's National Ukrainian Army in Civil War, created a a new identity as a worker at the Kharkhov Tractor Plant after his father's arrest. W. I. Hryshko, "An Interloper in the Komsomol," in *Soviet Youth: Twelve Komsomol Histories* (Munich, 1959), series 1, no. 51, p. 96.

[45] *Sudebnaia praktika*, 1929 no. 8, p. 15.

he had rejected his parents' values after going away to school and wanted a "Soviet" identity.[46]

Such cases were invariably complex, since they brought into play all the tensions inherent in the relationship between parents and their growing children. The daughter of a priest left home and "broke all ties" with her parents, first living with her brother, an agronomist, and then working as a nurse in order to realize her dream of going to medical school.[47] A merchant's son, also a university student, argued before a purge commission that he had broken all "political ties" with his father, constantly quarreled with him about politics and thus should not be considered to share his class identity.[48]

Young people often made unsuccessful efforts to get their parents to change their class position.

> No matter what we say or how we curse the old man [and tell him] to give up being a priest (bros' svoe popovstvo), it's just deception of the public, he doesn't want to listen. He's taken his stand; he says: "You make your own decisions, and so will I. What will I do at my age if I give up being a priest?" You just can't budge him.[49]

Some children of social aliens "broke ties" with their parents, or even resorted to public announcement of the fact ("I, as the son of a former priest, break all ties with the clerical caste. [Signed,] Iurii Mikhailovskii, teacher").[50] In one case, a man whose prospects in the party were blighted by his alien social origins took even more desperate action:

> Veit [a party member since 1923] concealed the fact that he was the son of a noble, a former assistant district police officer. When Veit's social position was disclosed, and he was expelled from the party for hiding it and for inactivity, his relations with his father worsened acutely, and in the end, Veit killed him.[51]

[46] N. Khvalynsky, "Life in the Countryside," in Soviet Youth, pp. 111–14.

[47] She got into medical school in Moscow a few years after leaving home in 1924, but was expelled four months before graduation (and sentenced to a term of imprisonment by a court) on grounds of concealment of social origin. It took several years of litigation to get both the university's and the court's decision reversed. Sudebnaia praktika, 1931 no. 16, p. 13.

[48] The investigator was skeptical about this because the student still lived at home. Krasnaia molodezh', 1924 no. 1, p. 126.

[49] From a Perm University student's interview with the 1924 purge commission, Krasnaia molodezh', 1924 no. 2, p. 127. For a similar case, see Khvalynsky, "Life in the Countryside," in Soviet Youth, p. 113.

[50] Izvestiia, 24 February 1930, p. 5.

[51] Biulleten' TsKK VKP(b)—NK RKI SSSR i RSFSR, 1927 no. 6–7, pp. 12–13.

Although it was relatively easy to misrepresent or invent class identity, it was also common for identities to be challenged, as happened in Veit's case, with damaging consequences to the individual. "Unmasking" of concealed or fraudulently claimed class identity was a great preoccupation of Communists in the 1920s and, as a result, a constant anxiety for some segments of the population. Apart from Nepmen, kulaks, priests, and members of the former noble and merchant estates, who were directly at risk, the issue of class identity was most troubling for white-collar wage and salary earners (*sluzhashchie*), who were particularly likely to have ambiguous class identities and to have made selective and creative use of the disparate data at their disposal.

The proletarian writers' slogan "Tear off the masks!" ostensibly referred to a literary technique by which the real person was revealed behind the social persona. In reality, however, the young Communists of RAPP (the proletarian writers' association) tore off the masks in order to reveal class enemies. It was this instinct that brought them success in the Communist milieu of NEP and lent credibility to their dubious claims to be proletarian. Fear of hidden enemies, and habitual suspicion that people might not be what they seemed, were already basic components of Soviet political culture in the NEP period.

> Once, passing through Tula, I happened to stop in at the GPU. I looked, and there was sitting the son of our former lord (*barin*). I was horrified. And then the train came in, and I had to go. I asked him: 'What's your last name?' But he saw that the train had already come in, . . . so he wouldn't say.[52]

Such encounters with the class enemy, real or imagined, were frightening to Communists, especially those who were uneducated and from the lower classes. One source of anxiety was fear that the more cultured class enemy might hoodwink and manipulate them. A semiliterate peasant chairwoman of a rural soviet described her alarm when, just after taking office, she saw what she thought was a familiar name in a document and asked someone to decipher it for her. It turned out to be the name of the daughter of the old *barin*, wanting an official signature for (the chairwoman presumed) some sinister purpose. "If I had signed the piece of paper and put the [soviet] stamp on it, who knows what she might have done with that piece of paper!"[53]

Because of these fears, the public unmasking of hidden class enemies seems to have been reassuring as well as exhilarating to many Communists. When Zemliachka, a member of the Central Control Commission,

---

[52] *Tret'ia sessiia Tsentral'nogo Ispolnitel'nogo Komiteta*, Bulletin 12, p. 13.
[53] Ibid., Bulletin 12, p. 13.

reported to a party congress on a recent purge of the Cooperatives, the engagement of her audience was palpable:

> [Those purged included] 109 former merchants (not people from merchant families, but the actual former merchants themselves), former nobles, hereditary Honored Citizens and persons of the clerical estate. Among those purged were 11 former Ministers from various governments *(Excitement in the hall)* and . . . 49 scions of former Tsarist *chinovniki*, Tsarist aristocrats, big landowners, manufacturers and merchants. 57 of those purged had criminal convictions under Soviet power; 22 had engaged in trade in the Soviet period, and 82 were former officers *(Excitement in the hall. Voices: "Aha!")* . . .[54]

• • •

This chapter has focused on a central paradox of NEP society: the fragility of individuals' class identity, on the one hand, and its great social and political significance, on the other. The paradox is important for historians of the NEP period because most of the contemporary sources reflect the Bolsheviks' Marxist, class-based approach to social analysis. If we take those sources at face value, we may overlook the fact that the class roles played by Soviet citizens during NEP were often precarious and unstable. If, however, we conclude that class is an artificial category in the Soviet context, we are in danger of missing an important and unusual dimension of NEP society, namely that presentation of a *class* self in everyday life was part of the common social experience.

A question that remains to be addressed is whether ordinary people internalized the class categories the new regime bestowed on them. Since these class identities were invoked so often in everyday life, it would be surprising if some degree of internalization did not occur. This would not preclude a sceptical approach to Soviet class categories or a sense of dual or multiple social identity. A peasant might regard himself simultaneously as a *bedniak* (if this was his Soviet persona) and as an ordinary peasant (for purposes of everyday interaction with other peasants in the village). A self-defined *intelligent* who pronounced the term "bourgeois specialist" in tones of mockery might still come to see himself as, in some essential way, bourgeois.

Moreover, we have the added complexity of what might be called event-related internalization of class identities. Whether or not a kulak class existed during NEP, Soviet society of the 1930s certainly contained a real-

---

[54] *XVI syezd Vsesoiuznoi Kommunisticheskoiu Partii (bol'shevikov), 26 iiunia—13 iiulia 1930 g. Stenograficheskii otchet* (Moscow, 1935), vol. 1, pp. 621–22.

life category of *raskulachennye*—that is, those who had suffered the dramatic event of dekulakization. Many kolkhoz chairmen in the 1930s were identified as "from the poor peasantry" (*iz bedniakov*), though the class of bedniaki had formally ceased to exist with collectivization. In the ranks of industrial management, similarly, people "from the working class" (*iz rabochikh*), promoted during the First Five-Year Plan, held an honored place.[55] It is true that the form of internalization of class identities varied according to the nature of the event ("promotion," on the one hand; expropriation and disgrace, on the other). A worker *vydvizhenets* who became a manager was likely to boast of his humble class origins, while anyone who had been dekulakized and escaped deportation was bound to try to hide his background. In terms of internalization, however, can there be any doubt that the "class consciousness" of ex-kulaks was even stronger, because more painful, than that of former workers?

[55] See *Sostav rukovodiashchikh rabotnikov i spetsialistov Soiuza SSR* (Moscow, 1936), where the breakdowns of industrial management distinguish not only former workers but those within the category who were workers at the bench in 1928.

CHAPTER FOUR

Class and *Soslovie*

To ascribe, according to one of the definitions offered by the *OED*, means "to enroll, register, reckon in a class." But there is no known process of enrollment in *Marxist* classes. A class in the Marxist sense is something to which a person belongs by virtue of his socioeconomic position and relationship to the means of production (or, in some formulations, the class consciousness engendered by socioeconomic position). In this it differs fundamentally from the kind of class to which one might be ascribed: for example, a social estate (*soslovie*, Rus.; *état*, Fr.; *Stand*, Ger.), which is first and foremost a legal category that defines an individual's rights and obligations to the state.

This chapter is about the peculiar conjunction of two incompatible concepts, ascription and Marxist class, that existed in Soviet Russia in the 1920s and 1930s. The conjunction was the product of a Marxist revolution that occurred in a country where class structure was weak and social identity in crisis. While the Marxist framing of the revolution required that society be properly "classed" in Marxist terms, the society's own disarray prevented it. The outcome was a reinvention of class that involved the ascription of class identities to citizens so that the revolutionary regime (a self-defined "dictatorship of the proletariat") should know its allies from its enemies.

I will argue in this chapter that the process of revolutionary ascription produced social entities that looked like classes in the Marxist sense, and were so described by contemporaries, but might more accurately be described as Soviet *sosloviia*. Whether, in addition to these "soslovie-classes," postrevolutionary Russian society was also in the process of making real Marxist classes is a question that lies outside my scope here. But I would tentatively suggest that processes of class formation in the Marxist sense were much inhibited in Soviet Russia in the 1920s and early 1930s, partly as a result of the ascriptive use of Marxist class categories.[1]

This chapter is a shortened version of my "Ascribing Class: The Construction of Social Identity in Soviet Russia," *Journal of Modern History* 65:4 (1993). I have edited it to focus more tightly on the theme of class and soslovie, eliminating discussion of other issue that are dealt with in more detail in preceding chapters in this section.

[1] This applies particularly to those Marxist concepts of class formation (e.g., E. P. Thompson's) that emphasize consciousness. Consider, for example, the problems of (re)for-

Soslovie and Social Identity in Early
Twentieth-Century Russia

Russian society was in flux at the turn of the century. The crisis of identity that had long preoccupied educated Russians extended to the basic units of social classification. At the time of the country's first modern population census in 1897, citizens of the Russian Empire were still officially identified by soslovie rather than occupation.[2] Soslovie categories (noble, clergy, merchant, townsman, peasant) were ascriptive and usually hereditary; historically, their main function had been to define the rights and obligations of different social groups towards the state. To all educated Russians, the survival of soslovija was an embarrassing anachronism, pointing up the contrast between backward Russia and the progressive West. Liberals asserted that soslovie had "lost its practical significance as a social indicator," and even claimed (unconvincingly) that many Russians had forgotten which soslovie they belonged to.[3]

Judging by the entries in the St. Petersburg and Moscow city directories, however, urban citizens of substance remembered their soslovie but did not always choose to identify themselves by it.[4] Many directory entries gave a soslovie description such as "noble," "merchant of the first guild," and "honored citizen" (or, even more frequently, "widow of . . . ," "daughter of . . ."). But those who had a service rank ("privy counselor," "retired general") or profession ("engineer," "physician") tended to list it, in rare instances adding soslovie if that lent weight to the persona ("noble, dentist").

The soslovie structure offended educated Russians because it was incompatible with the modern, democratic, meritocratic principles they saw emerging and admired in Western Europe and North America. They assumed—not entirely accurately, as historians have recently pointed out—that the Russian soslovija had no vitality or raison d'être other than tradi-

---

mation of the Russian working class in the early Soviet period, given the Bolsheviks' appropriation for their party of a version of "proletarian consciousness" that actual industrial workers neither wholly accepted nor wholly disowned.

[2] Form "A" of the 1897 population census is reproduced in V. Plandovskii, *Narodnaia perepis'* (St. Petersburg, 1898), Appendix 1. Respondents were required to give their "Social estate, status, or title" (soslovie, *sostoianie, ili zvanie*), as well as the branch of the economy in which they worked (agriculture, industry, mining, trade, and so on).

[3] Plandovskii, *Narodnaia*, p. 339. The only example cited is that of peasant respondents to the 1897 census, who were unable to identify their families' pre–1861 status (*razriad*, not soslovie) under serfdom, that is, whether they were manorial serfs, state peasants, or so on.

[4] *Vsia Moskva* and *Ves' Peterburg*, published annually or biennially from the turn of the century.

tion and state inertia.[5] Following Kliuchevskii and other liberal historians, it was fashionable in the early years of the twentieth century to condemn the Russian soslovie system, past as well as present, as an artificial creation that the Tsarist state had foisted on society.[6] (The estates of early modern Europe, by contrast, were seen as "real" social groups whose existence and corporate life were independent of the state's imprimatur.) Dissatisfaction with the soslovie system focused particularly on its failure to incorporate the two "modern" social entities that were of particular interest to educated Russians: the intelligentsia[7] and the industrial working class.[8] This was regarded, not without reason, as a reflection of the regime's suspicion and fear of these groups.

It was taken for granted in educated circles at the turn of the century that the soslovie system would soon wither entirely, even in backward Russia, and that a modern class society on the Western pattern would emerge. While this reflected the popularity of Marxism among Russia's intellectuals, it was by no means only Marxists who thought that a capitalist bourgeoisie and industrial proletariat were necessary attributes of modernity. The belief was widespread; even Russia's conservative statesmen and publicists shared it, though they had a different value judgement of modernity. Even though Russia was still lacking one of the two great classes of modern society, the notoriously "missing" bourgeoisie, this did not disturb the general assumption of educated Russians that when (as must inevitably happen) classes finally superseded sosloviia as the struc-

[5] For discussion of the general problems of soslovie, see Gregory L. Freeze, "The Soslovie (Estate) Paradigm and Russian Social History," *American Historical Review* 91:2 (1986); Leopold H. Haimson, "The Problem of Social Identities in Early Twentieth Century Russia," *Slavic Review* 47:1 (1988); Alfred J. Rieber, *Merchants and Entrepreneurs in Imperial Russia* (Chapel Hill, 1982), pp. xix—xvi; and idem., "The Sedimentary Society," in Edith W. Clowes, Samuel D. Kassow, and James L. West, *Between Tsar and People: Educated Society and the Quest for Public Identity in Late Imperial Russia* (Princeton, 1991); and Abbott Gleason, "The Terms of Russian Social History," in Clowes et al., *Between Tsar and People*, pp. 23–27.

[6] See V. O. Kliuchevskii, *Istoriia soslovii v Rossii; Kurs, chitannyi v Moskovskom Universitete v 1886 g.* (St. Petersburg, 1913).

[7] The intelligentsia emerged out of the nobility in the mid-nineteenth century as a distinct group of educated Russians not in (or not committed to) government service. Its non-noble members, many of whom were sons of clergy, were sometimes given the estate classification of "raznochintsy" (various ranks). As separate professions such as law and medicine became more important in the society in the late nineteenth century, the state showed some inclination to treat them as new sosloviia—a development to which Russian intellectuals, already focused on Marxist classes as the necessary "modern" unit of social aggregation, paid little attention.

[8] The rapid growth of the urban industrial working class was a result of Russia's pellmell industrialization under the leadership of Count Witte from the 1890s. Most industrial workers, recent or not-so-recent migrants from the villages, were legally peasants by soslovie.

tural underpinning, Russian society would have made the transition from the "artificial" to the "real."[9]

The definitive transition to a class society came—or seemed to come—in 1917. First, the February Revolution created a "dual power" structure that looked like a textbook illustration of Marxist principles: a bourgeois, liberal Provisional Government dependent for its survival upon the good-will of the proletarian, socialist Petrograd Soviet. Class polarization of urban society and politics proceded apace in the months that followed: even the Cadet party, traditionally committed to a liberalism that was "above class," found itself inexorably drawn to the defense of property rights and an image of politics as class struggle.[10] In the summer, the land-owning nobility fled the countryside as peasants began to seize their es-tates. In October the Bolsheviks, self-described "vanguard of the proletar-iat," drove out the Provisional Government and proclaimed the creation of a revolutionary workers' state. The centrality of class and the reality of class conflict in Russia could scarcely have been more spectacularly demonstrated.

Yet the moment of clarity about class was fleeting. No sooner had word reached the outside world that Russia had experienced a Marxist class revolution than its newly revealed class structure started to disintegrate. In the first place, the revolution deconstructed its own class premises by expropriating capitalists and landowners and turning factory workers into revolutionary cadres. In the second place, the turmoil attendant upon revolution and civil war led to a breakdown of industry and flight from the cities that, in one of the great ironies of revolutionary history, tempo-rarily wiped out the Russian industrial working class as a coherent social group.[11] The proletarian revolution had indeed been premature, the Men-sheviks crowed, and within the Bolshevik Party harsh words were ex-changed about the vanishing of the proletariat ("Permit me to congratu-late you on being the vanguard of a nonexistent class," an opponent

[9] On this perception, see Freeze, p. 13. Yet, as Leopold Haimson has pointed out ("The Problem of Social Identities," pp. 3–4), if sosloviia were the state's representation of society, so Marxist classes were essentially an "alternative representation" offered by a quasi-dissi-dent intelligentsia on the basis of observation of Western rather than Russian society.

[10] See William G. Rosenberg's comment that "for a brief historical moment, at least, dominant identities allowed the lines of social conflict to be very clearly drawn" ("Identities, Power, and Social Interactions in Revolutionary Russia," *Slavic Review* 47:1 [1988], p. 27) and the data on liberal perceptions of class polarization in his *Liberals in the Russian Revo-lution* (Princeton, 1974), esp. pp. 209–12.

[11] On the demographic process, see Diane P. Koenker, "Urbanization and Deurbanization in the Russian Revolution and Civil War," *Journal of Modern History* 57:3 (1985); on its political significance, see Sheila Fitzpatrick, "The Bolsheviks' Dilemma: The Class Issue in Party Politics and Culture, in Fitzpatrick, *The Cultural Front*.

taunted the Bolshevik leaders in 1922).[12] But in a sense the debacle was even worse: in addition to leading a premature revolution, it appeared that the Bolsheviks had achieved a prematurely "classless" society in which the absence of classes had nothing to do with socialism.

RECLASSING

For the Bolsheviks, it was imperative that Russian society be "reclassed" forthwith. Their preferred classification system was, of course, the Marxist one, certainly not the old soslovie system of Tsarist times. Indeed, sosloviia were officially abolished, along with titles and service ranks, within a month of the October Revolution.[13] Yet from the very beginning there was a hint of soslovie in the Soviet approach to class—perhaps the result of a spontaneous popular recasting of unfamiliar categories in terms of the familiar. The white-collar "employee" class, for example, was anomalous in strict Marxist terms. White-collar workers should by rights have been put in the same "proletarian" category as blue-collar workers (and sometimes were, for purposes of academic Soviet-Marxist analysis),[14] yet popular usage persisted in giving them a separate class status, distinctly nonproletarian in political flavor. The pejorative term "meshchanstvo," derived from the lower urban soslovie of *meshchane* and denoting a petty bourgeois, philistine mentality, was so regularly used by Bolsheviks to describe white-collar office workers as to suggest that the new class of *sluzhashchie* was in effect a Soviet version of the old estate of *meshchane*.

Priests and members of clerical families constituted another anomalous "class" in Soviet popular usage that was clearly a direct descendant of the old clerical soslovie.[15] In contrast to the "employee" class, which was merely an object of suspicion and disapproval, priests belonged to a stigmatized class deemed unworthy of full Soviet citizenship. They figured prominently in Soviet thinking about potentially counterrevolutionary "class enemies" in the 1920s; efforts were made to prevent the class ene-

---

[12] *XI syezd RKP(b). Mart-aprel' 1922 g. Stenograficheskii otchet* (Moscow, 1961), pp. 103–104.

[13] Decree of TsIK and Sovnarkom, 11 (24) November 1917, signed by Sverdlov and Lenin, "Ob unichtozhenii soslovii i grazhdanskikh chinov," in *Dekrety sovetskoi vlasti*, vol. 1 (Moscow, 1957), p. 72.

[14] See, for example, the detailed class breakdown of Soviet society, based on census returns, in *Statisticheskii spravochnik SSSR za 1928 g.* (Moscow, 1929), p. 42.

[15] In a context of serious social-statistical analysis, however, priests and other religious servitors (*sluzhiteli kul'ta*) were subsumed under the category of "free professionals" (*litsa svobodnykh professii*).

mies' children, who were also stigmatized, from getting higher education or "penetrating" (in the terminology of the time) the teaching profession. The assumption that priests were ipso facto class enemies was so strong that large numbers of village priests were "dekulakized"—that is, stripped of their property, evicted from their homes, and arrested or deported along with the kulaks—at the end of the decade.

In the courts, the principle of class justice meant that defendants identified as "bourgeois" or "kulak" would receive heavier sentences, if convicted, than those identified as proletarian. For this reason, defendants sometimes tried to have themselves reclassified: as a legal journal reported,

> Relatives, and sometimes the accused themselves, obtain documents after the trial to *change their economic and social position*, and the supervisory committees permit them [to raise] the question of transferring from one [class] category to another.[16]

Such legal reclassification was nonsensical if one thinks of class in Marxist terms, but made perfect sense on the assumption that class was actually a revolutionary way of talking about soslovie.

In the higher educational system, too, class identities were often contested by persons refused admission on class grounds or expelled in the course of social purges. The whole issue of class discrimination in education was a painful one to Bolsheviks old enough to remember the time when, in a policy shift universally condemned by Russian radicals, the Tsarist government had sought to restrict the educational access of members of lower sosloviia ("children of cooks and washerwomen"). Nobody went so far as to raise the issue of a new Soviet *soslovnost'* (soslovie order) explicitly in public debates, but the "quota politics" that developed in education in the 1920s had disconcerting overtones. When, for example, teachers pressed a government spokesman on the issue of "parity of rights with workers" in regard to university admissions,[17] it was almost as if a time warp had plunged Russia back to 1767 and Catherine the Great's Legislative Commission was arguing about soslovie privileges.

Hints of soslovie surfaced, too, in the "genealogical" approach whereby an individual's "real" class was determined by the class he came from, not the class position he currently occupied by virtue of occupation. The "genealogical" approach to class was mocked by the party's intellec-

---

[16] *Sovetskaia iustitsiia*, 1932 no. 1, p. 20. (My emphasis.)

[17] The government spokesman was Lunacharsky, People's Commissar of Education, who was being questioned at a teachers' conference in 1929. (He advised the teachers to rely on the goodwill of the admissions boards rather than pushing their luck by trying to get this enacted into law.) Gosudarstvennyi Arkhiv Rossiiskoi Federatsii (GARF), f. 5462, op. 11, d. 12, l. 37.

tuals[18] and disdained by the Central Committee's statisticians, whose determinations of the class status of a Communist used the two indicators of "social position" (usually defined in this context as an individual's basic occupation in 1917) and current occupation. In general, Communists in the 1920s used genealogical terms relatively sparingly in their discussion of proletarians: it was, of course, a matter of pride to be a "hereditary worker" (*potomstvennyi rabochii*), but the fact that so many workers, including worker-Communists, had in fact been born peasants was no doubt an inhibiting factor, as were the nonproletarian origins of many of the party's leaders. As Central Committee's statistical department put it, with regard to party members it was not so important who the parents of a Communist were, for this "lays a less bright imprint on his whole spiritual profile" than his own immediate class experience and occupational history.[19] Genealogy was invoked mainly for purposes of stigmatization. Regardless of occupation or convictions, it was very difficult for a priest's son to shed his "from the clergy" label (in effect, his inherited membership of the *dukhovnoe soslovie*), and almost as hard for a noble's son to live down his aristocratic origins.

If Soviet class-discriminatory laws were creating new "sosloviia-classes," however, this was an involuntary process that went unnoticed by the Bolsheviks. Russian Marxist intellectuals were deeply committed to the belief that classes and class relations were objective socioeconomic phenomena, and that gathering information on them was the only way to gain a scientific understanding of society. It was in this spirit, undoubtedly, that even before the Civil War was over, Lenin was pressing for a population census that would provide the data on occupations and class relations.[20]

A national population census, designed and analyzed according to impeccable Marxist principles, was conducted in 1926 and published in fifty-six volumes. Its basic socioeconomic categories were wage and salary earners (proletariat), on the one hand, and "proprietors" (*khoziaeva*), urban and rural, on the other. In the latter group, which included the entire peasantry[21] as well as urban artisans and businessmen, those em-

---

[18] See Fitzpatrick, "Bolsheviks' Dilemma," in *The Cultural Front*, p. 28.

[19] *Sotsial'nyi i natsional'nyi sostav VKP(b). Itogi vsesoiuznoi perepisi 1927 goda* (Moscow, 1928), p. 26.

[20] The failure of the 1897 census to provide such data had been a source of great frustration to Lenin when he was writing *The Development of Capitalism in Russia*. A census was duly taken in 1920, during the last stages of the Civil War, but because of the social turmoil and dislocation of the period its occupational data turned out to be of little value. *Massovye istochniki po sotsial'no-ekonomicheskoi istorii sovetskogo obshchestva* (Moscow, 1979), p. 24; V. Z. Drobizhev, *U istokov sovetskoi demografii* (Moscow, 1987), pp. 47–48 and 53.

[21] With the exception of landless agricultural laborers.

ploying hired labor (capitalists!) were rigorously differentiated from those working alone or with the assistance of family members.[22] The census, which was exhaustively analyzed and studied by contemporary demographers, sociologists, journalists, and politicians, constituted a major step in the Marxist "classing" of Russian society.[23] Of course, it did not and could not create classes in the real world, but it created something that might be called *virtual classes*: a statistical representation that enabled Soviet Marxists (and future generations of historians) to operate on the premise that Russia was a class society.

PASSPORTS AND STALINIST *SOSLOVNOST'*

At the end of 1932, the Soviet government introduced internal passports for the first time since the fall of the old regime. This was a reaction to the immediate threat of a flood of peasant refugees from the famine-stricken countryside overwhelming the towns, which were already drastically overcrowded as a result of the large-scale out-migration associated with collectivization and the rapid expansion of industry under the First Five-Year Plan. But it also turned out to be something of a milestone in the evolution of new Soviet soslovie order (soslovnost'). Just as Tsarist passports had identified the bearers by soslovie, so the new Soviet passports identified them by "social position"—in effect, by class.[24]

Notable features of the new passport system were that the passports were issued to urban inhabitants by the OGPU (forerunner of the NKVD and KGB), along with city residence permits (*propiski*), and that passports were not automatically issued to peasants. As in Tsarist times, peasants had to apply to the local authorities for a passport before departing for temporary or permanent work outside the district, and their requests were not always granted. Kolkhoz members also needed permission from the kolkhoz to depart, just as in the old days of *krugovaia poruka* they had

[22] See *Vsesoiuznaia perepis' nasleniia 17 dekabria 1926 g. Kratkie svodki*, vyp. 10 (Moscow, 1929): *Naselenie Soiuza SSR po polozhenie v zaniatii i otrasliam narodnogo khoziaistva.*

[23] On the general question of the uses of statistics for purposes of social construction and control, see Ian Hacking, *The Taming of Chance* (Cambridge, 1990), and Joan Scott, "Statistical Representations of Work: The Politics of the Chamber of Commerce's Statistique de l'Industrie à Paris, 1847–1848," in her *Gender and the Politics of History* (New York, 1988).

[24] The basic coordinates of personal identity given in the passports of the 1930s were age, sex, social position (*sotsial'noe polozhenie*), and nationality: see resolution of TsIK and Sovnarkom USSR of 27 December 1932, "Ob ustanovlenii edinoi pasportnoi sistemy v SSSR," published in *Pravda*, 28 December 1932, p. 1. "Social position" remained as an entry in Soviet passports until 1974.

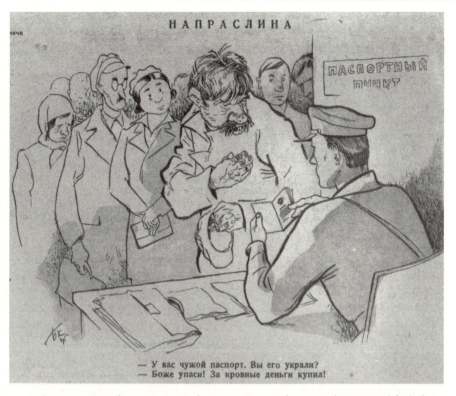

Figure 3. "You have someone else's passport. Did you steal it?" "God forbid! I bought it with hard-earned money!" Drawing by B. Klinch from *Krokodil*, 1935 no. 23, p. 14.

needed permission from the mir.[25] It was hard to ignore the soslovie overtones, once the peasantry was placed in such a juridically distinct (and, of course, inferior) position. The rules on passports were not significantly changed in the course of the 1930s, despite the equality-of-rights principle that was declared to be a foundation of Soviet law and government by the Constitution of 1936.

The normal passport entries under the "social position" heading in the 1930s were worker, employee, kolkhoznik, and, for members of the intelligentsia, a designation of profession, such as doctor, engineer, teacher, or factory director.[26] With the exception of "kolkhoznik," these passport

[25] Collective responsibility for redemption and tax payments of households in the peasant commune in the post-Emancipation era.

[26] "Passports," entry in *McGraw Hill Encyclopedia of Russia and the Soviet Union*, ed. Michael T. Florinsky (New York, 1961), p. 412; information from Harvard Refugee Inter-

listings seem usually to have been an accurate representation of the individual's basic occupation.[27] No doubt the fact that passports came under NKVD jurisdiction improved their accuracy, but in addition it should be noted that, with the decline of class-discriminatory laws and procedures, there was a corresponding decline in contestation of social identity. No stigma in the old sense attached to any of the class identities given in passports. "Kolkhoznik" and "edinolichnik" (noncollectivized peasant)—the two juridical categories of peasant in the 1930s, which replaced the three quasi-legal, quasi-economic categories of the 1920s—were certainly inferior statuses in Soviet society, but neither can be regarded as having the pariah status of the old "kulak."

When the Communist Party and Soviet society emerged from the maelstrom of collectivization and cultural revolution in the second quarter of the 1930s, the depth and sincerity of the leaders' commitment to Marxist principles on class had noticeably waned. As has already been noted, the regime started moving away from practices of class stigmatization and class discrimination, and, if this meant little in the case of the new Constitution, real changes in Soviet practice occurred in other areas: for example, educational opportunity and elite recruitment via Komsomol and party membership. The decline of genuine concern about class was also manifest in the abrupt collapse of social statistics, a major research industry in the 1920s, in particular the disappearance of the formerly ubiquitous tables showing the class breakdown of every imaginable population and institution.

All the same, it would be misleading to leave the impression that the Soviet authorities no longer bothered to collect data on social origin and class background. The concerns about hidden enemies discussed in the previous section were reflected in Soviet recordkeeping practice, but this was mainly in the context of personal dossiers. As Malenkov told a national party conference as late as 1941, "when an official is appointed in many party and economic organs, despite the Party's instructions, people spend more time establishing his genealogy, finding out who his grandfather and grandmother were, than studying his personal managerial and political qualities [and] his abilities."[28] The standard questionnaire filled out by all state employees and party members in the 1930s pursued every possible circumstance bearing on social identity, including class origins

---

view Project cited in Alex Inkeles and Raymond A. Bauer, *The Soviet Citizen: Daily Life in a Totalitarian Society* (New York, 1968), pp. 73–74.

[27] "Kolkhoznik" falls into a special category because the passport-holding kolkhoznik was almost by definition not occupied fulltime in kolkhoz agriculture. As in the Tsarist period, this was often the designation of a former peasant who had in practice become an urban worker, but had not yet succeeded in changing his legal status.

[28] Reported in *Pravda*, 16 February 1941, p. 3.

(former soslovie and rank, parents' basic occupation), occupation before entering state employment (or, for party members, occupation before joining the Communist Party), year of first job in state employment, and current social status.[29]

The population censuses of the 1930s, in contrast to the 1926 census, dealt briskly and briefly with social position. In a sense, this simply reflected changing external circumstances, notably the expropriation of kulaks and other private employers of hired labor. But it was also clear that, in an unarticulated reversion to the spirit of the 1897 census, the question about class (identical in the 1937 and 1939 censuses) had suddenly ceased to be complicated and become almost as straightforward as the old question about soslovie. Class position no longer had to be deduced on the basis of painstakingly assembled and analyzed economic data; for a large part of the population, it was conveniently written in the passport and just had to be reported. In the 1937 and 1939 question on social position, respondents were simply required to say which of the following groups they belonged to: "workers, employees, kolkhozniks, edinolichniki, craftsmen, free professionals or servants of a religious cult, and non-toiling elements." In addition, in an evocative turn of phrase that would not have displeased Peter the Great, they were asked to identify their present "service" (*sluzhba*)—that is, their branch of employment if they worked for the state.[30]

The term "class" was not used in the census forms, suggesting some uncertainty about its continuing relevance as a category.[31] In the mid 1930s, after all, the Soviet Union had officially reached the stage of socialist construction (*sotsialisticheskoe stroitel'stvo*): it was possible, despite the lack of theoretical clarity about the relationship of socialist construction to socialism, that this implied that the achievement of a classless society was imminent. Stalin, however, confirmed that classes did indeed remain in Soviet society, although they were classes of a special, nonantagonistic kind due to the ending of exploitation and class conflict.[32] He did not bother to justify this assertion with elaborate theorizing[33]—and in-

---

[29] GARF, f. 5457, op. 22, d. 48, ll. 80–81 (personal dossier [*lichnyi listok po uchetu kadrov*] of P. M. Grigorev, member of knitting workers' trade union, 1935).

[30] See census forms for 1937 and 1939 censuses, published in TsUNKhU pri Gosplane SSSR, Vsesoiuznaia perepis' naseleniia 1939 g., *Perepisi naseleniia: Al'bom nagliadnykh posobii* (Moscow, 1938), pp. 25–26. The 1937 census was suppressed and never published because the population total was unacceptably low.

[31] Instead, a completely new term was introduced: "social group" (*obshchestvennaia gruppa*).

[32] "O proekte konstitutsii Soiuza SSR" (25 November 1936) in I. V. Stalin, *Sochineniia*, vol. 1 (14), ed. McNeal (Stanford, 1967), pp. 142–46.

[33] "Can we, as Marxists, evade the question of the class composition of our society in the Constitution?" he asked rhetorically. The laconic answer was: "No, we cannot." Stalin, "O proekte," in *Sochineniia*, vol. 1 (14), p. 169.

deed, theorizing about his new categories would have taken him into awk-ward territory: take class exploitation away from the Marxist concept of class and what remains looks less like Marxist class than Russian soslovie.

In the spirit of Catherine the Great clarifying the principles of soslo-vnost' in the eighteenth century, Stalin laid out the three major groupings of Soviet society: two classes, workers and peasants (*kolkhoznoe krest'i-anstvo*), and a stratum, the intelligentsia.[34] In fact, Stalin's three entities were a reasonable adaptation to contemporary Soviet circumstances of Catherine's four basic sosloviia divisions.[35] Its practical innovation with respect to Soviet precedents was the dropping of the old "employees" category, which was subsumed together with the intelligentsia and the Communist administrative elite to form a single white-collar conglomer-ate called "the Soviet intelligentsia."

By the end of the prewar period, Soviet citizens had become completely accustomed to the idea that "class" (whatever that might mean) was part of their public identity. As the authors of the postwar Harvard Interview Project reported with a touch of perplexity, their Soviet refugee respon-dents had no difficulty at all identifying themselves in terms of class,[36] despite the fact that they "showed only a modest degree of class hostility or conflict" and thus presumably possessed "only mild class conscious-ness."[37] The perplexity arose out of the Harvard scholars' assumption that Soviet classes were classes in the Marxist sense, defined in terms of exploitation and in relation to each other. In fact, of course, Stalin's "two classes and a stratum" were not classes in the Marxist sense at all—like sosloviia, they were defined by the relationship of each group to the state, not by their relationship to each other. Soviet citizens possessed a clear and nonproblematical recognition of class, just as their ancestors had had of soslovie, because they were used to being asked to identify themselves in these terms.

One of the more striking findings of the Harvard project was an appar-ent confirmation of Stalin's assertion that the sosloviia-classes of the two-and-a-half formula were not mutually antagonistic. Given the lively class antagonisms of the 1920s, especially of lower classes against "bourgeois specialists," it comes as a surprise to find that lower-class respondents

[34] Ibid., p. 142. For reasons of doctrinal orthodoxy, Stalin called the first two groups "classes" and the third (which was not defined by relation to the means of production) a "stratum" (*prosloika*). This was sometimes referred to irreverently as the "two-and-a-half" formula.

[35] Nobility, clergy, urban estates, peasantry.

[36] Alex Inkeles and Raymond A. Bauer, *The Soviet Citizen. Daily Life in a Totalitarian Society* (New York, 1968), p. 74.

[37] Alex Inkeles, "Images of Class Relations among Former Soviet Citizens," *Social Prob-lems*, vol. 3 (January 1956), p. 193.

interviewed in the West after the war expressed so little antagonism to the intelligentsia, part of the society's new elite. No, the majority responded, they did not think the intelligentsia or any other social group had undue access to privilege. Only "the party" had that.[38] This position implies a belief on the respondents' past that the (party-)state had taken over the role of the old exploiting classes of Tsarist times. It suggests, too, that one of the unintended consequences of the state's assault against "enemy" classes at the end of the 1920s had been to defuse those very social antagonisms that the assault had been supposed to mobilize.

It would, of course, be an exaggeration to claim that a full-blown soslovie system emerged in the Soviet Union in the 1930s. Nevertheless, there were many signs of a tendency toward soslovnost' in Soviet social organization at this time, starting with the entry of social position in internal passports discussed above. The peasantry had the most clearly defined soslovie characteristics. Unlike the other basic soslovie-classes, workers and intelligentsia, peasants did not have the automatic right to passports and thus had special restrictions on mobility. They bore a *corvée* obligation to the state to provide labor and horses for roadwork and logging from which the other soslovie-classes were exempt. On the positive side of the ledger, peasants were alone in having the collective right to use land,[39] and they also had the right, denied to other Soviet citizens in the 1930s, of engaging in individual trade.[40]

More subtle distinctions in the rights and privileges of different social groups also existed in Soviet society in the 1930s. Some of them were enshrined in law: for example, the right of noncollectivized peasant households—in contrast to kolkhoz households and members of urban sosloviia—to own a horse, and the right of "worker" and "employee" households to the use of village plots or urban allotments of a designated size.[41] Cossacks, one of the traditional minor *sosloviia* under the old regime, recovered quasi-soslovie status with regard to military service privileges in 1936, after twenty years in disgrace because of their opposition to Soviet power during the Civil War and collectivization.[42] Kulaks deported

[38] Inkeles and Bauer, *Soviet Citizen*, pp. 304–12, 324.

[39] Noncollectivized peasants had an individual (household) right in their native village, though not elsewhere.

[40] This right was limited to certain designated spaces, the "kolkhoz markets" in towns to which individual peasants and kolkhozy brought surplus produce.

[41] Note that for most practical purposes, "employees" (*sluzhashchie*) were still treated as a separate estate in the 1930s, despite Stalin's "two-and-a-half" formula.

[42] See the letter from Cossacks of the Don, Kuban, and Terek pledging loyalty to the Soviet regime in *Pravda*, 18 March 1936, p. 1, and the statute on their new status passed by the Central Executive Committee of the Congress of Soviets of the USSR on 20 April 1936, cited in *Bol'shaia sovetskaia entsiklopediia*, 2nd ed., vol. 19 (Moscow, 1953), p. 363 (entry on "Kazachestvo"). It is possible that the new Cossack "soslovie" also received the

at the beginning of the 1930s and other "special settlers" (*spetspose-lentsy*) in Siberia and elsewhere must also be regarded as a separate estate, since their rights and restrictions as agriculturalists and industrial workers were carefully spelled out in laws as well as secret instructions.[43]

We can also distinguish at least one "proto-soslovie" whose existence was recognized by custom and official statistical classification, if not by law. This was the new Soviet upper class, the administrative and professional elite that constituted the top layer of the general white-collar group that Stalin called "intelligentsia." The formal designation of this elite, used in statistical analyses of the 1930s that were usually unpublished, was "leading cadres and specialists."[44] Members of the group enjoyed a range of special privileges including access to closed stores, chauffered cars, and government dachas.[45]

In this connection, it should be noted that the whole economy of scarcity and "closed distribution" networks that developed in the 1930s tended to encourage the trend toward soslovnost'.[46] This applied not only to the new upper class of "leading cadres and specialists" but also to groups lower in the social hierarchy that also enjoyed access privileges of various kinds. At the beginning of the 1930s, for example, the closed distribution and public dining room system in factories often distinguished three categories: the administrative-professional ITR (*inzhe-nerno-tekhnicheskie rabotniki* or engineering-technical personnel),[47] privileged workers,[48] and ordinary workers.[49] Later, with the development of

---

right to own horses, a much-coveted privilege in the 1930s, but I have so far been unable to determine this.

[43] See V. N. Zemskov, "Spetsposelentsy (po dokumentatsii NKVD—MVD SSSR)," *Sotsiologicheskie issledovaniia*, 1990 no. 11, pp. 3–17, and (on the removal of legal restrictions from this group in the 1950s), Zemskov, "Massovoe osvobozhdenie spetsposelentsev i ssyl'nykh (1954–1960 gg.)," *Sotsiologicheskie issledovaniia*, 1991 no. 1, pp. 10–12.

[44] *Rukovodiashchie kadry (rabotniki) i spetsialisty*. See *Sostav rukovodiashchikh rabotnikov i spetsialistov Soiuza SSR* (Moscow, 1936); "Iz dokladnoi azpiski TsSU SSSR v Prezidium Gosplana SSSR ob itogakh ucheta rukovodiashchikh kadrov i spetsialistov na 1 ianvaria 1941 g." in *Industrializatsiia SSSR 1938–1941 gg. Dokumenty i materialy* (Moscow, 1973), pp. 269–76; and other surveys cited in Nicholas de Witt, *Education and Professional Employment in the USSR* (Washington, D.C., 1961), pp. 638–39. In industrial statistics of the 1930s, the category of "ITR" (engineering-technical personnel) was used in the same way: it included administrators as well as professionals, but excluded lower-status office-workers, who were put in a separate "employees" category.

[45] See Mervyn Matthews, *Privilege in the Soviet Union: A Study of Elite Life-Styles under Communism* (London, 1978), ch. 4.

[46] That is, distribution of rationed and scarce consumer goods via workplaces and professional organizations.

[47] On ITR, see above, note 44.

[48] "Shockworkers" (*udarniki*), rewarded for high achievement as workers.

[49] See Leonard E. Hubbard, *Soviet Trade and Distribution* (London, 1938), pp. 38–39 and 238–40.

the Stakhanovite movement in the latter part of the decade, Stakhanovites and *udarniki* came to constitute a distinct stratum of workers who received special privileges and rewards for their achievements.[50] In theory, Stakhanovite status was not permanent but dependent on performance. But it is clear that many workers perceived it as a new "honored worker" status—comparable perhaps with the "honored citizens" soslovie of Tsarist times?—that, once earned, was bestowed for a lifetime.[51]

. . .

I have argued in this chapter that class became an ascribed category in Russia after the Revolution. The main proximate causes were the legal and institutional structures that discriminated on the basis of class and the societal flux and disintegration that made an individual's "real" socioeconomic class elusive and indeterminate. More generally, one can say that the Soviet practice of ascribing class arose out of a combination of Marxist theory and the underdeveloped nature of Russian society.

In a sense, class (in its Soviet form) can be seen as a Bolshevik invention.[52] The Bolsheviks, after all, were the rulers of the new Soviet state and the framers of class-discriminatory legislation, and Marxism was their professed ideology. All the same, it is too simple to give the Bolsheviks all the credit for the Soviet invention of class. This invention also had Russian popular roots: after all, it was the popularly created workers' soviets of 1905 and 1917 whose class-based franchise set the pattern for the restriction of voting rights in the 1918 Constitution, and thus indirectly for the whole corpus of class-discriminatory legislation of the early Soviet period. Moreover, the soslovie overtones of class in the 1920s—particularly evident with regard to the "class" status of the clergy and the meshchane-like category of "employees"—also suggests popular rather than Bolshevik imagination.

Where a specifically Bolshevik (or Marxist intellectual) construction of class was most evident was in the realm of social statistics. Convinced

[50] On Stakhanovism, see Lewis H. Siegelbaum, *Stakhanovism and the Politics of Productivity in the USSR 1935–1941* (Cambridge, 1988).

[51] See, for example, the heartfelt complaint from an illiterate woman worker in the flax industry who wrote (via her literate daughter) to Maria Kaganovich, the national head of her trade union, to complain of the gross injustice committed when she was deprived of Stakhanovite status (and forbidden, therefore, to sit in the front row at the factory club) just because her health declined and she could no longer work as well as she used to. GARF, f. 5457, op. 22, d. 48 (letter of November 1935).

[52] This is essentially the position taken by two scholars who long ago drew attention to the problems inherent in Soviet class classification of peasants in the 1920s: Moshe Lewin in *Russian Peasants and Soviet Power* (London, 1968) and Teodor Shanin in *The Awkward Class* (Oxford, 1972).

that a scientific analysis of society required class categories, Soviet statisticians of the 1920s painstakingly built such categories into their data, including the volumes of the 1927 population census dealing with occupation. In this chapter, I have suggested that the great corpus of social statistics of the 1920s was part of the creation of a "virtual class society"—that is, a representation whose purpose was to sustain the illusion of classes. The inference to be drawn is, of course, that historians should be extremely wary of taking these statistics at face value.

The explosive charge associated with class reached its apogee at the end of the 1920s and beginning of the 1930s, but even as interest in class as a weapon of warfare declined, the unintended soslovie characteristics of Soviet class structure became more marked. Class was still a basic category of identity for Soviet citizens, and this was institutionalized in a new way when internal passports including a "social position" entry were introduced at the end of 1932. This "social position" entry was an almost exact counterpart of the old "soslovie" notation in Tsarist identification documents. No longer a matter of contestation or (with the dismantling of legal and institutional structures of class discrimination) of stigma, Soviet "class" increasingly assumed the meaning of Imperial "soslovie."

The full implications of a "Stalinist soslovnost'" model of Soviet society cannot be adequately explored here, but it may be useful to suggest a few of the important problems it might illuminate. One such problem is the strange "state and society" relationship of the Stalin period, particularly the primacy of the state and the definition of social groups in relation to the state rather than in relation to each other. The totalitarian model provides an explanation for this in terms of the political system; a "Stalinist soslovnost'" model would offer an alternative (or complementary) explanation in terms of social system.

A second problem is that of social hierarchy. While it has often been pointed out that an unmistakable social hierarchy reemerged in the Stalin period, its nature remains conceptually blurred. While it is easy to agree with Trotsky and Djilas that a new upper class, strongly associated with office holding, emerged in the Stalin period, it is much more difficult to accept the Marxist proposition that this was a new *ruling* class rather than simply a privileged one.[53] Within the framework of "Stalinist soslovnost'," this class would become a latterday "service nobility" (as has already been suggested by Robert C. Tucker, Richard Hellie, and others).[54]

[53] See L. Trotsky, *The Revolution Betrayed* (London, 1937); M. Djilas, *The New Class* (London, 1966).

[54] See Robert C. Tucker, "Stalinism as Revolution from Above," in Tucker, ed., *Stalinism: Essays in Historical Interpretation* (New York: Norton, 1977), pp. 99–100; Richard Hellie, "The Structure of Modern Russian History: Toward a Dynamic Model," *Russian History* 4:1 (1977), pp. 7–9.

The same framework should provide a way of understanding and relating such characteristic and apparently disparate Stalinist phenomena as social pageantry (the colorful parade of "all classes and peoples of the Soviet Union" that was reported in the press with every new session of the Supreme Soviet), ritual gatherings of Stakhanovite workers, and the peculiar "happy peasant" discourse of Stalinism which celebrated not only the kolkhoz but also, in a clear throwback to premodern concepts of social order, the satisfactions of the kolkhoznik's lot.

PART II

Lives

CHAPTER FIVE

Lives under Fire

> *"I am a petty bourgeoise, born in 1901. My father was . . ."*
> [sic]
>   *The opening of the purge meeting . . . has acquired a stan-*
> *dard form. The meeting usually starts with someone standing*
> *up . . . to recount his autobiography.* Confused people, espe-
> cially women, who have absolutely no reason to be ashamed
> of themselves or their parents, get nervous and upset. Some,
> the more self-assured and confident, describe in the most de-
> tailed fashion their actual or imagined merits . . .
>   [The purge becomes] *a kind of clumsy popular ritual of*
> *confession. . . .* In my presence, an elderly woman, by all ac-
> counts an exemplary worker and excellent colleague, . . . tear-
> fully related details of her past unhappy family life. Insults
> which she suffered at the hands of her husband many years
> ago. *What is the point of this?* (from a newspaper report on
> the government purge of 1929)[1]

Soviet citizens of the 1920s and 1930s were used to telling the story of their lives in public. Numerous interactions with the state required presentation of an autobiographical narrative—for example, seeking employment, applying for admission to higher education, or undergoing the periodic personnel checks of state employees and party members known as purges (*chistki*). The Life, an all-purpose Soviet identity card, was a work of art, polished to a high gloss. Naturally, it represented a selective, partial summary of biographical data, and its public presentation, though habitual, was not an inconsequential action. There was always the possibility that the Life might be challenged, even rejected, by its listeners. "Unmasking" (*razoblachenie*) was the Soviet term for those occasions when

---

This is a slightly expanded version of "Lives under Fire: Autobiographical Narratives and their Challenges in Stalin's Russia," published in *De Russie et d'ailleurs. Mélanges Marc Ferro* (Paris, 1995). The present version was first published in Russian (author's translation) as "Zhizn' pod ognem. Avtobiografiia i sviazannye s nei opasnosti v 30-e gody," in *Rossiiskaia povsednevnost' 1921–1941 gg.: Novye podkhody* (St. Petersburg, 1995).

[1] *Nasha gazeta*, 5 July 1929, p. 3. The italics are in the original.

an autobiographical narrative faltered in the face of a challenge and its author's self-representation was discredited.

Class was the central component of Soviet identity and autobiographical narrative.[2] In the Bolsheviks' Marxist perspective, the key attribute of an individual was his social class, for this indicated his probable political allegiance. Someone who came from a proletarian or poor peasant family was likely to be a supporter of the Revolution and Soviet regime. By the same token, someone who had belonged to the privileged classes under the old regime was likely to be an opponent. The same applied to priests and kulaks (prosperous peasants regarded by the Bolsheviks regarded as exploiters of the poor). Apart from class, important identity markers were political history, religious belief, foreign connections, nationality, and military service. To be a religious believer or have relatives abroad was always negative. Nationality (Russian, Georgian, Uzbek, and so on) was usually a neutral attribute—but not invariably, as we shall see later. Military service in the Red Army was a plus, especially for those who had been Civil War volunteers, but service as an officer in the White Armies was a serious blot on the record.

People with taints such as noble background, White Army service, or membership of the Tsarist police were stigmatized and often faced legal discrimination. Thus there was a strong tendency to suppress such information in order to avoid stigmatization. If there was a high probability that the discreditable fact would emerge, however, it was better to include it in the Life rather than risk being caught out at question time. Concealment was the cardinal sin of Soviet autobiographical narrative, harshly penalized and usually interpreted in the most sinister light.

In his discussion of biography in the context of stigma, Erving Goffman notes that "we assume that an individual can really have only one [biography]," and comments that "this embracing singleness of life line is in sharp contrast to the multiplicity of selves one finds in the individual in looking at him from the perspective of social role."[3] In postrevolutionary Russia, however, such "singleness of life line" could not be assumed. Revolutions cut lives in half, often creating a sense of two separate lives, two identities. Many Soviet citizens publicly presented a Life that suppressed or censored their old identities. Prudence was not the only reason for this: those who concealed "alien" social background often desperately wanted to repudiate it and be accepted as a normal Soviet citizen. But the knowledge that something was concealed or glossed over was a source of insecurity. The narrators of such Lives were not sure that they deserved them.

---

[2] For elaboration of the discussion of class that follows, see above, chapter 2.

[3] Erving Goffman, *Stigma: Notes on the Management of Spoiled Identity* (New York, 1963), pp. 62–63.

Even for those without an uneasy conscience, telling an honest Life was not easy. Class, a crucial element in the Life, turned out to be remarkably elusive as a marker of individual identity in a part modern, part traditional society that had recently been thoroughly shaken up by war and revolution. Was an individual's real social position the one he had been born into? The one he held at the time of the October 1917 Revolution? The one he currently occupied? (These questions were not academic, for a common sequence in Communist life histories in the 1930s was peasant birth, proletarian youth, and postrevolutionary "promotion" into the white-collar elite.) Furthermore, if class and political behavior were inherently related, how did an individual's political biography affect his class status? Could a son or daughter of the bourgeoisie renounce his or her class, or annul it by fighting for the Revolution?

Successful challenges to a Life could bring various consequences. From the early days of Soviet power, identifiable "class enemies" such as kulaks, priests, and former Tsarist gendarmes belonged to a special legal category of the disenfranchised (*lishentsy*), whose civil rights were restricted. In the context of state personnel reviews in the 1920s and early 1930s, a government employee was likely to lose his job if it were found that he had concealed bourgeois class origins or fought for the Whites in the Civil War. In a Communist Party context, failure to satisfy a purge commission meant expulsion or demotion to candidate membership; by the mid-1930s, it sometimes also meant arrest. During the Great Purges of 1937–38, an individual who was "unmasked" as an enemy of the people was likely to be imprisoned, sent to Gulag, or even executed.

In this chapter, I will examine some cases of identity under fire that come from the minutes of a trade union congress held in January 1938—that is, at the height of the Great Purges.[4] Here the recitation of Lives was not part of a *chistka* (purge) but of an election process. Each candidate nominated for membership of the union's Central Committee had to recount his or her Life and then take questions from the floor; if the answers were unsatisfactory, a vote was taken on whether to drop the nominee from the list. Although Soviet elections normally ran smoothly according to prepared lists, this was not so during the Great Purges. Challenges to nominations were expected and even required in 1937–38, since it was assumed that any high-level body such as a trade union Central Committee was likely to include some hidden "enemies of the people." Thus, we are dealing with a specific type of Soviet election, generic to 1937–38, in which a quasi-democratic tone of *glasnost'* (a catchword of Stalin's Great

---

[4] The verbatim (stenographic) report of the Second All-Union Congress of the Union of Employees of State Institutions is in GARF, f. 7709, op. 8, dd. 1–2. The election process takes up a large part of the second volume (d. 2) of proceedings.

Purges long before its resurrection by Gorbachev in the 1980s) was combined with a strong intimidatory character.[5]

While the setting was typical of the era, the trade union in question
(state employees) had some unusual characteristics. First, it was a white-
collar union. State employees were still considered less trustworthy as a
group than blue-collar workers, as they had been since the Revolution.
Employees in state trade were a particularly suspect category. Second, it
was a union in whose leadership and membership non-Russians, especially Jews, Volga Germans, Tatars, were unusually prominent. At the
congress we will be examining, Jewish and Volga German candidates
seem to have been particularly likely to be cross-examined and criticized,
especially with regard to foreign and emigré connections.

Many autobiographical narratives were challenged at the Congress,
though in only a few cases were the challenges so successful that the
candidate withdrew his name from nomination or was dropped from the
list. One of the most common grounds of questioning was family class
status; candidates from peasant families, in particular, were frequently
asked to clarify whether their parents had been poor peasants, middle
peasants, or kulaks. One candidate questioned on these lines was Pyshkin
from Leningrad. Born a peasant in 1902, Pyshkin had several stints as
an industrial worker, served in the Red Army, studied at night school,
and became an engineer—an apparently exemplary Soviet Life. But some
of his listeners wondered why, on being demobilized from the army in
the mid 1920s, he returned to his native village, not to the factory. (The
unspoken challenge, which he managed to rebuff, was whether his parents had a kulak farm.)[6]

Some candidates tried to forestall such questioning by addressing the
issue in their original autobiographical statement. Molchanov from Stalingrad, born in 1904 in the family of middle peasant, hastened to explain
that its possession at the time of his birth of a horse, a cow, and a wooden
house was not excessive in view of the large family size—ten persons.[7]
Sudak from Kuibyshev admitted that an uncle had been dekulakized in
1930, though he said his own parents were middle peasants. After an
intensive inquisition about the uncle, his candidacy survived.[8] Gorichev
from Nikolaev had a similar stain on his social identity: his father, who
died in 1907, had inherited his own father's business a few years before
his death, but quickly drank it away and went bankrupt. As the narrator

---

[5] The peculiarity of these elections has been pointed out by J. Arch Getty, "State and
Society under Stalin: Constitutions and Elections in the 1930s," *Slavic Review* 50:1 (1991).
Note that my interpretation differs somewhat from Getty's.

[6] GARF, f. 7709, op. 8, d. 2, ll. 194–95.

[7] Ibid., l. 256.

[8] Ibid., ll. 333–35.

admitted, this damaging fact had led to his own expulsion from the party in 1933, but he had since been reinstated. Perhaps because of the candor of his narration, perhaps just because it was late in the session and the delegates were tired, Gorichev's Life did not provoke challenges.[9]

Childhood poverty featured prominently in the Life recounted by Ablikov of Mordovia. Born in 1889 in family of carpenter who died when he was eight, he went to work as a swineherd and then as an apprentice to a rural stovemaker from age eleven. At fifteen he got a job at a match factory, but was fired in 1905, wandered from job to job and place to place, and ended up as a hairdresser, becoming head of the hairdressers' trade union in 1919 and a Communist in 1925. Of course, a vigilant Marxist-trained audience could not be satisfied with merely knowing a man's trade. It was necessary to clarify whether Ablikov's practice of that trade had been capitalist (owning his own business), artisan (working alone or with family labor), or proletarian (working for wages in someone else's business).[10]

Women candidates, of whom there were quite a number, were more likely than men to be asked personal questions—usually, it seems, because the questioner was inquisitive rather than suspicious. "Are you married?" someone asked 35-year-old Bogadirova, president of the union's Central Committee. "No," she answered shortly.[11] But other women included such information in their autobiographical statements without prompting and responded almost confessionally to personal questions. Bogushevskaia of Kharkov, for example, volunteered that her father was a teacher and her mother a housewife. "I have no brothers and sisters. I had one brother, but he shot himself in 1921." This naturally aroused the delegates' curiosity, which Bogushevskaia willingly satisfied.

Question Why did your brother shoot himself?

Answer I don't know exactly. We [heard] that he was working as an agent for the district food commission, there was an attack by bandits on the food commission, and his right arm was shot up. Perhaps that influenced him.[12]

Another nominee, Kozin from Novosibirsk, had a more serious problem concerning a brother, though he managed to surmount it. Kozin's autobiography followed one of the standard Soviet models: an orphan's "road to life."[13] A former street child (*besprizornyi*) brought up in a Soviet or-

[9] Ibid., ll. 434–35.

[10] Ibid., ll. 368–69. Ablikov's answer made him an artisan.

[11] Ibid., ll. 185.

[12] GARF, f. 7709, op. 8, d. 2, l. 233.

[13] *Road to Life* (*Putevka v zhizn'*) was a popular Soviet movie of the early 1930s on the rehabilitation of juvenile delinquents.

phanage, Kozin joined the Komsomol at fifteen and went on to a successful career. His father, a peasant in the Volga region, was a First World
War casualty, and the family farm was ruined in the Volga famine of 1921.
Kozin's mother fled to Siberia with her children, but was forced to abandon the boy in Omsk. Despite his adolescence in the orphanage, Kozin
had kept in touch with his family, and his Life offered much more information about family members than was usual for a man. Initially, however, he mentioned his brother only in passing ("My brother is in the
kolkhoz in our home village"). During questioning, the reason for this
reticence soon became obvious:

> *Question* Did you know about your brother's expulsion from the
> Party?[14]
> *Answer* Of course I knew, although I haven't had any news of him
> for a year and a half . . . In 1933 there was news from my brother
> that he had been convicted . . . It seems that the conviction has been
> annulled, but on account of the conviction he was at one time ex-
> pelled from the party. I don't know if he has been reinstated now or
> not . . . I know that he is now working in a kolkhoz.[15]

Another nominee who rebuffed a serious challenge was Gaffner (Haffner), a Volga German from peasant family who had been one of the found-
ing members of his kolkhoz. The family's economic status had been middle peasant before the 1921 famine, he explained carefully, but after the
famine, they were poor peasants. This Life rung some alarm bells in the
audience. In the first place, German colonists were famous for their agricultural skills: perhaps his family had really been kulaks before the Revolution. In the second place, German Mennonites from the region had
emigrated, accompanied by much unwelcome international publicity, in
the early 1930s at the time of collectivization: perhaps members of the
Haffner family were among them.

> *Question* What part did you take in the organization of the collective
> farms—[which was happening] at the very time when Volga Germans
> were leaving for America?
> *Answer* I myself was the first to join the kolkhoz . . . In that same
> year I joined the Party and took part in the unmasking of those people
> [i.e., the would-be emigrants].
> *Question* How many of your people left?
> *Answer* From our village nobody left.[16]

---

[14] There was no mention of this in Kozin's original statement.
[15] GARF, f. 7709, op. 8, d. 2, l. 371.
[16] Ibid., ll. 364–65.

Among the small number of nominees voted down by the congress was Ruzniaev of Gorky, who presented a Life stressing his working class origins and work experience. Ruzniaev's problem was that, despite his proletarian credentials, the Revolution seemed to have left him cold. Promoted from private to a junior officer's rank in the old Army during the First World War, he took no part in the October uprising in Petrograd, did not volunteer for the Red Army after his demobilization in 1918, and never joined the Party. Another delegate, Belykh, chipped in to say that he knew, from having been in a neighboring unit in October 1917, that Ruzniaev's unit had been specially charged with the defence of the Kerensky government. This was damaging, and Ruzniaev's candidacy was voted down by a large majority. (When Belykh's turn came, however, he was subjected to a tough interrogation on his own military service in 1917 that his candidacy barely survived.)[17]

Two members of the existing union Central Committee, Zektser and Furman, failed to survive challenges to their candidacies. Both were Jewish, which may or may not have been a coincidence (as already noted, there were a number of Jews in the union's leadership). In Zektser's case, the attack was led by a fellow member of the union Central Committee, Liubimova, who stated that Zekster was something of a toady and a tricky character who had had too much access to union funds as a result of his friendship with its (former?) chairman. A third Central Committee member, Zelenko, tried to defend Zektser, but was himself accused of trying to "suppress criticism," and Zektser's nomination voted down (by 205 votes to 36).[18]

The other defeated nominee, Furman, gave a spirited account of his early life, stressing his prerevolutionary struggle for an education in face of the obstacles before him as a Jew, but withdrew his candidacy after a series of damaging challenges: in the first place, his class identity was dubious (his father, who died in 1905, had employed three hired workers in his tailor's shop—a bourgeois!), and in the second place, his party record was flawed (he had been suspended from the Party for a year in 1921 for double dipping on rations and making himself a suit out of an officer's greatcoat).[19]

The most dramatic event of the congress was the challenge to the nomination of Ulianova of Odessa. Born in 1898 to a poor family of Jewish agricultural colonists in the Odessa region, Ulianova, whose father died when she was four, was sent away to work as a domestic servant in town at the age of ten. When her mother fell ill a few years later she was called

---

[17] Ibid., ll. 296–97, 306–10.
[18] Ibid., ll. 318–25.
[19] Ibid., ll. 383–87.

back to the village and worked in the fields as well as tutoring children in Yiddish. When the Reds took the nearby town of Pervomaisk in 1920, she went there, joined the Komsomol, and started working for the Cheka. She married a Communist, from whom she later separated, and had a son. After the Civil War, she was sent off to finish her education, joined the Party, and then worked for many years in the NKVD. She had recently been sent by the party to head the Odessa branch of the union. It was an exemplary biography except for one thing: Ulianova had three sisters living abroad. Two of them had emigrated with their husbands before the war, fleeing the pogroms of the late Tsarist period; the third had left in 1924 on a Soviet passport, joining her husband, who had also been a prerevolutionary emigré.[20]

Questions came thick and fast. Why had her sisters emigrated? Had she not tried to dissuade them, especially the third? ("We have to remember—and I speak as an old NKVD cadre—what it means to be a Chekist and to let your own sister go abroad instead of keeping her here," was one sanctimonious contribution.)[21] Did she still correspond with this sister? How come she knew Yiddish? Why did she go by the (Russian) name Ulianov when she had been born Buber?[22] Why was she separated from her husband? What did "separated" mean, anyway? Were they divorced, or what? Was there a political reason for their separation? Could it be that her husband, a Communist, left her because he could not stand being married to a woman who had let her sister emigrate?

Some voices were raised in her defense, but Ulianova herself seemed panic-stricken and close to collapse under the relentless cross-examination.

Why don't I live with my husband? That's something that you don't talk about at a Congress.

Comrades, I didn't get an official divorce in ZAGS.[23] I would suggest that you don't get into family problems. I can only say that he visits, but I don't live with him. He came back, but then he went away again. Men are like that [. . .] I don't know how to judge [. . .] It's three or four years since we lived together.

We separated [. . .] Well, all sorts of things happen. He left in 1926. It was just that he was sent to work in [name of town, omitted in

---

[20] Ibid., ll. 269–70.

[21] Ibid., l. 278.

[22] Ibid., ll. 270–78. As Ulianova explained (l. 273), she had actually taken the name Ulianova as a nom de guerre, at her bosses' instructions, when she joined the Cheka; far from trying to conceal her original name, she had gone by Ulianova-Buber in her passport until the last exchange of party documents, when "they crossed out Buber and left only Ulianova."

[23] The state agency for registration of births, death, marriages, and divorces.

minutes]. He worked there for a year and then came back. We lived together, but then he went away again, he worked in Novosibirsk. He married another woman. She had a child, but he doesn't live with her either.[24]

The more frightened and confused she became, the more relentlessly the hunters pursued her and the louder the hounds bayed for blood. Finally, the meeting voted 261 to 4 to drop her from the list of candidates. But this was not all: voices from the floor called for "political conclusions" to be drawn.

> Odessa oblast is on the Rumanian frontier. The question arises, should Ulianova be chairman [*sic*] of the [Odessa] party committee?[25]

This amounted to a call to unmask Ulianova as an enemy of the people. Once such a call had been issued, in the context of the Great Purges, only a very brave or reckless person would intervene to save the victim. Remarkably, however, someone *did* intervene in this case. Ulianova's defender was the session's chairman, Zelenko—the same Zelenko who had tried to defend his Central Committee colleague, Zekster, under fire. After the session, when Ulianova's nomination had already been voted on and formally defeated, Zelenko went and rang up her former husband (then the state prosecutor in Tula) and asked him to vouch for her. This the former husband did, confirming that Ulianova had indeed opposed her sister's emigration and that their separation had nothing to do with political differences. Zelenko relayed this new information to the Congress, suggesting that Ulianova's nomination be resurrected, but he was voted down. The next day, however, after who knows what late night deal was cut behind the scenes, the final list of candidates for the new Central Committee was read out and Ulianova's name was on it.[26]

. . .

The Soviet ritual of public recounting of Lives, in which an individual's self-presentation was open to challenge by the audience, created the possibility of high drama in the unmasking of hidden enemies—the equivalent of those moments in Salem or early modern Europe when a suspect broke down under public interrogation and was revealed unmistakably as a witch. In our story, Ulianova was on the very brink of such a break-

---

[24] Ibid., ll. 279–82.

[25] Ibid., l. 281.

[26] Ibid., ll. 397, 426. Whether this saved Ulianova in the long run is not known. After such fierce public criticism, her situation was perilous regardless of the outcome at the congress.

down, and her audience was on the brink of unmasking her as an enemy of the people.

More often, however, the records of such Soviet interrogations are reminiscent less of witch-hunting than of schoolyard bullying. A scapegoat is selected (or emerges in the course of the meeting), and the pack fastens on him, taunting him with unanswerable questions, distorting his answers, shouting him down, jeering.[27] For the schoolyard scapegoat, as for the witch, there is no real possibility of self-defense. The difference is that those who are bullying the scapegoat do not care whether or not he is guilty (evil, tainted). They go after him, and not someone else, because they smell weakness and vulnerability.

There are many people who, in such circumstances, refuse to succumb to the excitement of the chase and oppose it passively by silence, but only a small number will take the risk of active opposition. In our story, Zelenko was such a man. For motives we can only guess at, he intervened twice, once in defense of Zektser (accused of personal corruption and abuse of power) and again, more dramatically, in defense of Ulianova. This was reckless conduct, particularly once it had been suggested that he was trying to "suppress criticism"—a phrase often used of officeholding enemies of the people during the Great Purges.

It is sometimes said that suspicion permeated Stalinist society to such an extent that those arrested as enemies of the people, even knowing themselves to be innocent, still assumed that others in the same situation were guilty. There is some truth to this, but it is not the whole truth. In addition to pervasive suspicion, there was also, at least in some segments of the society, a pervasive uneasiness about identity that made people suspect *their own* worth and credentials as Soviet citizens.

In the tense atmosphere of the Great Purges, the ritual of public recitation of Lives could end badly for virtually any Soviet citizen. True, there were people who explicitly noted that their Lives were untainted:

I was never convicted of a crime. I have no dekulakized or repressed relatives.[28]

I have never deviated from the general line of the party. I never participated in any Opposition.[29]

But was there anyone who could relate his Life completely confident that there was nothing in it that could possibly arouse suspicion—no dubious

---

[27] For a classic example, see the way Bukharin was handled at the February–March (1937) plenum of the Central Committee: *Voprosy istorii*, 1992 no. 4–5, pp. 3–36.

[28] GARF, f. 7709, op. 8, d. 2, l. 418.

[29] Ibid., l. 246.

relatives or ancestral taints, no political deviations, no brushes with the law, no contacts (even accidental ones) with "enemies of the people"?

By contrast, the number of Soviet citizens whose Lives had some potential vulnerabilities was very great. One person's father had been a priest, another's uncle a kulak, a third was descended from the nobility, a fourth had once been prosecuted for selling applies on the street, a fifth had happened to live in territory occupied by the Whites during the Civil War . . . Such people could hope to pass as good Soviet citizens, but they could not count on it. They might seem exemplary citizens to others; they might even, in their own hearts, be passionate loyalists of Soviet power. But their security could vanish in an instant if that weak point in their Lives— the shameful "taint" that they tried to keep hidden—should suddenly be brought to light. Then their Soviet masks would be torn off; they would be exposed as double-dealers and hypocrites, enemies who must be cast out of Soviet society. In the blink of an eye, as in a fairy tale, Gaffner the kolkhoz pioneer would become Haffner the Mennonite kulak. A clap of thunder and the face looking back from Ulianova's mirror would be that of Buber the wicked witch, an Enemy of the People.

CHAPTER SIX

The Two Faces of Anastasia

Anastasia Plotnikova was a perfectly ordinary woman. Her life was not mysterious or especially dramatic, at least in the context of her times. Born in a village in the Leningrad region in 1893, she became a Communist in 1920. By the mid 1930s, she had held senior administrative positions in Leningrad for almost a decade. In 1936 she was president of a district soviet in Leningrad and a member of the Leningrad city soviet. Her husband, whom she had married just before the First World War, had a party job in a factory in the Vyborg district of the city; they had two sons in the twenties, both members of the Komsomol serving in the Red Army. From the little we know about her character, she seems to have been practical, clear-headed, resourceful, unreflective, generous, and liked by her colleagues.

Why, then, did Anastasia Plotnikova have an identity problem? It happened in a very ordinary Soviet way, through a denunciation that gave a different version of her life from the one in her official curriculum vitae. This led the NKVD to investigate to see whether she had misrepresented herself. It should be emphasized that, while the affair could have had serious consequences for Plotnikova, it was not a case of gross misrepresentation, scandalous discoveries, or a disreputable double life. The circumstances were mundane. Plotnikova had not hidden anything more about herself than any other Soviet citizen—but that was enough for her, like so many others, to be in danger of unmasking.

Unmasking took many forms. A person's account of herself might be challenged by a written denunciation, as was Plotnikova's, evidently; in the course of a routine personnel review, such as was periodically conducted in government offices and the Communist Party; in connection with a promotion, a nomination to elective office, or an application for membership in a trade union, the Party, the Komsomol, or even the Young Pioneers; or in many other circumstances. In the face of a challenge to the narrative of personal identity, the narrator could either admit fault and

This chapter, originally presented as a paper at the AAASS meeting in Washington in October 1995, was first published as "The Two Faces of Anastasia: Narratives and Counter-Narratives of Identity in Stalinist Everyday Life," in Berthold Unfried, Irene Herrman, and Brigitte Studer, eds., *Parler de soi sous Staline: La construction identitaire dans le communisme des annees trentes* (Paris, 2002).

engage in self-criticism (*samokritika*), in the hope that the offense would be overlooked, or try to rebuff the challenge and rebuild the original self-representation. Sometimes the rebuilding was successful, sometimes not. It was more difficult to rescue an identity under siege in times of intense witch-hunting like the Great Purges than in ordinary times. But Anastasia Plotnikova was lucky. The challenge to her identity—or at least the challenge we know about from the archives—came in the spring of 1936, before the hysteria of the Great Purges took hold.

While unmasking was an everyday practice in Stalin's Russia, these contestations of identity were not trivial. Even in ordinary times, they could result in expulsion from the Party or dismissal from a job—and then those black marks, too, had to be kept out of one's curriculum vitae if possible. The Soviet ritual of "criticism and self-criticism"—in contrast, it seems, to the Chinese Communist version, and certainly to analogous confessional rituals in the Christian tradition—did not allow an individual's "sins" to be washed away. The black marks remained on the record, even if on a particular occasion the individual's self-criticism was judged satisfactory.[1] It was because there was in this sense no second chance in Soviet life that it was so important, on the one hand, to hide things, and on the other hand, to prevent the incipient black mark drying on the page.

Communist discourse about identity in the 1920s and 1930s was Manichean. You were either an ally or an enemy of Soviet power—*soiuznik ili vrag*. This absoluteness applied with special force and particularly bizarre effect to class identity: you were either "proletarian," in which case you were innately an ally, or "bourgeois," hence innately an enemy. These were allegedly objective and scientific categories—your own subjective view of Soviet power or your own class identity was irrelevant.

Of course, this was absurd, both for theoretical and pragmatic reasons. No Marxist intellectual could seriously argue that class identities are absolute, let alone that they are "genealogically" determined. Old Bolshevik intellectuals periodically rebuked the crude assumption, made so often in everyday Soviet life, that heritage was destiny as far as class was concerned ("If your father was a bourgeois, you are bourgeois"). Even Stalin finally repudiated this position.[2] An absolutist approach to class identity was particularly inappropriate to Russia in the first third of the twentieth century because of the enormous social turmoil, flux, and mobility associ-

---

[1] With regard to criminal convictions, the government tried to overcome this problem in the mid 1930s by legislating that certain categories of conviction be retrospectively canceled (*sniatie sudimosti*), but this only produced argument among jurists about whether the fact that a conviction had been retrospectively canceled should be entered on the record. But there was no procedure, in any case, for "canceling" black marks like an émigré relative, noble origins, or a past vote for the Opposition.

[2] For a more detailed discussion of these issues, see above, ch. 2.

ated with war, revolution, and Stalinist "revolution from above" at the end of the 1920s.

Nevertheless, in Communist discourse the world remained divided into sheep and goats—or, more exactly, into sheep, goats, and the infamous "wolves in sheep's clothing" whom it was a Communist's duty to discover and unmask.[3] But the very rigidity and impracticality of this framework meant that there had to be ways of getting round it. One of these ways was *semeistvennost'*, mutually protective "family circles" within the Communist bureaucracy in which the distinction between "ours" (*svoi*) and "others" (*chuzhye*) was made on a more personalistic basis. One did not unmask members of one's own *semeistvo*. If somebody else tried to unmask them, one did one's best—if only for reasons of self-protection—to prevent this. We can see this impulse, as well as the Manichean zeal to unmask that it partially frustrated, in the unfolding of the story of Anastasia Plotnikova's two faces.

• • •

Like all Soviet citizens in the 1930s, at least all who were wage or salary earners or belonged to the Communist Party, Plotnikova had a curriculum vitae (*avtobiografiia*) that she periodically updated. It was an official document kept in her personal file along with the formal questionnaires (*anketa*, *lichnyi listok*) whose thirty to forty questions covered social origin, education, army service, political involvements, and employment history. By convention, the Autobiography dealt with the same range of issues as the questionnaires, but it was freeform and might include discussion of such topics as formative experiences, personal philosophy, family life, and so on.

Plotnikova's Autobiography, dated 22 May 1936, was notable for its clarity, precision, and absence of personal-confessional motifs.[4] Relatives and their places of residence were named in full, places of work were clearly identified. Loose ends were neatly tied up, and the narrative often seemed to anticipate the reader's possible queries and provide answers. Technically, it was a model Autobiography. The life story it told was also exemplary in Soviet terms.

The account of herself Plotnikova gave was as follows. She was born Anastasia Khoreva in 1893 in the village of Ponizove in Novgorod prov-

---

[3] This metaphor really had wings in the 1930s; it crops up everywhere. For Stalin's use of it in connection with "enemies of the people" in 1937, see I. V. Stalin, *Sochineniia*, ed. McNeal, vol. 1 [14 in Soviet sequence] (Stanford, 1967), p. 190. For popular usage, see below, p. 171.

[4] Tsentral'nyi gosudarstvennyi arkhiv istoriko-politicheskoi dokumentatsii g. Leningrada (TsGA IPD, formerly the Leningrad party archive), f. 24, op. 2v, d. 1833, ll. 87–88: "Avtobiografiia. Plotnikova, Anastasiia Mironovna."

ince, not far from St. Petersburg. The family was poor: "In the village [my parents] were considered poor folk (*bobyli*), since they had no land; my father shared a hut with his brother. Sometimes he had a cow." The father, Miron Khorev, had worked for wages since he was twelve, and Anastasia identified him as "a worker" (*rabochii*) in her narrative. His trade was carpentry, which he practiced sometimes in the village but usually in various industrial enterprises in the St. Petersburg area. His wife resided permanently in the village and (as was usual in peasant-worker families like the Khorevs') did not accompany him when he went away to work in the city. She sometimes worked as an agricultural laborer (*batrachka*), probably for prosperous fellow villagers.

Anastasia was one of five children. Her two brothers followed their father's trade and became carpenters, working fulltime in St. Petersburg; one of them showed his proletarian-revolutionary mettle by joining the Red Guards in 1917. There were also two half brothers, her mother's sons by another marriage, who were likewise carpenters. Anastasia's two sisters were kolkhoz members at the time of writing, one in her native village, the other, Matrena, in Siberia. Starting from the age of eleven, Anastasia worked for wages. First, she worked away from home as a childminder (*nian'ka*), living at home only in the winter. From ages thirteen to nineteen she worked as an agricultural laborer (*batrachka*).

At age twenty, Anastasia left the village and went to St. Petersburg, where she married and worked in various shoemakers' workshops. In summers, when there was less work at the workshops, she worked at peat and lumber plants. Her husband, Plotnikov, was a shoemaker by trade; since the age of seventeen, "after the death of his mother," he had lived on his own. In 1915 Plotnikov was arrested. No reason for this is given in the Autobiography (though presumably it would have been given, had it been a political offense and thus, in Soviet context, a biographical asset), but it led to his being drafted into the army and sent to the front. In 1916 Anastasia almost succeeded in getting a job as a worker at the famous 'Treugol'nik' plant under the *soldatka* (soldier's wife) quota. But at the last minute she was refused on the grounds that she was not a real soldatka, but the wife of a man who had been sent to the front as a criminal. With two young sons (born 1913 and 1915) in tow, Anastasia went home to the village and worked as a field laborer until September 1917.

In September 1917, after Plotnikova's husband was invalided home from the front to a hospital in the city, she returned to Petrograd and went back to work in a shoemaking business. Early in 1918 her husband, still unable to walk, was sent home from the hospital with a bad case of scurvy, and in May 1918, the family—Anastasia and her husband, with their two small children, plus Anastasia's sister Matrena, who had recently lost her job as a worker at the Treugolnik plant—left for Siberia. They headed for the village of Katkovo in Tomsk province where some peasants from their home village had migrated a few years before the war.

The arrival in Siberia is a turning point in Plotnikova's narrative. Up to this point, her life story had contained no references to politics—the February and October revolutions were not even mentioned in her narrative. But politics enters abruptly with the family's arrival in Siberia, although there is no indication of an event or conversion experience that would explain this. "In view of Kolchak's seizure of power, we lived semi-legally," is the Autobiography's first sentence on the Plotnikovs' Siberian life from June 1918, as if the two of them had revolutionary pasts that made this self-evidently necessary. The Autobiography goes on to describe the Plotnikovs' activity in the Bolshevik opposition movement in Siberia. Working as farmhands and laborers on the railroad, Anastasia and her husband

> developed contact with workers of Kemerovo mine—comrade Korenev, a member of the Bolshevik Party, Loskutov and others—on whose instructions we worked among the poor peasants, mobilizing the *aktiv* to overthrow Kolchak; we searched out and collected weapons . . . My husband and I were members of Shevelev-Lubkov's partisan unit . . .[5]

In 1920, after Kolchak's defeat and the establishment of Soviet power in Siberia, both Plotnikovs formally joined the Bolshevik Party. At that point, they already held a variety of local offices: she was a women's organizer, her husband was secretary of the local (*volost'*) party committee and chairman of a kolkhoz (*kommuna*) they had organized in Katkovo, the village where the family was based.

In January 1923 the Plotnikovs returned to Leningrad (with the prior agreement of their Siberian party organization, as the Autobiography is careful to note) and found jobs there. At first Plotnikova worked as a lathe operator in a factory, but after a year or so she moved into organizational work and became secretary of a factory party organization. By the end of 1928, she had risen to the position of department head in a district soviet in Leningrad. From 1930 to 1935, she was party secretary at a big Leningrad plant, "Krasnoe znamia." Her husband, meanwhile, held various positions in factories of the Vyborg district of Leningrad. In the Autobiography, Plotnikova did not specify her exact current position: "Since 1935," she wrote modestly, "I have been working in the soviet of Petrograd district." In fact, she was chairman of the district soviet, which meant that she was the top official in an important subunit of Leningrad's city government.[6]

---

[5] Ibid., l. 80.

[6] Petrogradskii raion. Note that the name of the district remained the same even after the city's name was changed from Petrograd to Leningrad.

The life that was presented in this Autobiography was a typical Soviet success story: a proletarian woman, exploited and underprivileged under the old regime, joins the Party soon after the Revolution, is promoted (*vydvinuta*) and rises to high position, still keeping contact with her peasant and proletarian roots. To be sure, there were points in the narrative where a careful reader might have asked questions. Was Anastasia's peasant father really so poor, if he was a seasonal worker earning wages as a carpenter? Was she glossing over something in her husband's background, about which little was said, other than the apparently insignificant fact that he left home after his mother died? What lay behind the Plotnikovs' sudden emergence as Bolsheviks in Siberia? Could one read significance into Plotnikova's omission of any mention of education (which might imply that she had more years of schooling than would be normal for a landless peasant's daughter), or fault her for failing to state explicitly, as Autobiographies of the period often did, that she had a blameless political record and had never been linked with any Party Opposition?

The challenge that came to Plotnikova's self-representation, however, was fundamental. It concerned the essence of her sociopolitical identity (*klassovoe litso*), rather than peripheral details. According to this counter-representation, Plotnikova's identity was not proletarian but capitalist (kulak).

The NKVD was the fashioner of the counternarrative of Plotnikova's life, which was presented initially in a memo sent to the Leningrad party organization on 1 March 1936.[7] It is not entirely clear from the archival file what caused the NKVD's interest in Plotnikova. The stimulus in the first instance may have been a denunciation written by an unknown person against Plotnikova's cousin, Lipina-Kazunina, which contained damaging allegations about Plotnikova.[8] Another possibility is that the trigger was the arrest of Olga Drobetskaia, a Communist who had been a colleague and probably a friend of Plotnikova's at the "Krasnoe znamia" factory. Drobetskaia, a former Oppositionist charged with "wrecking," was interrogated in prison about Plotnikova, and her testimony was one of the NKVD's main sources for the counternarrative.[9] Another important source was testimony from Grigorii Shchenikov, a peasant from Plotnikova's native village, who was summoned later by the police to give information about her childhood and family origins.[10]

[7] TsGA IPD, f. 24, op. 2v, d. 1833, ll. 74–75: "Spravka na Plotnikovu Anastasiiu."

[8] This document, not in the file, is mentioned in the report of the head of the raion militia to Luk'ianov, 29 May 1936 (l. 80).

[9] "Spravka UGB UNKVD LO—iz pokazaniia restovannoi za kontrrevoliutsionnoi deiatel'nost' b. chlena VKP(b) b. rabotnitsy fabriki 'Krasnoe Znamia' Drobetskoi Ol'gi Vasil'evny, 10.IV.1936" (ll. 76–77).

[10] "Protokol doprosa 25.V.1936 g. svidetelia Shchenikova, Grigoriia Petrovicha . . ." (ll. 82–83).

In the counternarrative, Anastasia Plotnikova was not the daughter of a humble landless peasant but the adopted daughter of a "big kulak." From the age of seven, she had lived in the home of her aunt Lipina, whose husband was a prosperous businessman who owned half a dozen barges as well as having a "kulak farm." She was the Lipins' adopted daughter, thus a member of a family of rural capitalists and exploiters.

As might be expected of a kulak daughter, Anastasia made a good marriage. The Plotnikovs had a prosperous capitalist shoemaking business, run by Anastasia's father-in-law with the help of her husband and his brothers and, after her marriage, by Anastasia herself. (Opinions differed slightly on this last point: some accounts suggested that Anastasia worked in the Plotnikov family business, others that she was co-proprietor, and the peasant witness, Shchenikov, claimed that Plotnikova "never worked anywhere, either in Siberia or before [after her marriage]."）[11] The shoemaking business survived right up to the family's departure for Siberia in 1918. Contrary to Anastasia's account in her Autobiography, the family party that went to Siberia included Plotnikov Sr., the biggest capitalist of all. (He also returned with them from Siberia in 1923, but tactfully removed himself to Ponizove, which was evidently his native village as well as the Khorevs' and the Lipins', and soon died.)

The NKVD's counternarrative shook some skeletons out of the Plotnikov and Khorev family cupboards. In addition to being a capitalist, Plotnikov Sr. turned out to have killed his wife and her lover in a crime of passion in 1909. He was subsequently convicted for the murder and spent a year in prison. All this, of course, was remembered and reported when the NKVD started asking questions (the lover, a journeyman in the Plotnikov shoemaking business, was a good accordionist, Shchenikov recalled), and it certainly cast a new light on Anastasia's passing comment in the Autobiography that her husband had not lived at home after his mother's death. The NKVD also found out that one of Anastasia's brothers had been convicted of attempting to rob the mail in 1929. (Unfortunately, it is not clear if this was the same brother mentioned in the Autobiography as a Red Guard in 1917.)

Moreover, the discreditable Lipin connection did not end with Anastasia's marriage and departure from the village. It was made all the more damaging because of the Lipins' dekulakization in 1930. Uncle Lipin had died around this time, but Aunt Lipina and her daughter had taken refuge in Leningrad with Plotnikova. Since they were illegal immigrants to the city, Plotnikova should have turned them in to the police; instead, she gave them shelter and helped them get the necessary documentation and jobs. She even helped her cousin, Lipina-Kazunina, join the Komsomol,

[11] Ibid., l. 84.

which made her an accomplice in the latter's concealment of her kulak origins and dekulakization.

This was not the only time Plotnikova had put family interests above those of the Party. Indeed, she had been exceptionally generous to her village relatives—Khorevs and Plotnikovs, as well as Lipins—whenever they decided to migrate to the town, both before and after collectivization. "Living in the city of Leningrad, Anastasia Mironovna turned her apartment into a kind of 'peasants' boarding house' (*dom krest'ianina*), to which her relatives came, beginning in about 1925–26, and lived for the time needed in the first place to find a job and then to find housing."[12] Fifteen to twenty relatives were said to have passed through the Plotnikov apartment in this way over the years.[13]

As might be expected from someone with a capitalist background, hiding her real class identity from the party, Plotnikova had political blots on her record as well. She was an ideological waverer, perhaps even a Zinovievite Oppositionist. She had "ties" with a member of the defeated Zinoviev Opposition and had tried to protect someone arrested as a "wrecker." (This was presumably her friend Drobetskaia, whose prison interrogation became part of Plotnikova's file.) After the XVII All-Union Party Congress, to which Plotnikova was a delegate, she had spread the rumor that "Stalin and Kirov were not elected unanimously in the voting for the Central Committee." She had also reportedly expressed sympathy for the disgraced Zinoviev after she ran into him at a sanatorium in Kislovodsk in 1933, saying he looked "hunted" and "exhausted."[14]

So which was her real face, the kulak or the proletarian? The NKVD had summarized the evidence against her, but it had not predetermined the outcome. A year later it would have been different, but as of July 1936, the verdict lay with the Leningrad city party committee, in particular the head of its personnel department, S. Lukianov—and Lukianov certainly looks like a friend of Plotnikova's, whom he would have known personally because of her position. His summing up strongly suggests that in the Plotnikova case, a Leningrad "family circle" was protecting its own.[15]

Lukianov found that there was convincing evidence that Plotnikova had misrepresented some aspects of her social background and milieu. In the first place, she had concealed information about her own class position by suppressing the Lipin connection in her Autobiography and representing her work in the Lipin household as that of a hired hand (*ba-*

---

[12] TsGA IPD, f. 24, op. 2v, d. 1833, l. 81.

[13] From the report of the head of the raion militia (l. 81).

[14] The main source for the information in this paragraph is the interrogation of Drobetskaia (see above, note 5).

[15] Memo of 19 July 1936 (ll. 78–79).

trachka). In the second place, she had been less than candid about her husband's class background, and had described herself as "working for wages" in Petrograd in the war years when she had actually been working in (or was one of the owners of?) the Plotnikov family business right up to the time of their departure to Siberia in 1918. In addition, Lukianov concluded, she had abused her position as party secretary in a factory to get a job for the Lipins' daughter and then to get her into the Komsomol (which meant concealing the fact that she was the daughter of parents deprived of voting rights).

It was true, Lukianov found, that Plotnikova had showed bad judgement in telling the story about voting at the XVII Congress and expressing personal sympathy for Zinoviev. But these, he implied, were rather minor offenses, and other charges (meaning the implicit accusation that Plotnikova was a Zinovievite?) had not been confirmed. His recommendation was that Plotnikova should be removed from her job as chairman of the Petrograd district soviet and transferred to a rank-and-file (nonadministrative) position.

Under the circumstances, this was a mild punishment. It was striking, moreover, that Lukianov dismissed the XVII Congress story so lightly. After all, Plotnikova was repeating a rumor that has often been thought to be a matter of extreme sensitivity to Stalin—though admittedly her version of it (that Stalin and Kirov *both* received fewer votes than was officially claimed) was not as potentially damaging to Stalin as the version that surfaced in the Khrushchev era.[16] It is hard to believe that, if Plotnikova's case had been reviewed by the Party Control Commission in Moscow, that body would have regarded Plotnikova's reported political lapses quite as tolerantly as Lukianov did.

Further circumstantial evidence that the Leningrad party organization's "family solidarity" was working for Plotnikova came later in the summer, when the Petrograd district committee balked at issuing a new card to Plotnikova in the exchange of party cards (i.e., purge of party membership) that was currently being conducted. The district committee's hesitation was perfectly understandable, indeed proper, in the case of someone

---

[16] In this version, presented, for example, in Robert Conquest, *Stalin and the Kirov Murder* (New York, 1989), Stalin received fewer votes than Kirov, was jealous of him, and probably killed him on that account: Even with the post–1991 opening of the archives, no conclusive evidence linking Stalin with the murder has emerged: see Matthew E. Lenoe, "Did Stalin Kill Kirov and Does it Matter?" *Journal of Modern History* 74:2 (2002), pp. 352–80, for a useful survey of the new data. Reports on popular reaction to Kirov's murder suggest that this was not part of the contemporary rumor mill but entered Soviet folklore at a later time: See Lesley A. Rimmel, "Another Kind of Fear: The Kirov Murder and the End of Bread Rationing in Leningrad," *Slavic Review* 56:3 (1997), pp. 481–88; Sheila Fitzpatrick, *Stalin's Peasants* (New York, 1994), pp. 290–93.

who had just been investigated by the NKVD and demoted as a result. But Lukianov intervened, ordering the immediate issue of a new party card to Plotnikova, "since the Petrograd district committee has no grounds for holding up her case."[17]

There is one more document in the archival file demonstrating both Plotnikova's resourcefulness and the endless possibilities of contestation about social identity. On 24 August 1936 the Ponizove soviet issued a new certificate (*spravka*) that, on internal evidence, was surely drafted by Plotnikova herself with the aim of defusing the Lipin/kulak issue and recovering her "good" class identity. The certificate attested to the fact that citizeness Anastasia Mironovna Plotnikova came from a "poor peasant" (*bedniak*) family, her father being a landless poor peasant (*bobyl'*) and seasonal worker (*otkhodnik*). "From an early age," the certificate stated, "[Plotnikova] worked for her living. From November 1906 to February 1913 she lived with her uncle Lipin as a hired hand (child-minder and worker [*rabotnitsa*])." But, it was explicitly stated, she was "not part of the Lipin household" (*nichego obshchego k khoziaistvu Lipinykh ne imela*).[18] Anastasia was no longer the Lipins' adopted daughter; she was once again their batrachka. For the time being, at least, her proletarian face was back in place.

• • •

Did the NKVD find out "the truth" about Anastasia Plotnikova? On the one hand, its counternarrative supplied biographical information that Plotnikova omitted from her Autobiography, though some of it was clearly biased. (Shchenikov's picture of a woman who never worked in her life, for example, is much less plausible than Plotnikova's self-representation as a woman who worked hard at various jobs from an early age.) On the other hand, the overall message of the counternarrative that Plotnikova was essentially a class enemy of Soviet power—not, as her own narrative implicitly claimed, a supporter whose allegiance was grounded in early experience of poverty and wage labor—seems highly unconvincing. Common sense leads to the conclusion Lukianov drew (whatever his motives for doing so) that the new information on Plotnikova was relatively trivial and did not change her basic status as an ally. The Plotnikova who emerges from both narrative and counternarrative is not someone who was dispossessed by the Revolution. She is one of its beneficiaries.

---

[17] Memo from Lukianov to F. Ivanov, 15 August 1936 (l. 89).

[18] Ponizovskii sel'sovet, 24 avg. 1936 g. Spravka dana grazhdanke Plotnikovoi, Anastasii Mironovnoi (l. 104).

Figure 4. "Roar as you will, but until you show me a document that you're a lion, I'm not going to believe you!" Drawing entitled "A bureaucrat in the desert" by L. Brodaty, from *Krokodil*, 1933. Reproduced from S. Stykalin and I. Kremenskaia, *Sovetskaia satiricheskaia pechat'* (Moscow, 1963).

But there were multiple ambiguities in Plotnikova's social background (and not hers alone) that meant that even the least biased narrative was likely to oversimplify. One set of ambiguities surrounded the position of a peasant-worker such as the carpenter Miron Khorev, who was landless but possessed a marketable craft skill. On the one hand, Khorev was a bedniak, supposedly on the bottom of the heap in the village. On the other hand, by virtue of his craft skill he might make a reasonable living as an otkhodnik, or even (like his fellow villager, Plotnikov the shoemaker) set up a small business in town. Khorev was one of a whole category of literate, skilled, wage-earning bedniaks whose existence confounded the attempts of Marxist sociologists in the 1920s to analyze the Russian village in terms of class exploitation.

Another ambiguity concerns the status of a village child taken into the home of relatives more prosperous than her parents, a not unusual situation in early twentieth-century Russia. Such children invariably worked from an early age, as they would have done in their parents' home, but the work for adoptive peasants tended to be more exhausting and exploitative. No doubt Plotnikova gave a one-sided picture of her relationship to the Lipins by describing herself as their batrachka. But it would run counter to everything we know of Russian village life to conclude that the Lipins' relationship with her was based purely on familial love, with no value put on Anastasia's labor. Perhaps, since Plotnikova later helped the

Lipins in their hour of need, we should conclude that she felt a special affection and gratitude to them. Since she tended to help any relative, however, the evidence is far from conclusive.

Perhaps the closest we can come to "the truth" about Anastasia Plotnikova is that, like most people, her life could have taken various different courses, and her "identity" (*litso*)—that is, her social position, and her own and others' sense of who she was—would have changed accordingly. If there had been no revolution, the Plotnikovs might have done well with their business after the war and she might conceivably have become solidly urban and middle-class. But that solidity was still far away for Anastasia in the war years, when she was in danger of losing her foothold in the better life and finding herself back in the village as a landless widow with two dependent small children.

As it turned out, Plotnikova ended up being upwardly mobile by the Bolshevik path, not the bourgeois one, but that, too, had a certain precariousness. She came close to losing her grip on Soviet bourgeois status in 1936. She must have been at high risk in the terror that was to come, not only because of the NKVD investigation and demotion but also because she evidently belonged to the kind of regional party "family circle" that was particularly targeted in 1937. So she may finally have acquired a third face, that of an "enemy of the people," and, if she survived that abrupt change in her life's course, a new social identity as a convict or exile in a place far from Ponizove and Leningrad. But the archival narratives of Plotnikova's life take us no further than 1936. It is up to the reader to imagine the rest of the story.

CHAPTER SEVEN

Story of a Peasant Striver

On 10 November 1938, Andrei Ivanovich Poluektov, a 52-year-old peasant from the Dzerzhinskii kolkhoz, Losevo raion, Voronezh oblast, sent
off a letter to the editors of *Krest'ianskaia gazeta*.[1] It belonged to the
common genre of "abuse" letters,[2] detailing the misdeeds and incompetence of the kolkhoz chairman, but it was by no means a standard letter
to come from a peasant. Its length alone set it apart: the copy of the letter
typed out by *Krest'ianskaia gazeta* ran to thirteen pages, at least four
times as long as the average "abuse" letter to the newspaper. Equally
striking were the individuality and intelligence of the author and the ambitious scope of his epistle, which included a history of the Dzerzhinskii
kolkhoz, an analysis of its social relations and ethnic conflicts, and the
author's life story, to which about half the letter was devoted.

Poluektov's document is a rarity in that it is a genuine peasant autobiography. Peasants rarely write autobiographies, even in times and places
more conducive than the Soviet 1930s to tranquil reflection about the
past. The urge to self-exploration and the quest for a meaning to one's
individual life that is inherent in autobiography seems generally absent in
peasants, at least as long as they remain in the village.[3] When peasants do
make public autobiographical statements about their lives, as Stakhanovite peasants were encouraged to do in the 1930s, they are usually nonin-

This is a revised version of the introduction to the publication of the full text of the letter
in "From *Krest'ianskaia gazeta*'s Files: Life Story of a Peasant Striver," *Russian History*
24:1–2 (1997).

[1] Rossiiskii gosudarstvennyi arkhiv ekonomiki (RGAE), f. 396, op. 10, d. 19, ll. 133–206.

[2] On the "Abuse" genre, see below, pp. 218–21.

[3] Of the few memoirs of Russian peasants, most were written after the subject had deportation or voluntary departure from the village: see, for example, Ivan Stoliarov, *Zapiski
russkogo krest'ianina*, eds. Valerie Stoliaroff and Alexis Berelowitch (Paris, 1986); Ivan
Tvardovskii, "Stranitsy perezhitogo," *Iunost'* 3 (1988); "Zhizn' i sud'ba krest'ianskoi do-
cheri Marii Karpovny Bel'skoi," in *Narodnyi arkhiv (Iz podvala). Al'manakh*, vyp. 1 (Moscow, 1993); and Dmitry Morgachev, "My Life," in *Memoirs of Peasant Tolstoyans in Soviet
Russia*, ed. William Edgerton (Bloomington, Ind., 1993). The ethnomusicologist E. N. Ra-
zumovskaia recorded short life-stories from peasant folksingers in the 1970s and '80s: see
"60 let kolkhoznoi zhizni glazami krest'ian," in *Zven'ia. Istoricheskii al'manakh*, vyp. 1
(Moscow, 1991), pp. 113–61. For a peasant diary for 1937 (dealing mainly with the weather
and work), see Véronique Garros, Natalia Korenevskaya, and Thomas Lahusen, eds., *Intimacy and Terror: Soviet Diaries of the 1930s* (New York, 1995), pp. 11–65 passim.

trospective and follow stereotyped patterns (e.g., comparison of the "bad life" before collectivization with the "good life" now).[4] But the life story Poluektov tells has nothing to do with these stereotypes.

Poluektov was born a peasant and presumably died one, but not for want of trying to improve his lot in life. It is probably this upward striving that gives him the perspective to look at himself and his life in a way that is untypical of peasants. Notable also is his adaptability and the many ways of advancement—commercial apprenticeship, accountancy, officer training, soldiers' committees and revolutionary speeches (1917), employment as a Soviet official—that he tried at different times. His efforts were often frustrated by the sudden shifts in the rules of the game that occurred during his lifetime. In the Soviet period, he was hampered by having a "bad" class background (his father was a Stolypin separator, which put him dangerously close to the kulak category in Bolshevik eyes), and by failure to join the Communist Party (he passed up an early chance of joining and was rejected later as a "Stolypinite"). In the final analysis, since he ended up in the village as a kolkhoznik, these attempts to achieve upward mobility must be accounted a failure. But Poluektov does not tell a story of failure; he had too much self-esteem and buoyancy of temperament to see his life in that way. Poluektov's autobiographical persona is that of a man of parts who has seen the world.

Poluektov's narrative can be divided into three parts: a history and sociological analysis of the Dzerzhinskii kolkhoz, an indictment of kolkhoz chairman Nikulshin for "abuse of power," and the autobiography. Since the autobiography gives little information on Poluektov's life between 1931, when the kolkhoz was founded, and 1938, when he wrote the letter, I will include a short summary of the first two sections to help fill in the blanks.

HISTORY OF THE DZERZHINSKII KOLKHOZ

According to Poluektov's account, the Dzerzhinskii kolkhoz was founded in mid 1929 by some Red Army men from Briansk gubernia, probably

---

[4] The Stakhanovite life stories, which generically resemble Latin American *testimonios*, were usually related orally at conferences of Stakhanovites. For a brief discussion, see my *Stalin's Peasants*, pp. 275–79. The genre is discussed, and examples given, in a book of Russian women's autobiographical narratives from the prewar Soviet period compiled by Yuri Slezkine and myself, *In the Shadows of Revolution* (Princeton, 2000). There are also some longer, published Stakhanovite autobiographies, for example, Fedor Dubkovetskii, *Na putiakh k kommunizma. Zapiski zachinatelia kolkhoznogo dvizheniia na Ukraine* (Moscow, 1951); P. Angelina, *O samom glavnom: Moi otvet na amerikanskuiu anketu* (Moscow, 1948), and *Liudi kolkhoznykh polei* (Moscow-Leningrad, 1952).

Communists, who were serving in Voronezh. The core lands and member-ship were those of the village of Tumanovka (formerly a serf village, owned by the landowner I. D. Tushnev), but households from the nearby village of Livenka also joined, as well as some others from the neighbor-hood, including a group of Ukrainian households from Losevo. As of 1938, the kolkhoz consisted of 140 households, the largest contingent (55 to 60 households) from Tumanovka, followed by the Livenka, Bri-ansk, and Losevo contingents, in descending order of size. (Poluektov, it should be noted, belonged to none of the major groups in the kolkhoz; he was from Losevo—though apparently not, like some of the Losevo contingent, Ukrainian—and became a member of the Dzerzhinskii kol-khoz in 1931.

The kolkhoz was well-equipped and diversified in its production: it had a mill, generating electricity; a hulling mill; a mechanized oil press; a brick factory; a fruit-drying plant; an apiary; and a greenhouse (not to mention the three Fordson tractors and threshing machine that the MTS comman-deered after a few years).[5] For most of the 1930s, it was the most prosper-ous kolkhoz in the area. This was reflected in its building of new houses and a new street, as well as its possession of a bathhouse and a clubroom with a film projector, neither of which were standard issue in the prewar period, its wealth of voluntary societies (assuming that Poluektov, a tire-less activist in his community, was not the only member of these). The presence of several Communists as permanent members of the kolkhoz is also a mark of its superior status.

As was to be expected with its diverse membership, there were various long-running conflicts within the kolkhoz. One was between the Tuma-novka families, the "old inhabitants," and the newcomers, particularly the Briansk activists who had founded the kolkhoz. The Tumanovka group had a lukewarm attitude, at best, to the kolkhoz; three families had been deported as kulaks during collectivization from this village, and relatives of the victims remained in the kolkhoz. As Poluektov writes, "the old inhabitants say [to the newcomers] 'the devil brought you here, if it weren't for you there would be no kolkhoz,' and the new residents say to the old ones, 'what's eating you they say it's not the *pomeshchik* Tushnev, to whom you used to bow like a god . . .' "[6]

Another conflict was between Russians (the great majority of kol-khozniks) and a handful of Ukrainian families, contemptuously called "khokhols" and subject to mockery despite warnings from the local NKVD against such behavior. The manifestations of "national discord"

[5] MTS = machine-tractor station. In the early 1930s, most tractors, harvesters, and other complex agricultural machinery in the possession of collective farms were transferred to MTS.

[6] Noble landowner, formerly serf-owning.

(*natsional'naia rozn'*) that Poluektov describes are actually rather mild, but they caught the eye of the *Krest'ianskaia gazeta* staffer, no doubt both for their exotic quality (few such complaints were to be found in the paper's mail) and the clear ideological violation involved.

Like many other collective farms in the 1930s, the Dzerzhinskii kolkhoz had a rapid turnover of chairmen. Poluektov gives a graphic account of this, describing the four chairmen in the period 1933–37 as all "self-suppliers" (*samosnabzhentsy*), who surrounded themselves with "toadies" (*podkhalimy*) and "embezzlers" (*rastratchiki*). A self-supplier was a person who used an official position to allow him access to kolkhoz stores and assets to feather his own nest; virtually all kolkhoz chairmen could be described in this way, though of course the scope of their extracurricular activities varied. "Rastratchik" was a term used both for officials who misappropriated funds and for those who were guilty of economic mismanagement. It also almost goes without saying that a kolkhoz chairman would surround himself with "his" people, appointing allies to the growing array of offices that meant release from field work and a higher rate of payment for each day worked. That was the way things were done on collective farms in the 1930s, especially if the chairman was a local man, as it appears the Dzerzhinskii kolkhoz's chairmen usually were.

Although Poluektov does not spell this out, it appears that one of the problems the kolkhoz had with leadership arose from the fact that kolkhoz chairmen coming from one or other of the major groups were likely to get rough handling from the other groups in the kolkhoz. The most recent chairman, K. V. Nikulshin, was a Livenka man who was criticized for favoring relatives and other Livenka families. "The kolkhozniks" (this surely means the village's *sel'kor*, Poluektov himself?) had written to the oblast newspaper, *Kommuna*, about his defects. This had provoked an investigation, but thanks to support from the raion and the rural soviet chairman, Nikulshin had got off with a reprimand.

ABUSE OF POWER

Once Poluektov broaches the subject of Nikulshin, his letter switches into the "abuse of power" genre of denunciation. The main accusation against Nikulshin in the letter is that under his leadership there was insufficient financial accountability and the kolkhoz's economic performance had sharply declined. Why this occurred is not wholly clear from Poluektov's account: the two main factors seem to be Nikulshin's ill-advised attempt to move the brick factory, which put it out of commission and required the kolkhoz to spend a lot of money buying bricks from outside, and the loss of five draught oxen through the carelessness of the herdsmen. The other offenses Poluektov describes fall into the category of more or less normal "self-supply," though the impact on kolkhoz opinion was exacerbated by the fact that, as a Livenka man, Nikulshin favored the Livenka kolkhozniks. He awarded himself a salary of 100 rubles,[7] and helped himself to honey, butter, eggs, and other goods from the kolkhoz storehouse; also he allocated manufactured and leather goods unfairly, favoring relatives and cronies. When piglets were given out to kolkhozniks, and some died, only Nikulshin's sister was given a new piglet in compensation. His own piglet, which he never paid for, was fed on oilcakes from the Livenka store (where he had personal connections) that should have gone to the kolkhozniks as a reward for butter deliveries. After the disaster that caused five oxen to be slaughtered, Nikulshin took four of the carcases to town and sold them, apparently keeping the proceeds for himself.

All this had provoked "the indignation of the kolkhozniks," who had written letters of complaint to raion and oblast newspapers and done their best to bring criminal charges. It is customary for writers of "abuse of power" letters against kolkhoz chairmen to invoke "the kolkhozniks," implying a unanimity of opinion that is unlikely to have existed in real life, given the factional divisions within many kolkhozy, including Poluektov's. We are given no real information about the strength and composition of the anti-Nikulshin forces in the kolkhoz. It is clear, however, that Poluektov was playing a significant role (and conceivably even acting on his own), given that, as the village correspondent for both the oblast and raion newspaper, he was the person writing the letters. To be sure, Poluektov's denunciation of Nikulshin's abuse of power is somewhat weakened by his own vivid description of the crimes and follies of Nikulshin's predecessors, which is likely to leave the reader unpersuaded that Nikulshin is any worse than the rest or that any replacement is likely to do better. Moreover, unusually for an "abuse of power" letter writer, he acknowledges that for all his faults, Nikulshin is "a man devoted to Soviet power and trying to do good for the kolkhoz." Nevertheless, the bottom line of the letter is that Poluektov, claiming to speak on behalf of "the kolkhozniks," is implicitly asking for Nikulshin's removal as kolkhoz chairman.

POLUEKTOV'S LIFE STORY

The autobiographical theme is introduced midway through the letter with the statement: "Now I will say what kind of person I am (*chto ia za*

---

[7] As of 1938, it was common but nevertheless still illegal for kolkhoz chairmen to be paid a fixed salary (they were meant to be paid on a labor day basis, which meant fluctuations dependent on kolkhoz income): see Fitzpatrick, *Stalin's Peasants*, pp. 191–92.

chelovek) and how I came (*kak ia popal*) from Losevo to the Dzerzhinskii kolkhoz." Of the hundreds of letters from peasants in the *Krest'ianskaia gazeta* file I have read, this is the only one that raises the question of individual identity in this way. It is not uncommon for peasant letterwriters to include a paragraph of self-identification to lend credibility to their complaints and accusations, but such passages normally confine themselves to social origin ("bedniak"), length of association with the kolkhoz, and activism (as a sel'kor or *obshchestvennik*). Poluektov, in contrast, takes a *Bildungs* approach to his life; he wants to show the complex factors and experiences that have made him what he is. He tells his life as an adventure story, with many unexpected twists and incidents. It is in this sense that he uses the word *popal* to describe his arrival at the Dzerzhinskii kolkhoz. For all the prominence of accidents in Poluektov's narrative, he never gives the sense of being a passive victim of an arbitrary and cruel fate (a common trope in peasant letters). Poluektov is a match for fate; one might almost say this is the leitmotif of his story.

Poluektov's father was a *bedniak* (poor peasant) from Losevo whose outside trade was floating timber down river to Rostov. Born in 1886, Andrei graduated from the village school at the age of eleven and the next year was apprenticed to a merchant in Pavlovsk, another somewhat bigger town in the vicinity. He remained there for more than two years, after which his father took him home to Losevo. Poluektov conveys his misery as an apprentice only obliquely, but establishes the bond of affection existing between him and his father ("You're my only son, he said, and it's hard on you here, nothing but tar and kerosene and coal").[8]

Not long after Poluektov's return, the family suffered a disaster: fire burned down their hut and destroyed virtually all they owned. They took refuge with Poluektov's maternal grandfather, "a solid middle peasant," and Poluektov went to work for a merchant in Losevo. This must have been around 1900–1901. He continued in this employment until he was called up for the European war in 1916. Poluektov had already decided that a life in commerce was better than a life as a peasant: in his first major effort at upward mobility, he aimed to become an accountant. He studied bookkeeping, taking courses and subscribing to journals. He finally qualified as an accountant when he was close to thirty years old, but then was called to military service before he could practice.

Poluektov's father, meanwhile, was trying to improve the family fortunes within the framework of peasant agriculture. He and Poluektov built a new hut and acquired a horse and a cow. When the Stolypin land

---

[8] There is a later mention of a "little brother" (*men'shii brat*) of Andrei, but he must have been much younger. The family had three adult members—Andrei and his father and mother—circa 1907 when his father consolidated the family plots.

reform came, his father was one who chose to separate, consolidating the plot to which Poluektov was entitled as well as his own and his wife's. According to Poluektov's story, he was against this, saying he did not need the land, but his father went ahead anyway, since he was pressuring his son to go back into agriculture. The last was no doubt true, but it is unlikely that Poluektov really opposed his father's desire to add a third plot to the family farm. The point of this story is to dissociate himself from his father's act of separation from the commune.

It is at this point in the narrative that we have the first inkling of something that was to be a great burden on Poluektov in later life: his status as a "Stolypinite." In Soviet ideological context, a Stolypinite implied a prosperous, perhaps even kulak, peasant; in village context, it carried the onus of a separator, one who had chosen to break with the commune. "Even today they call me a Stolypinite," Poluektov writes. This pejorative label was brought up whenever he criticized fellow villagers in the wall newspaper or at the general kolkhoz meeting, and it was even rumored that at some unspecified (but Soviet) time he had run away from Losevo to escape arrest (presumably as a kulak).[9]

When called up for military service in 1916, Poluektov saw new ways of bettering himself. He became a junior noncommissioned officer and was trying to get promoted to senior NCO when the February Revolution came. This event brought another adjustment in Poluektov's goals and perhaps also in his worldview. (While the narrative implicitly advances the latter claim, it was so much in Poluektov's interest to present himself in this light that one is inclined to reserve judgement.) His first instruction in revolutionary matters came from a Moscow worker with whom he became friendly while they were stationed in Mtsensk, Orel province; the two of them were elected as deputies at a soldiers' meeting. Then, sent to the front, Poluektov was again elected to the company's soldiers' committee. This seems to have been a period in which Poluektov spread his wings: he was also elected to the cultural commission of his regiment as well as becoming librarian of the machine-gunners' detachment, "where I began to read contemporary revolutionary literature." While the machine-gun left its mark on his imagination,[10] it sounds as if his detachment did little or no actual fighting in the time between February and October 1917 when they were "at the front."

Between the February and October Revolutions of 1917, Poluektov tried his hand at public speaking, arguing against the continuation of the war at an army meeting, "for which they wanted to arrest me, but I hid."

[9] This is a murky part of the story. Elsewhere in the narrative, Poluektov refers to the time (1918 or 1919) when Cossacks occupied Losevo and he hid out to avoid being arrested by them as a Soviet sympathizer. He says he returned to Losevo only after their departure.

[10] Note the romantic-heroic image of the "12-muzzle gun" at the end of his letter.

In October 1917 his regiment was sent to defend the Provisional Government in Petrograd, but on the way "disintegrated into Bolshevism (*razlozhilsia v bol'shevizme*)," as Poluektov eloquently puts it. Demobilized after October, he returned to Losevo wearing revolutionary colors, as did so many other soldiers. He was elected to the first Losevo soviet and put in charge of the commission for confiscation of bourgeois property, "where the first thing I did was to confiscate the property of my [former] master."

The better future now lay in entering Soviet service. This is what Poluektov did in 1919, working for the next three years in Pavlovsk (a city in Voronezh province) as a low-level official in various state agencies and ultimately achieving the position of head of the *uezd* department of craft industry. The problem was that he had too many dependents (though the number sixteen that appears in the typed version of the letter seems improbably high) and there was not enough food. With four children with him in Pavlovsk (and others in Losevo), "I was terribly hungry and had to leave employment in Pavlovsk and return to Losevo." He had "neither horse nor cow" at this point, and we hear no further mention of his "Stolypinite" father (who could conceivably have been expropriated in this period as a kulak). With four comrades (all drawing salaries as Soviet employees in Pavlovsk), he had organized a kolkhoz of 125 households in Losevo, but it had collapsed after an attack by bandits when the male organizers were absent at the city jobs.

It was at this point that Poluektov had the chance to join the party, but bungled it. Clearly, it was a setback for an ambitious man, and he recounts it with some (but not excessive) regret. (The lack of intensity at this point suggests that Poluektov's revolutionary conversion, for what is was worth, may never have had a specifically Bolshevik coloration. If it was SRs (members of the Socialist Revolutionary Party) he encountered in 1917, he had every reason to edit this out of his life story later.) When, circa 1922, all district officials in Pavlovsk were invited to apply for party membership, Poluektov wrote an application for admission, "but my comrade, with whom I shared an apartment, so destroyed my desire that I tore up that application." Later, Poluektov notes baldly, "it turned out that that comrade was dekulakized and deported to Karaganda." (What Poluektov thought of his comrade's misfortune is not stated, but at least this fills in a gap in Poluektov's subsequent account of collectivization: it tells us that at least one friend [or former friend] of his fell victim to dekulakization.) As for the business of joining the Party, Poluektov continues that story with a rather wooden bow to the proprieties ("I of course later recognized the role of the Party in the socialist revolution") and the information that he later wrote and submitted a second application, but they brought up the old black mark of "Stolypinism" and rejected him.

Despite his failure to join the Party, Poluektov did well in the 1920s. He became a member of the Losevo credit union, charged with reorganizing it on Soviet lines; he "organized trade, as a specialist in that matter" (it is unclear whether his "trade" was private, cooperative, or state); he became a financial auditor, and then worked for two years as an auditor for the Losevo district consumer union. In general, it appears that he was working mainly as an accountant in this period, while continuing to maintain a farm to feed his family and supplement his salary.

Then came collectivization. Poluektov was by now in his early forties, a senior member of the local community, with grown or nearly grown sons. He describes himself as an early (1929) and voluntary entrant to the "Red Losevo" kolkhoz, serving first as kolkhoz accountant and deputy chairman, then (on the order of the local party committee) becoming accountant of the Losevo cooperative store. He was "one of the first to collectivize agricultural inventory and draft power," he says. This implies that he was a real kolkhoz enthusiast, and so he may have been, given that he had tried to organize a kolkhoz back in the Civil War period. It is also possible, of course, that he was willing to collectivize inventory and draft power because he did not possess much of either.

In 1931 two of Poluektov's sons, both tractor drivers, were invited to transfer to the Dzerzhinskii kolkhoz in Tumanovka, since the Losevo kolkhoz had more tractor drivers than it needed. They did so, and as a result, Poluektov also moved. This meant that he had to give up his work in the Losevo store, at the request of the Dzerzhinskii commune, at the beginning of 1932. Poluektov does not tell us whether or not he regarded this as a desirable turn of events. On most reckonings, running the local store was a highly advantageous job (because of access to goods), though not necessarily a prestigious one (because anything to do with trade had a lowly status). In the Dzerzhinskii kolkhoz, in any case, Poluektov became first a field specialist (*polevod*), an ambiguous job designation whose real-life meaning may have been anything on the spectrum from agronomist to fieldwork; then head of the dairy farm; and then secretary of the kolkhoz board (a clerical-managerial job with a more promising ring than the two earlier ones).

As of 1938, Poluektov was head of the kolkhoz laboratory hut and biological laboratory. What these titles meant in real life is something of a mystery. Laboratory huts were much ballyhooed in the 1930s as bearers of science to the countryside. Run by nonprofessionals, they seem to have been a mixture of agronomy station (sorting and preparing seeds for sowing, for example) and education-and-propaganda organ.[11] Although Po-

---

[11] The 2nd edition of the *Bol'shaia sovetskaia entsiklopediia* (v. 15, Moscow, 1952) defines *khata-laboratoriia* (later, *Dom sel'sko-khoziaistvennoi kul'tury*) as follows: "an experimental institution of the kolkhoz, organized for the study of concrete economic conditions

luektov expressed enthusiasm for the job and stressed its importance, it may have appealed to him as much as a safe haven as for any other reason. Heading the laboratory hut, like running the kolkhoz reading room, had something of the flavor of a retirement job. In addition, Poluektov undertook an impressive list of voluntary activities: drama group, choir, amateur radio, literacy school, societies to aid civil defense and international revolution, not to mention the agricultural circle, of which he was head ex officio.

Yet Poluektov was still very much the activist, particularly through his writing as a sel'kor, which made him a thorn in the flesh of a succession of kolkhoz chairmen. It was the sel'kor's job to provide information on kolkhoz life, but that "information" was often accusatory. When the status of sel'kor was first thought up in the 1920s, kulaks were the main targets of the sel'kors' denunciations; by the 1930s, with kulaks gone, kolkhoz chairmen had moved into the sel'kor firing line. Poluektov was a sel'kor for the raion newspaper (*Krepi kolkhoz*) and the oblast paper (*Kommuna*), not to mention occasional correspondent of the national peasant newspaper (in the letter that is the subject of this chapter) and writer of the kolkhoz wall newspaper. This had landed him in serious trouble in the past, when as chairman of the kolkhoz auditing commission in 1932, he conducted a "serious audit [that] touched various people," and as a result "fell into the hands of the NKVD and sat [in prison] for two months." It is not hard to imagine why local authorities might have feared him. Not only was he confident, experienced, and articulate, he was also an accountant by training. To have a sel'kor/accountant like Poluektov auditing the books was surely every kolkhoz chairman's nightmare.

Now Poluektov was again experiencing harrassment, of which he had complained to the district paper and the provincial prosecutor. Once again, a kolkhoz audit was coming up, and Poluektov had been invited to chair it, but prudently declined, pleading the demanding nature of his job as head of the laboratory hut. He was, however, serving as a member of the auditing commission, and was to all appearances ready to give battle. The dangers of the coming battle were clear to Poluektov: he knew that people were always ready to "take what you say in the wrong way, and even label you a counterrevolutionary." But his rhetoric against "the army of toadies" who "have so much grown into untruth that you can't take them out with a 12-muzzle gun" suggests that he approached them with relish as well as apprehension. "I write openly [about abuses] and

---

and for the inculcation into the collective production of the kolkhoz of the achievements of agricultural science and progressive practice." One clue as to the activities of Poluektov's laboratory hut lies in his reference early in the letter to the kolkhoz's recent achievements in developing Michurinite varieties of apple and other fruits.

sign correctly with my own name." "I consider that one can write the truth everywhere . . . and therefore that's just what I do all the time." Thus, the answer Poluektov implicitly gives to the question with which he began his autobiography, "What kind of man I am," is two-sided: a troublemaker in the eyes of authority, a truth teller in his own.

CHAPTER EIGHT

Women's Lives

Women's autobiographies (so recent scholarship tells us)[1] tend to focus on private rather than public matters, favor confession over testimony, show the authors in relation to a significant male Other such as a husband, and even question their right to tell an independent life story. But the life stories told by twentieth-century Russian women scarcely fit this mold. The typical autobiography by a Russian woman in the interwar period (1917–41) belongs to the genre of testimony—bearing witness to the times—not confession; it deals more with public matters than private, familial ones.[2] If there is a preoccupying Other in these stories, it is more likely the state than a husband or father. Russian women often write of themselves as victims, though not usually on account of their gender: they (and their menfolk) are victims of Communism, Capitalism, or simply History. But a surprisingly large number portray themselves and their female relatives as strong women—not dependents but tough and savvy survivors, morally and even physically stronger than their men.[3]

This is a revised version of my introduction ("Lives and Times") to *In the Shadow of Revolution: Life Stories of Russian Women from 1917 to the Second World War*, eds. Sheila Fitzpatrick and Yuri Slezkine (Princeton, 2000), pp. 3–17. The original introduction referred mainly to women's autobiographies published in the book; I have expanded it by extending the range of reference to other autobiographical sources and collections.

[1] See, for example, Mary G. Mason, "The Other Voice: Autobiographies of Women Writers," in James Olney, ed., *Autobiography: Essays Theoretical and Critical* (Princeton, 1980); Shari Benstock, ed., *The Private Self: Theory and Practice of Women's Autobiographical Writings* (Chapel Hill, 1988); Bella Brodzki and Celeste Schenck, eds., *Life/Lines: Theorizing Women's Autobiography* (Ithaca, 1988); Shirley Neuman, ed., *Autobiography and Questions of Gender* (London, 1991).

[2] I use the term "autobiography" to cover the whole range of writing or speaking about lives, including memoirs, not in the specialized sense of self-exploration proposed by Karl Weintraub in "Autobiography and Historical Consciousness," *Critical Inquiry* (June 1975).

[3] On the "strong woman," see Vera Sandomirsky Dunham, "The Strong-Woman Motif," in Cyril E. Black, *The Transformation of Russian Society: Aspects of Social Change since 1961* (Cambridge, Mass., 1960). On the tensions for women in the revolutionary era between the "masculine" pole of equality/independence and the "feminine" pole of supportiveness/nurturing/dependency, see Elizabeth Wood, *Baba and Comrade: Gender and Politics in Revolutionary Russia* (Bloomington, Ind., 1997). For discussion of the interesting but exceptional case of Nadezhda Mandelstam, a strong and assertive character who presents herself as wife and helpmeet in her autobiography, see Beth Holmgren, *Women's Works in Stalin's Time: On Lidiia Chukovskaia and Nadezhda Mandelstam* (Bloomington, Ind., 1993).

These women seem to have few doubts about their ability to bear witness. Asked shortly after the Revolution about how she viewed the new government, Tatiana Varsher replied challengingly: "With the wide-open eyes of a historian."[4] As it happens, Varsher actually was a professional historian, but other women expressed similar sentiments. "I . . . want to write about the way those [revolutionary] events were perceived and reflected in the humble and distant corner of Russia that was the Cossack town of Korenovskaia," wrote Zinaida Zhemchuzhnaia; describing a Civil War battle in the town, she notes that "curiosity kept me outside."[5] For other women, the urge to testify comes from a desire for justice or revenge: "I would very much like for my [story] to be published, if only because of all our suffering and undeserved torment," wrote a peasant victim of collectivization, Maria Belskaia.[6]

The penchant for testimony runs across the spectrum of Russian women's autobiography: émigré, Soviet, internal émigré, and post-Soviet. Russian women (and Russian men, too) wrote about their lives in the context of the times because they perceived their times as remarkable, overshadowing private concerns, impossible to ignore. They had the misfortune, as the Chinese proverb has it, to live in interesting times, and that is reflected in the way they tell their lives; their autobiographies are often like war stories. They remembered their lives and structure their narratives in terms of great public events—the Revolution, the Civil War, collectivization, the Great Purges, and the Second World War—rather than the personal milestones of marriage, childbirth, divorce, and widowhood.

Despite the common thread of testimony, there is great variety in the way Russian women saw their lives and times. To start off with, some of the women wrote their memoirs as émigrés, and their perspective naturally differed from that of Soviet citizens. There were differences among the émigrés, too, notably between those who emigrated soon after the Revolution and those who left the Soviet Union during the Second World War. Of the Soviet life stories, some were composed for a Soviet public in a spirit of Soviet patriotism, others were written "for the drawer" or for unofficial (*samizdat*) circulation by alienated Soviet citizens who might be called internal émigrés. The date of writing is often significant in Soviet memoirs. In telling her life story, Fruma Treivas, for example, frequently contrasted the way she understood things in the 1930s with the way she understood them at the time of writing (in the 1990s). If she had recorded

---

[4] Tatiana Varsher, "Things Seen and Suffered," in *In the Shadow of Revolution*, p. 116.
[5] Zinaida Zhemchuzhnaia, "The Road to Exile," in *Shadow*, pp. 82, 89.
[6] Maria Belskaia, "Arina's Children," in *Shadow*, p. 234.

a life story in 1936 (or in 1926 or 1946), it would undoubtedly have been very different.[7]

It is important to understand the constraints that shaped the writing of Soviet memoirs. Those written for publication were all subject to censorship, the severity of which changed over time.[8] In the Stalin period, censorship was very severe: topics like the Great Purges were taboo, disgraced revolutionary leaders like Trotsky were unmentionable. After Stalin's death in 1953, the Khrushchev thaw melted some of the ice, allowing the publication of memoirs such as Anna Litveiko's relatively unstereotyped account of a working girl's revolution and Lidia Libedinskaia's memoir of youth in an intelligentsia family with aristocratic antecedents.[9] Even during this period of relaxation, however, censorship still shaped the way people told their life stories: to note only the most important prohibition, it was possible to make only the most cursory and euphemistic references to the disappearance of family members and friends in the Great Purges.

Soviet ideological controls began to crumble in the mid 1980s during *perestroika* and then disappeared altogether with the collapse of the Soviet Union in 1991. This is not to say that autobiographies published in Russia in the 1990s were free from external influences, for what publishers and readers wanted at that time were the life stories of victims of the Soviet regime. Similar market constraints operated in the West in the interwar years, when Bolshevik atrocities were a basic feature of the genre of Russian emigré memoirs. In the 1970s, similarly, dissent and opposition were standard components in the popular Western publishing genre of Soviet dissident memoirs.[10]

In Evgenia Ginzburg's autobiographical writings, we can see the influence both of censorship and of genre and perceived audience. Ginzburg published two memoirs of school and university days in the Soviet youth

[7] Fruma Treivas, "We Were Fighting for an Idea!" in *Shadow*, pp. 324–30. For a similar dual perspective, see Raisa Orlova, *Memoirs*, trans. Samuel Cioran (New York, 1983). See also the successive versions of the life story of an Uzbek woman discussed in Marianne R. Kamp, "Three Lives of Saodat: Communist, Uzbek, Survivor," *Oral History Review* 28:2 (Summer/Fall 2002), pp. 21–58.

[8] For an excellent discussion of censorship and internal censorship of Soviet memoirs, see Hiroaki Kuromiya's "Soviet Memoirs as a Historical Source," in S. Fitzpatrick and L. Viola, eds., *A Researcher's Guide to Sources on Soviet Social History in the 1930s* (Armonk, N.Y., 1990).

[9] Anna Litveiko, "In 1917," in *Shadow*, pp. 49–65; Lidia Libedinskaia, "The Green Lamp," in *Shadow*, pp. 286–301.

[10] For a discussion of the specific characteristics of émigré and dissident memoirs, see Hiroaki Kuromiya, "Émigré and Dissident Memoir Literature," in Fitzpatrick and Viola, eds., *Researcher's Guide*, pp. 257–60.

journal *Iunost'* in 1965 and 1966 before going on to complete her two great volumes of Gulag memoirs, published abroad in 1967 and 1979.[11] The *Iunost'* pieces, lightly ironic and affectionately detached in tone, are written in the then popular genre of Soviet nostalgia for the pre-Stalin period: "How many times later, in hard times, I remembered that first dawn of the 1920s and drew strength from those memories. Our great, pure, young 1920s . . ."[12] In the university memoir of Kazan at the beginning of the 1920s, Ginzburg recalls how eagerly she and her fellow students studied Marxism. *Journey*, which Ginzburg initially hoped might be published in the USSR, reflects that hope, with the author writing within the framework of repudiation of the "cult of personality" and return of "the great Leninist truths."[13] In *Within the Whirlwind*, completed after the definitive Soviet rejection of *Journey*, Ginzburg no longer uses the "Leninist" persona or invokes Soviet nostalgia. Indeed, her comment that she and other Gulag victims "receive[d] our long-dreamed-of freedom through the establishment, as it is called nowadays," with its self-conscious use of a foreign term unfamiliar to many Russian readers, suggests that she may have already had a Western (or at least Russian émigré) public in mind.[14]

Russian women told their life stories in many different genres, written and oral. Among the important Soviet genres were revolutionary lives, workers' lives, and life stories of Stakhanovites. Lives of revolutionaries, drawing on a prerevolutionary tradition of exemplary lives, were particularly popular in the 1920s.[15] In the early 1930s, a project called "History of Factories and Plants," sponsored by the writer Maxim Gorky, collected

---

[11] Evgeniia Ginzburg, "Edinaia trudovaia . . . ," *Iunost'* 1965 no. 11, and "Studenty dvatsatykh godov," *Iunost'* 1966 no. 8; Ginzburg, *Journey into the Whirlwind*, trans. Paul Stevenson and Max Hayward (San Diego, 1967), and *Within the Whirlwind*, trans. Ian Boland (San Diego, 1981).

[12] "Edinaia," p. 99. Note the hint ("hard times") of her later suffering in the terror, the most that could be got through the censorship at that period, but still fully comprehensible to her readers.

[13] *Journey*, pp. 417–18. There is a fascinating description in this epilogue of the workings of Ginzburg's "internal censor" when she was hoping for Soviet publication.

[14] *Within the Whirlwind*, p. 411. This discussion is not meant to imply that Ginzburg was not a true Marxist and Communist in earlier times, or that her authorial stance in *Whirlwind* was insincere, but only to elaborate her own point (see above, note 12) that the story one tells changes according to one's perception of audience, and that censorship exaggerates this process.

[15] For a good example of a revolutionary life, written with maximum impersonality by the revolutionary herself, see Nadezhda Krupskaia, "Autobiography," in *Shadow*, pp. 111–12. On the genre of revolutionary lives, see Jeffrey Brooks, "Revolutionary Lives: Public Identities in Pravda during the 1920s," in Stephen White, ed., *New Directions in Soviet History* (Cambridge, 1991), pp. 27–40.

life stories of workers.[16] Participant accounts of revolution and Civil War emphasizing the heroism of the struggle were another major genre.

Stakhanovites—workers and peasants rewarded for outstanding production results—sometimes wrote their life stories, as in Pasha Angelina's case, but more often recited short accounts of their lives at the public meetings where Stakhanovites' achievements were celebrated. This was one common type of Soviet success story; another was the story of a woman of humble origins who rose to prominence after (and as a result of) the Revolution. Both resemble the genre known in Latin America as *testimonios*, in which men and women from revolutionary liberation movements testify about their participation in the struggle, portraying themselves less as individuals than as representatives of a collective experience.[17]

The 1960s and '70s saw a spate of Soviet publication of participant accounts of collectivization and the industrialization drive of the 1930s, often with a particular regional focus.[18] "Participants" in this context meant activists, often party and Komsomol members, and their stories were told in a spirit of celebration. Those who participated as victims—for example, peasants who were expropriated during dekulakization—had no public voice in Soviet times, and in the rare instances where their stories were recorded, they could not be published.[19] It was not until the post-Soviet 1990s that oral history, often victim-focused, flourished. A new People's Archive was established in Moscow to collect such documents, and similar initiatives to collect personal documents and testimony sprang up all over Russia.[20]

[16] See S. V. Zhuravlev, *Fenomen "Istoriia fabrik i zavodov": Gor'kovskoe nachinanie v kontekste epokhi 1930'kh godov* (Moscow, 1997). A collection of women's autobiographies from this project was published as *Rabotnitsa na sotsialisticheskoi stroike*, ed. O. Chaadaeva (Moscow, 1932).

[17] On *testimonios*, see Doris Sommer, " 'Not Just a Personal Story': Women's *Testimonios* and the Plural Self," in Brodzki and Scheck, ed., *Life/Lines*.

[18] For example, *Uchastnitsy velikogo sozidaniia* (Moscow, 1962).

[19] For examples of such peasant life stories, recorded by a Leningrad ethnomusicologist in the 1970s and '80s but published only in the 1990s, see the narratives by Nenila Bazeleva, Efrosinia Koslova, et al. in *Shadow*, pp. 241–42 and 322–23.

[20] For a collection of women's autobiographies from the the People's Archive, see *Zhenskaia sud'ba v Rossii: Dokumenty i vospominaniia*, comp. T. M. Goriaeva (Moscow, 1994). Various oral history projects have been conducted and published: notably Barbara A. Engel and Anastasia Posadskaya-Vanderbek, eds., *A Revolution of Their Own: Voices of Women in Soviet History* (Boulder, 1998); *Memories of Revolution: Russian Women Remember*, ed. Anna Horsbrugh-Porter (London, 1993), which contains oral histories of women who were longtime émigrés in England; and *Na korme vremeni: Interv'iu s leningradtsami 1930–kh godov*, ed. M. Vitukhnovskaia (St. Petersburg, 2000) (13 out of 15 of these interviewees are women). Interviews with peasant women are the data base of David L. Ransel, *Village Mothers: Three Generations of Change in Russia and Tataria* (Indiana, 2000), and *Golosa*

All through the Soviet period, Soviet citizens had the habit of writing to newspapers and political leaders with appeals and complaints, and it was customary to include a short autobiographical statement in such letters.[21] Only in rare cases were such letters published, but Soviet institutional and newspaper archives are full of them. Recently opened Soviet archives contain other interested autobiographical material, notably the narrative curricula vitae (*avtobiografii*) that were in the personal files of all Soviet citizens, along with personal questionnaires (*ankety*).[22] Another genre found in the archives—particularly interesting because of its specificity to Soviet-type political systems—is the public autobiographical statement made in a context of public interrogation, such as party purges, where the validity of the life story was liable to be challenged.[23]

MILESTONES OF PUBLIC LIFE

The revolutions of 1917 were central events in many autobiographies. The February Revolution was remembered as a joyful, carefree, bloodless event by memoirists from all parts of the society. An upper-class woman remembered the euphoria when a Cossack detachment passed through a crowd of demonstrators without dispersing them: "Everyone went wild. Some people started crying, others hugged each other . . . It's the revolution! It will prevail! Even the Cossacks are with the people!"[24] A worker's memories were in a similar vein: "The people from the calico printing factory came over and started shouting, 'Close down the factory!' We thought it was a strike and went out into the street, but there everybody was yelling 'It's an uprising,' so we got really excited . . . We saw two boys escorting a policeman, and he did not resist—just followed them to the station. We went marching through Moscow singing songs. Those were beautiful times . . ."[25] While the October Revolution was dutifully foregrounded by Soviet memoirists, the tone was less euphoric: as one Bolshevik memoiries admitted, "there was none of the pure devil-may-care joy of the kind that we had felt after the February Revolution. Then we had had nothing to worry about . . . But now we were in power, and

krest'ian. Sel'skaia Rossiia XX veka v krest'ianskkh memuarakh, ed. E. M. Kovalev (Moscow, 1996).

[21] On the genre of letters to authority, see chapter 9.

[22] For discussion of Communist *avtobiografii* in personal files, see Igal Halfin, *Terror in My Soul: Communist Autobiographies on Trial* (Cambridge, Mass., 2003).

[23] See Halfin, *Terror*, and chapter 5, this book.

[24] Ekaterina Olitskaia, "My Reminiscences," in *Shadow*, p. 34.

[25] Praskovia Komarova, in O. M. Chaadaeva, ed., *Rabotnitsa na sotsialisticheskoi stroike. Sbornik avtobiografii rabotnits* (Moscow, 1930), p. 140.

we were responsible for everything."[26] The worker Praskovia Komarova remembered October as "scary." "Soon I went to the village to join my husband—I got scared after all the shooting."[27] Émigré memoirists did not usually accord October the status of an event: they remembered rather a drift into chaos and brutality, culminating in Civil War, in which their familiar world was destroyed.

The Civil War was a time of upheaval for almost everyone, and chaotic movement and flight for many. Some memoirs described the flight to the south or east and the struggle to survive in areas that were successively under Red and White control.[28] Other memoirists fought for the Reds and related these experiences in the heroic mode of Soviet Civil War partici-pants' accounts.[29] Soldiers' wives described their travails, as in M. I. Nes-gorova's tale of Civil War hardships, in which she relates laconically that "they took my children to an orphanage, but when my husband came back from the Red Army, we got them back."[30] Some memoirists were orphaned and homeless until kind strangers took them in.[31] Young Jewish women made their way out of the *shetl* to new lives in Moscow.[32]

Collectivization looms large in the memoirs of rural women as well as the young urbanites sent to carry it out, but memories and perceptions of it differed greatly. For Pasha Angelina, collectivization was a fight be-tween the poor peasants of the village, led by the Angelin family, and the kulaks; for Antonina Solovieva and Elizaveta Nikulina, Komsomol collectivizers recounting their memories in a Soviet publication of the 1960s, "kulaks" were the people who put Valentin in hospital, murdered Marusia, and threw Elizaveta off a bridge into icy water and left her to drown. But Valentina Bogdan's classmate Fedia committed suicide rather than continue as a collectivizer, and victims of dekulakization like Nenila Bazeleva remembered bitterly that "if you were a good farmer you got dekulakized—that is, you had everything taken away from you." Maria Belskaia, writing in the 1990s, told a harrowing tale of dekulakization in which the family, evicted from their home in the village, wandered misera-

[26] Litveiko, "In 1917," in *Shadow*, p. 64.

[27] Chaadaeva, *Rabotnitsa*, p. 141.

[28] See, for example, Zhemchuzhnaia and Olitskaia memoirs in *Shadow*.

[29] See, for example, Anna Andzhievskaia, "A Mother's Story," and Zinaida Patrikeeva, "Cavalry Boy," in *Shadow*, and other memoirs in the book from which they came, *Zhen-shchina v grazhdanskoi voine: Epizody bor'by na Severnom Kavkaze i Ukraine v 1917– 1920 gg.* (Moscow, 1938); also *Zhenshchiny Urala v revoliutsii i trude* (Sverdlovsk, 1963).

[30] From A. V. Vlasovskaia et al., "Speeches by Stakhanovites' Wives," in *Shadow*, p. 365.

[31] Nina Nikoaevna Staroselets, "Moia zhizn'," in Z. M. Rogachevskaia, ed., *Zhena in-zhenera (K Vsesoiuznomu soveshchaniiu zhen ITR tiazheloi promyshlennosti)* (Moscow-Leningrad, 1936), p. 28.

[32] See, for example, Treivas, "Fighting," in *Shadow*, p. 324, and Inna Shikheeva-Gaister, "A Family Chronicle," pp. 376–78; Ulianova, whose story is told in chapter 5, above.

bly across Russia for years before finding a place to settle. Anna Gantse-vich's family left the village, too, but less traumatically: "We . . . had man-aged to get papers (*bumazhki*) and lived in Krasnoiarsk." For Ekaterina Pravdina, an orphan living with her aunt's family in the village, papers were crucial in another sense. "They [the aunt's family] were missing some papers. But if they had had time to adopt me, I would have been dekulakized too."[33]

The terror of 1937–38 was a taboo subject in Soviet publishing during the Stalin period and for many years after, but *perestroika* in the late 1980s brought forth an outpouring of memoirs by Gulag survivors and their relatives that continued in the 1990s. The desire to bear witness to horrors seen and experienced was often cited as the stimulus to writing.[34] Those who were themselves victims usually have particularly vivid memo-ries of the shock and confusion of their arrests and early days in prison. Olga Adamova-Sliozberg, in total denial of what was happening, worked diligently on a report for her boss for four hours while her apartment was searched, and had to be reminded by the arresting officer to say goodbye to her children; when the NKVD came for Fruma Treivas, four months pregnant, she said, "I left my son sleeping there, idiot that I was! I should have at least called my sister. But I did not have time: I had to hurry and go to prison!" When 21-year-old journalist Hava Volovich was arrested, she "didn't think that they would keep me long." Yet, she adds poi-gnantly, "at the same time I understood that my life was ruined for good."[35] Both Hava and Fruma initially thought their cell-mates in prison must be guilty: "My God, what was I doing there, among such people?" was Fruma's reaction on arrival at Butyrka prison. "They, of course, were guilty, but I was not." Yet a spirit almost of sisterhood among the arrested women is often recalled, all the more because elite wives often found themselves clustered together. In a memoir published in the early 1990s, theater director Natalia Sats recounted her arrival in a Butyrka cell crowded with elite women prisoners almost as if it were a social occasion:

[33] Pasha Angelina, "The Most Important Thing," in *Shadow*, pp. 309–10; Antonina Solo-vieva, "Sent by the Komsomol," pp. 235–40; Valentina Bogdan, "Students in the First Five-Year Plan," pp. 271–73; "Peasant Narratives (1)," p. 240; see also *Zhenshchiny Urala v revoliutsii i trude* (Sverdlovsk, 1963), pp. 323–24 (Nikulina story); Maria Belskaia, "Arina's Children," in *Shadow*, pp. 219–34; *Golosa*, p. 333 (Gantsevich); *Na korme vremeni: In-terv'iu s leningradtsami 1930-kh godov* (St. Petersburg, 2000), p. 75 (Pravdina). For a sum-mary of the memories of collectivization supplied by informants in Ransel's oral history project on fertility, see Ransel, *Village Mothers*, pp. 235–36.

[34] See, for example, Simeon Vilensky, ed., *Till My Tale is Told: Women's Memoirs of the Gulag* (Bloomington, 1999), pp. 2, 172, 335–36; Ginzburg, *Journey*, p. 417, and *Whirl-wind*, p. 417.

[35] Vilensky, *Tale*, pp. 246–47.

" 'Is it really Natalia Sats herself?' 'When did she manage to go grey?' . . . 'If they've got Natashka as well, there are no surprises left.' "[36]

Indeed, the reader of women's memoirs of the Great Purges sometimes has a similar feeling that it's a small world: in one freight car transporting women prisoners across the country to Magadan, there were actually *two* future chroniclers of the event: Katia Olitskaia and Zhenia Ginzburg. In their memoirs, written after surviving decades in Gulag, each remembered the other, though without special affection: Katia was an SR (Socialist Revolutionary), one of the comparatively few genuine opponents of the regime among the prisoners, while Zhenia belonged to the elite Communist group for whose past privilege and present delusions Katia had scant sympathy.[37] Friction between Communist women and SRs and Mensheviks is also reported in the Butyrka memories of Adamova-Sliozberg: the latter were the old hands, "experts on all the rules, knew how to stand up for their rights," confident in their condemnation of the regime and prediction of its collapse, "greet[ing] each new batch of arrested Communists with ill-concealed joy: people who had condemned their views and actions now had to share the same fate along with everyone else."[38]

Yet for many women not directly affected by terror, this world was unimaginable. In interviews conducted in the 1990s, respondents without personal or family involvement rarely expressed strong reactions to the Great Purges: some, like Khadycha Iakubova, a Tatar student in Leningrad, remembered having "no interest in politics," but basically accepting "public opinion" about the "enemies of the people": "We thought that obviously they ought to be punished, if they were against the people." The terror of 1937–38 "somehow . . . didn't affect me much," Ekaterina Pravdina confessed, even though she personally liked several of her bosses at the factory who were arrested. She went to the obligatory purge sessions, but "How to tell you, I was just a girl. I simply didn't listen because . . . I had no interest in it . . ." Natalia Kolokoltsova, a girl from the village who became first a domestic servant and then a factory worker, denied even hearing about the repressions.[39]

None of these 1990s interviewees remembered being strongly hostile to the alleged "enemies," but such hostility does show up in other kinds of life stories. When M. K. Razina, a militant milkmaid, was telling her

[36] Olga Adamova-Sliozberg, "My Journey," in Vilensky, *Tale*, p. 6; Treivas, "Fighting," in *Shadow*, pp. 327–28; Vilensky, *Tale*, pp. 246–47 (Volovich); Nataliia Sats, *Zhizn'—iavlenie polosatoe* (Moscow, 1991), p. 299.

[37] See Ginzburg, *Journey*, part 2, esp. p. 286 (for a somewhat unflattering description of "Katya Orlitskaya"[sic]) and 292–96; Ekaterina Olitskaia, "My Reminiscences (3)," in *Shadow*, pp. 431–34.

[38] Vilensky, *Tale*, p. 21.

[39] *Na korme vremeni*, pp. 279, 93–94, 154.

life story at a Stakhanovite conference in the mid 1930s, she expressed pleasure at the downfall of a state farm director who had earlier perse-cuted her. There was similar *Schadenfreude* in the comment (overheard by Bogdan) of a cleaning lady on the arrest of regional party leader, Ev-dokimov, and his wife's suicide:

"Who is Evdokimov?
"Don't you know? He was a member of the Provincial Executive Com-mittee and our delegate to the Supreme Soviet. His wife was a big Com-munist, too."
"Then she got what she deserved."[40]

Not all the memories are of horrors. Many women, telling their life stories in a variety of formats in the post-Stalin period, remembered childhood and youth in the 1920s and 1930s as times of happiness, infused with a sense of boundless possibilities. Part of this can surely be attributed to the universal tendency to look back with nostalgia on one's youth—a ten-dency intensified, Yuri Slezkine has argued, by the devastating impact of a parent's arrest in the Great Purges, which for a number of elite memoirists abruptly ended a "happy and peaceful childhood."[41] But not all the depic-tions of childhood happiness can be linked to a traumatic eviction from paradise in the late 1930s. For Raisa Orlova, war and the death of a beloved young husband marked the caesura, and her evocation of the youthful happiness of a Soviet "true believer" can scarcely be considered nostalgic, given that she wrote her memoirs as a dissident to whom such belief had become thoroughly alien. " 'Heute fuehl' ich mich so wun-derbar!' 'How happy I am today!' we sang in imitation of Franziska Gaal [in the German film *Peter*, shown in Moscow cinemas in the 1930s]"; and in her memories she emphasizes not only that she was "very happy in my youth" but also that she felt then "this was the way it was supposed to be, that this was the normal way, that man was born for happiness. Whereas unhappiness and grief were deviations, anomalies."[42]

The Leningraders interviewed in the 1990s about their youth in the 1930s also tend to have very positive memories, and to link them with a broader sense of optimism and national purpose. Iakubova remembered a cheerful student life at Leningrad University, in which people who had come from all parts of the country (often, like her, via affirmative action), felt a "union . . . of spiritual interests" and idealism: "We thought that we

---

[40] N. I. Slavnikova, et al., "Speeches by Stakhanovites," and Bogdan, "Memoirs of an Engineer," in *Shadow*, pp. 339 and 408.

[41] Yuri Slezkine, "Lives as Tales," in *Shadow*, p. 30. The quotation is from Shikheeva-Gaister, "A Family Chronicle," in ibid., p. 383.

[42] Orlova, *Memoirs*, pp. 36, 14.

would actually and seriously be building human society itself." Bronislava Kogan agreed: "We were young, we were drawn to the Komsomol, drawn to the new. And the party people were drawn to the new. We thought that a real era of freedom was dawning." Maria Shamliian from Armenia, another *vydvizhenka* and an orphan, described a life at apprenticeship school and the factory in which her Komsomol and party activism gave great personal satisfaction as well as rewards: not only were they "always promoting me" but also "people [*narod*] liked me very much."[43]

PERSONAL LIFE

Testimony is so important in twentieth-century Russian women's autobiography that it is hard to find instances of the confessional mode. Anna Iankovskaia's oral history about her redemption from a life of crime, recorded at the Belomor labor camp in the early 1930s, fits the confessional genre, as does Paraskeva Ivanova's dramatic account of her seduction and induction into a life of promiscuity by a Communist superior.[44] But it is Agrippina Korevanova's autobiography—a product of Gorky's project for publishing the lives of ordinary people—that is the real exception to the dominance of testimony.

> What made me want to write? I think there were two main reasons.
>
> First of all, my life was so sad that I kept thinking of suicide, and so I decided to describe all my sufferings, so that after my death people would discover my notebooks and find out what had me me want to kill myself.
>
> The second reason was my rage and horror at the unfairness of life; my protest against the oppression of women; and my hatred for a fat wallet. I wrote about all this in poor literary style but with great bitterness and passion. There was no practical use in it, of course, but at least it provided some relief . . .[45]

[43] *Na korme vremeni*, pp. 276, 215, 57–58. Note that the emotional tenor of the Engel and Posadskaya interviews, done at roughly the same period, is generally quite different, suggesting that interviewees in both surveys responded in part to what they perceived as the expectations of their interviewers. The small Engel and Posadskaya group, consisting disproportionately of women who had suffered for their "alien" class background in the 1930s, said little of youthful happiness, though they did report a higher degree of satisfaction and identification with the Soviet regime than their interviewers seemed to expect.

[44] Anna Iankovskaia, "A Belomor Confession," in *Shadow*, pp. 282–85; Paraskeva Ivanova, "Why I Do Not Belong in the Party," in ibid., pp. 213–18. The Ivanova statement appears to have been written as a letter to the editor (not clear which newspaper); it was originally published in L. Sosnovskii, ed., *Bol'nye voprosy (zhenshchina, sem'ia i deti)* (Leningrad, 1926).

[45] Agrippina Korevanova, "My Life," in *Shadow*, pp. 177–78.

Of course, personal life coexists with public life in many autobiographical narratives. Occasionally, as in the poignant account by Civil War fighter Anna Andzhievskaia of the loss of her infant daughter, it intrudes vividly and almost destabilizes the testimonary character.[46] But more often, especially in Soviet narratives, personal information is minimized or omitted. "Are you really interested in these trivial details of my life—my childhood, my family, how I became involved in the revolutionary movement?" Sofia Pavlova sternly asked interviewers in the 1990s. The story she wanted to tell was of her public life; she talked about personal matters unwillingly, and then only with the promise that it not be written down.[47] In her autobiography, the Stakhanovite Pasha Angelina mocked the American biographer who wanted to know the date of her wedding, and she did not even mention the name of her (divorced?) husband.[48] To be sure, Soviet editors often removed personal material from autobiographical writing, but its absence is also a product of the writers' own sense of autobiographical propriety.[49] "I long doubted whether it was appropriate to write of such a personal matter in a book of memoirs devoted to our shared sufferings and common shame," wrote Evgenia Ginzburg about falling in love with her second husband in Gulag. She finally decided to include him on the grounds that she could "show through his image that the victim of inhumanity can remain the bearer of all that is good."[50]

There are many autobiographies of self-presented "strong women." Princess Volkonskaia takes the lead, with an intrepid clandestine journey into Civil War Russia to rescue her imprisoned husband. Zina Patrikeeva, a nurse who dressed as a man to ride with Budennyi's cavalry in the Civil War, was a counterpart on the Red side. In many autobiographies published in the Soviet Union, women presented themselves as feistily independent, equal or superior to men even in traditionally male activities. Anna Shchetinina, a sea captain interviewed by a Soviet women's journal in the 1930s, compared herself favorably to one of her male counterparts

[46] Anna Andzhievskaia, "A Mother's Story," in *Shadow*, pp. 79–81. Note that the title is the editors', the memoir's initial genre—and that of the collection from which it comes, *Zhenshchina v grazhdanskoi voine: Epizody bor'by na Severnom Kavkaze i Ukraine v 1917–1920 gg.* (Moscow, 1938)—was that of celebration of women's heroism in revolution and war.

[47] Engel and Posadskaya-Vanderbeck, eds., *A Revolution of Their Own*, pp. 48, 62.

[48] "The Most Important Thing," in *Shadow*, pp. 305–21. Angelina did mention her parents and siblings—all Soviet activists—as well as her three children, the youngest of whom was called Stalina.

[49] See, for example, Catriona Kelly, "The Authorised Version: the Auto/Biographies of Vera Panova," in *Models of Self. Russian Women's Autobiographical Texts*, eds. Marianne Liljestrom, Arja Rosenholm, and Irina Savkina (Helsinki, 2000), pp. 73–76.

[50] Ginzburg, *Within the Whirlwind*, p. 122. Thanks to Kiril Tomoff for pointing this out to me.

in the merchant navy, "a dandy and a weakling, [who] often made mistakes [and] used to wear a flower in his lapel." Bilia Misostishkhova, a bumptious young Kabardian, boasted at a Stakhanovite conference in the mid 1930s of her mountain-climbing achievements and promised that "in parachute jumping I am also going to be ahead of the men."[51] The enthusiasm for revolutionary emancipation of women that underlay such claims is most noticeable in prewar memoirs, giving way in the postwar period to celebration of women as the stronger sex, with greater powers of emotional and physical endurance. "When the hard times came it became clear that the women who had affected the part of lady or little bird were the main organizers of daily life and, indeed, were the builders and mainstay of the family . . . The women were always stronger than the men, as everybody sees well enough today," Nadezhda Mandelstam wrote in the 1960s. The peasant Anna Gantsevich's description of herself in an oral history of the 1990s as "strong, able to endure things, fearless" implied the same belief—despite the fact that, like Mandelstam, she considered her husband her intellectual superior.[52]

The memoir literature abounds in portrayals of strong women other than the authors. Elena Bonner's indomitable grandmother Batanya is the classic example, with Lidia Libedinskaia's formidable aristocratic grandmother giving her lively competition, while in Shikheeva-Gaister's autobiography, a family servant steps into the "indomitable grandmother" role after her parents' arrest. Maria Belskaia dedicated her memoir to her steadfast peasant mother, Arina, who kept the family together after dekulakization; Evgenia Ginzburg presented her mother-in-law as a font of homely wisdom and clear thinking.[53] A different kind of strong woman, the sexually liberated revolutionary, is presented in Ekaterina Bogdan's portrayal of her college contemporary Olga as willful, independent, free-spirited, and sexually adventurous.[54] Women whose work and public commitments are so central to their lives that they hardly have time for their children show up in several daughters' memoirs.[55] And several émigré memoirists give us the obverse view of the strong Communist

[51] Sofia Volkonskaia, "The Way of Bitterness," in Shadow, pp. 140–65 (originally published in London under the same title in 1931); Zina Patrikeeva, "Cavalry Boy," pp. 118–22 (first published in Zhenshchina v grazhdanskoi voine in 1938); Anna Shchetinina, "A Sea Captain's Story," pp. 350, 352; Slavnikova et al., "Speeches," p. 341 (Misostishkhova).

[52] Nadezhda Mandelstam, Hope Abandoned, trans. Max Hayward (New York, 1974), p. 105; Golosa, p. 320 (Gantsevich).

[53] Elena Bonner, Mothers and Daughters, trans. Antonina W. Bouis (New York, 1993), pp. 13–17, 87–89, and passim; Libedinskaia, "The Green Lamp," in Shadow, pp. 287, 295–96; Shikheeva-Gaister, "A Family Chronicle," in ibid, pp. 382–83; Belskaia, "Arina's Children," in ibid.; Ginzburg, Journey, pp. 20–24.

[54] Shadow, pp. 263–64, 269–70, 404–5.

[55] For example, Bonner, Mothers and Daughters; Shikheeva-Gaister, "Family Chronicle."

woman in their pen portraits of de-sexed fanatics who are even more ruthless than their male counterparts.[56]

At the opposite end of the spectrum, victimhood is also an important theme of twentieth-century Russian women's autobiography. The peasant Efrosinia Kislova struck a typical "victim" note, beginning her 1970s oral history with the plaint "I had more sorrows than anybody else." The folksongs Kislova sings for the interviewer seem to be mainly about suffering at the hands of men, but in her story, and that of other peasant interviewees, it is the state that is the victimizer: "The government got all the grain, and we got the ashes"; "then this government came along, and dekulakized us."[57] In Belskaia's memoir, a veritable saga of a peasant family's victimization by the state, written under the influence of *perestroika*, this is developed into an indictment of Stalin ("Our very 'great' thanks to him for such a 'happy childhood'," she writes sarcastically).[58] The memoirs of first-wave émigrés also often tell a story of victimization by the Bolsheviks and the Soviet state, and, *nolens volens*, virtually all Great Purges memoirs have the same thrust.[59] As Vera Shulz wrote of her arrest in 1938, "it is impossible ever to forget this kind of cruel and senseless blow which affects the whole of one's life. Impossible to forget that one might at any moment become a powerless, humiliated pawn."[60]

However, as Catherine Merridale noticed in talking about experiences of repression to her respondents in the 1990s, survivors were often unwilling to tell their lives purely as victimization stories: "most people talked about survival. . . . They found ways of their own of dealing with their losses—human and material—and they are proud, up to a point, of their endurance."[61] The same desire to portray oneself as an endurer instead of (or as well as) a victim is evident in the peasant oral histories recorded in the 1990s. "There are times when you curse and cry," a peasant woman told interviewers, but still, she learnt something, even from such nightmarish experiences as her deportation as a kulak.[62] "My life has been sorrowful," another peasant woman said, remembering particularly her experiences in collectivization. "Not only has it been hard, but I also suf-

---

[56] For example, Varsher in *Shadow*, pp. 113–15; Volkonskaia, in ibid., p. 351.

[57] *Shadow*, pp. 323 (Kislova), 241 (Bazeleva). For more on the victim's plea, see Golfo Alexopoulos, "The Ritual Lament: A Narrative of Appeal in the 1920s and 1930s," *Russian History* 42:1–2 (1997).

[58] Fitzpatrick and Slezkine, *Shadow*, p. 223.

[59] For example, Volkonskaia, "The Way of Bitterness," in *Shadow*; P. E. Melgunova-Stepanova, "Where Laughter is Never Heard," in ibid., pp. 66–72 (from *Gde ne slyshno smekha . . .*, published in Paris in 1928).

[60] Vera Shulz, "Taganka," in Vilensky, *Tale*, p. 152.

[61] Catherine Merridale, *Night of Stone: Death and Memory in Twentieth-Century Russia* (Harmondsworth, Middlesex, U.K., 2001), pp. 17–18.

[62] *Golosa krest'ian*, p. 343.

fered many abuses . . . But however harsh the times were, anyway I brought up all my children and got them an education . . ." [63]

There are versions of the victim story that indict perpetrators other than the Soviet regime. One genre that was cultivated in Soviet autobiography (particularly that of working-class and peasant women) was the testimonio, focusing on oppression under Tsarism and comparing a miserable prerevolutionary life with the happiness and opprtities of the Soviet present.

> I will tell you about my life and about how I used to live . . . When I was eleven, I lost my mother and became an orphan. When I was twelve, I was given as a nanny to the village kulaks, and then, when I was fourteen, to the manor house, to look after their children . . . I couldn't read or write. My life was very bad, and I didn't know that there was a different, better life.[64]

There are, of course, women whose autobiographical narratives focus on victimization by men, though this is not characteristic of twentieth-century Russian women's autobiography. Agrippina Korevanova pointed the finger at her father, father-in-law, and husband, not to mention assorted male Soviet officials who mistreated her in later life. Some of this was put in a frame of prerevolutionary exploitation, but it is clear that for Korevanova exploitation was gendered. Even when she was assaulted by unknown assailants, she assumed the assailant was male and warned him that on her death "I will leave behind not one, not two *women* [my emphasis] loyal to the revolution, but perhaps hundreds." Anna Litveiko described her mother's victimization by a drunken husband and her own decision to throw her father out of the house—"my first independent act, and I was very proud of it" (though later she had wondered whether she had made her mother happier or unhappier by her action).[65]

Women are usually very reluctant to criticize husbands in their memoirs, even clearly unsatisfactory ones like Orlova's second.[66] Even in interviews in later life, respondents were notably uneasy when pressed for details about former husbands, implicitly rebuffing the interviewers' desire to be told the worst. Something of the same reticence can be felt even when the interviewer is clearly encouraging such criticism.[67] Despite their education and skills, the upper-class and intelligentsia women tended to

---

[63] Ransel, *Mothers*, p. 238.

[64] M. K. Razina, in *Shadow*, p. 338.

[65] *Shadow*, pp. 170–206 (quotation from p. 200) (Korevanova); 51 (Litveiko).

[66] Orlova, *Memoirs*, p. 32. In Bonner's autobiography, similarly, her first husband gets only the most cursory mention as the father of her children (*Mothers and Daughters*, p. 330), and is not even named.

[67] For example, Engel and Posadskaya, *Revolution*, pp. 70–71, 94–96.

be deferential to their husbands, according to their own self-depictions, and rarely report significant conflicts within the family on the issue of work outside the home.[68] In the portion of her memoirs covering the period after her marriage to writer Iurii Libedinskii in the early 1940s, Lidia Libedinskaia makes a striking switch in self-representation from the independent, albeit childish, actor of the first half of the memoir to a devoted spouse whose own life and work are totally subordinated to her husband's. Similarly, one of the intriguing aspects of Nadezhda Mandelstam's first memoir, *Hope against Hope*, is the contradiction between her expressions of deference and subordination to her poet husband and the unmistakable strength of own personality and self-assertion that the narrative itself conveys.[69]

Family conflict, usually involving husbands' attempts to restrict or control their wives' activities outside the home, was reported much more frequently by lower-class women; indeed, the theme of marital opposition was a standard component in the life stories of women activists. After six months of marriage, the husband of Moscow worker Anna Balashova "realized that I was not submissive enough." Their marriage started to fall apart, and he left her while she was in hospital after delivering their child, leaving no note but "taking quite a few of my personal things with him." Another Moscow worker, Anastasia Bushueva, ran away from a drunken husband who "beat me up so hard I could not work": her Party cell found her temporary housing until the factory could provide permanent accommodation.[70] Speaking to a women's journal in the mid 1930s, Stakhanovite Anna Smirnova also told a story of unresolvable marital conflict once she became an activist: "he started to give me a hard time about 'coming home late.' And I was always at a meeting, at a class, on duty in the cooperative store or the hospital . . . In the end, I got fed up with his needling. We separated. I have lived alone since 1924."[71]

Peasant women Stakhanovites, similarly, often had stories of oppression by husbands that frequently ended in divorce, represented as emancipation and the beginning of a "conscious" Soviet life. Gadiliaeva, a milk-

---

[68] In *Shadow*, Zhemchuzhnaia and Bogdan are exemplars of the educated but deferential wife.

[69] Lidiia Libedinskaia, *Zelenaia lampa* (Moscow, 1966), pp. 149–407; Mandelstam, *Hope against Hope*.

[70] These stories, originally published in O. N. Chaadaeva, ed., *Rabotnitsa na sotsialisticheskom stroike: Sbornik avtobiografii rabotnits* (Moscow, 1932), pp. 110–11, 150, come from the big Soviet oral history project of the early 1930s, *Istoriia fabrik i zavodov*; the Balashova extract is translated in Fitzpatrick and Slezkine, *Shadow*, pp. 249–50. That women's activism often had "serious problems with their husbands" is confirmed by Korevanova in *Shadow*, p. 206.

[71] *Obshchestvennitsa*, 1937 no. 1 (19), p. 27.

maid from Bashkiria, "was married off against my will" at sixteen. "Having lived with my husband for a year and a half, I divorced him and began working in the kolkhoz on my own." For the Armenian peasant Budagian, such problems were solved automatically by a payment structure in the kolkhoz that rewarded those who worked harder: "How can your husband exploit you when you make more money than he does? That usually shuts him up."[72]

The statements quoted above are from the testimonios of Stakhanovites. Women who testified not as Stakhanovites but as Stakhanovites' *wives* naturally struck a different note, representing the purpose of their lives as support for their husbands, and sometimes (surprisingly, in view of the usual Soviet celebration of women's employment) mentioning that the task was easier now that their husbands' increased earnings allowed them to quit the work force. Many of these women, however, portray themselves as distinctly superior spouses—more cultured, motivated, and organized than their menfolk—who have to keep potential backsliding husbands up to the mark. Vlasovskaia was angry when her husband, who had "kind of let himself go," initially failed to become a Stakhanovite. Nesgorova noted her role in protecting her husband from drinking and "bad influences." Poliakova pushed her husband to become a Stakhanovite, forced him to listen to her reading aloud in the evenings, even when he wanted to go to bed, and tested him to see if he had stayed awake at the theater and the movies. "I wanted him to be a cultured person," she said. "I didn't want him to lag behind other men."[73]

In Alla Kiparenko's autobiographical story of pioneering life in the Far East, her friend in the city's Komsomol committee tells her the story of how a good Komsomol girl redeemed a ne'er-do-well: "the newlyweds were given a room and a lot of good wishes, but a decision was made not to let them out of sight. Then a miracle occurred! Nobody could recognize the former hooligan; he tried his best to catch up with his wife, and soon his productivity began to approach hers."[74] Even Princess Volkonskaia's story, ostensibly one of total devotion to her husband, manages to convey a whiff of the same patronizing attitude toward husbands: in her memoirs, Prince Peter, henpecked by his mother, passive, and apparently too refined to express (or feel?) any strong emotion, cuts a drab figure beside

---

[72] *Shadow*, pp. 337, 336. These materials were originally published in *Geroini sotsialisticheskogo truda* (Moscow, 1936).

[73] A. V. Vlasovskaia et al., "Speeches by Stakhanovites' Wives," in *Shadow*, pp. 359, 365, 362 (originally published in *Zhenshchina—bol'shaia sila. Severnoe kraevoe soveshchanie zhen stakhanovtsev* (Arkhangelsk, 1936).

[74] Alla Kiparenko, "Building the City of Youth," in *Shadow*, p. 280.

his dashing wife.[75] Had he been a locomotive driver, like Vlasovskaia's husband, he too might have needed coaching in self-assertiveness.

CLASS

Since class—the difference between the noble Princess Volkonskaia and the proletarian Vlasovskaia—had enormous resonance in everyday Soviet life, it figures prominently in autobiographies. For many women, class seems to have been a matter of more vital interest and anxiety than gender, which is hardly surprising given its salience in creating dangers and opportunities for families and individuals. In her memoirs, Zinaida Zhemchuzhina remarked on the Bolsheviks' adherence to a "rigid, preconceived pattern" that required all citizens to be identified by class and treated accordingly: "you were either a member of the bourgeoisie, who should be robbed and murdered, or a proletarian, who deserved all the good things in life."[76] Irina Elenevskaia described how her apartment house in Petrograd in the early 1920s was divided by class, each household "identifying with either the 'bourgeoisie' or the 'toilers.' " (She herself, of intelligentsia/service nobility origins, belonged to the "bourgeoisie").[77]

Memoirists were aware how much life chances depended on ascribed class position. Lidia Libedinskaia was almost expelled from the Young Pioneers because of her "bad" class origins, while a schoolfriend of Valentina Bogdan's was denied admission to college because his parents were "disenfranchised."[78] Four of the eight interviewees in Engel and Posadskaya's oral histories belonged to a stigmatized class and suffered a variety of problems as a result, their origin hanging over them "like the sword of Damocles," as one of them put it.[79] Describing the class-discriminatory policies of Soviet universities in the 1920s, Evgenia Ginzburg, daughter of a physician, notes: "I was lucky—I wasn't among the 'others' [i.e., the fourth (stigmatized) category]. But belonging to the third category, where children of intelligentsia families belonged, was also not such a great joy. This didn't restrict one's rights, but some sort of 'guilt complex,' something like a sense of original sin, poisoned life." After being rejected for Komsomol membership on class grounds, the young Raisa Orlova concluded "that there was something inferior and insufficiently firm within

---

[75] Volkonskaia, "Way of Bitterness."

[76] Zhemchuzhina, "Road to Exile," in *Shadow*, p. 87.

[77] Irina Elenevskaia, "Reminiscences," in *Shadow*, p. 133.

[78] Libedinskaia, "Green Lamp," in *Shadow*, p. 291; Bogdan, "Students," in ibid., p. 254.

[79] Engel and Posadskaya, eds., *Revolution*. The four were Dubova and Dolgikh (daughters of "kulaks"), Fleisher (daughter of a priest), and Berezhnaia (daughter of a landowning noble).

me. I was an 'intellectual,' and had to struggle against it without fail. I had to weed it out."[80]

Of course, there was an obverse side to this discrimination. Proletarians "deserved all the good things in life," in Zhemchuzhnaia's phrase, and that meant that they were beneficiaries of positive discrimination and affirmative action. The life story celebrating upward mobility and thanking the Soviet regime for making it possible was one of the standard autobiographical genres of the Stalin era. As the Stakhanovite tractor driver Pasha Angelina put it, Soviet upward mobility was of a special type: instead of "rising *from* the people," like a capitalist Lord Beaverbrook, people like her rose *with* the people. Testimonios offered on such public occasions as International Women's Day celebrated Cinderella-like transformations from little apprentice Zhenka, beaten by her cruel mistress, to Evgenia Fedorovna, technical director of a Soviet textile plant.[81] Half a century later, women of the same cohort expressed pride and satisfaction at their translation from "Simochka" to "Serafima Iakovlevna," and, while they no longer gave thanks to Stalin, they did speak warmly of the bosses at the factory who promoted and nurtured them back in the '30s.[82]

Although the Bolsheviks often treated class as a self-evident quantity, this was far from the case in the experience of many autobiographers.[83] Zhemchuzhnaia noted the contortions the Bolsheviks in Cossack lands had to go through to make local social groups fit in a Marxist framework (priests, teachers, and Cossacks were assigned to the bourgeoisie; non-Cossack peasants to the proletariat). Both she and Olitskaia had the problem that their male relatives, as noble landowners, were now seen as exploiters rather than as enlightened men who had tried to help the peasants. Class was also a puzzle for the young Libedinskaia, whose grandmother was both noble and an enthusiast for the revolution. Praskovia Dorozhinskaia's father was expropriated as a kulak even though he had belonged to the local Committee of the Poor. Olitskaia notes that "dekulakization" on her father's former estates during the Civil War was a farce: when Bolsheviks pressured the villagers to identify their kulaks, they simply "elected" someone unpopular or dispensable to that status.[84]

[80] Ginzburg, "Studenty," p. 87; Orlova, *Memoirs*, pp. 12–13.

[81] Angelina, "Important," in *Shadow*, p. 307; *Trud*, 8 March 1936, p. 2 (interview with E. F. Dudina). See also Maslennikova, "The Story of My Life," in *Shadow*, pp. 391–93.

[82] See stories of Maria Shamliian and Serafima Kogan in *Na korme vremeni. Interv'iu s leningradtsami 1930-kh godov*, ed. M. Vitukhnovskaia (St. Petersburg, 2000), esp. pp. 53, 62–63, 114–15, 123.

[83] On this problem, see chapter 2, this book.

[84] *Shadow*, pp. 87, 85 (Zhemchuzhnaia), 37, 39-40 (Olitskaia), 287, 296 (Libedinskaia), 241–42 (Dorozhinskaia).

Class hatred, a sentiment much in vogue in the first decades after the Revolution, is only rarely expressed in autobiography. The unhappy Korevanova, writing in the mid 1930s, is an exception: her revolutionary epiphany occurred when her heart "ached with hatred" after hearing an account of White atrocities. Ten years later, Korevanova's women's brigade (with the exception of one "tender-hearted" member) evicted class enemies from their apartments in a mood of grim satisfaction: they were getting what they deserved! Writing in the post-Stalin era, Anna Litveiko remembered conducting "class hatred" propaganda in the early days, but distanced herself from it (her text was a pamphlet called *Spiders and Flies*, describing bosses as spiders who drank the blood of the workers by appropriating their labor, whose content she recounted to her workmates "the way I used to tell them about Nat Pinkerton").[85]

By the 1990s, class hatred had virtually disappeared from the life stories recounted by elderly women. Those who came from the lower classes usually express only good feelings for the upper class; their reminiscences of encounters with "social aliens" (in Stalinist terminology) in the 1920s and 1930s tend to be sympathetic, especially if the latter were victims of repression. Olga Filippova, a nurse of working-class origins, recalled that in the expulsions from Leningrad after Kirov's death, the police arrested "the most cultured people, we were sorry for them." Maria Novikova, daughter of a cook, remembered her German colonist neighbors as "so kind" amd recalled that when they were deported "we all wept so much." Ekaterina Pravdina sewed for the lone noblewoman in her working-class communal apartment—"Well, she was really nice, sociable." *Vydvizhenka* Maria Shamliian had a room in the apartment formerly owned by a noblewoman, the widow of Tsarist General Izmailov, who still lived there. "They called me into the district party committee several times [about Izmailova, and] . . . I always gave a positive evaluation. 'About her origins, I said, you decide yourself, but as director, as a person she deserves only a positive evaluation.' "[86]

Izmailova was one of those "former people" who did not try to hide her origins. So was Lidia Libedinskaia's father, an economist of noble birth who continued to carry business cards identifying him as "Count Tolstoy," explaining that "just as only a scoundrel would have been ashamed of his proletarian origin before the revolution, so it did not become a decent person to deny his gentry background after the revolution."[87] But many women memoirists and the people they encountered

---

[85] *Shadow*, pp. 181, 202–3 (Korevanova), 54 (Litveiko). The Nat Pinkerton detective stories were very popular in Russia in the teens and twenties. The Litveiko memoir was first published in *Iunost'*, 1957 no. 3.

[86] *Na korme*, pp. 239, 196, 80, 65.

[87] *Shadow*, pp. 286–87.

did feel obliged to disguise their social class. Sometimes it was a literal disguise, as when Princess Volkonskaia, making her adventurous foray back into Soviet territory to rescue her husband, donned a scarf in order to look like a humble schoolteacher.[88] But often the disguise was more complex—a new biography to suit a new identity, or at least the blotting out of certain episodes in the past. Bogdan's landlady in her college days had to hide the fact that her late husband had fought for the Whites in the Civil War (making her the widow of a "counterrevolutionary"); Zhemchuzhnaia and her husband, formerly an officer in the White Army, hid the same secret after their move to Moscow at the end of the Civil War.[89]

Natalia Kolokoltsova's secret was that she was the daughter of a Tsarist policeman (*uriadnik*) executed by the Bolsheviks in 1919, though she had been only one year old at the time and by virtue of her own occupation as a factory worker could claim proletarian status.[90] For Anna Dubova, who managed to escape from the village to the city during collectivization, the secret was that her family had been dekulakized; Ekaterina Dolgikh, the daughter of a "kulak" sent away to an aunt for her education, was forced to renounce her parents; Vera Fleisher, also sent away to relatives to escape the stigma of being the daughter of a priest, felt under pressure to cut all ties: "We weren't even supposed to correspond with our parents. It was like having a tie with an 'alien element.' But of course we continued to correspond with them, and once in a while we visited them. But it was very difficult."[91]

THINGS

In revolutions, some people lose things and others gain them. This happened in the Bolshevik Revolution, and both loss and gain had a great impact on individual lives. To be sure, it is hard to find an autobiographer who foregrounds the transfer of material possessions in her life story, since most people who grew up in Russia in the first third of the twentieth century seem to have subscribed to the notion that possessions were unimportant and concern for them unworthy of a Russian *intelligent* (or Soviet citizen, depending on primary allegiance). Nevertheless, things lost and gained showed up on the periphery of women's life stories. In their memoirs, members of the old privileged classes who lost possessions during the Revolution generally emphasized the cultural/sentimental aspect of

[88] *Shadow*, p. 141.
[89] *Shadow*, pp. 254–55.
[90] *Na korme*, 146, 152.
[91] Engel and Posadskaya, *Revolution*, pp. 27–30, 163–66, 91.

their loss rather than the material. Those who gained things often saw them as entitlements, obtained from the state (not their former owners) only after much effort and anxiety. Both losers and gainers stressed that they were not the kind of people who really cared about material things.

The first great transfer of assets were the revolutionary confiscations of property that occurred in 1917 and during the Civil War years. Volkonskaia, one of a number of émigré memoirists who were victims of revolutionary confiscations and house searches, admitted that it was extremely unpleasant to see strangers handling her possessions, but retreated to philosophical detachment with the comment that "our sense of property has been developed in us for generations; the inverse process will probably take as long—if not longer." Zhemchuzhnaia's commentary on the confiscation of her personal property by the Bolsheviks during the Civil War was noticeably more bitter than Volkonskaia's; she was infuriated when the confiscators lectured her on her lack of "consciousness" in failing to sacrifice her possessions voluntarily. She called this her "Soviet baptism," for it was then that she learned that her life as well as her property had ceased to belong to her—"They had become the 'people's' and were transferred to the state . . ."[92] Describing the process of confiscation, both she and Olitskaia express their disdain for the personal greed of the confiscators—and these simple workers and soldiers, in their turn, are reported as showing astonishment at the "bourgeois" women's lack of covetousness and indifference to the valuables in their houses.[93]

Envy of possessions is vividly reported in one of the Leningrad oral histories of the 1990s, when village-born Ekaterina Pravdina describes it as the root cause of her aunt's dekulakization during collectivization.

> That aunt of mine—they lived in the town too before the revolution, and during the revolution they all left. Well, they took some furniture—of course, they were used to not sleeping on the floor, already behaved differently, not like everyone else . . . In our house everything was different—there were Viennese chairs and cupboards and dressers. They brought everything from the town and slept on sheets. And when my aunt would wash the sheets, she would hang them to dry. And people would throw dirt—ah, you sleep on sheets! She would have to wash them again.[94]

Maria Belskaia described the experience of having property confiscated in the course of dekulakization. Officials came round and made an inventory of property in the house ("father's old sheepskin coat . . . , the table,

[92] *Shadow*, p. 105.
[93] *Shadow*, pp. 115–16, 159 (Volkonskaia), 105 (Zhemchuzhnaia), 40, 45–46 (Olitskaia).
[94] *Ha korme*, pp. 75–76.

the two benches, the stools, the pots, and the oven forks, . . . the pillows, the saddlecloth, and the blanket"), and later an auction was held in our yard, as the family "gathered by the wall of the house, crying and sniffling. Dema had his boots on—the ones Father had made for him as the oldest son. He was a young man of fifteen, after all, who had already started going to dances and dating girls. Anyway, a village soviet representative walked up to him with a kind of smirk, pulled the boots off his feet, and added them to the pile."[95]

It is rare to find a life story that includes an episode of confiscation from the standpoint of the confiscator. An exception is Anna Litveiko's 1957 memoir, which describes Civil War confiscations as a necessary measure to deal with hoarding and empty stores. "Tania and I had to go on searches and go through other people's chests, cellars, and hideaways, and drag out sackfuls of sugar, grain, flour, and sometimes even weapons. We did not mind. 'How come they're hiding all this when people are starving?' Some people welcomed us with saccharine smiles: 'Feel free to look around. We have nothing to hide.' Leaving was often a very different story. We drew up inventories of what had been confiscated and made them sign. Let them see that we were taking it for the state."[96]

Librarians were sometimes drafted for requisitioning, librarian Berta Alianskaia told an interviewer in the 1990s, "but I didn't take part in requisitions of that kind . . . Those were very bad. Bad, disorganized, and who knew where the books ended up." She did, however, participate in appraising and sorting requisitioned books, a taxing job, but appropriate for "specialists." The father of Marina Buskova, née Mushinskaia, an engineer, also found himself briefly participant in requisitioning during the Civil War. "They went in, you know, in leather jackets, with weapons belts and Mausers, and since Papa was literate, unlike the rest, he wrote the protocols and wrote up the inventories of property . . ." In this life story, there was a clear acknowledgement of the quid pro quo: housing for the Mushinskii family ("Well, as a requsitions worker they gave him this room. The room was dark, damp, but in general we got used to it and lived there"). But usually the crude fact of property transfer from the old ruling class to the new one was glossed over in autobiographical accounts. The worker Anna Balashova and her mother were allocated a good, large room, which in her account had become available when the former "bourgeois" residents "ran away." Alianskaia's brother got a good apartment, too. "He got it because of his job (po dolzhnosti). He worked in the Defense Commissariat, and they gave him that apartment." The activist Maria Shamliian received her room by regular bureaucratic

[95] *Shadow*, p. 226.
[96] *Shadow*, p. 65.

process, according to her account: she simply put her name on the list and was allocated space in the apartment of General Izmailov's widow, a mutually beneficial arrangement.[97]

As the autobiographical narratives move into the 1930s, we start to see other kinds of goods in new hands. There are inheritors who take a straightforward pleasure in their new identity as possessors of goods, notably the Stakhanovites, who proudly report on the *crêpe-de-chine* dresses and sewing machines they have received as rewards for their high productivity.[98] Valentina Bogdan reported with pleasure, albeit less naively stated, at her acquisition of a good apartment in a new building for Communist administrators, engineers, and Stakhanovites. (She is one of the few memoirists of this period who would not object too much to being called "bourgeois.") Bogdan's friend Tania also had good luck with housing in Leningrad:

> Our apartment not only came fully furnished, it actually had dishes, linen, dresses, and even playing cards! The previous owners must have been some kind of old-regime people: in their trunk we found some very old-fashioned dresses with spangles and lace, and lots of silverware— spoons, glass-holders, candlesticks, and so on. They had all been arrested and, I guess, sent to a camp, so we inherited the apartment the way they had left it on the day of their arrest.

Valentina is shocked by this, but Tania takes it in stride: "I never even think about it. They weren't arrested because of us, after all!"[99]

"Neither [parent] ever owned any real estate or other property," Nadezhda Krupskaia (Lenin's widow) stated in her autobiography.[100] This pride in nonpossession was widespread among Bolsheviks, and it caused some complications as a new generation of Communists—spurred on, Trotsky tells us, by their wives—assumed a privileged lifestyle.[101] Fruma Treivas explains how, at the time, she and her husband did not perceive themselves as privileged, despite their access to special stores, a chauffeur-driven car for her husband, a good apartment. After all, her husband was "killing himself working long hours at an important job, all for the glory of the Motherland and Stalin"; he needed the car to drive him to work. His salary was limited by the "party maximum." Their furniture belonged

[97] *Na korme*, pp 367 and 369 (Alianskaia), 286 (Buskova), 64 (Shamliian: see also above, p. 144); *Shadow*, pp. 247–48 (Balashova).

[98] *Shadow*, pp. 333 (Slavnikova), 334 (Vinogradova), 339 (Razina), 341 (Misostishkhova).

[99] *Shadow*, pp. 394, 414.

[100] Nadezhda Krupskaia, "Autobiography," in *Shadow*, p. 111 (originally published in *Entsiklopedicheskii slovar' Granat* [1929]).

[101] Trotsky, *The Revolution Betrayed* (London, 1967), pp. 102–3.

to the state, not to them; they paid little attention to money and posses-sions.[102] Sofia Pavlova insistently made the same point when interviewed in the 1990s: "We didn't buy anything . . . We had so absorbed, not so much a negative attitude but an indifference to comfort, to coziness, and the like, to going out and buying some particular thing, and that attitude has remained with me to this day . . . We lived very simply . . . And we always had very simple furnishing. Always . . ."[103] Khadycha Iakubova, student enthusiast of '30s, expressed a similar attitude when asked about clothes in a 1990s interview. "The thing was that I was the kind of girl who *despised* fashion. Komsomols, you know, we despised fashion . . . We went round in some kind of football shirts (*futbolki*), skirts . . . I despised fashion all my life and considered that 'it is unworthy of an intellectual.' "[104]

Inna Shikheeva-Gaister's family lived in an elite four-room apartment in the newly constructed House of Government, and her father, a Deputy Commissar of Agriculture, was able to buy a two-story dacha on the Mos-cow river "which my mother's brother, Veniamin, not without jealousy, used to call the 'villa.' " One of her father's friends ("forthright and hon-est to a fault. He always refused to accept the so-called money envelope—the party salary bonus") disapproved of "my father's eager acceptance of Stalin's little gifts, such as the beautiful apartment in the House of Government, the dacha, or the car that my mother did not mind using herself . . ." Gaister defends her father against his friend's criticisms in similar terms to Treivas: he worked hard for his benefits; the furniture in the apartment was not fancy and belonged to the government; the only personal valuables were a grand piano and a refrigerator brought from America. "There was no cult of things in our household," Gaister reas-sures the reader.[105]

• • •

As noted at the beginning of this chapter, most Russian women autobiog-raphers writing of the period from 1914 to 1941 told their life stories as part of the story of their times. Sometimes this was an imperative of the genre: for example, the Soviet success stories ritually presented in public by Stakhanovites and vydvizhenki require the narrator to recount her life this way. Angelina declared that her story was the story of the people.

---

[102] *Shadow*, p. 326. Elena Bonner gives a similar picture of her Communist mother and stepfather in *Mothers and Daughters*.

[103] Engel and Posadskaya, *Revolution*, pp. 70, 74.

[104] *Na korme*, p. 276.

[105] *Shadow*, pp. 368, 372, 375–76.

Figure 5. "Girl in a football shirt" (1932) by A. Kh. Samokhvalov. Reproduced from *50 let sovetskogo iskusstva* (Moscow, 1967).

Maslennikova recounted her story not because of its individuality—"there is nothing particularly remarkable about my biography"—but because of its representativeness. The stories of Great Purge victims and émigrés, though in many ways totally different from the success stories, share this characteristic of reporting not so much "what happened to me" as "what happened to people like me, to my generation." It was not just "my story" but "stories like mine" (in Korevanova's phrase) that are important.[106]

The almost total avoidance of the confessional genre suggests that living through civil upheavals may not be conducive to self-exploration. It is not just that the outside world demands attention but also that individual identity is destabilized. The Revolution itself set out to produce "new Soviet men" (and women), meaning that old personae had to be discarded. The thief Anna Iankovskaia was "reforged" into a new self; the boyfriend of Ekaterina Olitskaia's working-class friend Niura took the name Waldemar and called Niura "Nellie," explaining: "We are the masters of the country now, . . . so our names should be noble too.' "[107] Perhaps, to paraphrase Marx, the task of revolutionary autobiography is not to understand the self but to record its change.

Scholars have recently drawn attention to the importance of Soviet self-fashioning—learning to "speak Bolshevik," perfecting one's identity as a real Soviet citizen.[108] Many autobiographers—notably those of the Stakhanovites and the vydvizhenki—are clearly practicing this art. During the Great Purges, the elderly mother of one of Valentina Bogdan's friends went so far in self-recreation as to edit her old diaries to emphasize her loyal Soviet persona.[109] As this last example suggests with particular force, the task of self-construction (or self-reconstruction) is very different from the task of self-exploration. Indeed, the two may be incompatible.

The binary scheme of "old life" and "new life," "then" and "now," is pervasive in Russian/Soviet twentieth-century autobiography. The break-point is the revolution (or some equivalent like emigration or collectivization), which cuts lives in half." This is where I finish the story of my old life and begin the story of my new life," said A. M. Zinovieva, of the marriage to a worker in 1923 that freed her from slavery to a cruel mistress. "That is when the second half of my biography begins," Maslennikova explained of her move from the village to Moscow in 1921. Varsher, an émigré memoirist, supplied another perspective on rev-

---

[106] *Shadow*, pp. 307 (Angelina), 391 (Maslennikova), 169 (Korevanova).

[107] *Shadow*, pp. 282–85 (Iankovskaia), 428 (Olitskaia).

[108] See Stephen Kotkin, *Magnetic Mountain: Stalinism as a Civilization* (Berkeley, 1995), chapter 5, and Jochen Hellbeck, "Fashioning the Stalinist Soul: The Diary of Stepan Podlubnyi (1931–1939)," *Jahrbücher für Geschichte Osteuropas* 44:3 (1996).

[109] *Shadow*, pp. 409–10.

olutionary transformation in her story of the metamorphosis of Concordia Gromova, a humble, kindly student, into comrade Natasha, a Bolshevik executioner.[110]

Many lives are double rather than binary, for self-fashioning as a Soviet citizen implies that there is a non- or anti-Soviet self that is being denied. These anti-selves are shadowy doppelgänger that sometimes rise up and threaten to engulf the Soviet self, as in the case of Ulianova and Plotnikova.[111] Even Soviet citizens unaware of a doppelgänger may suddenly find themselves slipping into another identity, that of enemy of the people. "I turned out to be a terrorist," Olitskaia's friend Niura told her on the way to Gulag—not an admission of guilt, for Niura asserted her innocence, but a factual report on an involuntary change of identity.[112]

Revolutions create "might have beens" for everyone who lives through them. But if one's life had gone differently, would one have been the same person? The "might have beens" make identity precarious: one may even feel, in the words of an old Russian woman interviewed in the 1990s, that one had lived "someone else's life," not the life one was born to live.[113] Even Bogdan, whose sense of self seems rocklike, turns out to have had a kind of double life: the title of her first volume of memoirs, *Students of the First Five-Year Plan*, implies a Soviet life, while the title of her second volume tells us this was only *Mimicry in the USSR*, the imitation of a Soviet life.[114] But how can the imitation life be distinguished from the real one? The most urgent task of autobiography, for many of those who live in troubled times, is to establish that the real Plotnikova is the proletarian, not the kulak's daughter, that the real Bogdan is the principled anti-Communist, not the privileged Soviet elite member. Self-understanding becomes irrelevant, even dangerous. Under such circumstances, the object of the autobiographical quest is not self-discovery in the normal sense, but rather the discovery of a *usable* self.

---

[110] *Shadow*, pp. 364, 392, 113–15.

[111] Ulanova's and Plotnikova's stories are discussed in chapters 5 and 6.

[112] *Shadow*, p. 429.

[113] Engel and Posadskaya, *Revolution*, p. 46 (Dubova interview).

[114] The original Russian titles are *Studenty pervoi piatiletki* (Buenos Aires, 1973) and *Mimikriia v SSSR: Vospominaniia inzhenera 1935–1942 gody* (Frankfurt/Main, n.d.).

PART III

Appeals

CHAPTER NINE

Supplicants and Citizens

"Which one of us had never written letters to the supreme powers . . . If they are preserved, these mountains of letters will be a veritable treasure trove for historians."[1] So wrote that sharp-eyed anthropologist of Soviet everyday life, Nadezhda Mandelstam, and as usual she was right. The letters lay heaped in the archives waiting to be discovered by historians in the 1990s (ironically, given their generally nonpolitical content, they were usually filed in the archives' secret sections).[2] Writing to the authorities, it turns out, was a major pastime in the 1930s. People usually wrote as individuals, since multiply signed letters might be confused with collective protest, now essentially outlawed. They sent their letters everywhere: to Politburo members, obkom secretaries, newspapers, and government agencies of all kinds, and even sometimes to celebrities (writers, scientists, Polar explorers).[3] They wrote petitions, appeals, complaints, denunciations, confessions, threats, and statements of opinion. Though they were writing to unknown public figures, their letters dealt with personal as well as public matters. Some letter writers wrote as supplicants (requesting housing, education, medical treatment, money, justice) from the authorities, others as citizens (expressing opinions, complaining about bureaucracy, denouncing corrupt officials).

This is a revised version of "Supplicants and Citizens: Public Letter-Writing in Soviet Russia in the 1930s," *Slavic Review* 55:1 (Spring 1996).

[1] Nadezhda Mandelstam, *Hope against Hope: A Memoir*, trans. Max Hayward (New York: Atheneum, 1970), p. 93. Thanks to Golfo Alexopoulos for calling this passage to my attention.

[2] Though note that some scholars had guessed their importance earlier: notably Merle Fainsod, *Smolensk under Soviet Rule* (London, 1958) (esp. ch. 20: "The Right to Petition"); Margareta Mommsen, *Hilf mir, mein Recht zu finden: Russische Bittschriften von Iwan dem Schrecklichen bis Gorbatschow* (Frankfurt, 1987); Nicholas Lampert, *Whistleblowing in the Soviet Union: A Study of Complaints and Abuses under State Socialism* (New York, 1985); A. Inkeles and K. Geiger, "Critical Letters to the Editors of the Soviet Press: Areas and Modes of Complaint," *American Sociological Review* 17 (1952), and, "Critical Letters to the Editors of the Soviet Press: Social Characteristics and Interrelations of Critics and the Criticized," *ASR* 18 (1953).

[3] On letters to Otto Schmidt and other Polar explorers, see John McCannon, "Positive Heroes at the Pole: Celebrity Status, Socialist-Realist Ideals, and the Soviet Myth of the Arctic, 1932–39," *Slavic Review* 56:3 (1997), pp. 360–62; for Academician Pavlov's urgent appeal to citizens to stop writing to him about their health problems, see his letter to the editor, *Izvestiia*, 22 January 1936, p. 6.

Letters to newspapers, though only one of many destinations for letters, deserve special comment because the point of them was different from what might be expected. Hardly any of these letters were published, though a lucky few were boiled down to a short paragraph each for the "Signals from the localities" or "Readers' letters" columns that some newspapers ran. What the newspapers did—and it was one of their most important functions—was to forward letters to the appropriate authorities for action. Sometimes journalists conducted their own investigations and published their findings as feuilletons. It was common for major newspapers like *Pravda* to compile collections of letters on particular topics that would be sent up to the Politburo: such letters were an important source of information about public opinion and the functioning of bureaucracy, rivaling the surveillance-based reports on "the mood of the population" regularly prepared by the NKVD.

While it is clear, as Mandelstam pointed out, that the letters are a goldmine for present-day historians, just as they were for the regime in the 1930s, there are some obvious limits to what they can tell us. When people write letters to authority (*pis'ma vo vlast'*) they usually write in the authorities' language, and what they write is not necessarily what they think.[4] This latter caveat, of course, applies in some degree to all first-person documents, even those ostensibly private such as diaries, but it clearly applies with particular force to "public" letter writing. Such letters may sometimes express private emotions like grief, but there are a range of topics that are rarely or ever mentioned of which love, friendship, sex, and religious belief and practices are the most notable.[5] Nevertheless, the variety of what *is* in the letters is remarkable.

My aim in this chapter is to describe and analyze this variety. Since my sample is eclectic in terms of archival location and does not lend itself to quantification, my approach to the material was not that of a census taker than rather that of a botanist exploring the variety of plant life in an unfamiliar terrain.[6] When I encountered a type of letter that was new to

---

[4] This is the title of two useful collections: *Pis'ma vo vlast' 1917–1927: Zaiavleniia, zhaloby, donosy, pis'ma v gosudarstvennye struktury i bol'shevistiskim vozhdiam* (Moscow, 1998) and *Pis'ma vo vlast' 1928–1939. Zaiavleniia, zhaloby, donosy, pis'ma v gosudarstvennye struktury i sovetskim vozhdiam* (Moscow, 2002), compiled by A. Ia. Livshin et al.

[5] Exceptions to this rule are the letters, usually from peasants, protesting the closure of churches in their districts. The beliefs and practices *not* mentioned in public letter writing include those that would normally be classified by intellectuals as superstition: sorcerers and the evil eye are as much taboo in this genre as Orthodox Christian beliefs.

[6] It is impossible to know exactly how many letters were sent to the authorities in the 1930s, what proportion of them survive, and to what extent the letters surviving in the archives reproduce the contours of the original population. The scattered quantitative data I have been able to gather can do little more than confirm the scope of the phenomenon. All Leningrad party and state institutions (probably excluding the NKVD) reportedly received

me, I noted it; once I had encountered the same type of letter repeatedly, I classified it as a species and gave it a name. It is the distinctive *properties and markings* of these species (genres), as well as their place in the natural ecology of their region, that constitute my subject.

The Genres

Pouring out the Heart

The first genre I will examine is the confessional letter (*ispoved'*). This is not confession in the Christian sense or in the broader meaning of an admission of guilt, which is the first definition of the word given in Dal's dictionary. It is Dal's second definition that is relevant: "a sincere and complete confession (*soznanie*) or explanation (*ob"iasnenie*) of one's convictions, thoughts, and actions"—that is, a personal statement from the heart.[7] I choose to begin with this, even though other genres such as complaints and denunciations were employed more frequently, so that readers will immediately sense the unmistakably personal flavor of many of the "public" letters people wrote to political leaders, and even to newspapers and government institutions. Such letters were written to Stalin, as one might expect, but he was not the only recipient and it was not purely a "Stalin cult" phenomenon. There seem to be similar letters in the archives of all Soviet political leaders, including regional party bosses.[8]

An archetypal confessional letter was sent to Zhdanov in 1935 by Ekaterina Burmistrova, a worker-*vydvizhenka* who was struggling in school and in trouble on this account with her local party committee. "Deeply respected comrade Zhdanov," she wrote in a rambling and emotional letter, "I beg you not to refuse to listen to my *ispoved'* and help me understand my actions and the atmosphere that surrounds me . . ." In contrast

---

about a thousand letters a day in 1936 (TsGA IPD, f. 24, op. 2g, d. 46, l. 13), and the newspaper *Krest'ianskaia gazeta* reported a figure almost as high a year earlier (see 10, 22, and 24 July 1935). Zhdanov, as Leningrad obkom secretary in 1936, was receiving 150–200 citizens' letters a day (TsGA IPD, f. 24, op. 2g, d. 46, l. 13), while Molotov, as chairman of Sovnarkom at the same time period, was getting about 30 a day (GARF, f. 5446, op. 82, d. 51, l. 259). In mid-1939, the Soviet State Prosecutor's office was receiving 1,500 complaints a day (GARF, f. 5446, op. 81a, d. 93, l. 17).

[7] *Tolkovyi slovar' zhivago velikorusskago iazyka Vladimira Dalia*, 2nd ed. (St. Petersburg, 1881), vol. 2.

[8] For example, in the Kalinin and Lunacharskii fonds in Rossiiskii gosudarstvennyi arkhiv sotsial'no-politicheskoi informatsii (RGASPI), the Molotov and Vyshinskii fonds in Gosudarstvennyi arkhiv Rossiiskoi Federatsii (GARF), the Kirov and Zhdanov (obkom) fonds in Tsentral'nyi gosdudarstvennyi arkhiv istoriko-politicheskoi dokumentatsii Sankt-Peterburga (TsGA IPD), and the Eikhe (kraikom) fond in Partiinyi arkhiv Novosibirskoi oblast (PANO).

to many letter writers, Burmistrova had no specific demands or requests, though she hoped for a personal meeting. Nor was she seeking punishment for those responsible for her unhappiness. She was simply expressing her misery, her confusion, and her sense of inadequacy and rejection. "I can't go on, I have no other resort . . . They have turned my whole soul upside down, my nerves will not stand it"—the letter is full of such phrases. As with many writers, feelings of isolation and abandonment came through clearly. Written diagonally in the margin on the last page are the words: "Comrade Zhdanov, I couldn't find a common language with them [members of her local party committee]").[9]

A request for "a personal conversation, even if only for five minutes" was also the postscript to a plaintive letter that Anna Timoshenko, wife of a party official in the Western oblast, wrote to the first secretary of the obkom, I. P. Rumiantsev. Timoshenko's subject was "my own unbearably tormenting family life." She had written Rumiantsev many letters in the past and never sent them ("they were all of a personal character"), but now she could not refrain from pouring out her heart, and begged Rumiantsev to find time to read her letter and reply.[10]

A wronged wife, Sedova, wrote to the West Siberian party committee protesting against her mistreatment by her husband, a member of the district party elite, and the brusque dismissal of her complaints by the district party committee ("They said he didn't beat you he didn't do anything particular. We can't force him to live with you . . . It is his private life"). Sedova's story was about her misery, and her plea was for a sympathetic ear: "I'm not asking the kraikom and the raikom for Sedov to live with me, but I am a human being I don't want to be thrown overboard and I don't want people to make fun of me . . . I am unhappy[,] if [you] push me away there will be no point to my life."[11]

A 1935 letter from a Leningrad *komsomolka* made an unusual confession about religion: writing anonymously, so as to avoid trouble for singing in the church choir, she asked Stalin to close down her church and thus "save youth from that infection . . . The church singing is so sad and comforting, it's a terrible temptation . . ."[12]

Some confessional letters came from men. "I am a member of your party and write to you openly what is in my heart," wrote a young Communist to Stalin in 1936. He and his wife, both Petrograd workers in 1917, had fought in the revolution and later volunteered as '25,000-ers' (workers who went to the countryside to help with collectivization).

[9] TsGA IPD, f. 24, op. 2v, d. 1522, ll. 215–18.
[10] Smolensk Archive, WKP 386, pp. 91–92.
[11] PANO, f. 3, op. 11, d. 41, ll. 172–73.
[12] TSGA IPD, f. 24, op. 2v, d. 1518, l. 106.

While they were out in the countryside, his wife had been savagely attacked by kulaks. She never regained her health, though they moved out of the city on doctors' orders, and had recently died.

> I miss her a great deal, comrade Stalin. And now I find myself alone in the depths of the provinces, far from the railroad, and moreover I have become very impressionable and neurotic. The wind whistling at the window of the izba and the black quietness are destroying me. If I were with my wife it wouldn't be so terrible . . .[13]

Cries for Help

> Help, they are throwing me out on to the street, my mother is 76, I lost three sons in the Civil War, [I have] a mentally ill child, my heart is weak, my husband is in a mental hospital. Help me quickly.[14]

This telegram, sent in 1940 to Sovnarkom, gives us a capsule version of the typical "victim" letter, written in huge numbers by citizens whose object was to obtain some kind of help or favor. Such writers usually represented themselves as weak and powerless, victims of a "bitter fate" and adverse circumstances.[15] The help they requested was of various kinds. Many simply told a hard-luck story and asked for money, which was sometimes given.[16] Eikhe, first secretary of the West Siberian kraikom, received many letters from women trying to trace husbands who owed child support. In Zhdanov's mail as Leningrad first secretary, almost a third of all citizens' letters were about housing—crowded apartments, damp and decaying apartments, fights in communal apartments, contested rights to living space, threats of eviction, pleas for a room from families currently renting a "corner" in a kitchen or corridor.[17]

A single mother asked Kirov to find her 9-year-old son a place in an orphanage "or else give him to the Red Army to be brought up." "I haven't even got enough for bread," she wrote. "My son and I go hungry, everything has been sold I have no bedding left, no pillows, and both of

[13] Ibid., d. 2224, ll. 44–48.

[14] GARF, f. 5446, op. 81a, d. 24, l. 69.

[15] See Golfo Alexopoulos, "Victim Talk: Defense Testimony and Denunciation under Stalin," *Law and Social Inquiry* 24 (1999), pp. 501–18.

[16] For examples of responses, see TsGA IPD, f. 24, op. 2v, d. 1514, l. 41. In one case, the sum of 100 rubles was specified.

[17] Calculated from TsGA IPD, f. 24, op. 2g, d. 4, ll. 3–6. The next most popular categories (in order) were requests for passports and Leningrad residence permits, appeals against judicial sentences, requests for work, appeals from prisoners for amnesty, and requests for places in educational institutions.

us are barefoot and in rags."[18] A laborer wrote to Molotov asking for cast-off linen for his family (and/or a job as an investigator for the NKVD).[19] Molotov's mail, like Zhdanov's, was full of pleas about housing.

Requests for favors came to Molotov from members of the Soviet elite as well as ordinary people: for example, Pavel Nilin and two other young members of the Writers' Union, professionally successful but poorly housed, wrote a joint letter begging for "normal" living conditions.[20] Such letters (discussed at length in chapter 10) belong to a special sub-genre of client-to-patron communications, for Molotov, like almost all Soviet political leaders, acted as a patron to a stable of regular clients from the intelligentsia.

Vyshinsky's mail as deputy chairman of Sovnarkom in 1939–40 included many appeals from wives, mothers, and daughters (and occasionally husbands, fathers, and sons) of arrested persons, mainly Great Purge victims. This reflected his previous position as State Prosecutor. "[My husband] did not commit any crimes, and from the condition of his health and his personal qualities is not capable of crimes. I have lived with him for forty years and know him as a man of crystalline purity," wrote the wife of a beekeeper from Saratov.[21] "My husband has been in prison almost a year and half," wrote the wife of one Hans Erman, probably a career Army officer. "A terrible reward for twenty years of honest, selfless toil!" "I ask of you truth and only truth, as a representative of the regime," this same letter concluded, "and I beg you for it, as a human being."[22]

Denunciations and Complaints

Denunciation—writing to the authorities to give damaging information about another person, with the intent that he/she should be punished—is the genre of public epistolary communication that comes first to mind in connection with the Stalin period. Since the genre of denunciation is dealt with in detail in chapter 11, I will not discuss it extensively here. Suffice it to say that denunciation was not one practice but many—a multipurpose tool that might be used for a whole range of purposes, including expressing loyalty to the regime; protecting oneself from the accusation of *not* denouncing; trying to settle scores with competitors, personal enemies, and tiresome neighbors; obliquely offering one's services to the NKVD as an informer; expressing outrage at corruption or other bureaucratic

[18] TsGA IPD, f. 24, op. 2g, d. 768, l. 117. For another plea to place children in an orphanage, see ibid., f. 24, op. 2v, d. 1554, l. 66.

[19] GARF, f. 5446, op. 82, d. 27, l. 28.

[20] Ibid., d. 77, ll. 9–10.

[21] GARF, f. 5446, op. 81a, d. 348, ll. 95, 101–2.

[22] Ibid., d. 93, ll. 319, 321, 323–24.

abuses; seeking justice and the redress of grievances, which the writer had been unable to gain through the courts or by other means.

Writers of denunciations usually headed them "Statement" (*Zaiavlenie*) or "Complaint" (*Zhaloba*). The difference between denunciations and complaints that involve criticism of persons lies in the centrality of the act of blaming, though the distinction is often a fine one. But there are also many letters of complaint that are just cries of outrage without any reference to guilty persons: for example, the letter sent to Molotov by a Moscow engineer, indignant after spending a whole day in the vain search for shoes for his child:

> Today I went round more than 40 shops and everywhere all you could hear was the answer NO. They turned up in one store but what kind of shoes were those, *crudely made and costing 45 rubles*. Of course that's nothing to you, but for a person earning 150–180 rubles or even 250 rubles a month it is very, very expensive . . .[23]

Opinions, Suggestions, and Advice

A wide range of suggestions was offered expressed in citizens' letters. For example: remove all "rab" and "slug" words from Russian language because of their servile connotations; pass a law against *blat*; limit the sale of alcoholic beverages near factories; prohibit betting at the racetrack; prevent discrimination against nonsmokers in offices; establish a socialist alternative to the Nobel Prizes to reward "heroism, great discoveries, [and] selfless struggle for the good of the world"; allow Old Believers premises for religious services; remove the stigma from "former people" and let those who were deported from Moscow and Leningrad return to their homes.[24] There were also occasional attempts to open an ideological discussion: a Siberian technicum student wrote to Eikhe in 1935 asking his opinion on an issue under dispute among his classmates—whether it was possible to "build communism in one country."[25]

While many of the "opinion" letters were essentially apolitical, others staked out political positions that ranged from strongly critical to ultra-loyal. The ultra-loyalists were those who not only accepted but even exaggerated regime values, especially with respect to watchfulness and suspicion of possible "enemies," "wreckers," and foreign spies. At the time of Kirov's murder, one Leningrader wrote offering to "avenge" Kirov by

---

[23] GARF, f. 5446, op. 82, d. 51, ll. 248–49.

[24] GARF, f. 5446, op. 82, d. 51, l. 144; ibid. op. 81a, d. 24, ll. 48–49; GANO, f. 47, op. 5, d. 120, l. 155; TsGA IPD, f. 24, op. 2g, d. 46, l. 10; GARF, f. 5446, op. 82, d. 108, ll. 19–22; TsGA IPD, f. 24, op. 2g, d. 46, l. 11; ibid., d. 47, l. 157; GARF, f. 5446, op. 82, d. 51, l. 276.

[25] PANO, f. 3, op. 9, d. 10, ll. 457–59.

personally carrying out the death sentences against his murderers. After Radio Moscow played the Funeral March from Chopin's B-flat Piano Sonata on the day Zinoviev and Kamenev were executed, a vigilant citizen wrote to alert Molotov to this coded Trotskyite signal, evidence that enemies had penetrated the state Arts Committee. Other writers warned that publishing statistics on pig iron production gave valuable information to the Fascists, and expressed dismay that Lenin's image had been cheapened by its reproduction on the new 30-ruble note.[26]

Among the critical letters (a larger group than the ultra-loyal), outright signed attacks on Stalin or his policies were rare but not totally unknown. In 1930, for instance, a Communist from Berezovka near Odessa signed his name to a letter to *Pravda* strongly criticizing Stalin's article "Dizzy with success" as a weapon in the hands of the Party's enemies, and expressing the hope that comrade Stalin would "recognize his mistake and return to the correct path."[27] To be sure, letters of such boldness are rarely encountered *after* 1930, but some later letters to Molotov and other political leaders directly criticized the addressee for specific actions or statements. For example, while the engineer who wrote to Molotov about children's shoes (above, p. 161) blamed "do-nothings in the commissariats" for shortages, he added that "this doesn't absolve you from responsibility." Molotov had

> loudly proclaimed to the whole USSR and the whole world that in the next two years prices would fall, but in a few months prices for shoes, clothing, and other things increased. Oy, how badly that turned out . . .[28]

More often, signed criticism of political leaders was directed at second-tier figures like Litvinov, Kollontai, and Lunacharsky (to name three popular targets, suspected by many Communists of "bourgeois" or "liberal" tendencies). The following, written in 1936, was one of many attacks on the Commissar for Foreign Affairs:

> What kind of person is Litvinov? A tricky fellow who long ago succumbed to the bourgeoisie. Soon he will put a monocle in his eye and play Bismarck. His opinion of I. V. Stalin is known to everyone here and abroad. . . . Litvinov wants the laurel wreaths of the bourgeoisie, not the praise of the proletariat, which nauseates him . . . Currying favor with bourgeois ministers is not diplomacy, it's shameful![29]

[26] TsGA IPD, f. 24, op. 2v, d. 727, l. 341; GARF, f. 5446, op. 82, d. 51, ll. 213–23; TsGA IPD, f. 24, op. 2v, d. 1554; GARF, f. 5446, op. 82., d. 56, l. 331.

[27] GARF. f. 3316, op. 16a, d. 446, l. 190.

[28] GARF, f. 5446, op. 82, d. 51, ll. 248–49.

[29] TsGA IPD, f. 24, op. 2g, d. 226, l. 38.

Regime policies on issues like education were often criticized, and sometimes such criticism had broader implications. For example, a low-level soviet official who described himself as "a Soviet patriot" for the past fifteen years wrote to Kirov at the end of 1932 to say that his loyalty was being severely tested by the regime's handling of food shortages. In particular, he said, he could not understand "why we have abandoned the children. My wife works in railroad school no. 5 in Pskov. She says that when a doctor inspected the children's health it turned out that about 90% were in a weakened state from malnutrition . . ." How could this happen when "we are building the future of all mankind"?[30]

Leningrad workers, distinguished by their proprietorial attitude to the regime and confident assumption of the right to reprimand it, were particularly likely to write admonitory letters. The Leningraders' criticisms were directed most frequently at elite privileges and the Party's growing alienation from the working class.[31] Sometimes they conveyed a veiled threat, as in the signed letter to Zhdanov, dated June 1937, in which a Communist worker (who had just been fired for drunkenness and absenteeism) complained that the factory bosses had become a new ruling caste, treating the workers even worse than the capitalists had done:

> Just think, comrade Zhdanov, how many of us are candidates for the Trotskyites, although I always struggled and will struggle for socialism against capitalism, but as for others in the same position as I am, I can't answer for them, only I hear them cursing Soviet power.[32]

Anonymous letters often expressed similar sentiments. Once such letter from Leningrad in 1935 complained that "the apparats . . . are filled with princes, aristocrats and clergy[.] These creatures sit in all the apparats and most have party cards, but the worker has no right to work in the apparats[,] they drive them all out so as not to be an eyesore . . ."[33]

The *anonimka* was a genre with its own characteristic tropes. One trope was anger, often explosively expressed, directed against members of the old and new privileged classes, foreigners, and Jews. The Russian Revolution was part of an international Jewish conspiracy and Stalin and Kirov had sold out to the Jews, according to one Leningrad anonimka of 1934. Workers were fed up with Jewish domination and would soon end it by another revolution, another asserted.[34]

The threat in the second letter was not unusual. After Kirov's murder, many *anonimki* made sinister reference to it, warning, for example, that

[30] Ibid., op. 1b, d. 449, l. 73.
[31] For example, TsGA IPD, f. 24, op. 2g, d. 48, l. 223.
[32] Ibid., op. 2g, d. 47, ll. 147–49.
[33] Ibid., op. 2v, d. 1518, l. 62.
[34] Ibid., op. 2v. d. 1518, l. 9, and d. 727, l. 367.

if prices were not lowered, other political leaders would share Kirov's fate.[35] A 1936 anonimka from a convict, complaining that "only women and orphans remain in Soviet collective farms and the husbands of these women all sit in damp jails like your Thälmann," warned that there might be uprisings and war if the regime did not release "at least the kolkhozniks" from prison.[36]

Sarcasm was another characteristic trope in anonimki. Often the writers focused their barbs on the gulf between the rhetoric of "great Soviet achievements" and Soviet reality, or played on the regime's hypocrisy in condemning capitalist governments for oppressing their citizens. "So this is a glorious epoch," wrote one anonymous writer in 1936,

> [but] for me the following thing remains incomprehensible . . . We have a colossal army of convicts, tens of millions of them, who are overflowing the jails, the camps, and the [labor] colonies . . . In the majority of cases the accusation against them is completely brazen, crass, and based entirely on lies . . .[37]

An anonimka sent to *Pravda* in 1930 noted sarcastically that the First Five-Year Plan had omitted to budget for the necessary building of prisons: "the supreme potentate (Caucasian Prince Stalin) and his faithful servant (peasant *starosta* Kalinin) forgot about that . . ."[38]

LANGUAGE

Modes of Address

Many letters used the comradely style of salutation: "Dear (*dorogoi*) comrade," as in "Dear comrade Vyshinsky" or "My dear comrade Stalin," though the more formal "respected/deeply respected (*uvazhaemyi/mnogo-uvazhaemyi*) comrade" was also used.[39] Communists and Komsomols often signed their letters "with Communist (Komsomol) greetings," or sometimes "with comradely greetings." Party members might give the number of their party card (especially when writing denunciations). Workers often identified themselves by factory as well as by name.

---

[35] Ibid., d. 1518, ll. 1, 14.

[36] Gosudarstvennyi arkhiv Novosibirskoi oblast (GANO), f. 47, op. 5, d. 206, l. 148. Ernst Thälmann was a German Communist leader whose imprisonment by the Nazis was the subject of many indignant articles in the Soviet press.

[37] GARF, f. 3316, op. 40, d. 14, l. 100.

[38] Ibid., op. 16a, d. 446, l. 100.

[39] For example, GARF, f. 5446, op. 81a, d. 93, l. 323; TsGA IPD, f. 24, op. 2v, d. 2224, l. 46.

In some letters, writers addressed political leaders with the familiar second-person singular (*ty*).[40] But a sense of intimacy was more often conveyed by other means. "Give some thought to this question, talk it over in the Kremlin," a Communist worker advised Zhdanov in letter on foreign policy.[41] "Ekh! Mikhail Ivanovich! Check this out . . ." wrote an anonymous denouncer of plots to President Mikhail Kalinin.[42] Some peasant or uneducated writers used the salutation "Good day!" One letter to *Krest'-ianskaia gazeta* began as if the writer had just knocked on the editorial door: "Good day, comrade staffers. A kolkhoznik is here to see you."[43]

Some letters attempted to blend the intimacy of comradeship with that of supplication, as in a Communist agronomist's appeal whose flavor is hard to convey in English: "*Tovarishch Zhdanov, chutkii, rodnoi—pomogi* (Comrade Zhdanov, dear sensitive one, help me)."[44] Others softened comradely criticism with a sense of shared historical mission, as in the exalted ending of a worker's complaint about elite privileges:

I remain, with respect and in the conviction of the victory of Communism,
  N. A. Kosoch.
  April 2, 1937, 3 o'clock at night.
  My five little ones sleep, and I write for the future.[45]

The comradely style could also take a belligerent turn. A Communist's denunciation of a low-level official sent to a regional administrator opened with a comradely "Good day, comrade Denisov," but ended harshly: "This bastard should be driven out of the trade union. If you don't take measures, I will write directly to the Central Committee of the party."[46]

Epithets like "leader of the proletariat" or "comrade-in-arms (*soratnik*) of Stalin" and grandiose terms like *vozhd'* (Leader) appeared in citizens' letters of the 1930s, though perhaps less often than one might expect. For example, a Leningrad worker petitioning "comrade Zhdanov" in 1937 addressed him as "leader (*vozhd'*) of Leningrad Bolsheviks [and] com-

[40] TsGA IPD, f. 24, op. 1b, d. 449, l. 72 (1932 letter to Kirov from a young worker-*vydvizhenets*).

[41] TsGA IPD, f. 24, op. 2g, d. 226, l. 38.

[42] GARF, f. 1235, op. 141, d. 2070, l. 4.

[43] The Russian, retaining the original punctuation and spelling, is "*dobry den, tavarichi robotniki. Kvam kolkhoznik.*" Rossiiskii gosudarstvennyi arkhiv ekonomiki (RGAE) f. 396, op. 10, d. 161, l. 289.

[44] TsGA IPD, f. 24, op. 2g, d. 47, l. 147.

[45] Ibid., d. 48, l. 223 (my emphasis).

[46] PANO, f. 3, op. 9, d. 801, l. 209. Despite the familiar greeting, the writer noted that he was not personally acquainted with Denisov.

rade-in-arms of the leader of peoples, comrade Stalin."[47] On the whole, however, the flattering "courtier's" style was more likely to come from the intelligentsia and the new privileged class than the lower classes, and to be found in ceremonial collective epistles rather than individual letters.[48] "Our dear and beloved Andrei Aleksandrovich," was how the painter Mark Shafran prefaced his request that Zhdanov pose for his portrait,[49] and a mathematician seeking support for his path-breaking work, *Bases of a New Algebra*, not only implored Zhdanov to extend his "personal protection and patronage (*zashchita i pokrovitel'stvo*)" but also sent in two acrostics he had composed on the names of Stalin and Kirov.[50] Simpler people used simpler methods of flattery. "Knowing your love and care for children . . ." wrote a mother of three to Zhdanov, asking for "material help" (that is, money); "Knowing your exceptional responsiveness (*chutkost'*) . . ." wrote a petitioner to Eikhe.[51]

The image of the political leader as a benevolent father who protects and pities his children, or as a trusted and understanding friend, is encountered often in the letters. "Be a good father" and protect us from the temptations of religion, the Leningrad Komsomolka appealed to Stalin. "I beg you as a father, as a friend of the people," the betrayed wife wrote to Rumiantsev. "My only friend, who deeply understands the human heart," the distraught widower quoted above (pp. 159–59) addressed Stalin.

Justice was regularly invoked by letter writers. "Where is truth and justice?" "Comrades, answer us please where we can find justice . . . ?" "If there is any justice in Soviet power, punish those people."[52] Duty appeared equally often, but only in one specific context—"I consider it my duty (party duty, duty as a citizen) to inform you . . ." was one of the standard preambles to a denunciation.[53]

Styles

While much research remains to be done on the relationship between Soviet letters to authority and prerevolutionary petitions, it is clear that

[47] TsGA IPD, f. 24, op. 2g, d. 47, l. 237.

[48] Congratulatory telegrams on International Women's Day sent to Zhdanov by branches of the wives' volunteer movement, *Obshchestvennitsa*, were full of flowery epithets like "loyal comrade in arms of comrade Stalin" and "leader of the toilers of Leningrad oblast." TsGA IPD, f. 24, op. 2v. d. 2219, ll. 185–88.

[49] TsGA IPD, f. 24, op. 2v, d. 2219, l. 1.

[50] Ibid., d. 1544, ll. 184–92.

[51] Ibid., op. 2g, d. 46, l. 2; PANO, f. 3, op. 9, d. 10, l. 1173.

[52] GARF, f, 5451, op. 14, d. 68 (4), l. 30; RGAE, f. 396, op. 10, d. 65, ll. 212–14; RGASPI, f. 475, op. 1, d. 2, l. 24.

[53] TsGA IPD, f. 24, op. 2g, d. 14, l. 84; TsGA IPD, f. 24, op. 2v, d. 1518, l. 97; GARF, f. 1235, op. 141, d. 2070, l. 4.

many letters of the 1930s used conventions that predated the Soviet regime. Construing authority as a "beloved father," appealing for justice (without reference to law), complaining to higher authority about local abuses, writing pathetically of "the crust of bread" that was so often lacking—all these are as standard in the repertory of nineteenth-century petitions as in the those of the 1930s.[54]

In the mid 1920s, a Soviet official categorized citizens' letters on taxes as follows: 1) typed petitions written by lawyers, citing laws and administrative instructions; 2) handwritten scribes' petitions ("big letters with curlicues") using emotional rather than legal argumentation; and 3) personal pleas, often with autobiographical details, clumsily written on dirty scraps of paper.[55] By the 1930s, the third type of letter was flourishing, the first had largely disappeared, while the second survived mainly in the countryside, where the scribes' familiar "curlicues" decorated some letters right up to the war.

It was not unusual for writers to embellish their letters with literary or historical references. "The voice of the kolkhoznik dies away, a voice crying in the wilderness," wrote a peasant (this was one of the comparatively rare biblical references in the letters). "[They are] driving me to the edge, as Nicholas I's black band of butchers drove Pushkin" declaimed another. A worker warned that leaders alienated from the masses might meet the fate of "the Greek hero of myths Antæus [who] severed himself from mother earth and suffocated in the air and his only strength was the mother earth who bore him."[56]

Drawing on literary and cinematic sources, Svetlana Boym has recently suggested that *grafomaniia*—the urge toward *pisatel'stvo* (writerliness) in those without literary talent—moved out of its nineteenth-century intelligentsia home to become an "all-people's" affliction in the Soviet period.[57] Leaving aside the red herring of literary talent or its absence, the urge to write *for the sake of writing* is very marked in popular letter writing of the 1930s. The letters often convey an exhilaration and delight in the power to use language that reminds the reader how recently some of their writers had acquired literacy. For the historian (and no doubt the original addressee as well), reading such letters can be a moving experience.

---

[54] For the nineteenth century, see Mommsen, *Hilf Mir*, pp. 54, 56, 104–5, and passim; for Soviet examples, see above, p. 166 ("father," "justice"), and GANO, f. 47, op. 5, d. 179, l. 170; Tsentral'nyi munitsipal'nyi arkhiv goroda Moskvy (TsMAM), f. 1474, op. 7, d. 72, l. 121; RGAE, f. 396, d. 128, l. 68 ("crust").

[55] RGASPI, f. 17, op. 84, d. 826, ll. 23–24.

[56] RGAE, f. 396, op. 10, d. 142, l. 177; ibid., d. 26, l. 139; TsGA IPD, f. 24, op. 2g, d. 48, l. 223.

[57] Svetlana Boym, *Common Places: Mythologies of Everyday Life in Russia* (Cambridge, Mass., 1994), pp. 200–205.

Figure 6. "An unruly kolkhoz meeting." Drawing from two kolkhozniks' letter of complaint to *Krest'ianskaia gazeta* about abuses in the kolkhoz leadership, 1938. Angry kolkhozniks are shown cursing out the kolkhoz board members, while the chairman tries to calm the meeting. From Rossiiskii gosudarstvennyi arkhiv ekonomiki (RGAE), f. 396, op. 10, d. 67, l. 33.

Writing letters to the authorities surely was, or at least could be, as much a form of popular culture and an expression of popular creativity as the amateur theatricals and balalaika playing that are usually listed under these headings. The line between popular letter writing and popular writing in the literary sense was a fine one, and there are signs that many amateur writers refused to draw it. The readers who deluged *Krest'ianskaia gazeta* with so many letters of complaint, denunciation, and enquiry were also spontaneously sending the newspaper "artistic" production—drawings (see figure 6), poems, and short stories—that they hoped would be published.[58] Sometimes the genre distinction simply melted away, and anonymous indictments of Soviet power were crafted in classical quatrains, while "abuse of power" letters came illustrated with cartoons. In

---

[58] *Krest'ianskaia gazeta*, 10 July 1935. In the period 5–8 July, the paper received ninety drawings and forty-five poems and short stories. Citizens also sent poems and other literary compositions to obkom secretaries: see, for example, TsGA IPD, f. 24, op. 2v, d. 1554, l. 66.

one such case, the writer/artist ended his letter by requesting a job as a caricaturist on the newspaper.[59]

An item in *Krest'ianskaia gazeta*'s mail that straddled the boundary between letter writing and popular art was an essay in *skazka* form under the title "Exploits (*podvigi*) of the hooligan knave S. M. Tychinkin."

> In the dark little village of M. Kemary . . . resounded the name of the "First of August" kolkhoz . . . Why it grew [*sic*] Communist kolkhoz chairman E. E. Vaseev was sent to it with Soviet spirit and Communist heart. Vaseev did not touch strong drink, all the masses loved Vaseev . . . , but for those who were stealing from the kolkhoz life became dreary. Vaseev would not let them steal from the kolkhoz, [so] they threw themselves on Vaseev, wanting to force him out, but the stalwart Communist pushed off the rascals. Who was the head of the rascals[?] Tychinkin Stepan Mikhailovich . . . There was no end to the beatings and hooliganism, there is not enough paper to describe all his tricks . . .[60]

The collective authors asked the newspaper "to publish our note (*za-metka*)."[61] This was a commonly expressed desire, despite the infrequency of its realization. Many writers to newspapers also indicated their commitment to publication by giving titles to their letters, usually modeled on headings in the Soviet press: "Which of them are class enemies?," "Take appropriate measures," "Illegal business," "Is this not wrecking?"[62] V. V. Smirnov, a kolkhoz veterinary feldsher (and perhaps, judging by his elegant script, a former scribe), headed his denunciation of the kolkhoz chairman (see figure 7) with whole array of decoratively inscribed slogans:

> A serious signal from "Red Potiagino" kolkhoz, Viatskii sel'sovet, Bol'-shesol'skii raion, Iaroslavl oblast.
> THERE CAN BE NO MERCY FOR ENEMIES OF THE SOVIET PEOPLE.
> THEY ARE PROTECTING ENEMIES ~~~ UNPUNISHED CRIMINALS.[63]

Even letters *not* written to newspapers were sometimes given titles by their authors.[64] This brings us back to an earlier question about the

---

[59] See RGASPI, f. 475, op. 1, d. 2, l. 79 for the quatrains and RGAE, f. 396, op. 10, d. 67, l. 33, and ibid., d. 129, unpag., for cartoons. The request for a job is in d. 129.

[60] RGAE, f. 396, op. 10, d. 26, ll. 137–39.

[61] There were six signatories, two identifying themselves as "sympathizers [of the Communist Party]" and four as "kolkhozniks."

[62] RGAE, f. 396, op. 10, d. 86, l. 406; PANO, f. 3, op. 9, d. 10, l. 295; RGAE, f. 396, op. 10, d. 142, l. 141; GARF, f. 3316, op. 64, d. 1854, l. 258.

[63] RGAE, f. 396, op. 10, d. 161, ll. 24, 29–32.

[64] See, the 1936 letter to Rumiantsev headed "A sel'kor's signal," Smolensk Archive, WKP 355, 219.

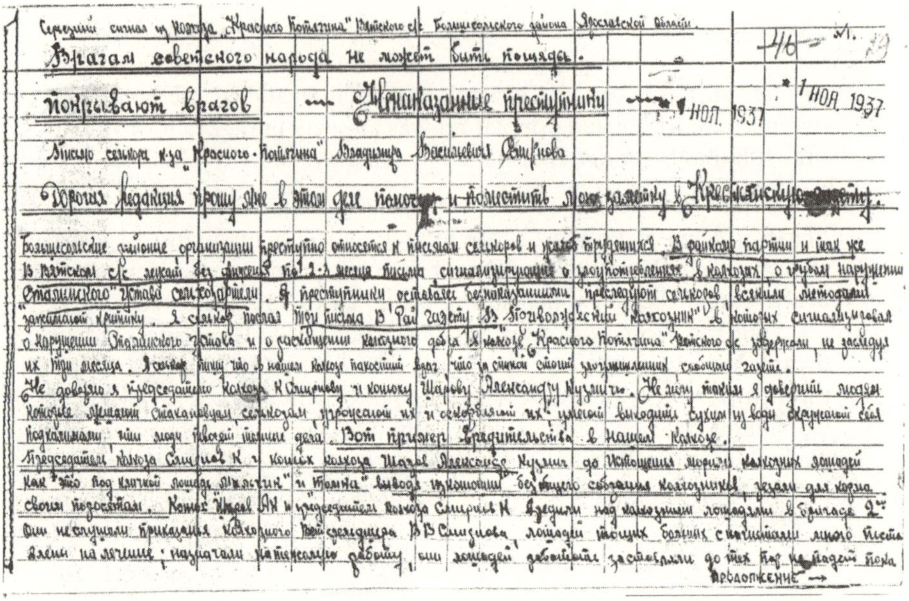
Врагам советского народа не может быть пощады.

Покрывают врагов — Ненаказанные преступники

1 НОЯ 1937

Дорогая редакция прошу вас в этом деле помочь и поместить мою заметку в Крестьянскую газету.

Figure 7. "No mercy for enemies of the Soviet people." Letter to *Krest'ianskaia gazeta* from kolkhoznik V. V. Smirnov, 1937, headed "There can be no mercy for enemies of the Soviet people. They are protecting enemies. Unpunished criminals." From RGAE, f. 396, op. 10, d. 161, l. 29.

"publicness" of public letter writing. Given the very small chance of getting a letter published, and the much larger chance of provoking some act of official response (investigation of a dispute, punishment of an offender, accelerated access to a scarce good), the rational goal of writing letters was not publication but official intervention.[65] Yet many letter writers persisted in asserting the contrary. This suggests that the flood of readers' letters to newspapers and journals in the era of Gorbachevian glasnost was no accident,[66] and that perhaps what Soviet letter writers wanted all along was to get their letters into print and their opinions into the public sphere.

Letter writers of the Stalin era did their best to master the language of *Pravda*. Soviet epithets, party jargon, and rhetorical devices were used exuberantly and sometimes incongruously:

[65] Of letters sent to *Krest'ianskaia gazeta* in 1937–38, less than 1% were published, but almost 60% were sent out for investigation, and responses (outcomes) were reported on 33%. RGASPI, f. 17, op. 114, d. 857, ll. 27–31 (Orgburo resolution "On the situation in *Krest'ianskaia gazeta*," 12 April 1938).

[66] See *Small Fires: Letters from the Soviet People to 'Ogonyok' Magazine 1987–1990*, selected and ed. by Christopher Cerf and Marina Albee with Lev Gushchin (New York,

"It is not a kolkhoz but a nest of gentry and gendarmes . . . A CLUSTER OF FORMER PEOPLE has gathered in the house . . . Degenerate elements have wormed their way onto the kolkhoz board . . . We are now waging decisive war with grabbers (*rvachi*) . . . Revolutionary legality was brazenly violated . . . They were deaf to [my] signals . . . [He] took the path of terror . . . More than once I unmasked [them] . . . , but the district leaders hide my unmaskings under the blanket . . . An incorrigible opportunist and hidden Trotskyite . . . A self-seeker (*shkurnik*) with a party card . . . This handful of kulak hold-outs (*nedobitki*) . . . White-guardists, Trotskyites, and wreckers."[67]

Quotations from Stalin are to be found in the letters of the 1930s, though less often (and more ambiguously) than one might imagine on the basis of the "model letters" occasionally published in the press.[68] A handful of phrases seem to have lodged firmly in the popular mind. "Cadres decide everything" was one of them, used both as boilerplate and as a pointed remark from mistreated employees.[69] Another was "Life has become better, life has become more cheerful"—sometimes used ironically.[70] But perhaps the most winged of all Stalin's words in the late 1930s was a borrowing from Aesop's fables, "wolves in sheep's clothing."[71] "Let them uncover who she is, tear off the mask . . . [from] the wolf in sheep's clothing." "Those wolves in sheep's clothing are happy to harm our party in the kolkhoz at every turn." "We need to know how to recognize the enemy in sheep's clothing who is conspicuously showing devotion to Soviet power but thinking like a wolf."[72]

1990), and *Dear Comrade Editor: Readers' Letters to the Soviet Press under Perestroika*, trans. and ed. by Jim Riordan and Sue Bridger (Bloomington, Ind., 1992).

[67] RGAE, f. 396, d. 128, l. 158; TsGAOR g. Moskvy, f. 1474, op. 7, d. 79, l. 86; GANO, f. 47, op. 5, d. 206, l. 76; PANO, f. 3, op. 9, d. 10, l. 1434; ibid., op. 11, d. 41, l. 31; RGAE, f. 396, op. 10, d. 161, l. 49; ibid., d. 87, l. 281; ibid., d. 86, l. 391; RGASPI, f. 475, op. 1, d. 10, l. 2; ibid., d. 9, l. 8; GANO, f. 47, op. 5, d. 206, l. 77; RGASPI, f. 475, op. 1, d. 9, l. 108.

[68] For a "model" letter allegedly from kolkhozniks, headed "Destroy the enemy without mercy," see *Krest'ianskaia gazeta*, 25 January 1938, p. 3. On the treatment of Stalin in Leningrad letters, see Sarah Davies, "The 'Cult' of the *Vozhd*': Representations in Letters from 1934–1941," *Russian History* 24:1–2 (1997), pp. 131–47.

[69] RGASPI, f. 475, op. 1, d. 2, ll. 39–40; TsGA IPD, f. 24, op. 2v, d. 1534, ll. 176, 183.

[70] See TsGA IPD, f. 24, op. 2v, d. 1514, l. 37, for a literal use (re: Leningrad's soccer team), and ibid., d. 3548, l. 62 (for popular comments on price increases reported by the NKVD).

[71] In his speech to the February–March plenum (1937), Stalin asked why "our leading comrades . . . have not managed to discern the real face of the enemies of the people, have not managed to recognize *wolves in sheep's clothing*, have not managed to tear the masks off them": I. V. Stalin, ed. McNeal, *Sochineniia*, v. 1 (14) (Stanford, 1967), p. 190 (my emphasis).

[72] TsGA IPD, f. 24, op. 2g, d. 14, l. 1; RGAE, f. 396, op. 10, d. 128, l. 159; GARF f. 3316, op. 64, d. 1854, l. 258.

Presentation of Self

STEREOTYPES

Like memoirists and actors, those who write letters to the authorities are involved in a sort of performance. Many cast themselves in particular roles and draw on established social stereotypes and rhetorical conventions in acting them out. There are many **orphans** in the Soviet letter files—perhaps even more than there were in real life.[73] Some writers cited their parentless state and upbringing in an orphanage as evidence of their impeccable Soviet values: "vigilance and justice were implanted in my childhood."[74] Others used it as a synecdoche for the powerlessness and vulnerability that must arouse compassion. The orphaned Churkov siblings, children of deported kulaks, played on this response when petitioning for the return of the family izba.[75] The presentation of the self as weak, poor, uneducated, powerless was perhaps most typically a woman's and children's ploy, but it was also used by peasants. "Comrades, help, we appeal to you for help, for mental capacity . . ." "We are uneducated (*malogramotnye*), it is easy to fool and rob us."[76]

Women writers frequently wrote as **mothers**. In many cases, this was because they were writing on their children's behalf, asking that a son or daughter be admitted to college, given medical treatment, or released from prison. Mothers of Red Army men had a practical purpose for identifying themselves thus, since a range of special benefits were available to them.[77] Some women cited the fact that their children were Communists, Komsomols, or vydvizhentsy as evidence of their own worth as Soviet citizens. Women asking for "material help" on the grounds of poverty invariably mentioned the plight of their children, barefoot and in rags, "without a crust of bread." A peasant woman writing anonymously to condemn cursing and hooliganism in her village signed the letter "Mother."[78]

Male letter writers often presented themselves as **patriots**. A statement of Communist Party membership was one obvious way of making this claim, but many reinforced it with references to specific services to the Revolution (for example, serving in the Red guards, volunteering for the Red Army, fighting bandits in the Far East or the Caucasus). As an episto-

[73] In seventeenth-century Russian petitions, virtually all petitioners refer to themselves as "orphans" of their lords (*siroty tvoi*). See *Krest'ianskie chelobitnye XVII v. Iz sobranii Gosudarstvennogo Istoricheskogo muzeia* (Moscow, 1994).

[74] TsGA IPD, f. 24, op. 2v, d. 1534, ll. 176, 183.

[75] Smolensk Archive, WKP 355, 129–32.

[76] From letters to *Krest'ianskaia gazeta* in RGAE f. 396, op. 10, d. 161, l. 289; ibid., d. 128, ll. 66–69 (paraphrase).

[77] See RGAE, f. 396, 7. d. 26, ll. 207–8.

[78] GARF, f. 3316, op. 41, d. 85, ll. 41–43.

lary trope, shedding blood in the Civil War had the greatest resonance. "I am a Communist since 1918, and lost my health (an arm) for the new life." "I have already paid my debt with blood fighting on the fronts of the Civil War." "[We] did not spare [our] blood and fought the parasites."[79] In anonimki, a favorite legitimizing device was to sign the letter "Veteran of the Civil War" or (in Siberia) "Red partisan."[80]

There were women patriots, too. One of them, asking Kirov's help on a family matter in 1934, described herself as "a member of the Bolshevik Party since March 1917" who had been arrested by Junkers in 1917, taken part in the battle of Pulkovo, and so on. Three years later, the same woman wrote to Zhdanov asking for help in a new family crisis. It is interesting to note that this time—no doubt in response to the public re-valuation of the family associated with the debate on abortion and anti-abortion law of 1936—she introduced a subtle change into her self-repre-sentation: not only a revolutionary patriot now but also a parent, she appealed to Zhdanov in 1937 "as a member of the Bolshevik party since March 1917 *and as the mother of three children.*"[81]

Another form of patriotic identification was as a **correspondent** from the factory or village (*rabkor*, sel'kor), that is, a public-spirited citizen who wrote in to the newspaper on a regular basis, voluntarily and without pay, "signaling" local bureaucratic inefficiency and "unmasking" wrong-doers. The rabkor/sel'kor movement of the 1920s had much in common with that of American whistleblowers in the 1970s, except that the Soviet targets were not corporate executives but anti-Soviet engineers and cor-rupt kolkhoz chairmen. During collectivization, a number of sel'kory were murdered by "kulaks" in their villages. Though the formal institu-tion was lapsing by the late 1930s, the image of the fearless truth teller retained its appeal, and many peasant authors of "abuse" letters adopted the sel'kor persona. "I am persecuted as a sel'kor" was a familiar refrain.[82]

The trope of past **oppression**—prerevolutionary poverty, misery, and exploitation—served both as an appeal to compassion and as evidence of pro-Soviet sympathies. Kolkhozniks described themselves as former poor peasants and batraks; Old Believers pointed out they they had been perse-cuted under the Tsar.[83] "I was illegitimate, my mother worked as a ba-

[79] GARF, f. 5446, op. 82, d. 51, ll. 248–49; TsMAM, f. 1474, op. 7, d. 72, l. 121; RGAE, f. 396, d. 128, l. 159.

[80] GARF, f. 5446, op. 82, d. 27, l. 172; GANO, f. 47, op. 5, d. 179, l. 170; PANO, f. 3, op. 9, d. 9, 126.

[81] Letters in TsGA IPD, f. 24, op. 2v, d. 727, ll. 335–36, and ibid., op. 2g, d. 47, l. 272 (my emphasis).

[82] RGAE, f. 396, d. 86, ll. 391–92; Smolensk Archive, WKP 386, 144–47.

[83] RGAE, f. 396, d. 128, l. 159, and Smolensk Archive, WKP 190, 26; TsGA IPD, f. 24, op. 2g, d. 47, l. 157.

trachka in Tver guberniia," wrote a Communist administrator embroiled in a local feud, seeking to establish her credentials as one who had suffered under the old regime. "In childhood [I] experienced great poverty," noted the wife of an arrested factory manager in her appeal on her husband's behalf in 1937.[84]

Self-identification as a **worker** was another way of establishing Soviet loyalties. In the eyes of "worker" writers, this status carried special rights, including the right to criticize the regime. Such men expected the authorities to listen to them, and the archival record suggests that their expectations were justified. They announced their worker identity proudly: for example, one writer signed himself "worker Slashchev, Vasilii Fedorovich, member of the union of river transport of Bobrovskii creek, employed continuously in river transport since 1908 up to the present day."[85] Of course, the "worker" label was also used manipulatively. Anonymous letter writers frequently signed themselves "Odessa worker," "Production worker," "Worker at the Putilov plant," "Old worker," and the like.[86]

In the course of the 1930s, writers increasingly often represented themselves as **achievers**. The quintessential achievers of the decade were shock-workers (*udarniki*) and Stakhanovites, over-fulfillers of norms who were singled out for rewards and public recognition. Three Komsomol workers from the Moscow Metro construction project added the phrase "decorated shockworkers (*udarniki-znachkisty*)" to their signatures on a denunciation of politicians in their native Southern Osetiia.[87] A woman writer identified herself as "an *obshchestvennitsa*, initiator of the movement of wives of engineering-technical personnel in the city of Leningrad, for which I was decorated by the government."[88]

To be a *vydvizhenets*—that is, someone promoted from the lower classes into a white-collar administrative or professional position—constituted achievement, and a number of letter writers described themselves in this way.[89] Usually, this conveyed pride in having risen from humble origins. But Sedova, the Siberian wronged wife encountered earlier (p. 158), gave it a different twist, perhaps unintentionally, in a poignant final sentence that made upward mobility seem just another form of uprooting: "I am a *vydvizhenka*, an orphan."[90]

---

[84] TsGA IPD, f. 24, op. 2v, d. 1514, l. 23; ibid., d. 2220, l. 10.

[85] GANO, f. 288, op. 2, d. 902, l. 6.

[86] GARF, f. 5446, op. 82, d. 42, l. 115; TsGA IPD, f. 24, op. 2v, d. 727, ll. 403–9; ibid., d. 1518, l. 8.

[87] GARF, f. 5446, op. 82, d. 42, l. 103.

[88] TsGA IPD, f. 3, op. 11, d. 41, ll. 172–73.

[89] Smolensk Archive, WKP 386, 322–23; TsPA IPD, f. 24, op. 2?, d. 15, ll. 92–93; ibid., op. 1b, d. 449, l. 72.

[90] PANO f. 3, op. 11, d. 41, ll. 172–73.

It would be misleading to leave the impression that all letter writers presented themselves as embodiments of a few recognizable social types. On the contrary, a distinct subgroup of writers stressed the individuality of their person and the particularity of their life experience. The repertoire of such writers might include philosophical reflection, irony (as distinct from the sarcasm that was a stock-in-trade of many exposé letters), introspection, emotional display, and analysis of psychology and motivation.

Confession (*ispoved'*) was the genre in which individualized autobiography and uninhibited emotional display were the norm. "I thirsted for boiling, vital activity," wrote a young Leningrader describing the spiritual odyssey that ended in her resignation from the Komsomol.

> I wanted to throw myself into work so as to forget myself as an individual (*kak individuum*), to lose count of time, to submerge myself in the worries, joys, and excitements of the collective. I thought that I could find all that only in the Komsomol collective. But from the first I was disappointed . . .[91]

Not all letters about emotional distress belonged to the confessional genre. A Communist schoolmaster wrote to Zhdanov in 1934, imploring him to find out the truth about the death of his daughter, an engineer on the Caucasus railway who had died in mysterious circumstances after enduring sexual harrassment from bosses and colleagues. The author's wife, in her grief, had become convinced that there had been some kind of cover-up, and would wake him in the middle of the night to ask where their daughter was, and whether she had been shut away in a mental hospital. The wife suspected her husband of involvement in the cover-up, even though he had sent letters and petitions in all directions. "Life has become hell," the letter concluded.[92]

Another man's life was hell for different reasons. Thirty-one years old in 1937, he was an orphan who had worked as a shepherd and agricultural laborer and lived on the street as a homeless *besprizornyi* before joining the kolkhoz and the Communist Party in the early 1930s. Despite his lack of education, he was promoted to head a rural soviet and then, in September 1937, to the much more formidable job of chairman of a district soviet. Here, coping with the aftermath of his predecessor's arrest as an enemy of the people, he was completely out of his depth, tormented by his "political and general illiteracy" and the mockery of unnamed people who called him "durak." By his own description, he was wracked by "nervous illness" and unable to eat ("In two and a half months of such a

[91] TsGA IPD, f. 24, op. 2v. d. 772, ll. 23–24.
[92] Ibid., ll. 248–52.

life . . . , I have lost as much as 10 kilograms from the weight of the organism"). He begged to be relieved of his position.[93]

An engineer who was the daughter of an Armenian father killed in ethnic strife during the Civil War and a mother who died as a refugee shortly afterwards described these circumstances and her privileged upbringing in her brother's apartment in the Dom Pravitel'stva in Moscow before outlining her immediate problem: she was about to be fired from her job for consorting with persons now exposed as Trotskyites (the year was 1937), even though her association with them was related to her work as an informer for the NKVD.[94] A woman wrote to Molotov protesting the Moscow Soviet's decision to evict her from the apartment she had occupied for twelve years on the grounds that only her former husband had claim to it. This was a true irony of fate, she wrote, because she had just managed to graduate with a degree in animal husbandry, seven years after her husband had left her with the "cruel words" that she was a mere housewife who had "lagged behind political life."[95]

An older woman sent Zhdanov an eight-page letter about her troubles at work, dwelling with a touch of wry humor on the conflicts provoked by her prickly and zealous character, and with sadness on her personal isolation and overdependence on the companionship of the workplace.[96] A man whose wife had been arrested as a spy wrote to Molotov explaining that this was something of which she was just temperamentally incapable:

> She is not a complex person, not someone who hides things . . . With my character, I might be able to conceal the fact that some misfortune had happened to me. She could not. She "unloaded" everything very quickly, indeed words were unnecessary—her feelings were too transparent not to see them even if you were not particularly looking. I cannot believe that she was hiding some kind of dark secret under a mask of simplicity . . .[97]

• • •

Since letters are texts that are read as well as written, it remains to consider the question of response. The degree and kind of response that could be expected from the authorities is obviously crucial to our understanding of the phenomenon of popular letter writing. If letters were written without any reasonable expectation of response, this was one-way

[93] Ibid., op. 2g, d. 48, ll. 197–203.
[94] Ibid., ll. 5–8.
[95] GARF, f. 5446, op. 82, d. 64, l. 206.
[96] Ibid., op. 2v, d. 1534, ll. 176–83.
[97] GARF, f. 5446, op. 82, d. 56, ll. 13–16.

communication that presumably had little significance in the general picture of state/society relations. If, on the other hand, citizens could reasonably (on the basis of experience) expect a response to their letters, the communication was two-way and the public significance of the process was much enhanced.

We have only incomplete and nonsystematic information on the responses of the authorities to citizens' letters. A stream of official instructions throughout the 1930s ordered all institutions to respond to citizens' letters in a timely and conscientious manner. Unfortunately, these same instructions note that many authorities failed to do this. By a rough estimate based on my work in various archives, perhaps 15–30% of the letters that have been preserved received some kind of response—that is, provoked some kind of bureaucratic action or order to act. The figure rises to 70% in some archives if we expand the meaning of "response" to include a bureaucrat's instruction to a secretary to type out a handwritten letter. What proportion of all letters survives in the archives is, of course, unknown.

For all the deficiencies of the data, however, it is clear that letter writing was indeed a form of two-way communication. Writers could reasonably hope for a response to their letters, and had the right to complain if they received none. Officials were supposed to respond and could be reprimanded for failing to do so. Of course, there were many forms of possible response. Responses could be perfunctory or involve serious investigations of citizens' complaints; they could support petitions or deny them; they could punish the target of a denunciation letter, or on occasion punish the denouncer.

We can get a sense of the range of responses by surveying the disposition of cases mentioned in this and a later chapter. Let us start with positive outcomes. The grieving widower trapped in the sticks (above, pp. 158–59) was given a job in Leningrad; the tormented *komsomolka* (p. 175) was sent to a sanatorium for a rest; the letter from the schoolmaster father (p. 175) was forwarded to the Caucasus for elucidation of the circumstances of his daughter's death. A kolkhoznitsa's demand for the immediate arrest of her kolkhoz chairman (p. 221) led the raikom to recommend, if not arrest, at least criminal prosecution. Two out of the three young members of the Writers' Union who asked Molotov for housing (p. 160) received it; and Zhdanov was sufficiently impressed by the sycophantic mathematician (p. 166) to call "urgently" for a "serious" report on his *Bases of a New Algebra*.

The Churkov orphans (p. 172) aroused a sympathetic response in Rumiantsev's office ("Fix things for the kids [*ustroi detishek*]," his assistant wrote to the local soviet chairman), although, as it turned out, even this was not enough to get them their izba back once the local boss had gotten his hands on it. Vyshinsky responded conscientiously to the appeals he received from prisoners' relatives, even though his responses did not usually help the victims. In the Erman case (p. 160), he called for a review by the Chief Military Prosecutor and then wrote to Erman's wife with the news that the eight-year sentence had been upheld. He tried to follow the same procedure in the beekeeper's case (p. 160), but when the report came in, it showed that the man had been summarily executed in Saratov in 1937. Perhaps understandably, Vyshinsky left the appeal of the beekeeper's wife unanswered.

Shafran's request to paint Zhdanov's portrait (p. 166) was dismissed with the curt notation "File (*Arkhiv*)," and there is no sign of any reply to the outpourings of the distraught vydvizhenka (p. 157) and the wronged wives (p. 158), the cry of distress from the *vydvizhenets* promoted beyond his abilities (pp. 175–76), or the letters of opinion from the angry engineer and the Litvinov critic (p. 162). In general, opinion letters rarely received replies. But that is not to say they were ignored. Newspapers regularly compiled summaries (*svodki*) of correspondence received on various topics for the information of government and party leaders. The letter about over-flowing jails (p. 164), for example, was included in a 1936 summary sent by *Krest'ianskaia gazeta* to the Constitutional Commission.

Letters could make trouble for their authors. A student's enquiry about the possibility of building communism (p. 161) provoked an immediate police investigation of Trotskyite influence in his school (though the writer himself was thought naive rather than dangerous). The feldsher's denunciation (p. 169) was investigated and found to be groundless—moreover, the report noted ominously, the writer himself had "a lot of disgraceful things (*bezobraziia*) and abuses" to answer for. With "abuse of power" letters, there was always the possibility that the denunciation would backfire and damage the author. Sometimes it was the denouncers, rather than their intended victims, who ended up in prison or under investigation by the NKVD.[98]

From this range of responses, it is evident not only that popular letter writing in the Stalin period was a two-way transaction but also that it could be a bit of a gamble for the initiator. But only some kinds of letters carried a real risk, just as only some kinds of letters were likely to bring their writers tangible benefits. To understand the distribution of outcomes, it is useful to think of letter writers in terms of two major categories, Suppli-cants and Citizens.

These two types of letter writer seem to inhabit different worlds, though their letters lie side by side in the archives and the writers themselves

[98] For examples, see RGAE, f. 396, op. 10, d. 64, l. 165; ibid., d. 68, ll. 77–78; ibid., d. 143, l. 211.

might be neighbors. The Supplicant was implicitly a subject rather than a citizen. He sent his private complaints, requests, petitions, and confessions to an authority figure imagined as a benevolent father (or father-confessor) or a patron. Women letter writers were often Supplicants, as were peasants. Supplicants' letters might ask for justice as well as mercy, but they did not invoke rights. They portrayed their authors as victims and dwelt on their miseries and misfortunes. Supplicants' letters, though sent to public figures and requesting them to act in their official capacity, dealt with private and personal concerns.

For Supplicants, letter writing was not a risk-taking enterprise, since the worst of the likely outcomes was that their letter would be ignored. Writing a Supplicant's letter was something like buying a ticket in the state lottery (another popular pastime in Stalin's Russia): it cost little, carried no obligations, and offered the chance, however remote, of a big win.

Supplicant letter writing, though widespread, was almost never discussed in Soviet media or official instructions. A rare exception was a 1936 article by the veteran party journalist, Lev Sosnovskii, urging newspapers and other recipients of such letters to be more responsive to the problems of the little man, while expressing the hope that little men would learn to approach the organs of Soviet power "not like timid supplicants, but like masters."[99] Obviously many Supplicants' letters were ignored, but there were also many that were not. My own impression from the archives is that obkom secretaries,[100] in particular, were surprisingly responsive to appeals from ordinary people—indeed, that harkening to the pleas of widows and orphans was one of the more satisfying aspects of a senior Communist administrator's job, providing reassurance that Soviet power really was on the side of the poor and humble, and leaving a glow of conscious virtue.

Another kind of Supplicant letter was part of a transaction between client and patron, with the client normally belonging to the cultural and scientific elite and the patron to the Communist political leadership. Elite Supplicants tended to be conspicuously deferential and generous with flattery. Patrons like Molotov responded to their clients' requests in a routine, businesslike manner that implied acceptance of the premise of patronage systems everywhere, namely that the patron's ability to look after his clients is an index as well as a prerogative of power.

[99] L. Sosnovskii, "Letter from the editorial board," *Izvestiia*, 5 May 1936, p. 4.
[100] The cases I know best are those of Eikhe in Novosibirsk (from PANO files), Kirov and Zhdanov in Leningrad (TsGA IPD), and Rumiantsev in the Western oblast (Smolensk archive).

The Citizen was a more "modern" figure than the Supplicant, and one that the regime was proud to acknowledge as a participant in Soviet democracy and watchdog against bureaucratic abuses.[101] He wrote letters to the editor or the Politburo to state opinions, criticize policies, suggest improvements, blow the whistle on corrupt officials, point out miscarriages of justice, and denounce wrongdoers in the name of "my duty as a citizen." He acted, or claimed to act, in the public interest; if he had private motives for writing, he concealed them. He used the language of rights, and among the rights he implicitly claimed was his right to be heard. The Citizen often addressed party leaders as "comrade," and was willing to remind them, particularly if he was an urban worker, of the promises of the Revolution. The majority of Citizen letter writers were male and urban, though the rural Citizen, in the person of the sel'kor, was a recognizable figure. Though their letters of Citizens were filed as "secret" in the archives, they were essentially public communications in form and content—and also in aspiration, judging by the stubbornly reiterated hope of publication.

Yet the Citizen, unlike the Supplicant, was taking a risk when he wrote his letter. He was more of a gambler than a buyer of lottery tickets. Many Citizen's letters had no possibility of a payoff that would directly benefit the author. Others might benefit him indirectly (e.g., by getting rid of a corrupt boss or abusive kolkhoz chairman), but could also damage him, if the target of a whistle-blowing letter found out his identity and retaliated. "Opinion" letters might make an impact via inclusion in a "public opinion" summary sent up to the Politburo. But they might also bring trouble upon the author's head if his opinions offended someone in authority. The NKVD made a practice of trying to discover the identity of the authors of anonimki, and that could spell trouble for those who put their anti-Soviet opinions on paper.

Behind the Supplicant and the Citizen are discernible other, less distinct figures—the Conman, assuming the persona of Supplicant or Citizen for his own nefarious ends;[102] the would-be Informer, using a denunciation as a scarf to trail in front of the secret police;[103] the Memoirist;

---

[101] For a summary of statements and instructions on this question, see Golfo Alexopoulos, "Exposing Illegality and Oneself: Complaint and Risk in Stalin's Russia," in *Reforming Justice in Russia, 1864–1996: Power, Culture, and the Limits of Legal Order*, ed. Peter H. Solomon Jr. (Armonk, N.Y., 1997).

[102] For a fascinating case study of a con man, a prodigious writer of petitions and denunciations who turned to playwriting when he found himself in prison facing a death sentence, see Golfo Alexopoulos, "Portrait of a Con Artist as a Soviet Man," *Slavic Review* 57:4 (1998); on con men in general, see chapters 13 and 14.

[103] For more on this topic, see below, p. 230.

the *Grafoman* . . . But these shadowy figures must await another inter-
preter. To borrow some conventional closing phrases from the letters,
"there is no end" to the richness of the subject, "there is not enough
paper to describe it." "It is only one tenth of what I could say . . . But I
am tired of writing."[104]

[104] Quotations from RGAE, f. 396, op. 10, d. 26, ll. 137–39; RGASPI, f. 475, op. 1, d.
16, ll. 182.

CHAPTER TEN

Patrons and Clients

> In 1930 in the little Sukhumi rest-house for bigwigs where
> we ended up through an oversight of Lakoba's, Ezhov's wife
> was talking to me: "Pilniak goes (khodit) to us," she said.
> "And whom do you go to?" I indignantly reported that con-
> versation to O. M., but he quietened me down: "Everyone
> 'goes'. Obviously it can't be otherwise. And we 'go'. To
> Nikolai Ivanovich [Bukharin]."[1]

Patronage relations were ubiquitous in the Soviet elite. The phenomenon
is perhaps most familiar in the political sphere, where local and central
leaders cultivated and promoted their own client networks (the often-
criticized "family circles" [semeistva]).[2] But it was not only rising politicians who needed patrons. Lacking an adequate legal system, Russians
relied on patronage alliances to protect "personal security, goods, career
and status, freedom of expression and other material interests."[3] These
words, written by David Ransel about Russian elites in the time of Catherine the Great, apply equally well to Stalinist society. Like blat connections,
patronage relations were part of the well-placed Soviet citizen's survival
kit. And no sector of the elite was more intensive in its pursuit of patrons,
or more successful in finding them in the heights of the party leadership,
than the Soviet "creative intelligentsia," whose clientelist practices are the
subject of this paper.

To say that patronage relations were ubiquitous in the elites of Stalin's
Russia is not to say that everybody had them. Not everyone is equally

---

This chapter was first published as "Intelligentsia and Power: Client-Patron Relations in
Stalin's Russia," in Manfred Hildermeier, ed., Stalinismus vor dem Zweiten Weltkrieg: Neue
Ansätze der Forschung/Stalinism before World War II: New Lines of Research (Munich,
1998).

[1] Nadezhda Mandel'shtam, Vospominaniia (New York, 1970), pp. 119–120.

[2] T. H. Rigby was the pioneer in studies of political patronage in the Soviet Union: much
of his work on the subject is collected in his Political Elites in the USSR: Central Leaders
and Local Cadres from Lenin to Gorbachev (Aldershot, 1990). On political patronage in
the Stalin period, see Graeme Gill, The Origins of the Stalinist Political System (Cambridge,
1990), esp. pp. 129–30, 315–16, 324–25.

[3] David L. Ransel, The Politics of Catherinian Russia: The Panin Party (New Haven,
1975), p. 1.

adept at the human skills involved in patronage and blat relations. Some members of the intelligentsia were virtual nonparticipants for lack of opportunity or aptitude; others avoided clientelist relations with highly placed Communists on principle. But nobody within the elites—and perhaps outside them, although that question remains to be investigated by scholars—could live in a patronage-free environment, anymore than he or she could live in a social environment that was free of blat. These two phenomena are intimately connected. Both involve the doing of favors based on some degree of personal relationship, for which there is no direct payment; the difference is that patronage connections exist between persons of unequal social status, whereas blat relations are nonhierarchical.[4]

Like blat, patronage was and remains a semitaboo subject with slightly shady overtones of corruption for Russians (at least when they are talking about themselves). Among intelligentsia memoirists, only the most sociologically inclined (like Nadezhda Mandelstam) or the most flagrant practitioners of clientelism (like Natalia Sats, former director of the Moscow Children's Theater) openly discuss their own relations with patrons from the political elites.[5] Most memoirists remain reticent, though they may note occasions where some important personage showed his nobility of character or devotion to the arts by intervening on their behalf. The same reticence is to be found in the language that Russians use to talk about patronage. While terms describing a patron's protection exist (*pokrovitel' stvo, protektsiia, ruka*), they tend to be pejorative and would rarely be used about one's own patronage relations. Most nonpejorative ways of referring to a patron are euphemistic and tend to present the patron-client relationship in terms of friendship. Verbs like "help" (*pomogat'*), "support" (*podderzhivat'*), and "come to the aid of" (*vyruchat'*) are often used to describe patronage transactions. Written appeals to patrons request their "advice" (*sovet*) and "help" (*pomoshch'*).[6]

There is an extensive comparative literature on clientelist/patronage relations in which these are defined as reciprocal, personal (conventionally involving affective ties), continuing (not one-off), and taking place between unequal partners.[7] The advantage to the client is that he obtains

---

[4] On blat, see Alena V. Ledeneva, *Russia's Economy of Favours: Blat*, Networking and Informal Exchange (Cambridge, 1998).

[5] See Nadezhda Mandelstam, *Hope against Hope* (London, 1970) and *Hope Abandoned* (London, Atheneum, 1974), both trans. Max Hayward (Russian titles *Vospominaniia* and *Vtoraia kniga*), and Nataliia Sats, *Zhizn'—iavlenie polosatoe* (Moscow, 1991), esp. pp. 377–92, 443–44 and 467, 479–80.

[6] Thanks to Yuri Slezkine and Alena Ledeneva for their advice on the language of patronage.

[7] Anthony Hall, "Patron-Client Relations: Concepts and Terms," in *Friends, Followers and Factions: A Reader in Political Clientelism*, eds. Steffen W. Schmidt, Laura Guasti,

goods, jobs, promotion, protection, and so forth from the more powerful and worldly connected patron. The advantage to the patron, as it is described in the literature, is that the patron has the loyalty and services of the client for a range of purposes ranging from work, protection of reputation, and provision of intelligence to support in elections. The client is the patron's "man." Many writers on clientelism see it as closely connected with insecurity and vulnerability: "One may posit that resort to patronage mechanisms will be the more pronounced where the weak are disproportionately weak, the strong disproportionately strong, and formal, alternative mechanisms for protecting citizens—laws, court systems, police, procedural rules of the game, etc.—remain embryonic, manipulable or perhaps imbued with little or no legitimacy."[8] It has also been suggested that, in situations of scarcity of goods and services, patronage may provide the necessary discriminatory selection basis.[9]

Much of this general theory of patronage fits the Soviet case very well, in particular the insecurity/vulnerability and preferential distribution arguments. Undoubtedly, patronage and blat were Soviet mechanisms for distributing scarce goods in the absence of a market. There was not enough housing, health care, etc. to go round; there was no market to set priorities via pricing; bureaucratic rules of allocation were clumsy and unsatisfactory; law functioned poorly, especially as a protection for the individual against arbitrary state action. In the real world, personalistic processes like patronage and blat were what often determined who got what.

Less clearly applicable to the Soviet case is the notion of reciprocity in patron-client relations. In the sphere of political clientelism, one can see possible forms of reciprocity in the form of loyalty, discretion, and mutual protection within the family circle: since *semeistva* landed local political leaders in big trouble during the Purges, their ubiquity presumably tells us that a local mutual-protection ring was an almost essential modus operandi in Stalinist politics, despite the dangers.[10] But in the multifarious

---

Carl H. Landé, and James C. Scott (Berkeley, 1977), 510; Ernest Gellner, "Patrons and Clients," in Ernest Gellner and John Waterbury, eds., *Patrons and Clients in Mediterranean Societies* (London, 1977), 4. On asymmetry, durability, and reciprocity see John Waterbury, "An Attempt to Put Patrons and Clients in their Place," in Gellner and Waterbury, eds., *Patrons*, pp. 329–32. On the personalistic aspect, see James Scott, "Patronage or Exploitation?" in ibid., p. 22.

[8] Waterbury, "Attempt," p. 336.

[9] Waterbury, "Attempt," p. 339.

[10] See Gill, *Origins*, pp. 129–30, on the ways in which "local control by a personalized network" could protect subnational leaders from both grassroots criticism from below and interference and investigation from above. The best concrete description of such a ring, based on regional party and NKVD archive material from Ekaterinburg (Sverdlovsk) is in James R. Harris, *The Great Urals: Regionalalism and the Evolution of the Soviet System*

patron-client relationships that linked the creative intelligentsia and the regime, it is hard to see what reciprocal benefits the clients could offer their patrons. Of what use would the loyalty of (say) Mandelstam have been to Bukharin, or of Vavilov to Molotov? And what "services" could these intelligentsia clients provide for their patrons?

On closer examination, this may not constitute a deviation of Soviet patronage from the general rule so much as point up a weakness in the articulation of the theory. There must, in fact, be many contexts in which patrons are unlikely to obtain tangible material benefits from his clients. As one writer notes, "a patron controlling bureaucratic favours may be victimised by his own power, unable to extract from his clients anything commensurate with the services he has rendered."[11] (I will consider the intangible benefits to the patron later in this chapter.)

Patronage is still an underdeveloped topic in modern Russian/Soviet historiography. Daniel Orlovsky has provided a valuable introductory overview of pre-Soviet patronage focused on the late Imperial period, and Daniel Aleksandrov and other young Russian historians of science have begun to investigate patronage in the sciences as part of their study of the everyday practices (*byt*) of Russian and Soviet science.[12] The present discussion is, as far as I know, the first attempt at an overview of client-patron relationships between members of the Soviet intelligentsia and members of the Soviet political elite. For reasons of space, the equally important topic of clientelist relations *within* the intelligentsia is not dealt with here.

Who Were the Patrons?

Officials were the people with access to resources in Soviet society; consequently, officials were the major source of patronage. Any office holder could function as a patron who did favors for clients, and it is hard to believe that there was any official who never did this. As for patronage of the intelligentsia, some political leaders were more involved, some less, but it is probably safe to assume that all members of the Politburo and

(Ithaca, 1999), chapter 6 (also published in slightly revised form in Fitzpatrick, ed., *Stalinism: New Directions*, pp. 262–85).

[11] Waterbury, "Attempt," p. 331.

[12] Daniel T. Orlovsky, "Political Clientelism in Russia: The Historical Perspective," in T. H. Rigby and Bohdan Harasymiw, eds., *Leadership Selection and Patron-Client Relations in the USSR and Yugoslavia* (London, 1983), pp. 175–99; D. A. Aleksandrov, "Istoricheskaia antropologiia nauki v Rossii," *Voprosy istorii estestvoznaniia i tekhniki*, 1994 no. 4. This article appeared in English translation in *Russian Studies in History* (Fall 1995), pp. 62–91.

obkom secretaries acted at least occasionally as patrons of members of the intelligentsia. This was not necessarily from a love of the arts and scholarship but a matter of *noblesse oblige*—the position and status required it.

From the existing memoir literature, it would be easy to get the impression that patronage of the intelligentsia—indeed, patronage in general—was the prerogative of a few particularly generous or culturally inclined party leaders: for example, Sergei Kirov, the Leningrad obkom leader; "Sergo" Ordzhonikidze, People's Commissar of Heavy Industry; Mikhail Kalinin, longtime President of the Executive Committee of the Congress of Soviets (TsIK); and Nadezhda Krupskaia, Lenin's widow, who was deputy Commissar of Enlightenment.[13] This is not the case, however. It must be remembered that in the Khrushchev and Brezhnev periods, when most of these memoirs of "unforgettable meetings" with "friends of science" and "friends of the arts" in the party leadership appeared, large numbers of former leaders—from Oppositionists of the 1920s like Trotsky and Kamenev to the "antiparty group" of the 1950s, including Molotov and Malenkov—were nonpersons whose names could not be mentioned in print.

It may be that "good" Communists like Kirov and Ordzhonikidze—along with Bukharin, whose patronage is attested by dissident and "samizdat" sources—really were particularly generous as patrons of the intelligentsia, but "bad" Communists like State Prosecutor Andrei Vyshinsky or Nikolai Ezhov, Genrikh Iagoda, and Iakov Agranov of the NKVD were also active patrons.[14] With the opening of the Soviet archives, we find that even Viacheslav Molotov, head of the Soviet government throughout the 1930s, who gets few if any mentions as a patron in the memoir literature (or, for that matter, in his own recollections, as recorded by Felix Chuev), was much sought after and responsive as a cultural patron.[15] (The next section of this chapter is largely based on Molotov's Sovnarkom archive.)

Stalin, of course, was in a category of his own. While his eminence tended to disqualify him from engaging in ordinary patron-client relations in the 1930s and '40s, he may be regarded as the universal and archetypal

---

[13] For a bibliographical survey of this literature, which incidentally provides a useful guide to the range of "acceptable" subjects of memoirs, see the section on "Deiateli Kommunisticheskoi partii i sovetskogo gosudarstva . . ." in *Sovetskoe obshchestvo v vospominaniiakh i dnevnikakh*, ed. V. Z. Drobizhev, vol. 1 (Moscow, 1987), pp. 26–101.

[14] See Arkady Vaksberg, *The Prosecutor and the Prey: Vyshinsky and the 1930s Moscow Show Trials*, trans. Jan Butler (London, 1990), pp. 3–7, 275–77; Iurii Elagin, *Ukroshchenie iskusstv* (New York, 1952), pp. 48, 52, and *Temnyi genii (Vsevolod Meierkhol'd)* (New York, 1955), p. 291.

[15] *Sto sorok besed s Molotvym: Iz dnevnika F. Chueva* (Moscow, 1991).

patron, as in this fantasy of the writer Mikhail Bulgakov (whom Stalin did in fact help):

> *Motorcycle* ... brrm!!! In the Kremlin already! Misha goes into the hall, and there sit Stalin, Molotov, Voroshilov, Kaganovich, Mikoian and Iagoda.
>
> Misha stands in the door, making a low bow.
>
> *Stalin*: What's the matter? Why are you barefoot?
>
> *Bulgakov* (with a sad shrug): Well ... I don't have any boots..
>
> *Stalin*: What is this? My writer going without boots? What an outrage! Iagoda, take off your boots, give them to him.[16]

High officials in the cultural bureaucracies played a special role as patrons of the intelligentsia. Anatolii Lunacharsky, as head of the Commissariat of Enlightenment (Narkompros), was notoriously generous in this regard, though the generosity of his response reduced the value of his interventions on behalf of clients.[17] As the writer Kornei Chukovskii recalled, as early as 1918 dozens of clients gathered every day outside Lunacharsky's apartment in Petrograd, "thirsting for his advice and help":

> Pedagogues, workers, inventors, librarians, circus clowns, futurists, artists of all schools and genres (from *peredvizhniki* to Cubists), philosophers, ballerinas, hypnotists, singers, Proletkult poets and simply poets, artists of the former Imperial stage—all of them went to Anatolii Vasilevich in a very long queue up the dilapidated staircase to the crowded room which finally came to be called the "reception room" (*priemnaia*).[18]

In the realm of cultural patronage, nobody was more important than Maxim Gorky. His position was anomalous, since he was neither a cultural bureaucrat nor a party leader. He established the role first during the Civil War by virtue of his long close acquaintanceship with Lenin and other Bolshevik leaders. Then, after his return to the Soviet Union at the end of the 1920s, Gorky was essentially given the job of patron extraordinaire by Stalin; indeed, this was probably one of the main incentives for him to return. Chukovskii's tribute to his "unforgettable role" as a patron of children's literature ("How stubbornly he helped us children's writers struggle with Leftist pedologists, how many times he saved our books from the then Narkompros, RAPP [the Russian Associa-

---

[16] Vitalii Shentalinskii, *Raby svobody: V literaturnykh arkhivakh KGB* ([Moscow], 1995), p. 120.

[17] See Sheila Fitzpatrick, *The Commissariat of Enlightenment* (London, 1970), pp. 131–32. Examples of Lunacharsky's activity as a patron may be found in RGASPI, f. 142, d. 647 (*Pis'ma akademikov, deiatelei nauki i kul'tury o pomoshchi* ... 1928–33).

[18] Kornei Chukovskii, *Sovremennniki: Portrety i etiudy* (Moscow, 1963), pp. 401–2.

tion of Proletarian Writers], and so forth") is one of hundreds.[19] There are more than 13,000 letters to Gorky from Soviet writers in the Gorky archive, a sizeable proportion of which approach him as an actual or potential patron, and his activities in this sphere in the first half of the 1930s were legendary.[20]

Finally, institutional sources of patronage outside the cultural bureaucracy should not be forgotten. Katerina Clark notes that in the early years of NEP, when Narkompros's budget was drastically reduced, the Komsomol assumed new importance as a source of patronage for Petrograd intellectuals.[21] The GPU/NKVD and its leaders also provided important patronage for some cultural and educational activities (Matvei Pogrebinskii's and Anton Makarenko's communes for delinquents, the writers' expedition to the White Sea canal that resulted in the *Belomor* volume, and so on).[22] For the artists of AKhRR (the Association of Artists of Revolutionary Russia, established in the mid 1920s), trade unions and the Red Army were the main sources of patronage. It should be noted that artists had access to private patronage in a fully traditional sense: the commissioning of portraits of patrons in the political world. The Army leader Klim Voroshilov was one of those whose portraits were painted by a client. Opponents of the AKhRR group claimed that AKhRR owed its success to a "policy of worming a privileged position by doing portraits of the establishment figures, who in turn passed on lucrative commissions to the Association on behalf of the organizations they headed."[23]

WHAT COULD PATRONS DO FOR THEIR CLIENTS?

There were three main categories of request from clients: 1) goods and services; 2) protection; and 3) intervention in professional disputes.

The first category is the one where we see patronage acting as a nonmarket mechanism for the distribution of scarce goods, above all housing.

[19] Chukovskii, *Sovremenniki*, p. 360.

[20] *Novyi mir*, 1968 no. 3, p. 6 (number of letters in arkhive). On Gorky's position after his return to the USSR and his patronage activities, see Shentalinskii, *Raby svobody*, pp. 302–77 passim, and Valentina Khodasevich, "Takim ia znala Gor'kogo," *Novyi Mir*, 1968 no. 3, pp. 11–66.

[21] Katerina Clark, *Petersburg, Crucible of Cultural Revolution* (Cambridge, Mass., 1995), p. 145.

[22] *Belomorsko-Baltiyskii kanal imeni Stalina* (Moscow, 1934).

[23] Elizabeth Valkenier, *Russian Realist Art. The State and Society: The Peredvizhniki and Their Tradition* (Ann Arbor: Ardis, 1977), pp. 151, 156; *Sto sorok besed s Molotovym*, p. 315. For another example of military patronage, see the discussion of LOKAF in Evgenii Dobrenko, *Metafora vlasti: Literatura stalinskoi epokhi v istoricheskom osveshchenii* (Munich, 1993), pp. 138–51.

Molotov's Sovnarkom archive of the 1930s is full of requests from members of the intelligentsia, writing to him as a patron (addressed by name and patronymic) and putting their requests on a personalistic basis, for help in obtaining a larger apartment.[24] The letter of Nikolai Sidorenko, a member of Writers' Union, was a typical if florid example that described pathetically how he lived with his wife and stepson of fifteen in a single attic room, damp, low and dark, 13 square meters, off the Arbat. As a result of the "everyday-life and moral torments of my family," his wife was suffering from severe nervous breakdown; the boy was growing up "abnormal, without his own corner"; his wife's father, a 72-year-old invalid, had to beg corners in strange apartments.[25] Writers, musicians, scientists, and artists were among those who approached Molotov, often successfully, for help in obtaining housing.[26]

The second category—even more common, at least in the Great Purge years—consists of requests for protection. In the Soviet case, this could mean intervention to stop the writer being harassed by colleagues or particular state institutions; help in reestablishing reputation after falling into political disgrace; help in getting an arrested relative released or his or her case reviewed, etc. Take a characteristic selection of items from the mailbags of Molotov and Zhdanov in the second half of the 1930s: Professor A. L. Chizhevskii appealed for protection from harassment by the Communist biologist B. M. Zavadovskii; Academician Derzhavin asked for help in resisting "persecution" at the hands of Academician Deborin; I. I. Mints asked him to squash a libelous rumor that Mints was a friend of the disgraced "Trotskyite" Leopold Averbakh (former leader of RAPP); the poet A. Zharov complained about the "death sentence" pronounced on his recent book in a *Pravda* review.[27]

There is no reason to think Molotov was unusual in the scope of his patronage activities (after all, as noted above, he is not celebrated as a patron in the annals of the literary intelligentsia). Similar "client" cases can be found in Ordzhonikidze's archives. In 1931, for example, the former Menshevik economist, O. A. Ermanskii, wrote to Ordzhonikidze ask-

---

[24] See Gosudarstvennyi arkhiv Rossiiskoi Federatsii (GARF), f. 5446, op. 82, d. 72, l. 114 for a letter of early 1938 from the housing officer noting that as soon as the NKVD releases the apartments and rooms it had sealed up after arresting their occupants, he will get back to Molotov with a response to the clients' cases Molotov had raised.

[25] Molotov sends this on to Bulganin with a request for action. GARF, f. 5446, op. 82, d. 72, l. 115.

[26] See, for example, GARF, f. 5446, op. 82, d. 77, ll. 9–10; d. 72, l. 34; d. 51 [no page] (case of Academician V. I. Vernadskii); d. 51, l. 286 (thanks from the Kukryniksy, cartoonists).

[27] GARF, f. 5446, op. 82, d. 51, l. 144 (Chizhevskii); Tsentral'nyi gosudarstvennyi arkhiv istoriko-politicheskoi dokumentatsii Sankt-Peterburga (TsGAIPD), f. 24, op. 2v, d. 2220, ll. 103–5 (Derzhavin); GARF, f. 5446, op. 82, d. 53, l. 130 (Mints); GARF, f. 5446, op. 82, d. 70, l. 165 (Zharov).

ing for his help in dissipating the "social isolation into which I have fallen."[28] There are many letters to party leaders in the archives from aggrieved actors, singers, and other performers complaining about being denied good roles.[29] Agranov of the NKVD, a patron of the Vakhtangov Theater, was the person to whom the actress Tsetsilia Mansurova regularly applied when her husband, a member of the aristocratic Sheremetev family, was disenfranchised or arrested because of his social origins. When the composer Dmitrii Shostakovich fell into disgrace over his opera *Lady Macbeth of the Mtsensk District* in 1936, he turned naturally to his friend and patron, Marshal Tukhachevsky.[30]

The third type of help for which clients appealed to patrons was intervention in professional disputes. Lysenko's feud with the geneticists, for example, was the subject of many appeals from both sides.[31] Physics, too, was a subject of appeals and counterappeals. For example, the militants at *Pod znamenem marksizma (PZM)*, M. B. Mitin, A. A. Maksimov, and P. F. Iudin, sought Molotov's support for their controversial attack on "idealism" in physics, while Petr Kapitsa wrote *against* the militants to Stalin, Molotov, and Mezhlauk, characterizing *PZM*'s intervention in physics as "scientifically illiterate" and deploring the assumption that "if you are not a materialist in physics, . . . you are an enemy of the people."[32]

Artists were perhaps even more prone to appeal to patrons to resolve professional disputes than scientists. At the beginning of 1937, Konstantin Iuon, Aleksandr Gerasimov (head of the Moscow Union of Artists), Sergei Gerasimov, and Igor Grabar asked Molotov to receive a delegation to adjudicate their quarrels with Kerzhentsev's Arts Committee, claiming that "extra and decisive interference of authoritative instances is necessary so as not to allow that union [of artists] to collapse completely."[33]

How to Acquire a Patron

The patron-client relationship requires the existence of some sort of personal connection. That connection may be social or familial; or

---

[28] Rossiiskii gosudarstvennyi arkhiv sotsial'no-politicheskoi informatsii (RGASPI), f. 85, op. 28, d. 77. Ermanskii's work on the scientific organization of labor was savagely attacked in 1930, and he was expelled from the Communist Academy along with other Mensheviks.

[29] See, for example, the letter to Zhdanov in TsGAIPD f. 24, op. 2v, d. 2679, ll. 28–30.

[30] Elagin, *Ukroshchenie*, pp. 52–53; *Testimony: The Memoirs of Dmitri Shostakovich*, ed. Solomon Volkov, trans. Antonina W. Bouis (New York, 1980), pp. 98–99.

[31] See, for example, the anti-Lysenko letter from two young biologists send to Molotov via his wife in 1939. GARF, f. 5446, op. 82, d. 112, ll. 281–92.

[32] GARF, f. 5446, op. 82, d. 65, l. 207 (the attack in question was launched in *PZM* nos. 7 and 11–12, 1937); P. L. Kapitsa, *Pis'ma o nauke 1930–1980* (Moscow, 1989), p. 151.

[33] GARF, f. 5446, op. 82, d. 53, l. 82. The meeting was duly held on 11 February 1937, Kerzhentsev also being present: GARF, f. 5446, op. 82, d. 53, l. 102.

have occurred through a chance meeting in a work context, in a train, at a resort, etc.; or through an introduction. Boris Pilniak was taken along to meet an early patron, Trotsky, by A. K. Voronskii (editor of *Krasnaia nov'*) in the early 1920s.[34] How he met a later patron, Ezhov, is unknown, but most likely it was through Isaac Babel, who was a friend and former lover of Ezhov's wife. Leopold Averbakh knew Iagoda because his sister married him; one of the sources of his (and Iagoda's) contact with Maxim Gorky was that his uncle, Zinovii Peshkov, was Gorky's adopted son. Meyerhold expanded his network of party and security police patrons through the salon run by his second wife, Zinaida Raikh.[35] Painters could acquire patrons by painting them: see, requests to pose from painters Mark Shafran (to Andrei Zhdanov) and B. V. Ioganson (to Ivan Gronskii).[36]

These are only the beginnings of chains by which a potential client could establish contact with a patron. There were political leaders who were known to specialize in certain types of clients on the basis of ethnicity, profession, avocation, etc.: Mikoian for Armenians,[37] Ordzhonikidze for Georgians,[38] Vyshinsky for lawyers and diplomats,[39] Voroshilov (an amateur singer) for opera singers . . . And there were also introductions from lower-level patrons: for example, when Pilniak was in trouble in the mid '20s after the publication of his scandalous novella, *Povest' nepogashennoi luny*, he approached a middle-level patron, Ivan Skvortsov-Stepanov, then editor of *Izvestiia*, who arranged a meeting with Rykov (who "advised me to write letters of contrition, which I did").[40] And people with contacts might pass on a letter "kuda sleduet," as Babel did when he handed Ezhov's wife a letter from Eduard Bagritskii's widow asking for the release from prison of her sister's husband.[41] Finally, major cultural institutions like the Bolshoi or Vakhtangov theaters would have their own sets of patronage connections that could be activated on behalf of a member in need.[42]

[34] From Pilniak's statement under interrrogation by the NKVD, 11 December 1937, cited Shentalinskii, *Raby*, p. 196.

[35] Elagin, *Temnyi genii*, p. 291.

[36] TsGAIPD, f. 24, op. 2v, d. 2219, l. 1; Ivan Gronskii, *Iz proshlogo . . . Vospominaniia* (Moscow, 1991), p. 142.

[37] After the arrest of her stepfather, the Armenian Gevork Alikhanov, Elena Bonner's mother appealed to Mikoian for help, even though they had not been particularly close friends judging by Bonner's recollections; moreover, Mikoian responded with an offer to adopt Elena and her younger brother. Elena Bonner, *Mothers and Daughters*, trans. Antonina W. Bouis (New York, 1993), pp. 123–4.

[38] RGASPI, f. 85 (Ordzhonikidze *fond*) contains many such letters.

[39] Arkady Vaksberg, trans. Jan Butler, *The Prosecutor and the Prey: Vyshinsky and the 1930s Moscow Show Trials* (London, 1990), pp. 3–4, 275.

[40] Shentalinskii, *Raby*, p. 197.

[41] From Babel's confession, in Shentalinskii, *Raby*, p. 50.

[42] See Elagin's many examples in *Ukroshchenie*, including his own case.

BROKERS

There were certain leading members of the cultural and scholarly professions—P. L. Kapitsa and S. I. Vavilov were examples in the natural sciences—who acted as representatives of a whole group of clients in dealing with highly placed patrons. They assumed this broker function because of their professional stature and their established connections with various government leaders: chairmen of the Academy of Sciences, secretaries of professional unions, directors of scientific institutes, etc. had it ex officio. Sometimes brokering was a matter of representing the professional interests of a group, as when Aleksandr Fadeev, secretary of the Writers' Union, wrote to Molotov in January 1940 to express the distress of the literary community that none of the the newly established 100,000-ruble Stalin prizes had been earmarked for literature.[43] Sometimes it meant interceding on behalf of subordinates, for example, when Graftio, head of a Leningrad hydroelectric construction trust, wrote to Leningrad leader M. S. Chudov in 1935 on behalf of engineers threatened with deportation.[44]

Many "broker" interventions had to do with arrests within the professional community that the broker represented. Kapitsa, for example, appealed to Valerii Mezhlauk (deputy chairman of Sovnarkom) and Stalin about the arrest of V. A. Fock in 1937 and to Molotov and Stalin about Landau's arrest (in 1938) and continuing imprisonment (in 1939).[45] S. I. Vavilov wrote to Beria in 1944 attempting to gain release of N. A. Kozyrev, a young astronomer from Pulkovo.[46] Gorky, of course, was famous for such interventions on behalf of Petrograd intellectuals during the Civil War, and continued the practice—though increasingly sparingly—in the 1930s. Meyerhold frequently appealed to his patrons, Avel Enukidze and Genrikh Iagoda, on behalf of arrested friends and acquaintances in the theater world—it was said of him that "he practically never refused anyone."[47] If this is not hyperbole, however, it suggests that Meyerhold lacked the quality of sober calculation of the odds that characterized the best brokers (there was no point in a broker using up credit with a patron on a hopeless case).

[43] GARF, f. 5446, op. 81a, d. 337, ll. 76–78.
[44] TSGAIPD, f. 24 op. 2v, d. 1515, ll. 64–65.
[45] TSGAIPD, f. 24 op. 2v, d. 1515, ll. 184–85.
[46] Paul Josephson, *Physics and Politics in Revolutionary Russia* (Berkeley and Los Angeles, 1991), p. 316. From Academy of Sciences archive.
[47] Elagin, *Temnyi genii*, pp. 294–95.

How to Write to a Patron

While other forms of initial approach to a patron existed (e.g., via a word to the patron about the client's needs from a family member or assistant), writing a letter was the standard way of communicating a clientelist request. The composition of such letters was a serious matter: Kapitsa "worked on letters to 'up there' no less seriously and responsibly than on an article or a paper" and often wrote four or five drafts before he was satisfied. Kapitsa, who was often writing as a broker for the physics community rather than for himself, wrote dignified, substantive letters with a minimum of flattery and little intrusion of the personal; some of his letters were so like articles that they contained separate headed sections and even on one occasion an epigraph. Like most clients, Kapitsa used a formal salutation with name and patronymic ("Much respected [*mnogouva-zhaemyi*] Valerii Ivanovich") for lower-level patrons like Valerii Mezhlauk, Karl Bauman, or Nikolai Gorbunov, ending his letter "Yours, P. Kapitsa." In writing to top leaders in the 1930s, however, he used the less common style of addressing his letters to "Comrade Stalin" and "Comrade Molotov" without further salutation, ending his letters simply with a signature.[48]

Natalia Sats approached the task of writing equally seriously. In 1941, visiting Moscow seeking intervention on her behalf in troubles in her theater work in Kazakhstan, she sat up all night in the bathroom of a friend's apartment in Moscow, writing on the window ledge, composing a letter to Aleksandr Shcherbakov, secretary of the Central Committee and a major force in cultural affairs. The letter went through fifteen to twenty versions. It was important to be brief, in Sats' view; on the other hand, it was also necessary to strike a personal note. In the letter to Shcherbakov, whom Sats did not know well, this meant slipping in a reminder of past contacts, however tenuous ("He probably knows me from past work. Once Aleksei Maksimovich Gorky mentioned me in a letter to him").[49]

Once the letter was finished, both Kapitsa and Sats agreed, it must be hand delivered. Kapitsa would send his wife, personal assistant, or secretary to deliver his letter to the Central Committee and obtain a receipt. Sats delivered her own letter by hand to Shcherbakov's assistant, asking him to give Shcherbakov the letter personally at once.[50]

[48] P. L. Kapitsa, *Pis'ma o nauke 1930–1980* (Moscow, 1989), passim and introduction by Kapitsa's former secretary P. E. Rubinin, pp. 11–12. In 1943 Kapitsa switched to "Much respected Viacheslav Mikhailovich" for Molotov and retained this style thereafter, using it also in his letters to Khrushchev, Mikoian, and Malenkov in the 1950s. Stalin remained "comrade Stalin" to the end, though from 1945 Kapitsa ended his letters to him with "Yours," or "Respectfully yours."

[49] Sats, *Zhizn'*, p. 446.

[50] Sats, *Zhizn'*, p. 446; Kapitsa, *Pis'ma*, pp. 11–12.

Although the approach to a patron was normally by letter, the reply, if there was one, usually came by telephone.[51] Two days after the delivery of her letter, Nataliia Sats received a telephone call from Shcherbakov's assistant giving her the good news that Shcherbakov supported her in the quarrels in the Kazakhstan theater world about which she had complained.[52] For a client to make his pitch to a patron over the telephone was apparently very rare, probably because this approach seemed insufficiently deferential. (There were exceptions, however. In 1937, the much-rewarded writer Aleksei Tolstoy had the nerve to telephone Molotov's secretary and request—though it came across almost as a demand—an eleven-room dacha in a particular location that he preferred to that of the dacha he had been offered.)[53]

THE HUMAN FACTOR: AFFECTIVE TIES BETWEEN PATRONS AND CLIENTS

In 1930 Mikhail Bulgakov received a telephone call from Stalin responding to his complaints about persecution and censorship and promising to remedy the situation. News of this call spread rapidly through the intelligentsia on the grapevine. As an anonymous police agent reported, the story had had an enormous impact on intellectuals' views of Stalin. "It's as if a dam had broken, and everyone around saw the true face of comrade Stalin." They speak of his simplicity and accessibility. They say that Stalin is not to blame for the bad things that happen; "he lays down the right line, but around him are scoundrels. These scoundrels persecuted Bulgakov, one of the most talented Soviet writers. Various literary rascals were making a career out of persecution of Bulgakov, and now Stalin has given them a slap in the face." Intellectuals were talking of Stalin "warmly and with love."[54]

The conventions of Soviet client-patron relations demanded that they be represented as based on friendship or at least mutual regard, or sometimes even in familial terms (the patron as father who "pitieth his children"). These conventions are most evident in the hagiographic memoir literature on great men—from political leaders like Ordzhonikidze to cultural figures like Maxim Gorky—in which the client-memoirist dwells affectionately on the deeply human traits (generosity, compassion, understanding, paternal

---

[51] K. Rossiyanov, "Stalin as Lysenko's Editor: Reshaping Political Discourse in Soviet Science," *Russian History* 21:1 (1994), pp. 49–63.

[52] Sats, *Zhizn'*, p. 446.

[53] GARF, f. 5446, op. 82, d. 56, l. 154. (Molotov approved this request, though he cut the dacha size down to ten rooms.)

[54] Shentalinskii, *Raby*, pp. 124–25.

solicitude) of the patron as well as emphasizing his high culture. Kalinin "looked up at me with sparkling eyes and smil[ed] his kind old-man's smile, as if his entire face had lit up in an instant." "Valerian Vladimirovich [Kuibyshev] was a many-sided man, a great connoisseur of art and literature, enchanting, uncommonly simple and modest in approach ... He liked nature and flowers very much. When we went out on the sea, he, with youthful animation, called us up on deck to enjoy the spectacle of the beautiful sunset. 'How sad that all this is so fleeting,' he said, when the multihued sky dulled and grey twilight descended."[55]

Although these memoirs were written for public consumption and, to a large extent, according to formula, we can find similar statements of affection for patrons in diaries.[56] This does not fully answer the question of how "sincere" such protestations were. But our interest is less in whether the emotions expressed were genuine than in the fact that their expression was conventionally required in a patronage situation. Even the irreverent Nadezhda Mandelstam writes of her husband's patron, Bukharin, with affection; and the cynical Shostakovich called Tukhachevsky his "friend" and "one of the most interesting people I knew," while acknowledging that, unlike other admirers of the Marshal, "I behaved very independently. I was cocky, [but] Tukhachevsky liked that."[57]

Evidence on patrons' attitudes to their clients is harder to come by than its obverse, but is not totally lacking: Molotov noted a "mutual liking" (*vzaimnaia byla takaia sviaz'*) between Voroshilov and his client, the painter Aleksandr Gerasimov. Khrushchev, whose connections with the intelligentsia in the 1930s seem to have been less abundant than those of many other leaders, emphasizes his personal regard in the few instances he recalls in his memoirs: for example, with regard to the engineer-inventor Paton.[58] Many client-memoirists describe their patrons as people whose happiness in life came from helping others (or specific categories of others, like young people or artists). As applied to Soviet party leaders, this may seem to us a bizarre characterization, yet for the leaders' own self-perception it surely had resonance. Given the harshness of Soviet rule in the 1930s, it cannot always have been easy for an obkom secretary or Politburo member to retain the sense (important for effective functioning as a

[55] Mikhail Sholokhov, "Velikii drug literatury," in *M. I. Kalinin ob iskusstve i literature: Stat'i, rechi, besedy* (Moscow, 1957), pp. 234–37; Galina Serebriakova, "V. V. Kuibyshev," in *O Valeriane Kuibysheve: Vospominaniia, ocherki, stat'i* (Moscow, 1983), pp. 219–21.

[56] For example, Galina Shtange on Lazar Kaganovich (patron of her women's group) in *Intimacy and Terror. Soviet Diaries of the 1930s*, eds. Véronique Garros, Natalia Korenevskaya, and Thomas Lahusen (New York, 1995), p. 184.

[57] Shostakovich, *Testimony*, p. 96.

[58] *Sto sorok besed*, p. 315; *Khrushchev Remembers*, trans. Strobe Talbott (Boston, 1970), pp. 116–19.

leader) of being basically a good man serving the interests of the people. Patronage activities, earning the gratitude, loyalty, and affection of clients and allowing a leader to demonstrate his own capacity for loyalty, generosity, and compassion, surely helped in this regard.

If a particular patron-client relationship was too distant for the notion of friendship to be appropriate, it was at least necessary to impart some touch of the personal. This is evident, albeit in stylized form, in the possibly anecdotal description that Vyshinsky's biographer provides of Vyshinsky's relationship with his client Aleksandr Vertinskii, a famous popular singer. After Vyshinsky had made possible Vertinskii's return from emigration in China, he supposedly attended one of Vertinskii's concerts, sitting "modestly in a side box hidden from inquisitive eyes behind velvet drapes. However, his presence was no secret to the artist on the stage. He knew perfectly well whom Destiny had appointed as his patron. When he started singing, as a token of respect he turned very slightly towards the box. Only very slightly but it was still noticeable. And he also bowed separately and with particular dignity towards the box."[59]

For Natalia Sats, exiled to the provinces in the 1940s, it was a matter of the highest importance to establish new clientelist ties in the towns to which she had been exiled. As her description makes clear, this meant trying by every means possible to arrange a meeting with a potential patron, and then—most important—somehow establishing personal rapport, however tenuous, in the course of the meeting. In Alma-Ata, for example, when Sats finally got to see Zhumbai Shaiakhmetov, second secretary of the Kazakhstan party, the success of the meeting—that is, the establishment of a personal connection—was demonstrated when Shaiakhmetov (who also knew how to play this game) playfully dispatched a messenger to Sats bearing the box of matches from his desk that, at their meeting, had momentarily distracted her attention. Later, when enemies in the Saratov theater were threatening to have her transferred further into the boondocks, she appealed "personally, tears running down my face," to the patron who had got her the job, G. A. Borkov, first secretary of the regional party organization.[60]

Hierarchies of Patronage

In his memoirs, Iurii Elagin tells the story of the epic "battle of patrons" between two well-connected theatrical figures, L. P. Ruslanov, administrator of the Vakhtangov theater, and A. D. Popov, director of the Moscow

[59] Vaksberg, *Prosecutor*, p. 237.
[60] Sats, *Zhizn'*, pp. 443–44, 479.

Red Army Theater. Ruslanov and Popov lived in the same apartment house, and the trouble arose when Popov hung flowerpots from his balcony that Ruslanov regarded as a potential danger to passers-by. Using his contacts, Ruslanov got an order from the head of the raion militia to remove the flowerpots; Popov trumped this by getting permission to keep his flower-pots from the head of the militia of the city of Moscow; Ruslanov then went to the chief director of militia of the whole Soviet Union for a removal order, to which Popov responded with a letter from Voroshilov instructing that he should not be further harrassed about his flowerpots. But Ruslanov was the winner when he went to Kalinin, president of the U.S.S.R., and obtained an order that the flowerpots should be removed.[61]

Apocryphal or not, this story is a nice illustration of the hierarchies of patronage that could be invoked by persistent and well-connected clients. The Vakhtangov theater, according to Elagin, had its set of middle-level patrons in the pre–1937 period—Maxim Gorky, Avel Enukidze, Daniil Sulimov (chairman of the Russian Council of Ministers), and Iakov Agranov (deputy head of the secret police)—"who were always ready to do everything possible for our theater." But there were also even more highly placed persons, notably Voroshilov and Molotov (both Politburo members, with Molotov as chairman of Sovnarkom) who could also be called on in extreme cases.[62] These middle-level patrons were themselves clients whose efficacy as patrons often depended on access to patrons at the very top. Thus, Gorky, for example, was effective as a patron only so long as Stalin, Molotov, Iagoda, etc. were prepared to honor his requests for his clients.

Naturally, in the politically perilous circumstances of the Soviet Union in the 1930s, a patron's status was not necessarily stable: he might rise and fall in the hierarchy of patronage; indeed he might even fall from the status of patron completely and become a client-supplicant.[63] Bukharin provides a good illustration of this process. As the sharp-eyed Nadezhda Mandelstam noted, "Up until 1928 he would cry 'Idiots!' and seize the

[61] Elagin, *Ukroshchenie*, pp. 66–69.

[62] Elagin, *Ukroshchenie*, p. 48.

[63] Note that patronage relations were not without risk to the client: the patron might be disgraced. In 1939 the young writer A. O. Avdeenko was blamed for his connections with unmasked "enemies of the people," the industrialist Gvkhariia and Urals party leader Kaba-kov (D. L. Babichenko, *Pisateli i tsenzory: Sovetskaia literatura 1940-kh godov pod poli-ticheskim kontrolem TsK* [Moscow, 1994], pp. 26–27). Pilniak was another whose connec-tions with Opposition figures were held against him. It has been suggested that the fall of theater director Vsevolod Meyerhold at the end of the 1930s was associated with his clien-telist ties to Trotsky and Zinoviev in the early 1920s (*Testimony*, p. 80) or to Rykov and other "Rightists" at the end of the decade (Elagin, *Temnyi genii*, p. 319), but Meyerhold had so many political patrons at various times that this is hard to judge (it is equally plausible to link his fate with that of his NKVD patrons of the 1930s).

telephone, but from 1930 he would frown and say: 'I have to think whom to ask (*komu obratit'sia*) . . . [*sic*].' " Molotov was one patron whom Bukharin successfully approached on Mandelstam's behalf in the early 1930s, and, although Bukharin did not know Gorky particularly well, he recognized his power as a patron in the early '30s and "kept wanting to go to 'Maksimych' in his search for 'transmission channels.' " Ordzhonikidze and Voroshilov were figures to whom he turned on his own behalf in the last years.[64]

Perils and Pleasures of Patronage

As already noted, there were no obvious tangible benefits to the Soviet patron in having clients. Soviet officials' tenure was not dependent on popularity or winning elections. Clients might praise their patrons' generosity, but too fulsome expressions of enthusiasm for a local leader could provoke the accusation that he was developing a local "cult of personality." Indeed, in the suspicion-laden world of Stalinist politics, there were definite risks associated with being too active or committed a patron. The pejorative words *khvosty*[65] and *semeistva*[66] were frequently invoked when local leaders were unmasked as "enemies of the people" during the Great Purges. An example of the possible pitfalls of patronage comes from the memoirs of Ivan Gronskii, *Izvestiia* editor, who was a patron of old-school realist artists in the 1930s. The day after a group of his "clients" escorted him home as a gesture of appreciation after his pro-realism intervention at an artists' meeting, Gronskii received a telephone call from Stalin with the abrupt and threatening query: "What kind of demonstration was that yesterday (*Chto vchera byla za demonstratsiia*)"?[67]

That patronage of the intelligentsia could be a negative in Stalin's eyes is confirmed by Molotov's reported comments on Voroshilov, who "loved to play a bit at being, so to speak, a patron of the arts (*metsenat*), a protector (*pokrovitel'*) of artists and so on." Stalin saw this as a weakness, "because artists, they're easily duped (*rotozei*). They are harmless in themselves, but around them swarm all kinds of dubious riffraff (*shantrapa*

---

[64] Mandel'shtam, *Vospominaniia*, p. 124; Gronskii, *Iz proshlogo*, p. 125; Anna Larina, *This I Cannot Forget*, trans. Gary Kern (New York, 1993), pp. 310, 328.

[65] Means entourage (literally, tails), as in "He brought his entourage with him when he took up the new job."

[66] Means mutual-protection circles (literally, family groups).

[67] Gronskii, *Iz proshlogo*, p. 143. Note, however, that despite this threatening preamble, Stalin was sympathetic to the artists when Gronskii described their situation and actively took up their cause, according to Gronskii's account.

polosataia). They exploit that connection—with Voroshilov's subordinates, with his family . . ."[68]

The archetypal example of a good Bolshevik ruined by his taste for patronage was Avel Enukidze, secretary of the Central Executive Committee of the Congress of Soviets (TsIK), whose dramatic fall from grace in 1935 was one of the harbingers of the Great Purges. Enukidze was well known both as a patron of the arts with a taste for ballerinas and as one of the party leaders who was most likely to be sympathetic to the plight of "former people," members of the old nobility and privileged classes who were liable to disenfranchisement and other forms of discrimination in the Soviet period.[69] The accusations made at the June 1935 plenum focused particularly on the latter: in Ezhov's words, "Enukidze created a situation in which any Whiteguard could and did get in to work in the Kremlin, often using the direct support and high protection (*pokrovitel'stvom*) of Enukidze." People got a job in the TsIK *apparatu* through friends and family connections, and Enukidze himself "was linked through personal, friendly relations" with many TsIK employees. Even when their alien social backgrounds and "anti-Soviet attitudes" were reported to Enukidze by the NKVD, he continued to shield them and refused to fire them. He used government money from TsIK's "secret fund" to support various unfortunates, including 600 rubles to "Stepanova, one of the wives of the writer [Nikolai] Erdman, exiled for a lampoon against Soviet power." All this made Enukidze "the most typical example of a degenerating and complacent Communist who not only fails to see the class enemy, but actually forms an alliance (*smykat'sia*) with him," in Ezhov's words.[70] It also led inexorably to corruption, sexual as well as financial.[71]

Defending himself at the closed session of the Central Committee, Enukidze regretted having involuntarily aided the class enemy in some in-

---

[68] *Sto sorok besed*, p. 315.

[69] The TsIK archive contains many instances: see, for example, GARF, f. 3316, op. 2, d. 918, ll. 1–13 (1930 memo from Enukidze to Stalin on abuses of disenfranchisement) and ibid., d. 1227, l. 101 (conflict between Enukidze and the Moscow OGPU in 1933 over denial of passports to "former people").

[70] RGASPI, f. 17, op. 2, d. 542, ll. 79–86 (stenogram with speakers' corrections of proceedings at the plenum). Thanks to Arch Getty for generously making this material available to me.

[71] Bribes and presents of a thousand rubles or more (evidently accepted by Enukidze's subordinates, not Enukidze himself) were mentioned in Ezhov's indictment. Sex is not explicitly mentioned in the surviving text of Ezhov's indictment, but it must have been there originally since Enukidze denied that he had "had affairs (*sozhitel'stvoval*) with any of those who were arrested" (RGASPI, f. 17, op. 2, d. 542, l. 128). For gossip about the sexual aspect of the Enukidze scandal, see "Dnevnik M. A. Svanidze," in *Iosif Stalin v ob"iatiiakh sem'i: Iz lichnogo arkhiva* (Moscow, 1993), p. 182.

stances, but still managed to convey that his patronage was needed and justifiable in human terms. "There were really a lot of people to whom I gave that help that is now characterized as my high protection in regard to certain persons. Unfortunately, circumstances were such that people appealed to me for everything: if they needed an apartment, material help, things (*veshchi*), or to be sent somewhere to a rest home. Through me, both our people (*nashi*) and people alien to us (*chuzhie*) received aid; I distributed that aid to everyone."[72]

What Enukidze personally got out of his patronage activities (before he lost his life for them) is not known. In general, however, what patrons got out of patronage were intangibles: prestige and status associated with the ability to act as a patron; a sense of *noblesse oblige* or a desire to play the great man as it was traditionally played; a desire to see themselves as good, generous people; a desire to receive flattery and gratitude from clients. "Tukhachevsky liked being a patron of the arts," wrote his client and friend Shostakovich. "He liked finding 'young talents' and helping them. Perhaps because the marshal himself had been a military *Wunderkind*, or perhaps because he liked demonstrating his enormous power."[73] Patronage is a traditional prerogative of power and also a visible mark of it. Writing of her refusal on principle to establish patronage connections, an informant in Ledeneva's blat study notes that "the nomenclatura people I met did not pay me any respect for that [refusal]. They respected those who made them feel powerful and helpful."[74] They would have thought better of her, she felt, if she had approached them as a humble client asking for favors.

There were added benefits in the case of patronage of the arts, viz access to the world of celebrity and glamor—famous singers and film actors, writers and scientists of international renown—to which members of Stalin's Politburo were drawn just as contemporary American politicians are often drawn to Hollywood and sports stars. Like rulers in many societies, Stalinist politicians obviously felt that contact with the arts and scientists adorned them. To some degree, patronage was an indicator of *kul'turnost'* for Soviet leaders. In the Gronskii story cited above, Gronskii portrayed himself as embarrassed but also flattered by the fulsomely expressed admiration of the artists—"famous old masters of painting," as he puts it.[75]

There was even some allure in the risk inherent in acting as patron to someone of high reputation in the cultural world who was under a cloud.

[72] RGASPI, f. 17, op. 2, d. 542, 139.

[73] *Testimony*, p. 98.

[74] Alena V. Ledeneva, "Formal Institutions and Informal Networks in Russia: A Study of Blat," Ph.D. diss., Cambridge University, 1996, pp. 105–6.

[75] Gronskii, *Iz proshlogo*, pp. 142–43.

This is most often seen in the case of middle-level patrons such as journal editors, who would take the risk of publishing a controversial poem or story because of the kudos to be gained within the intelligentsia through such boldness. But the same dynamic may have operated at a higher level: for example, in Vyshinskii's patronage of the former émigré singer Vertinskii, whose semidisgrace was underlined by the ban on publicizing the concerts that he was occasionally allowed to give after his return.[76]

. . .

Patronage networks are important to the functioning of many societies, and patronage of the arts exists in some form in virtually all, but how much patronage matters in the day to day life of clients and patrons depends on the seriousness and frequency of the clients' need for protection. Stalin's Russia was a dangerous place to live in. Insecurity and the ever-present danger of a major personal calamity were a fact of life in the elites as much as (perhaps more than) lower social strata. It was not uncommon, even in the privileged intelligentsia, for a person suddenly to find himself in truly desperate straits as a result of the loss of an apartment or ration privileges, or an accident at work that was construed as "wrecking." Arrest or the public besmirching of reputation that might lead to loss of employment and arrest were also common occurrences. Having a patron to "go to" could make the difference between surviving or failing to survive.

This was one of the features of Soviet patronage that distinguished it from patronage in late Imperial Russia or most other modern societies. Another distinguishing feature was that goods and services were in chronically short supply in the Stalin period, and the party-state had monopoly control over their distribution. If one had the misfortune to be without a decent apartment in Moscow, how else could one obtain it without recourse to a patron? If one's child suddenly fell critically ill, how else could one get access to the right doctor and the right hospital to treat her? If one lost one's job or was arbitrarily denied access to the "closed" food store, how would one remedy the situation except by appeal to a patron? The malfunctioning of the Soviet legal system was another of the features of Stalinist society that made patronage practices—as well as their humbler counterpart, petitioning—essential.

One of the fascinating aspects of patronage in Stalinist society is its strange relationship to official ideology. On the one hand, the patron-client relationship exemplified the personalistic interests of officialdom that were routinely deplored and sometimes harshly punished as corrup-

[76] Vaksberg, *Prosecutor*, p. 237.

tion. On the other hand, this same relationship exemplified the human and familial motif that was at the heart of Stalinist discourse about rulers and people.[77] In the familial metaphor, the whole Soviet Union was a family (*sem'ia*) with Stalin as the father, and it is only a short semantic step from "sem'ia" to "semeistvo" (the pejorative applied to political patronage relations). If Stalin was "father" and "benefactor" of his people, was he not by the same token the universal "patron" of Soviet citizens, bound by ties of mutual affection to his "clients"? Were not all the *vozhdi*, local and regional, construed as benevolent patrons of the citizenry, ready to respond to need and rescue from distress? It may be argued that patron-client relations in the everyday world were exactly what gave that rhetoric a grounding in reality for Soviet citizens, making patronage practices a kind of intuitive proof of the ideological premise that the Soviet regime was the people's benefactor.

[77] My thinking here is indebted to discussion with Yuri Slezkine as well as Katerina Clark's treatment of the "Great Family" myth in *The Soviet Novel. History as Ritual* (Chicago, 1985), pp. 114–17.

PART IV

Denunciations

CHAPTER ELEVEN

Signals from Below

> DENUNCIATION (donos). A weapon of war of reaction-
> ary forces of the bourgeoisie and Black Hundreds against the
> revolutionary movement—information [given] to the Tsarist
> or other reactionary government about revolutionary acts
> that were secretly being prepared. [Examples] *Acting on a de-*
> *nunciation from a traitor, Tsarist gendarmes broke up an un-*
> *derground Bolshevik organization. Fascists threw a group of*
> *Komsomols into prison on the basis of a provocateur's*
> *denunciation.*
> SIGNAL (signal). 2. A warning about something undesir-
> able that may happen, a putting on guard (predosterezhenie).
> [Example] *The Bolshevik Party demands sensitivity to the sig-*
> *nals coming from below by way of self-criticism.*[1]

Denunciation—the voluntary reporting of wrongdoing by other citizens
to the authorities—is a highly ambiguous practice. In some contexts, a
denunciation may be read as an exemplary act of civic virtue, motivated
by altruistic concern for the public good. More often, however, denunciations are construed as acts of betrayal, motivated by venality or malice.
Language reflects these ambiguities and complexities. Two different
terms for the practice may exist simultaneously, one neutral or positive
(French, *dénonciation*; Stalinist-period Russian, *signal*) and the other pejorative (French, *délation*; Russian, *donos*). Euphemisms abound, like
the contemporary American "whistle-blowing." The related and almost
universally despised practice of informing—that is, regular denunciation
that is paid or otherwise rewarded—has generated whole hosts of colloquial pejoratives.

How to distinguish "good" denunciation from "bad" has exercised
many writers. Contemplating the moral status of practices of public accu-

---

This is an abridged version of "Signals from Below: Soviet Letters of Denunciation of
the 1930s," first published in *Journal of Modern History* 68:4 (1996) and reprinted in *Accu-*
satory Practices: Denunciation in Modern European History, 1789–1989, eds. Sheila Fitzpatrick and Robert Gellately (Chicago, 1996).

[1] *Tolkovyi slovar' russkogo iazyka*, ed. D. N. Ushakov, 4 vols. (Moscow, 1935–40):
Donos entry.

sation (delation) in ancient Rome, an early twentieth-century edition of the *Encyclopedia Britannica* concluded that the key distinction was between interested and disinterested accusation: "When exercised from patriotic and disinterested motives, [the] . . . effects [of delation] were beneficial; but the moment the principle of reward was introduced, this was no longer the case."[2] Diderot's encyclopedia suggested a more complex division based on intention: "One is inclined to think that the delator is a corrupt man, the accuser an angry man, and the denouncer an indignant man," while noting that "these three personages are equally odious in the eyes of the people."[3]

Denunciation has attracted less attention from twentieth-century thinkers than it did from those of the eighteenth century. When it has been discussed in English-speaking countries, it is usually in the context of totalitarianism and in a tone of confident moral superiority that recalls an older liberal-protestant Anglo-Saxon tradition of writing about the Inquisition.[4] Yet denunciation is a phenomenon of everyday life that exists in every society, albeit with great variation in type, visibility (the degree to which the practice is recognized and problematized) and rate of incidence. The Soviet Union of the 1930s, with its multiplicity of types of denunciation, strong visibility, and high incidence, provides a rich but by no means unique case study.

There were well-established traditions of denunciation in Russia long before the Bolsheviks took power in 1917.[5] The Bolsheviks and other Russian revolutionaries despised these traditions and associated them with the corruption of the old regime, as their counterparts in the French Revolution had done before them. Yet, at the same time it quickly became clear to the Bolsheviks, just as it had to the Jacobins, that *revolutionary* denunciation was both necessary and virtuous. It was necessary to encourage citizens to denounce enemies, spies, and plots because of the danger of counterrevolution. Within the revolutionary party, moreover, denunciation of backsliders and hypocrites was the duty of every member, a guarantee of the continued purity and transparency on which the revolution depended. Unlike the Jacobins, the Bolsheviks did not philosophize about

---

[2] *The Encyclopaedia Britannica*, 11th ed., vol. 7 (New York, 1910): Delator entry.

[3] *Encyclopédie ou Dictionnaire Raisonné des Sciences, des Arts et des Métiers, par une Société de Gens de Lettres Mis en ordre et publié par M. Diderot*, vol. 10 (Lausanne/Berne, 1779).

[4] The locus classicus is Henry Charles Lea, *A History of the Inquisition of Spain in Four Volumes* (London, 1906).

[5] On denunciation in the Muscovite and Petrine periods, see A. M. Kleimola, "The Duty to Denounce in Muscovite Russia," *Slavic Review* 31:4 (December 1972); Richard Hellie, "The Origins of Denunciation in Muscovy Law," *Russian History*, 24:1–2 (1997); Evgenii Anisimov, "Donos," *Rodina*, 1990 no. 7.

the principle of denunciation, but they instinctively adopted the practice, just as every other sect of revolutionary or religious enthusiasts has done over the ages.[6] There can be no secrets in the community of saints.

With time came routinization. The Bolshevik Party's concern for purity was institutionalized in the periodic party "cleansings" or purges of the 1920s and 1930s, in which each member had to give a public account of himself and respond to questions, criticisms, and accusations. The practice of denunciation of Communist by Communist was embedded in this ritual, though it also existed independently of it.

As for popular denunciation, the type actively encouraged by the regime was citizens' denunciation of wrongdoing by officials. This was conceived as a kind of popular monitoring of bureaucracy that was also a form of democratic political participation. One institutional product was the workers' and peasants' inspectorate that was much on Lenin's mind in his last years. Another was the recruitment of worker and peasant correspondents for newspapers, volunteer amateur stringers whose job was to serve as "the eyes and ears of Soviet power," reporting local abuses of power by Soviet officials as well as keeping watch on the activities of class enemies like kulaks and priests. A third product was the institution of "self-criticism" in factories and enterprises to stimulate the airing of workers' grievances and denunciation of wrongdoing and incompetence on the part of managers and specialists.[7]

Denunciation as a social practice was greatly encouraged by the regime's decision in the late 1920s to expropriate, deport, and otherwise punish whole categories of class enemies. Such enemies, who were prone to conceal their identity, had to be "unmasked," and denunciation was an important part of this process. A few years later, denunciation acquired its official hero and martyr in Pavlik Morozov, a young Pioneer (or so the story had it) murdered by relatives after denouncing his own father for trying to cheat the Soviet government by hoarding grain. For more than fifty years, until his monuments were (literally) toppled by resentful citizens in the Gorbachev era, Pavlik remained an exemplar of the virtuous Soviet child who put public interests above private and family loyalty.[8]

The Great Purges of 1937–38 gave further impetus to popular denunciation, as citizens were exhorted to watch out for spies and saboteurs and unmask hidden "enemies of the people," a term applied primarily to dis-

[6] See Colin Lucas, "The Theory and Practice of Denunciation in the French Revolution," in *Accusatory Practices*, pp. 22–39.

[7] In Bolshevik jargon, "self-criticism" originally meant the self-criticism of the collective. But the meaning it acquired in practice was public criticism of bosses by the rank-and-file, and the bosses' acceptance of such criticism (q.v., Ushakov's definition of "Signal," above).

[8] On the cult of Pavlik Morozov, see Robert Conquest, *Harvest of Sorrow* (New York, 1986), pp. 293–96, and Fitzpatrick, *Stalin's Peasants*, pp. 254–56.

graced Communist bosses. Soon the tide of denunciation rose so high that party leaders became disturbed by its disastrous impact on government efficiency and industrial output, and started to inveigh against "false (*lozhnye*) denunciations," meaning accusations that were hysterical and unfounded or that served the denouncer's private interests rather than the public good. It should be noted, however, that citizens' denunciations constituted only one of a number of sources of what was known in Soviet parlance as "compromising information."[9] The Soviet secret police was a large organization, and in addition to its network of regular informers (*sekretnye sotrudniki*) it also collected a great deal of the material used against "enemies of the people" through interrogation of prisoners and members of the free population.

For the purposes of this discussion, a denunciation will be defined as a written communication to the authorities, voluntarily offered, that gives damaging information about another person.[10] Contrary to the stereotype of denunciations in a police state, Soviet denunciations were not addressed exclusively or even mainly to the secret police.[11] Communist denunciations of other Communists were usually sent to some organ of the Communist Party.[12] Other denunciations were sent to the government and

[9] A Russian scholar working with materials from the KGB archives in the Urals reports that most denunciations in investigatory files are statements obtained by the police in the process of investigation, and only a few are voluntary "signals" from members of the public: S. M. Popova, "Sistema donositel'stva v 30-e gody [K probleme sozdaniia bazy dannykh na materialakh Urala]," *Klio*, 1991 no. 1, pp. 71–72. (Thanks to Hiroaki Kuromiya for alerting me to this article.)

[10] This follows the definition of denunciation (*donos*) given in a standard Soviet dictionary, namely a secret communication to a representative of the regime or a superior about somebody's illegal activity (S. I. Ozhegov, *Slovar' russkogo iazyka* [Moscow, 1964]). I have substituted "damaging information" for "illegal activity" because the latter is too narrow to cover the range of proscribed, hence denunciable, behaviors. (It was not illegal, for example, to have been a supporter of Trotsky in the 1920s, yet many Communists were denounced for this in the 1930s.) Note that my definition covers only letters written by citizens on their own initiative and in a private capacity. It excludes the following types of written document: reports (*doneseniia*) by regular police informers or by officials writing in the line of duty, and denunciatory statements (*pokazaniia*) solicited from citizens and prisoners by the NKVD in the course of interrogation or otherwise.

[11] The denunciations used in this chapter came from a large variety of party and government archives, but unfortunately the NKVD (now FSB) archive was not accessible to me. However, judging by Vladimir Kozlov's study of denunciations sent to the secret police in the 1940s, these denunciations are of similar type to those in other archives (Vladimir A. Kozlov, "Denunciation and its Functions in Soviet Governance: A Study of Denunciations and their Bureaucratic Handling from Soviet Police Archives, 1944–1953," in *Accusatory Practices*, pp. 121–52).

[12] The Central Committee, the Central Control Commission (Commission of Party Control) and its regional branches, regional party committees, the political administrations of the Red Army and other quasi-militarized sectors, etc.

to individual government agencies such as Rabkrin, the People's Commissariat of Workers' and Peasants' Inspection. Some people sent their denunciations directly to Stalin, Molotov, or another Politburo member, or to the first party party secretary in their region, who was often the object of a regional "cult of personality" similar to Stalin's. Citizens also sent denunciations directly to the procuracy and the NKVD, or, as in the case of other letters to authority, to newspapers. Many denunciations were sent to newspapers *and* the relevant government and party bodies, even though each letter cost the sender 20 kopeks in postage.

There were *practices* of denunciation in Stalin's Russia, not just a single practice. While the most familiar might be called the politically motivated "Pavlik Morozov" denunciation, in which a citizen performed his duty of informing the state of a threat to its security, several less familiar types are equally important. Subaltern denunciations—"weapons of the weak," in James C. Scott's phrase—were an important category of denunciation: they allowed ordinary people to accuse powerful people of malfeasance and abuses.[13] Private interest denunciations—those intended to produce some specific benefit or satisfaction for the writer—often mimicked the forms of "Pavlik Morozov" and subaltern denunciations, but had as their purpose the disgrace of a professional rival or competitor in village politics, the eviction of a neighbor from a crowded communal apartment, or the settling of scores with a personal enemy.

Political disloyalty, class origin, and abuse of power are the three main types of accusation made in denunciations of the 1930s. A fourth type, immorality, is much less common in the prewar period. Let us examine each of these in turn.

DISLOYALTY

There were many ways in which a person could be compromised politically, the most important being past membership of an opposition within the party (Trotskyite, Zinovievite, Rightist) or of another political party such as the SRs or the Mensheviks. Other allegations of disloyalty run the gamut from "anti-Soviet conversation" to terrorism and counterrevolutionary conspiracy. "Compromising facts" commonly cited include supporting the White armies during the Civil War, participating in uprisings against Soviet power, and connections of any kind with Oppositionists, foreigners, or émigré relatives.

[13] James C. Scott, *Weapons of the Weak: Everyday Forms of Peasant Resistance* (New Haven, 1985).

It was the duty of Communists to make known to the Party any compromising information about other Communists that came to their attention. Some writers of loyalty denunciations used the formulaic preamble "I consider it my party duty to inform you . . ." But many dispensed with any introductory phrase or used the more ambiguous "I consider it necessary to inform you . . ." Many such denunciations were evidently written out of fear of the consequences of *not* writing, especially during the Great Purges, when the volume of loyalty denunciations increased markedly.

Some "loyalty" denunciations appear to have been written in a spirit of public service, though such subjective evaluations of decontextualized texts are obviously fallible. For example, the Leningrad Communist writer Vera Ketlinskaia conveyed a kind of civic spirit, albeit on the hysterical side, in her letter to Leningrad party secretary Andrei Zhdanov about enemies in the Communist leadership of Komsomolsk, a new town in the Soviet Far East from which she had just returned in the fall of 1937.[14] In more measured terms, a group of young South Osetian Komsomols working on the construction of the Moscow Metro wrote a collective letter addressed to Stalin, Kaganovich, Molotov, and Kalinin warning them of the degeneration of the party leadership in South Osetiia as a result of Mensheviks and "opportunists" worming their way in.[15]

Other denunciations had a sound of genuine outrage. One indignant citizen, probably a young engineer, wrote to Nikolai Ezhov[16] in 1936 asking him to "pay attention to some outrageous facts" about the director of the "Red Flag" factory in Leningrad who made fun of young Communist engineers, mocked the factory party committee, helped people who had been arrested as terrorists by the NKVD, and on top of that was of alien social origin—the son of a rich merchant under the old regime.[17]

As might be expected, malice made itself felt in many denunciations, though no doubt the more skillful writers were able to conceal it. Perhaps more disconcerting than everyday malice was the spirit of the Young Avenger that imbued some denunciations from adolescent vigilantes. A fourteen-year village Komsomol member, for example, wrote to Stalin in 1937 in terms of excited self-congratulation and bloodlust about the local Trotskyites that remained to be arrested in his district, not to mention the bandits in the forest. This boy, eager to make his mark in the Pavlik Morozov mode, boasted that he had already "bagged" one kolkhoz chairman.[18]

---

[14] TsGA IPD, f. 24, op. 2v, d. 2222, ll. 202–8.

[15] GARF, f. 5446, op. 82, d. 42, l. 103.

[16] The same Ezhov who headed the NKVD during the Great Purges. This denunciation, however, was sent to him (by name) at his earlier post in the Commission of Party Control.

[17] TsGA IPD, f. 24, op. 2v, d. 1570, ll. 216, 219.

[18] The verb *posadit'*, whose colloquial meaning is to cause to be imprisoned, fortunately has no English analogue. TsGA IPD, f. 24, op. 2v, d. 2226, ll. 78–79.

During the Great Purges, as in several earlier periods of Russian history, failure to denounce could have very serious consequences, particularly for a Communist. The archival files for 1937–38 contain many denunciations from Communists that were surely written from fear, or at least to be on the safe side, rather than out of any real sense of duty, outrage, or even malice. One such denunciation was sent to Gamarnik, head of the Red Army's political administration, in 1935.[19] Its subject was an anti-Soviet conversation at a drinking party the previous summer. In the presence of the writer (and "a lot of other comrades"), "comrade Smirnov, having had a bit to drink, made a speech in defense of Zinoviev and especially Trotsky." He said that "if Lenin were alive, Trotsky, Zinoviev, Bukharin and the others would be in the Politburo and would have worked for the good of the party, and that in general the wheel of history would probably have turned in another direction," and he called Trotsky "exceptionally talented," second only to Lenin in the Party. The comments were sufficiently rash that at least one listener was likely to pass them on, which meant that the others present would be in trouble for keeping silent. The writer's basically self-defensive motivation and lack of enthusiasm for his task was palpable: "I cannot, as a party member, fail to report this, despite the fact that it was at an evening party (*vecherinka*) and despite the fact that Smirnov was half drunk." The letter ended on a fine note of bathos: since Smirnov was reportedly "a professor of dialectics," the writer concluded, he "should not make such remarks even when drunk."

The Great Purges stimulated many denunciations about conspiracies and sinister signs and connections whose full import (the authors write) had only just become clear. In Siberia a semiliterate woman farmworker wrote to the regional party committee in 1937 to say that reading "all those articles by comrade Zhdanov and Vyshinsky"[20] had made her wonder about the loyalty of a party organizer who had worked at her state farm in 1933: his mother-in-law, who came from Latvia, used the prerevolutionary salutation "Sir" (*gospodin*), and the man himself inherited sixty dollars from a Latvian relative.[21]

Early in 1937, a local prosecutor wrote in, apropos of the recent suicide of the Leningrad oblast prosecutor, Palgov, to say that he had just thought of something sinister: Palgov had a friend called Nechanov, also a prosecutor, whose wife had once denounced or threatened to denounce her husband as a Trotskyite. Were Palgov and Nechanov involved in some

---

[19] TsGA IPD, f. 24, op. 2v, d. 1518, l. 94.

[20] Andrei Zhdanov was the party leader who took over in Leningrad after Kirov's assassination. Andrei Vyshinsky was the State Prosecutor in the famous show trials of former opposition leaders held in Moscow in 1936, 1937, and 1938.

[21] PANO, f. 3, op. 11, d. 41, l. 97.

sort of plot together? Might this not explain both Palgov's suicide and Nechanov's strangely rapid promotion?[22]

An engineer wrote a loyalty denunciation about an official named Uralov who was in charge of purchasing aircraft and determining their routes. Uralov always made the wrong decisions, and the writer had many conflicts with him. "At the time it seemed to me that Uralov was simply ignorant, uninformed, not a real engineer but just an incompetent," the engineer wrote to the Political Administration of the Northern Sea Routes in November 1937, "but after my investigation of the Tiumen air route I analyzed a number of facts and came to the conclusion that *Uralov is an enemy, a wrecker.*"[23]

Such illumination was sometimes conveyed in exalted tones. "I accuse Popovian, a party member since 1918, of being an enemy of the people, a Trotskyite," wrote M. P. Gribanova, a Communist, to her local party committee in October 1937. Gribanova had worked with Popovian when he was chief physician in a hospital on the island of Spitzbergen. She remembered that he and his wife had a very suspicious meeting behind closed doors with a Norwegian who came to the hospital at eight o'clock in the morning: "The conversation was conducted rather quietly, in English and sometimes in German. Before [the Norwegian] left, Popovian gave him a package and added something in German, but I don't know what it was."[24]

Sometimes there was a note of urgency, almost desperation, about the fact that an obvious enemy had so far escaped detection. "I don't understand why up to the present time S. P. Vaniushin still enjoys honor and respect . . . Who is protecting him?" asked one baffled denouncer in May 1938.[25] "I have already written eight times to various places, but for some reason Vaniushin still survives unscathed." Given the facts cited in the letter, notably Vaniushin's close contacts with prominent Communist leaders who had been shot as enemies of the people, it was indeed surprising that Vaniushin remained at liberty. Such people were not only in great danger themselves but also constituted an involuntary danger to all around them. This was perhaps why the author, probably a colleague of Vaniushin's, was so anxious for Vaniushin to be removed from his environment.

Similar concerns are evident in one of the most striking denunciations I have encountered, a letter sent to the editor of *Pravda* (Lev Mekhlis) by a Komsomol student of a Leningrad technical institute in 1936.[26] The

[22] TsGA IPD, f. 24, op. 2v, d. 2478, ll. 25–26.

[23] RGASPI, f. 475, op. 1, d. 10, ll. 356–57 (emphasis in the original).

[24] RGASPI, f. 475, op. 1, d. 10, l. 2.

[25] RGASPI, f. 475, op. 1, d. 16, ll. 180–82.

[26] TsGA IPD, f. 24, op. 2v, d. 1628, ll. 79–82.

student was in "torment," he wrote, because N. V. Kitaev, another student at his institute, had just been reinstated in the Party despite having supported Zinoviev in the party debates of 1925–26 and, worse, having been a co-worker and perhaps even friend of one of the Leningrad Oppositionists executed for complicity in Kirov's murder.

> How can a parasite WHO ALWAYS SOBS WHEN HE HEARS LENIN'S NAME AND GROANS WHEN HE HEARS STALIN'S (those are not just words, comrade Mekhlis, but the appalling truth), how can such a person be allowed to remain within the walls of the institute, how can we, comrade Mekhlis, shelter such a snake in our bosom?

Since he became "so agitated" about Kitaev's continued presence, the author wrote, Mekhlis might suspect that he had some personal grievance against Kitaev.

> No comrade Mekhlis, it's much worse—for four years, until February 1935, we venerated him as a "real party man," politically highly developed, an activist, someone who always spoke up at every meeting and assembly, who could quote Lenin and Stalin and in our (the Komsomol members') eyes was the INCARNATION OF PARTY CONSCIENCE, ethics, and PARTY SPIRIT.

It was painful to recall that the Komsomol students of the Institute had defended Kitaev a few years earlier when the Institute tried to expel him for academic failure, but now this previous admiration had turned to hatred.

> Since Kirov's murder, [Kitaev] arouses an animal fear in me, an organic disgust. Just as I previously venerated him and respected him, now I fear him and expect him to do something terribly evil, some irreparable harm to the whole country. If you could have seen the unfeigned joy we all felt . . . when we learned of his expulsion [later revoked] from the Institute after the execution of Zinoviev and Kamenev . . . It is impossible and criminal to allow him to finish his studies at the Institute, because comrade Mekhlis even THE CAMPS OF THE NKVD WILL NOT REFORM HIM . . . I am terribly sorry now that he was not sitting next to his hero Zinoviev and Kamenev [in the court that ordered their execution].

CLASS ORIGINS

As grounds for denunciation, class origins were popular with urban and rural citizens alike. Among urban writers, somewhat unexpectedly, non-

Communists seem to have been more likely to write class denunciations than Communists, and their letters often hinted that party and government leaders were too lenient on questions of class.

A good proportion of class denunciations simply stated that someone who was a member of the party or held a responsible position was of alien class origin and ought to be expelled from the party and dismissed from his job. For example, a person identifying himself as nonparty wrote to the Leningrad party committee in 1935 to say that there were many class enemies (whom he named) in the local soviet: two daughters of a rich kulak who had been arrested and died in prison were working in the education department, the daughter of a former landowner was employed as court secretary, there were kulaks in the agriculture department, and "no fewer than three kulaks" in the State Bank.[27]

A more passionate denunciation came from nine "old party members, civil war veterans" who wrote to Molotov in 1934 (see figure 8) about class enemies in responsible positions in the Crimean party organization: four merchants' sons; two priest's sons, including one who was a former Tsarist officer; three mullah's sons, one of them rector of the local Communist University, and so on. Everybody knew about this, but kept quiet. The authors were afraid to sign their letter for fear of retaliation. But if Molotov did not respond to their letter, they wrote, "then we will appeal to comrade Stalin, and if comrade Stalin does not take measures, then one must say straight out that our regime is not socialist but KULAK."[28]

A Siberian miner wrote to the regional party secretary to denounce the chairman of the local trade union, whom he had just heard was "the son of a big merchant," married to a kulak's daughter, who had got into the Party by changing his name and concealing his real identity. "This bastard should be driven out of the trade union," the miner wrote. "If you don't take measures, I will write directly to the Central Committee of the party."[29]

The implied threats in these last two denunciations were atypical but by no means unique. A small but distinct subgroup of denouncers seemed to enjoy the sensation of bullying the important man to whom they addressed their letter and/or hinting that he, and perhaps the regime as a whole, shared the sins of the individual being denounced.

The underlying theme of many class denunciations was resentment that "they" (the formerly privileged and powerful, who had retained at least part of their power under the new regime) "still treat us as they used to in the old days." When the Siberian Waterways Administration was going

---

[27] TsGA IPD, f. 24, op. 2v, d. 1518, ll. 164–66.
[28] GARF, f. 5446, op. 82, d. 27, l. 172.
[29] PANO, f. 3, op. 9, d. 801, l. 209.

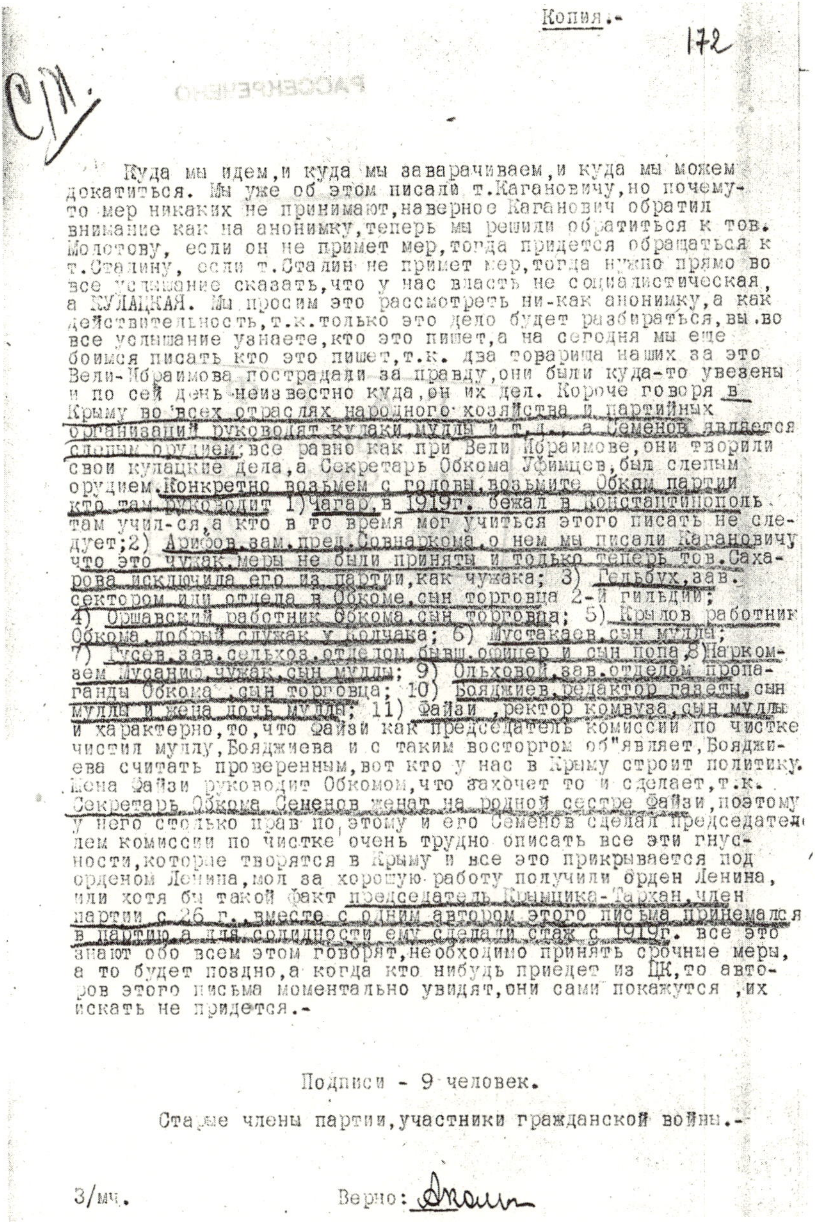

Копия.-

172

РАССЕКРЕЧЕНО

Куда мы идем, и куда мы заварачиваем, и куда мы можем докатиться. Мы уже об этом писали т.Кагановичу, но почему-то мер никаких не принимают, наверное Каганович обратил внимание как на анонимку, теперь мы решили обратиться к тов. Молотову, если он не примет мер, тогда придется обращаться к т.Сталину, если т.Сталин не примет мер, тогда нужно прямо во все услышание сказать, что у нас власть не социалистическая, а КУЛАЦКАЯ. Мы просим это рассмотреть ни-как анонимку, а как действительность, т.к. только это дело будет разбираться, вы. во все услышание узнаете, кто это пишет, а на сегодня мы еще боимся писать кто это пишет, т.к. два товарища наших за это Вели-Ибраимова пострадали за правду, они были куда-то увезены и по сей день неизвестно куда, он их дел. Короче говоря в Крыму во всех отраслях народного хозяйства и партийных организаций руководят кулаки мулы и т.д. а Семенов является слепым орудием; все равно как при Вели Ибраимове, они творили свои кулацкие дела, а Секретарь Обкома Уфимцев, был слепым орудием. Конкретно возьмем с головы, возьмите Обком партии кто там руководит 1) Чагар, в 1919г. бежал в Константинополь там учил-ся, а кто в то время мог учиться этого писать не следует; 2) Арифов, зам.пред.Совнаркома, о нем мы писали Кагановичу что это чужак. меры не были приняты и только теперь тов.Сахарова исключила его из партии, как чужака; 3) Гельбух, зав. сектором или отдела в Обкоме. сын торговца 2-й гильдии; 4) Оршавский работник Обкома. сын торговца; 5) Крылов работник Обкома, добрый служак у колчака; 6) Мустакаев, сын муллы; 7) Гусев. зав. сельхоз. отделом, бывш. офицер и сын попа 8)Наркомзем Мусаниц. чужак. сын муллы; 9) Ольховой. зав. отделом пропаганды Обкома. сын торговца; 10) Бояджиев, редактор газеты. сын муллы и жена дочь муллы; 11) Файзи, ректор комвуза, сын муллы и характерно, то, что Файзи как председатель комиссии по чистке чистил муллу, Бояджиева и с таким восторгом об"являет, Бояджиева считать проверенным, вот кто у нас в Крыму строит политику. Жена Файзи руководит Обкомом, что захочет то и сделает, т.к. Секретарь Обкома Семенов женат на родной сестре Файзи, поэтому у него столько прав по этому и его Семенов сделал председателем комиссии по чистке очень трудно описать все эти гнусности, которые творятся в Крыму и все это прикрывается под орденом Ленина, мол за хорошую работу получили орден Ленина, или хотя бы такой факт председатель Крымщика-Тархан, член партии с 26 г. вместе с одним автором этого письма принадлежал в партию. а для солидности ему сделал стаж с 1919г. все это знают обо всем этом говорят, необходимо принять срочные меры, а то будет поздно, а когда кто нибудь приедет из ЦК, то авторов этого письма моментально увидят, они сами покажутся, их искать не придется.-

Подписи - 9 человек.

Старые члены партии, участники гражданской войны.-

З/мч.   Верно: *[подпись]*

Figure 8. "If comrade Stalin does not take measures, then one must say straight out that our regime is not socialist but KULAK." Anonymous denunciation sent to V. M. Molotov, chairman of Council of People's Commissars, 1934. From Gosudarstvennyi arkhiv Rossiiskoi Federatsii, f. 5446, op. 82, d. 27, l. 172.

through a routine purge in 1930, several workers with memories of the old days wrote to the purge commission to denounce "bourgeois specialists," holdovers from the equivalent prerevolutionary bureaucracy. These were people who had been responsible for having sailors flogged and workers arrested before the Revolution, the letters stated. They had served Kolchak's (anti-Bolshevik) administration willingly in 1918; they were protectors of counterrevolutionaries. "This citizen Gavril Meshkov is cunning," one worker wrote about the specialist who had headed the Waterways Administration under the Tsar. "I know his tricks since 1905 as well as I know my own five fingers." According to the writer, Meshkov pretended to be loyal to Soviet power, but in fact his record showed that he would work for any regime—Tsarist, Kolchak's, or Soviet.[30]

Women workers at the Leningrad Knitting Plant wrote to a newspaper in 1931 to denounce the manager of their plant, a former entrepreneur (they claimed), whose associates were of the same bourgeois ilk. This "former petty boss" (byvshii khoziaichik) treated the workers like any capitalist,

> making them have hysterics, and he answers just like a little capitalist, "If you don't like it you can leave, [and] I will hire others in your place."[31]

In similar vein, a group of peasants denouncing their kolkhoz chairman in 1938 recalled that his father, a labor contractor, had always exploited and cheated poor peasants:

> That's how Romanenkov's father carried on the whole time up to the Revolution, and made people's lives miserable and beat them like a Fascist contractor; the old people in the district know that, but the rural soviet [leaders] themselves, being young, don't know it.[32]

Many class denunciations had the aim of invoking a specific legal or administrative sanction against the person denounced. For example, a trade unionist wrote to the Central Electoral Commission in 1929 arguing that a woman living in his neighborhood should be deprived of the vote because she was not an unskilled laborer, as she claimed, but a former nun who made a good living trading in icons and crosses. Another denunciation was sent to the Commission on Passportization in 1933 with the aim

---

[30] GANO, f. 288, op. 2, d. 902, ll. 4–5; ibid., l. 6.
[31] Tsentral'nyi gosudarstvennyi arkhiv goroda Sankt-Peterburga (TsGA S-P), f. 1027, op. 2, d. 860ob, l. 52.
[32] RGAE, f. 396, op. 10, d. 128, ll. 66–69.

of preventing the issue of passports to persons the author claimed were class aliens.[33]

When Communists wrote denunciations on class grounds, the purpose was usually to unmask another party member who was concealing "alien" class background. In one such letter (1935), an old Communist (Civil War vintage) wrote to the regional party committee to denounce a Communist woman called Khomlianskaia, a resident in Novosibirsk. According to the writer's information, Khomlianskaia claimed to have joined the party organization in his district in 1922. That was impossible, he said, because he knew her to be the sister of a rich wool and leather merchant who had fought against the Reds in the Civil War and subsequently had been exiled. Evidently, therefore, she had obtained her party card fraudulently and lied about her social origin. Moreover, the writer added, she was probably still in touch with her capitalist brother, in whose home she had been reared and educated, for "according to my information Khomlianskaia's brother at the present time is also in Novosibirsk and trades in cigarettes in a kiosk opposite the Soviet Hotel."[34]

Vigilance about class enemies was particularly strong in the late 1920s and early 1930s, the time of collectivization, dekulakization, expropriation of urban Nepmen, and mass arrests of priests. Any Communist worth his salt was going to be watching local "kulaks" closely, as did the Komsomol from Kuntsevo who wrote to the district OGPU in 1933:

> Pay attention to the citizens living in Usovo village, Stepan Vasilevich Vatusov and his wife Nadezhda Senafantevna, since according to my observations of them they . . . are like kulaks working *by stealth*; up to 1930–31 they had their own separate farm with about five hectares of land which they worked by exploiting the bedniak population. The land has now been transferred to the kolkhoz, but [the Vatusovs] are making money on their well-appointed house, which has all kinds of extensions, by renting it out to vacationers . . . In all probability they have gold because when they come from Moscow they bring all kinds of packages whose wrapping could only be from Torgsin.[35]

Some "class" denunciations have the look of preemptive strikes by people whose own origins made them vulnerable to attack. For example, in 1937 a statistician denounced the party secretary of his district, a man he had apparently known from childhood, saying that he was the son of

---

[33] TsMAM, f. 1474, op. 7, d. 79, ll. 86–87; ibid., f. 3109, op. 2, d. 2140 (thanks to Viktoria Tiazhelnikova for making available the latter document.) On petitions against disfranchisement, see Alexopoulos, *Stalin's Outcasts*.

[34] PANO, f. 3, op. 9, d. 801, l. 10.

[35] GASO, f. 88, op. 2, d. 62, ll. 125–26. In the early 1930s, state Torgsin stores sold scarce goods for hard currency, gold, and silver only (no rubles).

a local scribe who had himself worked as a scribe (a damaging sign of willingness to serve the old regime, despite the lowly status of the job) and had also rented out part of his house as a commercial teahouse. The writer added that this same man had been spreading slander about *his* social origins.[36]

Despite the 1936 Constitution's transcendence of class discrimination, old class stigmas and suspicions were not forgotten even in the late 1930s.[37] Reading in 1938 of the appointment of V. S. Tiukov as deputy chairman of the State Bank, an alert resident of the village of Maksimovka in Voronezh oblast realized that a class enemy might have penetrated the highest ranks of government. He wrote to Molotov to warn him that this could be Valentin Tiukov (or perhaps his brother Vitalii), son of a big local landowner, Stepan Tiukov, who had suddenly vanished from the district with his entire family around 1925.[38] As late as December 1940, several years after the party had dropped class criteria in admissions, a Communist wrote in to complain that one Mikhailov, recently admitted to candidate membership of the party, was ineligible for party membership on class grounds "since his parents were former owners of furnished rooms and commercial bathhouses in the city of Tambov."[39]

ABUSE OF POWER

"Abuse of power" (*zloupotreblenie vlasti*) is one of the most interesting categories of Stalinist denunciation.[40] These letters in fact straddle the boundary between denunciation (where the emphasis is on wrongdoing by another person) and complaint (where the emphasis is on injury to the writer). In the Soviet period, as before the Revolution, most writers of "abuse" denunciations were peasants, though one sometimes encounters urban denunciations of similar type against small-town bosses, factory directors, and so on.[41] Kolkhoz chairmen were by far the most popular target of peasants' accusations. These denunciations are quintessen-

---

[36] TsGA IPD, f. 24, op. 2g, d. 15, ll. 3–8.

[37] See above pp. 47–49.

[38] GARF, f. 5446, op. 82, d. 65, l. 53.

[39] GARF, f. 5446, op. 82, d. 65, l. 53; RGASPI, f. 475, op. 1, d. 28, l. 395.

[40] For a more detailed discussion of abuse letters from peasants, see Fitzpatrick, "Readers' Letters to *Krest'ianskaia gazeta*, 1938," *Russian History* 24:1–2 (1997), pp. 149–70. In the *Krest'ianskaia gazeta* archive (RGAE, f. 396, op. 10 and 11), such letters are collected in files headed "Wrecking and Abuse in the Collective Farms" (*Vreditelstvo i zloupotrebleniia v kolkhozakh*) or variants thereof.

[41] For example, PANO, f. 3, op. 11, d. 41, ll. 31–36, TsGA IPD, f. 24, op. 2g, d. 48, ll. 22–25.

tial "weapons of the weak," containing many references to the writers' powerlessness and poverty, and invoking natural justice rather than formal law.

Unlike the peasant petitions from the 1905 period analyzed by Andrew Verner, Soviet "abuse" letters rarely came from the whole village community, though it was not uncommon for more than one kolkhoznik to sign (but not more than five or six).[42] But it was equally rare for an "abuse" letter to be written as if it represented only the opinion of the individual writer. "All the kolkhozniks are indignant," is a standard phrase. Often an individual author will name other kolkhozniks who have denounced the same offender to the authorities, or list the names of kolkhozniks who will back up his version of events, or even enclose a copy of the minutes of a kolkhoz meeting censuring the offender.[43]

The "abuse" letter of the 1930s had a Soviet as well as a prerevolutionary antecedent, namely the reports sent to newspapers by rural correspondents (sel'kory) in the 1920s.[44] By the late 1930s, however, that movement had withered. Only a small minority of peasant writers to the newspaper Krest'ianskaia gazeta in 1938 called themselves sel'kory or had the sel'kor's typical self-identification with Soviet power and the Communist Party, though a larger number had borrowed something of the style of the sel'kor reports published in newspapers over the years, using Soviet terms like "unmask" and "wrecker," and occasionally providing titles for their letters (for example, "Who is plundering kolkhoz assets?") Most writers of "abuse" denunciations in the late 1930s were just ordinary peasants with grievances against the kolkhoz leaders. The purpose of writing the denunciation was to get the chairman or brigade leader dismissed from his job (or, for those of more vengeful character, arrested).

Unlike the "disloyalty" and "class" denunciations discussed earlier, the typical "abuse" denunciation does not focus on a single or central attribute or action. Instead, it is a grab bag of all the crimes, shortfalls, mistakes, defects, and black marks that can plausibly be attributed to the denouncee, particularly those that are likely to weigh heavily with higher authorities. At the top of the list in my sample is "stealing" from kolkhozniks. This is not ordinary theft (usually) but, rather, the kind of misappropriation of kolkhoz funds that was easily done by kolkhoz chairmen and accountants: cheating kolkhozniks on labor day payments, confiscating their animals, imposing illegal fines and a variety of other forms of

[42] See Andrew M. Verner, "Discursive Strategies in the 1905 Revolution: Peasant Petitions from Vladimir Province," *Russian Review* 54:1 (1995).

[43] RGAE f. 396, op. 10, d. 161, ll. 289, 128; ibid., d. 142, ll. 493, 496–97.

[44] For a detailed study of sel'kory, see Steven R. Coe, "Peasants, the State, and the Languages of NEP: The Rural Correspondents Movement in the Soviet Union, 1924–1928," Ph.D. diss., University of Michigan, 1993.

extortion, treating the kolkhoz horses as personal property, drawing money out of the kolkhoz bank account for personal use, and so on.

One such denunciation described how kolkhoz leaders refused to give a deserving kolkhoznik twenty-four kilos of flour, extorting his fur coat in payment:

These kulak scum take grain themselves, they sell sixteen kilos [on the market] for fifty rubles a *pud*, while honest toilers go hungry. Comrades, where is your vigilance? Twenty years of Soviet power and this kind of abomination and terrorizing of the dark masses continues.[45]

Next on the list of offenses cited in rural "abuse" denunciations was "suppression of criticism," a catch phrase that covered a range of arbitrary and tyrannical practices on the part of the chairman.

Kolkhoz chairman F. A. Zadorozhnyi does not allow kolkhozniks to talk at the meeting, if somebody tries to say something he Zadorozhnyi says why are you trying to disrupt the meeting you are not our man; because of that kolkhozniks don't go to meetings, they say why should we go if Zadorozhnyi won't let us speak and stifles criticism and self-criticism.[46]

Writers of such denunciations often complained that the chairman in question was a district appointee who had been forced on the kolkhozniks against their will. No less frequent were indignant reports of the chairmen's and brigade leaders' offenses against the peasants' dignity: treating kolkhozniks with contempt (*izdevatel'stvo*); insulting, beating, and cursing them ("He curses out all the kolkhozniks in foul language; he can't find words bad enough to call the kolkhozniks").[47] Chairmen were also accused of favoring relatives and drunkenness.

Just as peasants quickly learned to use the term "kulak" to discredit kolkhoz chairmen with higher authorities, so also they were quick to pick up the preferred rhetorical terms of indictment of the Great Purges period: "enemy of the people," "terrorist," "Trotskyite."

The position in our kolkhoz is pitiful. Comrades, answer us please where we can find justice. We often read the papers and see in them what great evil has been done in our Soviet Union by enemies of the people of the rightist-Trotskyite bloc, how widely it has spread, how they wrecked agriculture, how many horses perished and pedigreed cattle . . . How many times we have told our local authorities about this, both the kolkhoz board and also the chairman of the rural soviet, Savoni, who has now been exposed as an enemy of the people and the

---

[45] RGAE, f. 396, op. 10, d. 128, ll. 158–59.
[46] Ibid., d. 86, ll. 71–73.
[47] Ibid., d. 161, ll. 84–87.

police chief Arkhipov who has also been taken away by organs of the NKVD . . . but there were no results.[48]

The peasants understood the mechanism of smearing by association and used it often when district leaders—who could always be more or less accurately represented as the patrons of lower-level bosses such as rural soviet and kolkhoz chairmen—were arrested as "enemies" during the Great Purges. For example:

> Many times I as a sel'kor have sent signals to Chistiakov, chairman of the rural soviet, and the Bol'shesol'skii district [leaders] about wrecking by the kolkhoz chairman and stableman, but they were deaf to these signals. Now the district soviet chairman Bugeev has been sent to prison as a wrecker [and it is] time to get all the other wreckers.[49]

Peasants who denounced their kolkhoz chairmen or other local office holders wanted them to be punished, "given what they deserve." They asked higher authorities to "help us purge the kolkhoz of these rascals," "help us to rid ourselves once and for all of these criminals," "deliver us from these enemies of the people who have got into the kolkhoz."[50] Some letters explicitly asked that the offender be dismissed from his post or prosecuted.[51] One writer, who had already sent material on her kolkhoz chairman to the local NKVD, was particularly forthright about the importance of arresting him. What the authorities needed to do, she wrote, was to "interview kolkhozniks on site, expose Bakaliaev as an enemy of the people, remove him from his job, prosecute him, and take him away from the kolkhoz."[52]

FAMILY AND MORALS DENUNCIATIONS

The intense publicity given to Pavlik Morozov's denunciation might suggest that denunciation of one family member by another was commonplace in Stalin's Russia, but the archives of the 1930s offer little support for this hypothesis. To be sure, there are individual cases of denunciation within the family. But in general this genre of denunciation is conspicuous by its absence. Thus, the story to be told in this section is essentially that of the dog that failed to bark.

---

[48] Ibid., d. 65, ll. 212–14

[49] Ibid., d. 161, ll. 29–32; see also ibid., d. 142, ll. 173–77.

[50] RGAE, f. 396, op. 10, d. 26, ll. 137–39 and 158–59; ibid., d. 87, ll. 125–26 and 281–84; ibid., d. 161, ll. 203–4; TsGA IPD, f. 24, op. 2v, d. 1570, l. 49.

[51] RGAE, f. 396, op. 10, d. 142, ll. 141–42; ibid., d. 161, ll. 84–89.

[52] Ibid., d. 161, ll. 84–89.

The archives of the 1930s do contain a large number of "family" letters that are *not* denunciations.[53] There are many letters from parents asking that their children be given medical help, admitted to technical schools and universities, or placed in orphanages (on the grounds that the parents lacked the means to support them). There are letters from wives asking that their absent husbands be traced and required to pay child support, and there are "confessional" letters (*ispovedi*) in which women write to a distant authority figure, usually a regional party leader, describing their misery at their husband's unfaithfulness or desertion. In the late 1930s, the archives contain an enormous number of appeals and enquiries from wives whose husbands have been arrested during the Great Purges, together with similar letters from the husbands, parents, and children of victims. Such letters almost invariably assert the innocence of the arrested relative and plead for his or her release.

In the last type of letter, we can perhaps find a clue to the rarity of denunciatory letters about family members. Reading these letters, it is difficult not to feel that, contrary to Hannah Arendt's "atomization" thesis,[54] family bonds in Russia were strengthened, not weakened, by Soviet terror.[55] But there were also practical reasons not to denounce a close family member during the Great Purges, as well as in the earlier rural terror associated with dekulakization. If one family member was dekulakized or branded an "enemy of the people," the whole family suffered. When kulaks were deported in the early 1930s, their families were deported with them. In the late 1930s, special camps were established in Gulag for "wives of traitors to the motherland."[56]

Of course, there are exceptions to all rules. In 1927 the wife of an assistant prosecutor in the Ukraine wrote to Stalin complaining about the abuse she had been suffering at her husband's hands since she had denounced him as an Oppositionist involved in preparing for an armed uprising(!).[57] In 1938 an angry ex-husband, denied custody of his young daughter by the court in the divorce settlement, wrote to the office of

[53] For more on these, see above, chapter 9.

[54] Hannah Arendt, *The Origins of Totalitarianism* (New York, 1951).

[55] In interviewing refugees from the Soviet Union after the war, the Harvard Project found respondents from all social levels were more likely to say that "under Soviet conditions the family drew closer together" than the reverse. This response was particularly common from members of families in which a close relative had been arrested by the secret police. Alex Inkeles and Raymond A. Bauer, *The Soviet Citizen: Daily Life in a Totalitarian Society* (New York, 1968 [1st pub. 1959]), pp. 211–13.

[56] For a good description of one such camp, see Anna Larina, *This I Cannot Forget: The Memoirs of Nikolai Bukharin's Widow*, trans. Gary Kern (New York, 1993), pp. 42–51.

[57] RGASPI, f. 17, op. 85, d. 492, l. 37.

President Kalinin to denounce his former wife for debauchery and for the fact that her lover had been arrested as an enemy of the people.[58]

Ex-spouses, of course, fall into a special category. Many people have grievances against former husbands and wives, and denunciation was one way to settle the score. This thought evidently occurred to someone in the Soviet propaganda machine. In mid-1937, just after the secret court martial of Marshal Tukhachevskii, General Iakir, and other leaders of the Soviet Army, *Pravda* announced that it had received a letter from the former wife of Iakir in which she "renounces and curses (*proklinaet*) her former husband as a traitor and betrayer of the motherland."[59] Like the Pavlik Morozov story, this had the look of an example for others to emulate. But a year later the newspaper changed its tune and deplored "false" (that is, malicious) denunciations from angry ex-spouses.[60] This may have been as much a response to popular objections to the gambit as to any flood of denunciations, since no such flood is visible in the archives, even at the height of the Purges.[61] Ex-wives, too, had self-preservation reasons to refrain from writing denunciations against their former husbands: the arrest of an "enemy of the people" could damage not only his current wife and children but also former wives and even the husbands and relatives of former wives.

As far as Pavlik Morozov's example is concerned, there certainly was a type of adolescent Young Avenger who wrote denunciations freely and recklessly in the hope of becoming a hero (see above, p. 210), but even would-be Pavliks did not usually write about their own fathers and mothers. The denunciations of this type I have encountered target people in the surrounding community—neighbors, teachers, schoolmates.[62]

While spontaneous written denunciations of parents by their children seem to have been rare, it was not uncommon during the Great Purges for

---

[58] GARF, f. 3316, op. 29, d. 312, ll. 12–13.

[59] *Pravda*, 18 June 1937, p. 6. This announcement was made in the "Chronicle" section. *Pravda* did not publish the text of the letter. According to Bukharin's wife, Anna Larina, who encountered Sarra Iakir in Gulag, she was much embarrassed by this publication and claimed it was a total forgery: Anna Larina, *This I Cannot Forget*, trans. Gary Kern (New York, 1993), p. 174.

[60] See, for example, the report in *Pravda*, 8 June 1938, p. 6, of a "false denunciation" from a former wife and her brother alleging that the husband had sold his passport to foreigners on a trip abroad.

[61] I have not come across any denunciations that are overtly by ex-spouses. The Leningrad Party archives contain some denunciations that, on internal evidence, could have been written by ex-spouses or spurned lovers, but the writers do not so identify themselves. See, for example, a woman's denunciation of a male Communist as a former Trotskyite and for other offenses: TsGA IPD, f. 24, op. 2v, d. 1516, l. 74.

[62] See TsGA IPD, f. 24, op. 2v, d. 2226, ll. 78–79; GARF, f. 5446, op. 81a, d. 335, l. 29; ibid., op. 82, d. 94, l. 19.

the school-age children of arrested "enemies of the people" to be forced to repudiate them orally in public at school or Komsomol meetings. Occasionally, as in the Iakir case, such repudiations appeared in print. But such practices evidently aroused popular revulsion. Despite the official endorsement of the Pavlik Morozov cult, in the spring of 1938 a regional newspaper, *Krasnaia Tatariia*, protested strongly against them. The occasion was the publication in a smaller local newspaper of a letter in which a young man accused his father, an agricultural laborer, of being an "enemy of the people" because he had stolen feed from the state farm where he worked. "The whole tone of the letter is obviously phony," *Krasnaia Tatariia* commented, clearly hinting that the district newspaper had fabricated the letter or forced the author to write it.

> This letter did not meet with the reader's approval. It only morally crushed the unfortunate father. What kind of joke is this, that a man's own son would publicly (*vsenarodno*) call his father an enemy of the people and repudiate him?[63]

Occasional denunciations of in-laws are to be found in the archives, though in most cases there is an obvious self-protection motive. One Communist had denounced his father-in-law as a kulak in 1930, when the older man fled the village and took refuge in the writer's city apartment. He did this unwillingly, and lived to regret it (as he wrote indignantly seven years later) when in 1937 his "kulak ties" (i.e., relationship with his father-in-law) led to his expulsion from the Party.[64]

Letters from wives about child support, as well as "confessional" letters from abandoned wives, sometimes had an element of denunciation, but this was not the predominant flavor. With rare exceptions, such letters did not ask that the delinquent husband be punished. The letters about child support were interested in collecting the money,[65] while the "confessional" letters asked for moral support, understanding, and the opportunity for a personal meeting with the addressee. No doubt women did not frame these letters as denunciations in the 1930s because the regime was still relatively uninterested in punishing people for moral delinquency. It

---

[63] *Krasnaia Tatariia* (Kazan), 5 April 1938, p. 2.

[64] PANO, f. 3, op. 11, d. 542, ll. 140–41. See also the quasi-denunciation of a father-in-law, recently arrested by the NKVD, from one of Molotov's stenographers in GARF, f. 5446, op. 82, d. 56, l. 22.

[65] One exception is the 1934 letter from a deceived and abandoned wife of a Communist, who, while noting that he had paid her nothing for child, seemed more interested in getting him punished or at least damaging his reputation than in the financial support. TsGA IPD, f. 24, op. 2g, d. 769, l. 78.

is true that the antiabortion law of 1936[66] introduced short prison terms for nonpayment of child support and raised the price of divorce, but "no fault" divorce remained. When a much stricter divorce law was introduced after the war, requiring demonstration of fault, the letters written by abandoned wives quickly acquired the character of denunciations.[67]

Questions of sexual morality were not major concerns in Soviet society in the 1930s, judging by their comparatively infrequent appearance in denunciations. After 1936, when it became a criminal offense punishable by imprisonment to perform an abortion or force a woman to have one, a few abortion denunciations appeared: for example, a 1938 denunciation of a kolkhoz chairman in Kursk included the allegation that he had forced his wife to have an abortion, from which she had died.[68]

Although male homosexuality was outlawed in 1934, I have encountered no denunciations for this or any other "deviant" sexual act. The only sexual offense that seems to have interested writers of denunciations was female promiscuity. Allegations that women administrators, or the wives of administrators, had lovers and rewarded them with favors and advancement were not uncommon. These letters follow the familiar "Catherine the Great" trope, in which a woman's power is juxtaposed with her unbridled sexual appetites, and both are condemned as perversions of nature.

"All this gossip about my past is meant to discredit me as a leader," wrote a woman party official in a complaint about denunciations that falsely accused her of having affairs with male colleagues.[69] One anonymous denunciation, written in block capitals by "An employee of the raikom [district party committee]" in 1935, dispensed with any talk of lovers and focused on a woman's undue sexual influence on her husband, who headed the district party committee in which she worked:

Zolina is Kasimov's second wife and therefore all the raikom staffers are in Zolina's hands, and if she doesn't like someone, then under the influence of a sweet minute in bed she only has to say [something] to Kasimov and the next day Zolina's request will be carried out and the staffers have to suffer . . . It is necessary to mount a campaign against sexual debauchery (razvrat) in the organizations and dismiss Zolina from the raikom.[70]

---

[66] Decree of 27 June 1936 "On the prohibition of abortions, . . . the strengthening of criminal penalties for nonpayment of alimony, and on certain changes in the legislation on divorce," Izvestiia, 28 June 1936.

[67] See this book, chapter 12.

[68] RGAE, f. 396, op. 10, d. 87, l. 207.

[69] TsGA IPD, f. 24, op. 2v, d. 1514, ll. 28–30.

[70] Ibid., d. 1518, l. 62.

Women rarely denounced men for sexual harassment (to use an anachronistic term). In the *Krest'ianskaia gazeta* archive, for example, there are very few denunciations of local officials by peasant women alleging that the men had forced the women to have sex with them, although we know from other sources that this was by no means an unusual phenomenon.[71] One of the rare exceptions, by a peasant woman named Suslova from Krasnodar, gave a vivid description of her attempted rape by a local official, Pavlenko:

> On 2 March 1938 [Pavlenko] came to Dakhovskaia stanitsa, drank himself stupid at eight in the evening came to the apartment of Elena Suslova and said: "Come to the soviet the NKVD summons you." The woman was frightened and asks why. He answers you won't come back from there, and on the way he says everything is in my hands I can save you Suslova. She began to implore him he throws himself on her and begins to do unspeakable things. Suslova began defending herself and begging him Pavlenko says if you are stubborn it will be worse we'll throw you in prison . . . Despite Pavlenko's threats Suslova still managed to run away home. He caught her and pulled at her, trying to rape her. Suslova continued to cry out and defend herself. Pavlenko seeing that he is losing takes hold of Suslova and tries to throw her in the well but because he was drunk he slipped and lost the chance. And Suslova ran into the house all beaten up after that she lay in bed all bruised, with swollen arms. But Pavlenko wasn't punished . . . I Suslova beg the editors of *Krest'ianskaia gazeta* to help me bring this criminal to justice.[72]

Manipulative Uses of Denunciation

The Soviet state was very responsive to denunciations. This responsiveness meant that it was always vulnerable to manipulation by denunciation writers with personal agendas. Regional officials were well aware that peasants were using mutual denunciation as a tool to pursue village feuds.[73] The newspaper *Krest'ianskaia gazeta* uncovered an elaborate confidence trick exploiting the convention of "abuse of power" denunciation. Two Belorussian conmen joined a kolkhoz in Krasnodar and set out to

---

[71] See, for example, the statements (*pokazaniia*) that the NKVD collected from five kolkhoz women in the course of a broader investigation of a kolkhoz chairman: Smolensk Archive, WKP 355, 48.

[72] RGAE, f. 396, op. 10, d. 66, l. 180. I have retained some of the grammatical and syntactical peculiarities of the original.

[73] See Fitzpatrick, *Stalin's Peasants*, pp. 259–61.

discredit the kolkhoz chairman. Their method was to encourage the kol-khozniks to criticize the chairman at kolkhoz meetings, and then to use these data to write plausible and circumstantial "abuse" denunciations. The aim was to force the chairman out of office, have their own man appointed, and get control of kolkhoz assets.[74]

A different kind of manipulative use of denunciations occurred in the cultural and scientific professions, which were often characterized by intense faction fighting as well as by close client-patron relations between leading members of the professions and political leaders. The use of denunciations as a weapon in the factional struggles of Soviet architects has been well illustrated from archival materials by Hugh Hudson.[75] A young Communist mathematician at Moscow State University was the author of a denunciation of the physicist Petr Kapitsa that, despite its postwar date, echoed the militant spirit of the Cultural Revolution of the early 1930s. Kapitsa, regarded with suspicion by many Communist and "nativist" colleagues on account of his Cambridge sojourn in the early 1930s, was accused of leading a Western-oriented clique that monopolized funds and appointments in physics, expressing anti-Soviet views, and behaving contemptuously toward Soviet physicists outside the clique, especially those who were Communists and Soviet patriots, of lower-class origin, and less cosmopolitan than Kapitsa and his friends. It is a measure of Kapitsa's standing with top party leadership that, despite the fact that these accusations were perfectly credible, the denunciation was dismissed by a high official as nothing more than a product of professional feuding and rivalry.[76]

Theaters, particularly the Bolshoi Theater in Moscow and the Kirov Theater in Leningrad, were notorious for the volume of mutual denunciation they generated. "Anonymous letters on the ballet company of the Kirov Theater are coming in almost every day to various institutions," stated a memo from a Leningrad official to Zhdanov in 1940. The agitprop files in Moscow contain many letters from leading actors, actresses, and opera singers denouncing the theater directors who had insulted them and failed to give them appropriate roles.[77]

[74] RGAE, f. 396, op. 10, d. 67, l. 219. For a similar case, see TsGA IPD, f. 24, op. 2v, d. 1534, ll. 105, 109.

[75] See Hugh D. Hudson Jr., "Terror in Soviet Architecture: The Murder of Mikhail Okhitovich," *Slavic Review* 51:3 (Fall 1992), pp. 455, 462–63.

[76] RGASPI, f. 17, op. 125, d. 361, ll. 19–31, 37–49 (Central Committee department of agitation and propaganda). The official who commented was Sergei Kaftanov of the Committee for Affairs of Higher Education. These documents come from 1945–46. Presumably, similar denunciations would have been found in the agitprop department's archives for the 1930s, but they are not available in RGASPI and may have perished during the war.

[77] TsGA IPD, f. 24, op. 2g, d. 226, l. 1; RGASPI, f. 17, op. 125, d. 216, ll. 33–35 and 51–54 (letters of 1941 and 1943).

"Apartment" denunciations provide a particularly good example of the manipulative uses of denunciation. In the former Soviet Union, even now, the term "apartment denunciation" is instantly comprehensible. The context it evokes is that of acute urban overcrowding that lasted for decades—in its most acute form, from the beginning of the 1930s to the 1960s. During this time, apartments formerly occupied by a single family became "communal," with one family per room and kitchen and bathroom shared by all the inhabitants. An "apartment" denunciation is the denunciation of neighbor by neighbor, often motivated by the desire to increase living space.

In 1933 I. A. Leontev, a resident of no. 19, Bolshoi Spasobolvanskii Lane, Moscow, wrote a denunciation about his neighbors.[78] Although his house was small, eighteen families lived in it. Most apartment denunciations focused on one person or family, but Leontev preferred the scattershot approach and gave all the damaging information he had on everybody. E. M. Dmitrieva, who had owned the house before it was municipalized and remained one of the residents, had been disenfranchised as a bourgeoise. Several other residents, relatives of Dmitrieva, were in the same "alien" class category. E. I. Tregubova was a formerly disenfranchised woman who had taken over the chairmanship of the housing council, the better to protect her own dubious relatives, also residents of the house; V. N. Suslin, an office worker, probably came from a priest's family; Z. E. Ekshtein, unemployed, "probably trades in something (you should check)"; V. G. Shenshev, a government employee, "has bourgeois inclinations, especially his wife," and so the list went on. Leontev addressed his letter to the Commission on Passportization, which was then (March 1933) issuing internal passports and urban registration permits to residents of the capital, and at the same time purging the city's population of "social aliens."

In another case, two Communists, husband and wife, each wrote a denunciation of a man named Volodarskii, also a Communist, who had lived in their apartment and still had legal claim to a room. When these denunciations were shown to Volodarskii, he said they were the result of a complicated quarrel about living space. According to his story, the wife wanted his room for her sister and had suggested an exchange, which he refused, causing bad feeling. Then he found a new job in another place and moved out, leaving the spouses in effective possession of his room— to which, however, he retained title. Then he was trying to organize an exchange that would bring a new permanent resident into the apartment—hence, Volodarskii implied, the denunciations.[79]

---

[78] TsMAM, f. 1474, op. 7, d. 79, ll. 86–87.

[79] RGASPI, f. 475, op. 1, d. 9, ll. 82–88. The wife denounced Volodarskii as a Trotskyite, the husband for his dissolute lifestyle.

An eloquent testimony to the power of apartment quarrels came in an appeal sent in 1939 to Andrei Vyshinsky, deputy chairman of Sovnarkom and former State Prosecutor. The writer was a Moscow teacher whose husband was serving an eight-year sentence for counterrevolutionary agitation. The family (parents and two sons) had lived for nineteen years in one comparatively large room—42 square meters—in a communal apartment in Moscow. "For all these years our room has been the apple of discord for all residents of our apartment," the teacher wrote. Neighbors sent an endless stream of denunciations to various local authorities. As a result, the family was disenfranchised, then the adults were refused passports, and finally the husband was arrested as a counterrevolutionary, leaving the rest of the family to fight eviction orders. When Vyshinsky called for a report on this case, the prosecutor's office conceded that denunciations by hostile neighbors lay at the root of the family's troubles. But the neighbors were hostile, the prosecutor explained, because the family was anti-Soviet.[80]

SECRECY

It is hard to form an accurate assessment of the proportion of denunciations that were anonymous, but it appears surprisingly small. According to the registry of incoming letters kept by the secretariat of the Leningrad party committee in the mid 1930s, fewer than one letter in a thousand was anonymous.[81] This is much lower than the proportion in *Krest'ianskaia gazeta*'s files for 1938, which is around 20 percent.[82] We should take account of the fact that a certain proportion of signed letters are signed with false names—that is, were in fact anonimki.[83] But even so, anonymous denunciations remain the exception.

The main reason for signing a denunciation was that it added verisimilitude. "We ask you to regard this not as an anonimka but as reality,"

[80] GARF, f. 5446., op. 81a, d. 94, ll. 207–9.

[81] TsGA IPD, f. 24, op. 2g, d. 13, ll. 3, 12–14; ibid., 46, ll. 31–77. The "letters" category includes appeals, complaints, and other types of letters from citizens, not just denunciations.

[82] Eighteen out of a sample of ninety-four denunciations from RGAE, f. 396, op. 10, were anonymous (count by Golfo Alexopoulos). A quick survey of the *Krest'ianskaia gazeta* files for the late 1920s (RGAE, f. 396, op. 6 and 7) suggests that, for unknown reasons, anonymous letters were more frequent then than a decade later.

[83] For example, the 1939 denunciation signed "A. Mitrofanov" in GARF, f. 5446, op. 81a, d. 154, l. 2. As an accompanying memo indicates, an NKVD investigation found that Mitrofanov was not the author of the letter, who remained unknown. See also TsGA IPD, f. 24, op. 2v, d. 1534, ll. 105–9 for a letter signed in the name of one kolkhoznik but actually written by a two others without his knowledge.

wrote one anonymous collective.[84] Writers of anonymous denunciations frequently addressed the possibility that their letters, as anonimki, would not be taken seriously, although on the basis of the available archival materials it is not clear that this was actually the case. Zhdanov's office in Leningrad, for example, seems to have handled anonymous communications in much the same way as signed letters.[85]

Some writers were coy about their anonymity, like the man who wrote to Moscow city authorities about a financial scam in 1933:

> I am obliged to write anonymously for the following reason—I am no coward, but this is my second letter to the OGPU for 1933, and after the first letter they ground me to powder although I had done a big service for the Republic—so I am fed up with being insulted and I decided not to give my name but if you guess it I will just congratulate you.[86]

Anonymous denouncers often promised to reveal their names as soon as they saw that action was being taken on their denunciations.[87] As "Unknown for the Time Being" wrote chattily to Kalinin in 1937 after informing him of a terrorist plot against Mikoian, "Ekh, Mikhail Ivanovich! Check this out, and when this group figures in the press I will make my appearance and unmask [them]."[88]

While most anonymous writers presumably wished to avoid the attention of the NKVD, some seemed positively to court it. "So long *until further work with you*, and [then] I will give you my name and everything," wrote one anonymous author of a denunciation, a man who claimed to have served as an informer before, not to mention having helped Kirov trap the Whites in Astrakhan and having a revolutionary pedigree that "went back to 1888 [*sic*]."[89] This writer seems to have been hoping for an invitation to work as an informer (*sekretnyi sotrudnik*) for the NKVD, which did in fact recruit informers from the writers of anonymous denunciations. In one such case (reported in passing in the Vyshinsky files), the writer was a high school student, whose subsequent reports as an informer—and presumably his original denunciation as well—turned out to be worthless fantasies, much to the NKVD's chagrin.[90]

[84] GARF, f. 5446, op. 82, d. 27, l. 172. See also GARF, f. 1235, op. 141, d. 2070, l. 4.
[85] TsGA IPD, f. 24, op. 2v, d. 1518 (1935 file of anonymous letters to the first secretary of the Leningrad party committee).
[86] TsMAM, f. 3109, op. 2, d. 2140.
[87] GARF, f. 5446, op. 82, d. 27, l. 172.
[88] GARF, f. 1235, op. 141, d. 2070, l. 4.
[89] TsGA IPD, f. 24, op. 2v, d. 945, l. 3 (my emphasis).
[90] GARF, f. 5446s, op. 81a, d. 94, l. 19 (1939 report).

Despite the fact that most writers of denunciations signed their names, secrecy still remained a major concern. Some denunciations are marked "Secret" or "Top secret" by the senders. Many writers stated that they feared retaliation, particularly when their bosses were the objects of denunciation.[91] Peasants denouncing kolkhoz chairmen and other rural officials were particularly anxious on this score (and, as we shall see, their fears were quite justified). Although they usually signed, their letters abound with anxious warnings: Don't let the district know our names because they will tell the kolkhoz bosses and "they will drive us out of the kolkhoz." Don't write directly to me "because the Doronins will get it." "Please don't make my name known, otherwise I will be in trouble."[92]

OUTCOMES

In March 1936 the Starodub district branch of the NKVD received a denunciation of the head of the local prison, Georgii Molotkov, an NKVD officer and party member since 1918.[93] Its author had encountered Molotkov on vacation and reported that in casual conversation Molotkov had slandered various named NKVD personnel, calling them "fascists," unworthy of their positions. Molotkov had also mentioned that he had a girlfriend in Moscow, Katia, who worked as a cook for a foreign consulate, and that through her he had met the consul and his wife.

This denunciation set in motion a complicated process. First, the Starodub party organization decided that Molotkov was a suspicious character and suspended his party membership. Since an exchange of party cards (i.e., a membership purge) was currently in process, this was done simply by failing to issue a new card. Then, because Molotkov no longer had a party card, he was fired from his NKVD job. Nobody told Molotkov the reason for this. He concluded correctly that he had been the victim of a denunciation, but made the wrong guess about who had written it. He thought the author was his boss, Strigo, head of the Starodub NKVD, and surmised that its content had something to do with a case of wrongful imprisonment that was currently under investigation. So he sent off his own counterdenunciation to Ezhov in Moscow, blaming Strigo for this and other similar occurrences.

[91] For such a statement in an anonymous denunciation of a factory director, signed "Production worker," see TsGA IPD, f. 24, op. 2v, d. 1518, l. 8.

[92] RGAE, f. 396, op. 10, d. 128, ll. 66–69, 158–59, and 262. See also ibid., d. 65, ll. 212–14; d. 86, ll. 71–73; d. 87, ll. 281–84; d. 142, ll. 40–41; d. 161, l. 289.

[93] Smolensk Archive, WKP 355, 10–11. The documents give two versions of Molotkov's first name, Georgii and Sergei, though agreeing on his patronymic, Grigor'evich.

The central office of the NKVD then ran a check on Molotkov and found he had a number of blots on his record, including expression of dissatisfaction with life in the Soviet Union and "praising the way of life abroad" in the presence of nonparty people. But it was Katia and her foreign employers that evidently bothered the investigators most: "We attach very serious significance to the materials received on Molotkov's links with one foreign consulate in Moscow." The outcome was a decision that Molotkov should no longer be employed in the NKVD.

It is rare to find so detailed a record of the outcome of a denunciation as this one. Often there is no information at all in the archival file about what action, if any, was taken in response to a denunciation. In other cases, the information consists only of a marginal note indicating the initial bureaucratic processing: "File (*Arkhiv*, i.e., no action)," "Send to the NKVD," "Send to the Prosecutor," or "Ask the raikom for information."

The *Krest'ianskaia gazeta* archive is one of the best sources of information on outcomes because of the assiduity with which the newspaper followed up on denunciations and complaints. The newspaper's statistics on its handling of letters suggests that out of every seven denunciations sent to *Krest'ianskaia gazeta* in mid-1935, one was successful (i.e., resulted in punishment for the person denounced), one was unsuccessful, and the other five fizzled without any particular result.[94] This ratio may not hold for all denunciations, since "abuse" denunciations from peasants seem to have had an abnormally high chance of backfiring on their authors. Nevertheless, the three types of outcome are universal. Successful outcomes usually involved dismissal from jobs, expulsion from the party, arrest, criminal charges, or a combination of the four. For example, a Siberian engineer denounced by two workers in separate letters in 1930 failed to get past the state purge commission and thus presumably lost his job. The head of department of the Central Committee denounced for softness on Trotskyism in 1937 was immediately dismissed from his position. A kolkhoz chairman was dismissed from his job, expelled from the party, and arrested by the NKVD following his denunciation by kolkhozniks for abuse of power. Criminal charges were brought against a band of hooligans terrorizing a kolkhoz as a result of a kolkhoznik's denunciation, and an audit of kolkhoz books was ordered after a denunciation of the accountant. A multitarget anonymous denunciation in 1935 against class enemies in a district soviet was spectacularly successful: at least four people lost their jobs after an immediate NKVD investigation.[95]

[94] Fitzpatrick, "Readers' Letters," p. 165.

[95] GANO, f. 288, op. 2, d. 902, ll. 4–5, 6; RGASPI, f. 17, op. 114, d. 822, l. 62; RGAE, f. 396, op. 10, d. 161, l. 53; RGAE, f. 396, op. 10, d. 121, ll. 52–55, and d. 142, ll. 493 and 496–97; TsGA IPD, f. 24, op. 2v, d. 1518, ll. 164–66. Note that in this case the investigation was so prompt and the endorsement of the anonymous denunciation so complete that one is inclined to suspect a ruse.

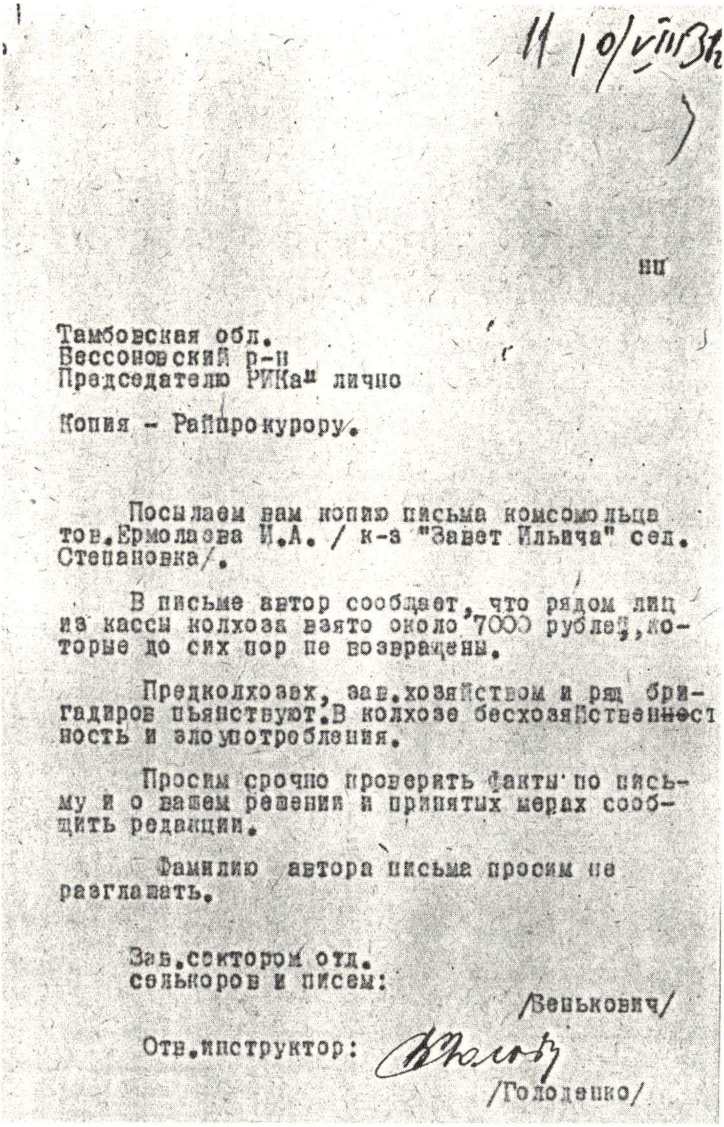

НП

Тамбовская обл.
Бессоновский р-н
Председателю РИКа" лично

Копия – Райпрокурору.

Посылаем вам копию письма комсомольца тов.Ермолаева И.А. / к-з "Завет Ильича" сел. Степановка/.

В письме автор сообщает, что рядом лиц из кассы колхоза взято около 7000 рублей, которые до сих пор не возвращены.

Предколхозах, зав.хозяйством и ряд бригадиров пьянствуют. В колхозе бесхозяйственность и злоупотребления.

Просим срочно проверить факты по письму и о вашем решении и принятых мерах сообщить редакции.

Фамилию автора письма просим не разглашать.

Зав.сектором отд.
селькоров и писем:
/Венькович/

Отв.инструктор:
/Голоденко/

Figure 9. "A denunciation is forwarded for investigation." Letter from *Krest'ianskaia gazeta* to district prosecutor requesting investigation of a denunciation, 1937. From RGAE, f. 396, op. 10, d. 142, unpag.

The most straightforward type of unsuccessful denunciation produced an investigation that concluded that the charges were groundless. For example, an anonymous denunciation, purporting to be from a worker at the Putilov plant, denounced a construction foreman as "a former contractor and exploiter" in 1934. The factory's party organizer, to whom the accusation was forwarded in 1934, said it was without foundation, and the case was dropped. A woman worker's denunciation of the director of a nursery for neglect and mistreatment of the children in her care was investigated in 1935 and found to be ill-founded, although the investigator admitted that the director's manner was stern and abrupt; no charges were brought. Suslova's accusation of attempted rape (see above, p. 226) was also dismissed by the local prosecutor, though in this case it is not clear that any real investigation took place: the key finding reported by the prosecutor to *Krest'ianskaia gazeta* was that "Suslova herself is the wife of an enemy arrested by organs of the NKVD"—that is, her complaint had no standing.[96]

Charges against kolkhoz chairmen in peasants' letters to *Krest'ianskaia gazeta* were often dismissed after investigation by the local authorities to which the newspaper had forwarded them. In addition, denunciations of local officials sometimes backfired, leading to the punishment of the author rather than the person denounced.[97] In the case of peasants who had written "abuse" denunciations, the criminal charges often involved stealing, slaughtering animals without permission, and similar economic offenses, but there was a specific criminal charge that could be brought for wrongful denunciation: slander. A Leningrader who denounced his Communist neighbors as "kulaks" and "Zinovievites" had an earlier conviction on his record for slander of these same neighbors, probably with similar allegations. A kolkhoznik was imprisoned, evidently on a conviction for slander, after his denunciation of a kolkhoz chairman was judged "clearly slanderous" and motivated by a desire for revenge after losing his job as head of the kolkhoz animal farm.[98]

Occasionally, even a successful denunciation backfired and resulted in criminal charges for the denouncer. For example, local authorities reported that, as a result of their investigation of a denunciation,

> kolkhoz chairman Manenkov has been dismissed from his job, and criminal charges have been brought against number of people, *among them being the author of the letter* . . . [who] is under arrest for antiso-

[96] TsGA IPD, f. 24, op. 2v, d. 727, l. 325; Ibid., d. 1534, ll. 166, 168–70; RGAE, f. 396, op. 10, d. 66, l. 180.

[97] For examples, see Fitzpatrick, "Readers' Letters," pp. 166–68.

[98] TsGA IPD, f. 24, op. 2v, d. 1516, ll. 88, 90; RGAE, f. 396, op. 10, d. 68, l. 78.

viet activities, obstruction of work in the kolkhoz, drunkenness, hooliganism, slander of honest workers, and so on.[99]

Prolonged investigations of a denunciation in which an initial outcome was reversed are occasionally recorded in the archives. A denunciation of a factory manager sent to the Leningrad purge commission in 1931 was investigated with great thoroughness: extra witnesses were sought out and interviewed, the background of the accusers was examined, and a lengthy statement was taken from the accused. At first it seemed that the denunciation had hit its mark, for the commission ruled that he should be dismissed from his job and not allowed to hold a senior position for three years, but this was reversed on appeal, and he evidently kept his job.[100]

A more dramatic version of the same pattern occurred after *Krest'ianskaia gazeta* forwarded a denunciation of a kolkhoz chairman to the district prosecutor in October 1937. The prosecutor had the chairman arrested and began criminal proceedings against him, but then the chairman was released—no reason is given, but presumably patrons in the district leadership intervened—and returned to his old job. Evidently he knew who had denounced him, because the denouncer (a kolkhoznik named Pavlenko) was immediately arrested. "There he sits in Ust-Labinskaia jail," Pavlenko's wife wrote pathetically to *Krest'ianskaia gazeta* in November, "and the other kolkhozniks say look what happens when you write to the paper and expose wrongdoing, you get sent where you don't deserve."[101]

. . .

We can think about the functions of denunciation in several ways. One way is to ask what a regime gets out of receiving denunciations from citizens. Another is to ask what citizens get out of writing these denunciations.

The first was the traditional approach in Sovietology, where denunciation was treated as a form of totalitarian control—in Merle Fainsod's words, "one of the important techniques developed by the regime to use the Soviet citizenry to spy on one another and to report on the abuses of local officialdom, to take the measure of popular grievances and to move,

---

[99] RGAE, f. 396, op. 10, d. 68, l. 325 (my emphasis).

[100] TsGA S-P, f. 1027, op. 2, d. 860ob, l. 52.

[101] RGAE, f. 396, op. 10, d. 68, ll. 77–78. After receiving Pavlenko's wife's letter, *Krest'ianskaia gazeta* sent a journalist to investigate, but he ended up agreeing with the district party committee's decision that Pavlenko's denunciation was malicious and the chairman essentially innocent.

where necessary, toward their amelioration."[102] Implicit in this approach was the assumption that denunciation was innately associated with totalitarianism, being a product of the climate of vigilance and mutual suspicion engendered by totalitarian regimes and a response to their insistence on ideological orthodoxy, conformity, and the exclusion of "alien elements" from the community.

This might be called the **surveillance** function of denunciation. While its traditional reference point was totalitarianism, it can be recast without difficult in Foucauldian terms.[103] In the Soviet context, it applies best to Communist-on-Communist "loyalty" denunciations, though there is also a type of "busybody" citizen denunciation that fits it well. In general, it is associated with the "Pavlik Morozov" category of denunciations discussed in the introductory section of this essay.

The second way of thinking about the function of denunciation is to take the citizen's perspective and ask what denunciation could do for the individual citizen and what he/she used this tool for. Jan Gross has made the intriguing suggestion that a totalitarian regime, by virtue of its willingness to receive denunciations from citizens, essentially put the coercive powers of the state at the service of the individual. The mechanism of denunciation, Gross writes, gave "every citizen . . . direct access to the coercive apparatus of the state," which could be used to "provid[e] an individual citizen with prompt settlement of some private dispute in his favor." In this sense, the totalitarian state was "at the disposal of every inhabitant, available for hire at a moment's notice."[104]

This might be called the **manipulation** function of denunciation. It applies particularly well to the category of private-interest denunciations—"apartment" denunciations and those connected with professional rivalries, village feuds, and the like—but obviously any genre of denunciation could be used for manipulative purposes. Those who use denunciation in this way usually lacked access to other social mechanisms, such as networks and "pull" (*blat, znakomstvo i sviazi*).

Manipulation for personal gain does not encompass the whole range of citizens' purposes in writing denunciations, however, in the Soviet Union or anywhere else. In all societies, there will be some citizens who use public accusation as a means of correcting injustice or protecting the interests of the community. These are the whistle blowers, familiar in a contemporary American context for their disclosures of wrongdoing in

[102] Merle Fainsod, *Smolensk under Soviet Rule* (Cambridge, Mass., 1958), p. 378.

[103] On the applicability of Michel Foucault's *Discipline and Punish*, see Robert Gellately, "Denunciations in Twentieth-Century Germany: Aspects of Self-Policing in the Third Reich and the German Democratic Republic," in *Accusatory Practices*, p. 185.

[104] Jan T. Gross, "A Note on the Nature of Soviet Totalitarianism," *Soviet Studies* 34:3 (July 1982), p. 375.

corporations and government departments.[105] They are the people who, in a French context analyzed by the sociologist Luc Boltanski, write letters to *Le Monde* exposing scandals and protesting against miscarriages of justice.[106] In the Soviet context, peasant "abuse of power" letters of the 1930s, continuing a long Russian tradition of peasant petition against unjust officials and landlords, constitute an important subgroup of whistle-blowing denunciations.

Writers of this kind of denunciation are attempting to exercise "the competence of justice," in Boltanski's phrase.[107] This **justice** function was characteristic of "subaltern" denunciations. Powerful people do not need to use denunciation as a way of seeking justice, any more than they need it for manipulative purposes.

Another way of thinking about the functions of denunciation is in terms of short cuts and surrogates for other social mechanisms. If bureaucracy works poorly and normal bureaucratic processes cannot be relied on, denunciation may function as a short cut, a way of getting around bureaucratic roadblocks. If the legal system is ineffective and judicial processes inaccessible, denunciation may serve as a substitute for law. Both these surrogate functions were operative in Russia in the Stalin period. In the case of law, the people's courts were unlikely to provide satisfaction for a citizen's grievance against an official, though they might be an adequate vehicle for his suit against another citizen. A great many denunciations were sent either directly or indirectly to state prosecutors, often leading the prosecutor to bring criminal charges against the denouncee. It is easy to see why a Soviet citizen might take this path, for the chances of success were undoubtedly greater in a legal action initiated by the prosecutor than one initiated in a lower court by a private plaintiff.[108]

Denunciations are never written in a vacuum. First and most importantly, they are letters to *authority*, and authority in any given context has its own codes, conventions, preferences, and spheres of action. People write the kind of denunciations they think are likely to be heard and acted upon by authority. One thing that this means in practice is that they denounce offenses that authority condemns and punishes. Societal interests also play a role, though one would guess a lesser one. After all, denuncia-

---

[105] On whistle-blowing, see Alan F. Westin, ed., *Whistle Blowing! Loyalty and Dissent in the Corporation* (New York, 1981).

[106] See Luc Boltanski, *L'Amour et la Justice comme compétences{{dagger}}: Trois essais de sociologie de l'action* (Paris, 1990), part 3, passim, and his article, with Yann Darré and Marie-Ange Schiltz, "La dénonciation," *Actes de la recherche en sciences sociales* 51 (1984), on which it is based.

[107] Boltanski, *L'Amour et la Justice comme compétences.*

[108] This raises the intriguing question of whether citizen denunciation is an integral part of all prosecutorial legal systems.

tion is typically a private transaction between an individual and the state. Only in exceptional situations does it assume functions of collective bargaining or conscious articulation of public opinion.

In Stalin's time, Soviet citizens denounced "class aliens" because alien social origin was punishable by disenfranchisement and other penalties. They denounced "kulaks" because kulaks were liable to expropriation and deportation, as well as disenfranchisement. They did not often denounce people for being Jews (as they would have done in Nazi Germany) because the Soviet regime in the 1930s did not marginalize Jews and condemned anti-Semitism. They did not often denounce people for sexual misbehavior, either because the authorities were perceived to be uninterested, or because it was not a dominant preoccupation in the society.

During the Great Purges, when Soviet authorities were calling for denunciations of many kinds, citizens responded generously, often used the party's nomenclature of "Trotskyites," "enemies of the people," "wreckers," and "spies." Yet it would be wrong to think of denunciation as something a regime can turn on and off at will, or order up with any precision. As we have seen, real-life Pavlik Morozovs seemed usually to denounce someone other than their parents, and this may have reflected their awareness that most people, even Communists, found this type of denunciation reprehensible. Ex-spouses generally found it more prudent to refrain from following the denunciatory example of General Iakir's ex-wife, despite *Pravda*'s encouragement.

Denunciation is always a matter of individual choice, whatever incentives regimes may offer and whatever personal advantages may be gained. The word "denunciation" (*donos*) was already pejorative in Russian in the 1930s, implying that many or most people condemned the practice.[109] If most people thought it was bad to write denunciations, why did so many people do it?

In the first place, not everybody wrote denunciations (or so we assume), and only a minority of people wrote denunciations often. Among those who wrote often, the historian comes to recognize some familiar types: paranoids, who felt they were being persecuted; people consumed by anger and malice, who wanted to hurt someone; graphomaniacs (perhaps a peculiarly Russian type),[110] who wrote for the love of writing and being read; and compulsive busybodies, who were always interested in other people's affairs and misdeeds.

---

[109] This is noted implicitly in Usakov's 1935 definition (see epigraph to this chapter) and explicitly in Ozhegov's *Slovar' russkogo iazyka* (1964). See also Kozlov, "Denunciation," p. 121.

[110] See Svetlana Boym, *Common Places: Mythologies of Everyday Life in Russia* (Cambridge, Mass., 1994), ch. 3.

In the second place, many writers of accusatory letters undoubtedly saw the practice as something other than denunciation. It is a familiar human trait to classify acts differently according to who performs them (If I write a denunciation, I am a public-spirited citizen; if my enemy writes one, he is a contemptible informer). Many of those who wrote "abuse of power" letters must have located them mentally in a category other than denunciation.[111] This was all the easier since Soviet citizens were in the habit of writing all sorts of letters to the authorities (complaints, petitions, appeals, and so on) that were not denunciations, and to which no odium was attached.[112]

Finally, a major reason for writing denunciations, even if one deplored the practice in principle, was that Soviet citizens had so few options for action. Law functioned poorly, the bureaucracy worse. There were few mediating institutions to deal with government on the individual's behalf, and those that existed, like the trade unions, were weak. In Stalinist society, some people were well connected and could pull strings to remedy injustices and mistakes or bypass bureaucratic roadblocks. But for the great majority who were not powerful or well connected, denunciation was one of the few available forms of agency, a way that the little man (as well as the malicious one) could hope to impose himself on his environment.

---

[111] The Russian scholar, Vladimir Kozlov, reports that, when writing his article on denunciation, he mentally used a nonpejorative label for the category of denunciation he identified as "disinterested." Kozlov, "Denunciation," in Fitzpatrick and Gellately, *Accusatory Practices*, pp. 130–31.

[112] On the range of citizens' letters, see above, chapter 9.

CHAPTER TWELVE

Wives' Tales

> *"The regulation of intimate relations by the Party has been
> an object of derision in the country for a long time. However,
> many Soviet women continue to consider party committee as
> final instances in which to force unfaithful husbands to stay
> with them, protect daughters from philanderers, and punish
> profligates of both sexes." (Shlapentokh, 1984)*[1]

In the 1930s, party committees do not seem to have concerned themselves
overmuch with the private lives and sexual morality of Party members.
This was not because of any ideological position protecting privacy: on
the contrary, the Party had always stated its right in principle to be interested in the private lives of citizens, especially Party members, and indeed
regularly exercised that right with regard to such specific matters as religious observance on the part of Communists and their families. But in
practice in the prewar period the Party did not want to hear about people's sex lives (or, by the same token, their drinking, if it was not totally
incapacitating), implicitly taking the view that there were other, more serious things to worry about.[2]

Fifty years later, Vladimir Shlapentokh describe a different situation,
one in which the Party was keenly concerned with its members' private
lives and women had developed the habit of appealing to the authorities
about private problems. This concern had been manifest "for a long
time," Shlapentokh says; certainly this was already the case in the 1960s,
when the balladeer Alexander Galich mocked it in his song "The Red
Triangle or Comrade Paramonova," told in the first person by Paramonova's luckless husband, whose escapades with a certain Nina have been
made known to his wife through an anonymous letter, leading her to quit
the marital home and appeal to the Party to punish him. Called into a

---

[1] V. Shlapentokh, *Love, Marriage, and Friendship in the Soviet Union* (New York, 1984),
p. 106.

[2] See, for example, Stalin's lack of enthusiasm for *"reklamnye vykriki protiv krainostei
v lichnoi zhizni"* (quoting with disapproval articles in a regional newspaper with headings
such as "Unrestrainedness in sex life is bourgeois," "One glass leads to another," and "Bandits of the double bed." From "Protiv oposhleniia lozunga samokritiki" (June 1928), in
Stalin, *Sochineniia* 11 (Moscow, 1952), 135.

party meeting, the husband admitted his fault ("I confessed the rotten West had been sapping / The foundations of my moral conceptions") and received a severe reprimand,[3] which both scared off Nina and allowed for a marital reconciliation under Party auspices.[4]

Just when and why this change in Party attitudes and practices occurred remains to be investigated, but it becomes visible in the 1940s, soon after the war. In the late '40s and early '50s, the archives of letters to the authorities show that, contrary to the situation in the 1930s, women frequently denounced their husbands to the authorities, citing not only marital misdemeanors but also other (sometimes criminal) offenses, and (in the case of men who were Party members), the Party and its control commissions were particularly popular addressees. At the same period, the Party seems to have become much more interested in listening to such complaints and punishing its members for "amoral behavior in everyday life" (*amoral'noe povedenie v bytu*) but also, more typically, counseling them on such matters—that is, assuming something like the role of a priest, a psychiatrist, or an Ann Landers in other societies. (Galich's song gives us a glimpse of this process, as conducted by a female party official, in his penultimate verse: "Side by side we're sitting in the Party office / And the lady says, all smiling and pleasant, / Well, he's had his reprimand, so let's drop it, / Now the pair of you should make up and mend things").[5]

The women's newly raised voices were angry and vengeful, the Party's response paternal, sometimes sympathetic with the erring male but also protective of the weak (women and children) and disapproving of disorderly lives and loose morals. The purpose of this chapter is to explore the change, comparing the ways wives talked to the authorities about themselves and their husbands in the pre- and postwar periods, and discussing possible sociopolitical and demographic causes for the change.

An Adulterous Love Affair

I will start with a story of an adulterous love affair and its denouncers that took place in Riga in 1952 and comes from the files of the Latvian Party Archives. On 17 June 1952, MGB Colonel G[6] wrote to the State

---

[3] Level 6 in the scale of party reprimands (see below, note 21).

[4] Aleksandr Galich, *Sochineniia v dvukh tomakh* (Moscow, 1999), pp. 217–19, "Krasnyi treugol'nik ili tovarishch Paramonova," dated 1964. The quotations are from the translations by Gerald Stanton Smith in G. S. Smith, ed., *Alexander Galich: Songs and Poems* (Ann Arbor, c. 1983), pp. 72–74.

[5] Ibid.

[6] I have substituted letters for the protagonists' real names, which are, of course, in the original archival document.

Prosecutor for the MGB armed forces in Riga reporting an adulterous love affair between MGB Colonel K, a married man in his early forties stationed in Riga, and a woman lawyer named S, aged forty-seven and resident in Riga. Colonel G's information came from the daughter of S, a student at Riga University, who had brought the case to the attention of the authorities by a telephoned denunciation (perhaps to him personally; he may have been a family acquaintance) in which she tearfully accused Colonel K of breaking up her parents' marriage and asked the republican military procuracy to intervene to punish him and save the marriage.[7]

Col. G accordingly started an investigation. His first step, taken on the daughter's advice, was to recruit S's best friend, "citizeness X,"as an informer (identified later in the file as U).[8] Citizeness X was willing, as long as her identity was concealed, because she disapproved of S's affair, thought K was too young for S, and feared the effect of any breakup of the family on S's sensitive daughter. She had told S of her concerns, but S would not listen to her. Even before Colonel G contacted her, citizeness X had made her own attempt to break up the affair: she had written an anonymous letter to K, appealing to him as "an officer and a Communist" to think of his wife and family and threatening to denounce the guilty pair to the Party and their employers. As citizeness X reported to Colonel G, the lovers were disturbed by the anonymous letter, but wrongly attributed its authorship to a former secretary in K's office.[9]

Col. G then called Col. K in for a talk. K admitted the affair, but said it wasn't serious. He promised to end his liaison with S and "not do anything like it again." Col. G was at first prepared to accept this assurance, but then changed his mind: it had become clear to him, he wrote, that "comrade K does not seriously intend to build his family life in Riga and still keeps thinking about the villa he has" in Simferopol (his wife was currently away in Simferopol, looking after her sick mother). "Living on two fronts, he turned out to be lacking in fortitude with respect to morals and family life and committed the dirty deed of interfering in the marital life of the S family," Col. G commented disapprovingly.[10]

Col. G's next step was to call in S, the adulterous wife, who spoke surprisingly freely (G may have been a personal acquaintance). She and K had agreed to keep the affair quiet, she said, but then K spilled the beans to Col. G—he was frightened for his career, and in S's evaluation "behaved childishly" (*po-mal'chisheski*). But S admitted that she was also

---

[7] LVA SPDN, f. 101, op. 15, d. 122, l. 93.
[8] LVA SPDN, f. 101, op. 15, d. 122, l. 93.
[9] LVA SPDN, f. 101, op. 15, d. 122, ll. 105–6.
[10] LVA SPDN, f. 101, op. 15, d. 122, l. 107.

at fault. "One well-known (*vidnyi*) party worker" had advised her earlier to break with K, and "some time ago . . . she tried to tell the Communists at that party meeting of her moral relapse, but at the last minute 'lacked the courage and determination.' " But it looked as if she lacked the desire as well as the will to break with K. She told Col. G that "if comrade K is severely punished, then if K's spouse refuses to follow him, she is determined to throw over her family and bear the responsibility before the party for following comrade K to his new workplace and mitigate her guilt before him."[11]

The outcome of Col. G's investigation was that K was sent away from Riga to a less desirable posting in the Russian provinces; K and S were told not to correspond, and agreed. They did correspond secretly, however, and this fact was duly passed on to the authorities.[12] But Col. G took no further action, and at this point, at least as far as Riga was concerned, the case was shelved.

THE PARTY AND PRIVATE LIFE

It is hard to pinpoint the moment when private life—or, in the terminology of the time, "so-called private life"—came to the fore as a Party concern.[13] Indeed, common sense would suggest that such changes normally come gradually, despite our ingrained Sovietological habit of always looking for a decree or authoritative ideological pronouncement to explain sociocultural shifts. The war and the attendant disruptions and marriage break-ups associated with wartime separation surely played a role. Rebuilding population after the staggering losses of the war was a major state concern, and, as the law of 8 July 1944 ("On increasing state help to pregnant women . . .") suggests, strengthening the family (as well as offering state support to children born outside wedlock) was assumed to be a prerequisite of population growth.[14] A brochure, *On the Moral Pro-*

---

[11] LVA SPDN, f. 101, op. 15, d. 122, ll. 108–10.

[12] LVA SPDN, f. 101, op. 15, d. 122, l. 116.

[13] "Tak nazymvaemaia chastnaia zhizn'." Two examples of this usage are given in the paragraph that follows. Note also the title of an article by D. Beliaev in *Pravda*, 4 July 1947, p. 3: "K voposu o 'chastnoi zhizni'."

[14] Decree "Ob uvelichenii gosudarstvennoi pomoshchi beremennym zhenshchinam, mnogodetnym i odinokim materiam, usilenii okhrany materinstva i detstva, ob ustanovlenii pochetnogo zvaniia 'Mat'-geroinia' i uchrezhdenii ordena 'Materinskaia slava' i medali 'Medal' materinstva'." For documentation of the party leadership's intense concern with population renewal in connection with the 1944 law, see Mie Nakachi, "The Patronymic of Her Choice: Khrushchev and the Postwar Family Law," chapter from University of Chicago Ph.D. dissertation in progress, "Replacing the Dead: The Politics of Reproduction in the Postwar Soviet Union, 1944–1955." For further discussion of the law, see below, p. 255.

file of Soviet Man, compiled in 1948 for the use of party propagandists and agitators, reminded Party members that "relations between the sexes are not only a personal affair," that "so-called private life demands an understanding of one's duty to the family," and that "in our society, dissolute behavior calls forth general indignation and contempt."[15] Newspapers periodically published stories deploring the bad behavior of men who abandoned their families, framing the issue in broader moral terms than had been the case with articles on desertion in the 1930s.[16] A feuilleton, "On the question of private life," published in *Pravda* in 1947 condemned work collectives that refused to intervene and discipline erring husbands in such cases on the grounds that "this has to do with his private life." Citing the case of a man who had not only left his pregnant second wife and their child for another woman but also tried to get them evicted from his apartment, the author noted that the offender, a candidate member of the Party, was in the process of applying for full membership—but "he forgot that one doesn't enter the sacred doors of the party with a clean collar and a biography that is tainted no matter in what respect—in the social [sphere] or in so-called 'private' life."[17]

As *Pravda*'s feuilletons usually originated in a denunciation or complaint sent in by a distressed citizen, the likely origin of this one was a letter from the wronged wife setting out her grievances. While the Riga story of an adulterous love affair discussed earlier was somewhat atypical in that the adulterous spouse is the wife rather than the husband, we find the same case originating in a similar way, through appeals and denunciations written by women (a telephone call from S's daughter; an anonymous denunciation from a concerned women friend). The procedure as we see it followed in the Riga case is that the authorities—in this case, military, since the man involved was a serving officer—then call in the protagonists, S and K, separately or together, and have a talk with them. In the Riga case, Col. G might have accepted K's assurance that he would break off the affair and dropped the case, but decided K was not leveling with him and therefore decided to pursue it further. S, when questioned, acknowledged that the proper course for her, a Communist (actually secretary of her local Party organization), would have been to confess the affair to her primary Party organization and receive its counsel for her "moral relapse."

[15] *O moral'nom oblike sovetskogo cheloveka: Sbornik materialov v pomoshch' propagandistam i agitatoram,* comp. A. S. Aleksandrov (Moscow, 1948), pp. 107–10.

[16] In the '30s, such articles typically focused on the practical question of preventing and punishing men who failed to pay child support. For examples, see Fitzpatrick, *Everyday Stalinism,* ch. 6.

[17] *Pravda,* 4 July 1947, p. 3.

We find similar an abundance of similar scenarios sketched out in the files of the Party's Central Control Commission (KPK), the agency in charge of disciplining individual party members. KPK investigations, too, almost invariably started with a denunciation[18] and led to the alleged offender, and often also the accuser, being called in for an interview with a KPK member.[19] During the war, such cases were few and KPK's interest level in moral issues was low: in 1943, for example, when the former wife of an important Party official—second secretary of the Voronezh obkom—complained about her husband's behavior, the KPK thought that the morals issue was adequately dealt with by calling the man in and getting his explanation, but worried that since his marital troubles had become widely known in Voronezh and perhaps undermined his authority, it might be better to move him to a similar position in another region.[20]

Many denunciations by wives arose out of a situation where the husband had taken a mistress, with whom he might be living, often with a child. The wives appealed to the authorities either to get him to return or to assert their entitlement to the marital apartment and child support. It was standard practice in the late Stalin period for the KPK or local Communist party bureau to call in the husbands and hear their explanation. Frequently, the explanation was accepted, perhaps with a promise from the husband to mend his ways, but occasionally the husband received an official rebuke.[21] Around 1952, for example, the bureau of the city Party committee in Gorky discussed an accusation from a woman Party member that her husband, also a Communist, a department head in the local militia, "conducts himself improperly in private life, has abandoned his family and lives with another woman." He received a level four reprimand.[22] High-ranking Communists with non-Party wives often got off

[18] One of KPK's files on such matters (RGANI, f. 6, op. 6, d. 1598) is headed "Materialy po proverki zaiavlenii o nepravil'nom povedenii v bytu, p'ianstve, khuliganstve" [January 1943—December 1950]. "Zaiavlenie" was one of the most frequent archival euphemisms for denunciation (see this book, chapter 11).

[19] The Komsomol also carried out such functions. See, for example, the case of a male student in Kuibyshev who dropped his de facto wife when she asked him to marry her and then married someone else, which earned the offender a rebuke entered on his Komsomol card. TsKhDNISO, f. 1683, op. 18, d. 181, l. 44 (excerpt from protocol of meeting of Kuibyshev Komsomol city committee, 16 February 1950).

[20] RGANI, f. 6, op. 6, d. 1598, ll. 2–3.

[21] The rebuke was usually a "vygovor," with or without "zanesenie v uchetnuiu kartochku." On the seven-level hierarchy of party reprimands (*partiinye vyskaniia*) that culminated in expulsion—1. *Predupredit'*; 2. *Ostavit' na vid*; 3. *Vygovor bez zaneseniia v uchetnuiu kartochku*; 4. *Vygovor s zaneseniem v uchetnuiu kartochku*; 5. *Strogii vygovor bez zaneseniia v uchetetnuiu kartochku*; 6. *Strogii vygovor s zaneseniem v uchetnuiu kartochku*; 7. *Iskliuchit'*—these stood in the middle. I have found no case in the postwar KPK archives where a morals accusation led to expulsion.

[22] See note 21, above, for the seven levels of Party reprimands.

more lightly. N, a former regional Party secretary, was denounced by his son for having a mistress and taking her and their young son rather than his wife to Moscow when he was sent on a training course. He explained that his wife, "who neither worked nor pursued further education, had fallen behind, become a philistine and surrounded herself with persons of the same kind, as a result of which the spiritual tie between them and his interest in her had disappeared," and stated self-righteously that he now felt "a moral obligation" to marry his mistress (formerly his secretary) and help bring up their child. The KPK found no reason to issue a reprimand.[23] Another wife asked the KPK to take action against her husband, a student at a higher party school under the Central Committee, who had allegedly abandoned her and their daughter. The KPK investigator found her to be a diagnosed schizophrenic whom her husband had sent back to her parents in the Far East and to whom he was making a large monthly payment. Called in for an interview, the husband said he had asked for a divorce and custody of his daughter, but that when his wife refused, he had dropped both requests. The investigator found no fault with his conduct.[24]

Another case that came to the attention of the Party several times in the early 1950s was that of a prominent Stakhanovite and industrial innovator of the 1930s, now become an engineer and Deputy of the Supreme Soviet, whom we will call G. G, whose story included three wives, children (including one of contested paternity), and serious alcoholism, received a Party rebuke for "unworthy conduct in everyday life" in 1950. In 1953 his second (de facto) wife, T, complained that he treated her and her child badly and asked the Party to take further disciplinary action. Having left his first wife and three children in 1941, G had been living in unregistered marriage with T and their second and only surviving child (whose paternity he contested) at his dacha, where he "got drunk and behaved outrageously, made scenes, and drove T and their child out of the dacha in the middle of the night," and then, to crown his offenses, finally officially divorced his first wife and went off and married a third woman. Called into the KPK, G admitted his alcoholism, for which he had received treatment, and his bad behavior to T (though making some counteraccusations, presumably having to do with the father of the second child), and promised to mend his ways. The KPK decided that no further disciplinary action was necessary.[25]

The high-ranking Communists with which the KPK habitually dealt usually paid some kind of child support and either ceded the apartment to their former wives (perhaps moving to the dacha, like G) or managed

[23] RGANI, f. 6, op. 6, d. 1598, ll. 100–103 (1949 case).
[24] RGANI, f. 6, op. 6, l. 3 (probably 1952 case).
[25] RGANI, f. 6, op. 6, d. 1666, ll. 74–75.

to find them other accommodation. Such was the case of another errant husband, L, who left his second wife in 1948 to live (evidently also at the dacha) with another woman, but paid her 5,000 rubles a month support for their two children (aged sixteen and ten), in addition to other financial support, and "had ceded to her their fine apartment in Moscow."[26] The second wife wanted more, however—namely, all the possessions acquired together in their Moscow apartment, and the dacha with all its furnishings, orchard, and building materials, "so that [L] would not put up any buildings on the plot for his other family" and his abandoned children would not have to suffer the new family's proximity. L, who obviously felt the original settlement was generous enough, was unconciliatory. The KPK's response is ambiguous: the woman who investigated the case, Abramova, was inclined to think he deserved a party reprimand, but Shkiriatov, the deputy head of the KPK, was evidently not fully convinced.

Housing was always a fraught issue in Soviet life, and sometimes an appeal to KPK was only one prong of a complex strategy for obtaining it. For example, the daughter of a government minister claiming an entitlement to a room in his Moscow apartment in an appeal to KPK was also suing him for this in the People's Court. We see some typical Soviet life paths in this story. D, the government minister involved, had an early provincial marriage that resulted in a daughter, born 1928, to whom he gave the resonant name of Sparta. Then in 1930 he went off to study in Leningrad and never returned to the family. Sparta moved from the provinces to Moscow in 1941, lived with an aunt, and in the years 1947–48, when she was a student at a technical college, her father made her an allowance of 300 rubles a month. Then in November 1938, D, who had a second wife and two children in Leningrad, acquired an apartment in Moscow. He moved his Leningrad family there, but also allowed Sparta to move in with them, probably as a way of getting her a Moscow residence permit. After less than a year, the second wife "drove Sparta out of the apartment." Sparta was married by this time, but she still wanted the room in D's apartment back. After calling in D and hearing his account of the matter, the KPK concluded that this demand was unjustified, though noting that the matter remained *sub judice*.[27]

Like Colonel G in Riga, the personal involvment of the KPK officials often and increasingly made itself felt in their reports, as the objective style characteristic of the first postwar years gave way to something less impersonal. Shkiriatov, in particular, becomes a distinct presence, as does the woman investigator, Abramova, and we hear more and more of the to-and-fro between KPK investigator and protagonists. Shkiriatov made

[26] RGANI, f. 6, op. 6, d. 1598, ll. 133–36.
[27] RGANI, f. 6, op. 6, d. 1599, ll. 29–33.

his own reactions almost the center of the story in his report to Central Committee secretary Nikita Khrushchev in June 1953 of a complaint from a woman, Z, against her former husband, N, a senior official working for the Central Committee. Z, who had remarried since the divorce from N, claimed that N had recently started to try to inveigle her into meetings with him and wanted to break up her new marriage. Instructed by the Central Committee Secretariat to investigate, Shkiriatov called in both Z and N for a conversation, but reported with disgust that the interview was pointless, since N did not deny the meetings but said that it was Z, the complainant, who had taken the initiative. Thus "it turns out to be impossible to clarify this issue and essentially there is nothing to investigate," concluded Shkiriatov, declaring the investigation closed.[28]

Abramova, whom we have already encountered as a sterner judge of a leading Communist's pecadillos than Shkiriatov in the case of L, tried her best for the women complainants, but not always successfully. In response to R's appeal to KPK "to preserve her family for her" after husband abandoned her and his daughters, Abramova had "many conversations with R and her husband, comrade S, but was unable to persuade him to return to his wife, "of which I have informed comrade R." Noting that S had already received a rebuke from his workplace Party organization, Abramova closed the file without recommending further action.[29] Another KPK investigator had a similarly frustrating time with Central Committee staffer N and his wife, who accused him of "unworthy behavior"—namely, having an affair with a woman staff member, A—and was in the process of divorcing him. N had already received a Party reprimand and been transferred from work in the Central Committee to a lesser job on the journal *Novosti*, but his wife was still not satisfied, though it was hard to work out what concretely she wanted. Finally, "when [A] was directly asked what she wanted from KPK, she answered that N should transfer living space to her, not tell lies about her in court, and have a better attitude to his daughter." He promised—with who knows what result, as KPK did not pursue the case further.[30]

MARITAL LOYALTY

Reading the denunciations of men by wronged women that were sent to the authorities in the postwar period—many of them full of anger and some of greed as well—it is easy to forget that, only a few years before,

---

[28] RGANI, f. 6, op. 6, d. 1666, l.128.
[29] RGANI, f. 6, op. 6, d. 1667, l. 48 (case of 1954).
[30] RGANI, f. 6, op. 6, d. 1667, l. 48 (case of 1954)

many wives were writing letters of a very different type about their spouses. For husbands arrested during the Great Purges of the late '30s, it was customary for wives to write passionate defenses, attesting to the husband's innocence and pleading for his release.[31] Although wives of "enemies of the people" were ipso facto at risk, and even had their own camps in Gulag[32] (though it was only the wives of very highly placed enemies who seem to have been routinely arrested), petitioning the authorities on behalf of one's husband evidently did not add to the risk; indeed, it seems to have been expected by the authorities and treated as perfectly natural that relatives would not only petition but also try to correspond, send parcels, and so on. The trope of the loyal wife, drawing heavily on the historical example of the Decembrists' Wives and the poet Nikolai Nekrasov's portrayal of their heroism, was very prominent in the Great Purge years, not just in petitions but in real life as well.[33]

In the postwar period, however, we encounter the loyal wife less frequently in the archives.[34] In the KPK files, the only example I came across was the wife of N, denounced by his son for taking a mistress (see previous). This wife, on being called into KPK, expressed astonishment at her son's letter, praised her husband, and said they had had a good marriage until recently and that she was unwilling to give written testimony against her husband "out of lack of desire to bring unpleasantness on [him]." (Her husband's ungrateful response to this was to label her a philistine—though, to be sure, she was refusing his request for a divorce.)[35]

One of the great disadvantages of letters to the authorities as a source is that they catch the writer at one moment, so that we see them frozen in a single stance—for example, that of the loyal wife—and we can scarcely imagine that they could play another role. In the case of S, however, heroine of the adulterous love affair in Riga discussed in an earlier section, we are more fortunate, thanks to information that S confided to Col. G in

---

[31] For examples of such letters, see above, p. 160. Marina Tsvetaeva's letter characterizing her arrested husband, Sergei Efron, as "incapable of treachery, double-dealing and perfidy" (quoted in Vitalii Shentalinskii, *Donos na Sokrata* [Moscow, 2001], p. 362) belongs to the same genre. Husbands wrote in defense of arrested wives too, though the occasion arose less often because women were less liable to arrest. For a touching example, see above, p. 176.

[32] See above, p. 222.

[33] In "Russkie zhenshchiny" (1871–72).

[34] In my (admittedly selective) reading of letters from citizens in the Latvian party archives 1945–52, I came across no petitions from wives on behalf of arrested husbands, although there were several such petitions from other family members (e.g., a sister protesting her brother's arrest on criminal charges in 1947: LVA SPD, f. 101, op. 10, d. 111, l.2; a daughter petitioning on behalf of her mother, imprisoned for assault, in 1952: LVA SPDN, f. 101, op. 15, d. 597, ll. 13–14).

[35] RGANI, f. 6, op. 6, d. 1598, l. 102.

the course of their conversations. Anxious to impress on Col. G that her relationship with K was really serious and long lasting, S told him that they had actually first met in the Ukraine in 1937–38, when both were posted there with their respective spouses. They had an affair and, according to S, K even proposed that both get divorced (though his wife was pregnant at the time) and marry each other. But then S's husband, an Army officer, was arrested. Telling K that "she did not have the moral right to leave her husband in such a position," S broke off the affair, and threw herself into the business of petitioning (*ser'ezno zanialas' khlopotami*) on her husband's behalf. Rather surprisingly, this worked: her husband was soon released from prison and his rank and party membership were restored.

By the 1950s, S's husband had shrunk into such insignificance (in her eyes, if not the eyes of her daughter) that he is scarcely mentioned in the voluminous documentation of her love affair and its aftermath.[36] But when he was arrested in the late 1930s, she had, in effect, cast him as a Decembrist and herself as a loyal Decembrist wife, ready to sacrifice everything for him. S retained her attachment to this trope even in the 1950s, but had to bend it rather drastically to make it fit the new circumstances: in a passionately romantic statement to Col. G, she said that if her lover (who, it will be remembered, had told the same interviewer that the affair was not really serious) were to be sent away as punishment for their affair, and if his wife were to refuse to follow him, she, S, would take up the mantle of womanly loyalty, give up her job and family life in Riga, and follow him as a gesture of atonement.

ANGRY WIVES

S's outburst of romanticism is a welcome diversion from the predominant mood of women's statements in the Riga archives, which is one of anger and resentment. The wronged wives writing in[37] often accused their husbands of other offenses, in addition to mistreatment of themselves and their children.[38] For example, a de facto wife accused her husband, a Com-

---

[36] According to a family friend, the husband, Major S, invalided out of the service, recently "left his job and was supposed to be having an affair with some woman." LVA SPDN, f. 101, op. 15, d. 122, l. 105.

[37] Almost all of them write in Russian and have Russian or Ukrainian names, no doubt reflecting the ethnic make-up of the Soviet ruling establishment in Riga, whose members (unlike the local Latvian population) were likely to feel entitled as well as inclined to write to the local Communist authorities on personal matters.

[38] Note that this archival source differs from the KPK files discussed earlier in that it is a record of letters received (with some information appended on outcomes), not of investiga-

munist cooperatives official, of embezzlement as well as bad treatment of herself and their son and forcing her to have an illegal abortion. (The husband had already received one Party reprimand about his "unethical attitude to the family.")[39] In another similar case, L, a 20-year-old wife of a Communist industrial manager wrote to the Latvian Central Committee: "The conduct of my husband is unworthy of a member of the Party: he comes home drunk, makes family scenes, insults me with obscene words and even movements of his hands, often does not come home at night, also claiming that he is busy at work[;] however on information at my disposal I know that my husband's position at work is far from good." He drinks samogon, L continued, and sleeps with employees at the plant, one of whom he got pregnant and forced to have an abortion; now he has abandoned L and their 2-year-old son, leaving them without means of support. (This denunciation earned the husband a reprimand from his local Party organization.)[40]

In some marriages, denunciation seems to have been become a standard ploy on the wife's part. P, a Communist, received several Party reprimands as a result of his wife's repeated denunciations: over a three-year period in the late '40s he had been dismissed or forced to leave his job five times for this reason. In 1950, when P's wife denounced him again for abandoning her and their 13-year-old son, a Party investigation followed—but then it was discovered that the couple was back together again, so no further action was needed.[41]

In addition to the angry denunciatory letters, the Latvian Party authorities also received appeals from wives—"weak, defenseless wom[en]," as one described herself—for protection.[42] V, wife of a high-ranking district official, wrote directly to the First Secretary of the Latvian Communist Party, Ian Kalnberzin, for "immediate help . . . in preserving [my] marriage": after thirty years of marriage, when "we are already on the threshold of communism," her "dear life's comrade," aged fifty-eight, had become entangled with a 26-year-old komsomolka, Z, who worked for him in the Ventspils district.[43] V's case was complicated by the fact that, in

---

tion prompted by such letters. The Latvian party archives also differ from other (mainly prewar) archives of citizens' letters that I have seen in being clearly labeled as denunciations, that is, letters containing "compromising data [*kompromat*] on members of the KPSS." Wives' denunciations form a significant proportion of all letters in these files.

[39] LVA SPDN, f. 101, op. 12, d. 290, ll. 4–7 (1949 case). The reprimand was a *preduprezhdenie* (level 1).

[40] LVA SPDN, f. 101, op. 12, d. 290, ll. 11–12 (1949 case). The reprimand was a *vygovor* (level 3 or 4).

[41] LVA SPDN, f. 101, op. 13, d. 387, ll. 155–59, 161.

[42] LVA SPDN, f. 101, op. 12, d. 290, ll. 172.

[43] LVA SPDN, f. 101, op. 15, d. 597, l. 1.

addition to his wife's appeal, his affair was denounced anonymously in the same month of 1952 by activists from the city of Ventspils, who complained that the district executive committee had become a brothel; the whole town was laughing at the affair and "even the countryside knows the whole story." V's wife having been dispatched to Moscow (a datum not mentioned in the wife's letter), Z was throwing her weight around in the office, "and there are rumors going round that [she] has a special mission to work over these kinds of bosses. After all, she also lived with his, that is V's, predecessors . . . and they were all married men. Tell us what the point of this is."[44]

Not surprisingly, V's version of events was different from his wife's. According to him, she had made scenes about his relations with Z even before there were any grounds: what she really wanted was to get back to Moscow, and she had now succeeeded. He wanted a divorce, and continued to insist on this when called in to an interview with a secretary of the Latvian Party. In light of his "refusal to continue his family life" with his wife, he was told to "resolve the situation on the basis of the law" (presumably to file a petition for divorce) and provide financial support to his family. It was also decided, no doubt in light of the anonymous denunciation, that "when the spring sowing ends, comrade V will be transferred to work in another district."[45]

Like the KPK in Moscow, the Latvian Party authorities wavered between their instincts to protect their own, that is, the errant husbands, and their sense of an obligation to protect "defenseless women." V's wife got scant sympathy from them, as did the young unmarried woman, A, who wrote in to accuse her former lover, C, a student, of moral degeneracy (moral'no-bytovoe razlozhenie) for seducing, exploiting, and abandoning her. A, who enclosed eleven love letters from him as material evidence, asked that he be given a severe Party reprimand for his conduct. Her story was as follows. Visiting her town as an intern, C had lived with her as man and wife in her parents' home for a month, and she gave him money, food, and other things. "Hiding under a mask of 'pure love' to me, he . . . was only interested in the material side and had ties to other women." He put off marriage, saying he needed to find an apartment and finish his studies, then disappeared. When she met him again, he was, alas, a changed man—"*khuligan,*" "*kham.*"[46] The local Party secretary who investigated the case, however, seemed more sympathetic to the young Don Juan than to his victim. It was true that C had deceived and abandoned A, but he had acknowledged his mistake to his school's Party organization

[44] LVA SPDN, f. 101, op. 15, d. 597, l. 2.
[45] LVA SPDN, f. 101, op. 15, d. 597, l. 11.
[46] LVA SPDN, f. 101, op. 12, d. 290, ll. 145–46.

and promised not to do it again. Moreover, the investigator reported, he had just married a staffer in the Kiev Party organization (clearly a step up socially from his small-town lover) and was currently away on his honeymoon. C got off with a warning, the lowest reprimand on the scale.[47]

Sometimes, however, the Party's condemnation was much sharper. Dr. A, a surgeon (judging by his name, ethnically Russian), was the object of repeated complaints and denunciations from his de facto wife, mother of his son, because he refused to marry her and did not pay for the child's upkeep. At first he received mild reprimands, but in the end he was actually expelled from candidate membership of the Party for "degenerate lifestyle (*bytovoe razlozhenie*) manifested in bigamy (*mnogozhenstvo*)" and "moral degeneration manifested in illegal cohabitation (*nezakonnoe sozhitel'stvo*)." What was meant by the last term remains obscure (cohabitation outside marriage was not usually described as "illegal"), but it appears that an important factor in the Party's decision was his failure to provide financial support for his son.[48]

Complicating matters in Latvian marital and personal conflicts brought to the attention of the authorities was the fact that Latvia was a recently acquired territory, formerly under German occupation and still incompletely Sovietized. This meant that—as in Russia in the 1920s—many people had "black spots" in their biographies due to family connections with émigrés and alleged collaborators ("Whiteguards"). Such connections, if known, made any accusations all the more credible and punishment more likely. In 1952, for example, T and M (a male and female teacher at a Party school, both married) were denounced by a woman student for adultery. An investigation showed that they had already received several official warnings about the impropriety of their conduct, but failed to heed them, and "demonstratively underlined their friendship, since they considered that the administration's reprimands and the opinion of the pupils on that question to be manifestations of philistinism (*obyvatel'shchiny i meshchanstva*)." Their defiance was already a very bad mark against them, but it turned out that there was worse: three of T's brothers were discovered to be "kulaks" and the fourth "a Whiteguard." T was dismissed from his position in the school as a result of this investigation.[49]

The converse was also true—namely, that a complaint, however justified, from someone with a black mark was unlikely to receive sympathetic consideration from the authorities. Thus in 1950, a district Party secretary

[47] Ibid., l. 157.
[48] LVA SPDN, f. 101, op. 11, d. 279, ll. 48–63 (1948 case).
[49] LVA SPDN, f. 101, op. 15, d. 598, l. 57.

reporting on his investigation following a wife's complaint against her husband noted that while "the husband, as Communist, bears a large part of the blame in the abnormal situation of his family life," at the same time the wife is "a politically untrustworthy, irresponsible woman" whose brother "has turned out to be a traitor to the motherland and has been convicted." This made the husband's wish to divorce her understandable, and the local Party organization supported his intention.[50]

THE PROBLEM OF DIVORCE

The war was a time when husbands and wives were often apart, fearing for each other's safety, uncertain if they would ever meet again. In addition to the millions of men (and some women) serving in the armed forces, millions of women had been evacuated to distant parts of the Soviet Union. Popular culture reflects the emotional turmoil of these years. There was an intense celebration of the women's loyalty, expressed both in the immensely popular song "Wait for Me"[51] and in Ilya Ehrenburg's paean to the "wives and girlfriends who waited—tenderly, sternly, with a strength worthy not of novels but of ancient tragedy—for their loved ones."[52] At the same time, men at the front feared that their women back home would find someone else.[53] Women had their own fears of their men's unfaithfulness with the so-called field wives—women on army (often medical) service. And, in the many cases where both spouses were absent from the prewar marital home, there was the additional shared fear that their apartment, which, with most of their possessions, was often occupied by an institution or strangers, would never be recovered.

When the war ended, the problems of resuming prewar life were scarcely less formidable.[54] It took some years to demobilize the whole contingent of conscripts. Those returning from evacuation to previously

---

[50] LVA SPDN, f. 101, op. 12, d. 290, l. 174.

[51] "Zhdi menia," words by Konstantin Simonov, music by Matvei Blanter, from the 1943 film of that name. The song suggests that if the loyalty of the woman at home is sufficient (if she "knows how to wait"), her man will survive and come back to her.

[52] Quoted from Ehrenberg's *Glaza Zolushki* in *O moral'nom oblike*, pp. 105–6.

[53] Diaries and letters from the front often express this concern: see, for example, "Frontovoi dnevnik N. F. Belova, 1941–1945 gody," in *Vologda. Kraevedcheskii al'manakh*, vypusk 2, ed. M. A. Beznin (Vologda, 1997), pp. 471–72, letter from A. D. Zharikov to wife (7 March 1943) in *Voenno-istoricheskii zhurnal* 4 (1995), p. 50. The film *Zhdi menia*, discussed above, featured an unfaithful as well as a faithful wife: the latter's husband survives the war, while the former's husband perishes.

[54] See Mark Edele, "A 'Generation of Victors?' Soviet Second World War Veterans from Demobilization to Organization, 1941–1956," Ph.D. dissertation, University of Chicago, 2004.

occupied areas were likely to find their homes destroyed, while those returning to other big cities like Moscow might find their apartments occupied by others who refused to move out and their possessions scattered, stolen, or vandalized. The kolkhoz, from which many men had been called up, was not necessarily an attractive place for them to return to. Millions of men had died in the war; women's deaths were proportionately smaller. In the age group aged twenty to forty, as the war ended, there were more than three women for every two men; for those forty and up in 1945, the ratio was more than two to one.[55] In other words, men were once again a deficit commodity, putting wives in an embattled position because of the numerical strength of the competition. Among the multitude of stories of women's disappointment when their men failed, for whatever reason, to return, one has particularly poignancy: that of the woman in Omsk who received word from her husband that he had been demobilized in Riga but who then lost him (to an accidental death? to another woman?) somewhere along the route home.[56]

The literature of the period provides many examples of painful readjustments when the couples did get together.[57] Obviously, the reaction of many in such situations—as in all the belligerent countries—was to consider divorce, but in the Soviet Union this was not so easy. Divorce, freely obtainable before 1936, had been made somewhat more difficult under the 1936 law. It was made yet harder to obtain by the wartime law of 8 July 1944, which, in conformity with the stated objective or "strengthening the Soviet family and marriage," for the first time since the Revolution required a court hearing and imposed a filing fee for divorce of 500–2,000 rubles (compared to 100–200 rubles under the 1936 law).[58] The courts were instructed not to approve "irresponsible" divorce petitions and told to try to achieve reconciliation of the parties wherever possible. To add to the formidable character that divorce proceedings had now acquired,

[55] Data from 1959 census, cited from Ernst Eisendrath, *Das Bevölkerungspotential der Sowjetunion* (Berlin, 1960), p. 34.

[56] LVA SPDN, f. 101, op. 10, d. 111, l. 52.

[57] For example, Vera Ketlinskaia's story "Nastia" (1945), in which an engineer, Pavel, returns after the war to his worldly, cynical "good wife" but longs for his wartime companion in Leningrad, discussed in Vera S. Dunham, *In Stalin's Time: Middle-Class Values in Soviet Fiction* (Cambridge, Mass., 1976), pp. 55–58; Wanda Wasilewska's *Prosto liubov'* (1945), on a man who returns to his wife hideously crippled, discussed in Anna Krylova, " 'Healers of Wounded Souls': The Crisis of Private Life in Soviet Literature, 1944–1946," *Journal of Modern History* 73:2 (2001), pp. 321–24, 327–29. The 1948 brochure *O moral'nom oblike* also addressed this question, noting that the "overwhelming majority" of such cases were resolved "courageously and humanely" by the women's readiness or even eagerness to take back their invalided husbands (p. 105).

[58] For a summary of the law's most significant provisions on divorce, see G. M. Sverdlov, *Sovetskoe zakonodatel'stvo o brake i sem'e* (Moscow-Leningrad, 1949), p. 64.

prosecutors—associated in popular mind with criminal (and political) cases rather than civil ones—were supposed to get involved in divorce cases where there was contestation and minor children were involved, interrogating the spouses and their witnesses (though it is not clear that this actually happened much in practice).[59]

The impact of the new law on the number of divorces was striking. In the city of Moscow just before the war, divorces were running at 10–12,000 annually. This dropped during the war to just under 4,000 per year in 1943 and 1944, but in 1945, after the introduction of the new law, it dropped precipitously to a total of 679 (less than 6% of the 1940 figure). By 1947–48 it was in the 4–5,000 range and in 1949–50 up to 7–8,000 per year, but it was not until the 1960s that the figure for 1940 was equaled.[60] All-Union figures dropped from 198,400 divorces in 1940 to 6,600 (about 3%) in 1945, rising to 41,000 in 1948.[61]

On the basis of materials in the Latvian Party archives, it would appear that in most postwar divorce petitions, men were the petitioners (often because they had found another partner); where there was resistance to divorce, it usually came from women.[62] This impression is reinforced by the sex breakdown of petitioners for divorce in cases considered by the USSR Supreme Court's college on civil cases in 1947: of the 103 petitioners who could be identified by sex, 89 (86%) were men.[63] Not that women were behindhand in bringing legal actions, for the courts were full of their petitions for child support. Nonpayment of child support in cases of separation and divorce had always been a problem in the Soviet Union, but now that problem was exacerbated: as a leading Soviet procuracy official noted, complaints to the procuracy about nonpayment rose sharply in 1946–47, and satisfaction of the women's claims was compli-

[59] See V. Tadevosian and S. Zagore, "Praktika primeniia ukaza Prezidiuma Verkhovnogo Soveta ot 8 iiulia 1944 g. o rastorzhenii braka," *Sotsialisticheskaia zakonnost'*, 1945 no. 8, pp. 6–7. Tadvosian and Zagore say that prosecutors ought to be involved, but in practice rarely are, because they don't know what they are supposed to do. I have come across no references to prosecutors' involvement in divorce material from the late 1940s.

[60] Figures from TsMAM, f. 2511, op. 1, d. 1.

[61] "Demograficheskaia situatsiia v SSSR v 40-e gody (po dokumentam 'osoboi papki' Stalina," *Otechestvennye arkhivy*, 1996 no. 2, p. 28. Note that, in Moscow, divorces were running substantially higher in the late 1940s than in the Soviet Union as a whole: Moscow's 1948 tally of divorces stood at 40% of the 1940 rate, compared to 20% for the Soviet Union.

[62] See LVA SPDN, f. 101, op. 12, d. 84, : *Obzor o sudebnoi praktike Verkhovnogo Suda Latviiskoi SSR po delam o rastorzhenii braka (sent.-noiabr' 1949 g.).*

[63] GARF, f. 9474, op. 5. The cases themselves were not available to this researcher; this count is made from the *opis'* or archival inventory (with thanks to Aleksandr Livshin for his assistance). The number of petitioners whose gender could not be ascertained by their last name was forty.

cated by the fact that many of the delinquents had simply taken advantage of postwar turmoil to vanish.[64]

One of the peculiarities of the 1944 law was that, while it required that the person seeking divorce needed to have serious grounds for the courts to grant his or her petition, it did not spell out what grounds it considered adequate.[65] In the great majority of filings by men, the real reason seems to be wanting to marry (and, in most cases, already cohabiting and having a child with) another woman. But sometimes the petitions cited abusive or slovenly behavior by the wife (for example, "cursing and threatening to shoot" the husband), or the wife's adultery.[66] Another approach was for the man to argue that he had grown apart from his wife because of her cultural backwardness. "I am a qualified engineer. I move in cultured society," F wrote in his divorce petition. "My friends—engineers, chess-players—often visit me at home. I am a chess lover. My wife is a backward, uncultured person. She works as a cook. Not only does she not read *belles-lêttres*, she reads even the newspapers very rarely. She can't play the piano, has no conception of chess and is not interested in it. I am ashamed before my comrades to have such a wife. I ask for a dissolution of our marriage."[67]

This last petition was a relatively easy one for the court to decide: it refused engineer F a divorce.[68] But other cases could be very difficult, all the more because of the lack of specificity in the law about grounds. Analyzing 400 cases from the first year of the law's implementation, one legal scholar concluded (approvingly) that the courts obviously thought mutual consent was adequate grounds for divorce, though they were sometimes unwilling to grant a divorce in contested cases when there were minor children, but otherwise it was hard to work out what their criteria

[64] Report of Chief Prosecutor of the USSR Gorshenin, 23 December 1948, in GARF, f. 8131, op. 37, d. 3805, l. 70. Gorshenin noted that one popular means of avoiding payment is "to cease contact with the family and hide one's whereabouts."

[65] As noted by V. Tadevosian, writing in *Sotsialisticheskaia zakonnost'*, 1944 no. 11, p. 41, the 1944 law "does not give a list of grounds serving as basis for the dissolution of marriage. The court decides that question in each individual case and taking into account the circumstances."

[66] LVA SPDN, f. 101, op. 12, d. 84, l. 12. The court did not believe this argument, concluding that the petitioner's real grounds for wanting a divorce were that he was living with another woman.

[67] Cited in *Sotsialisticheskaia zakonnost'*, 1949 no. 3, pp. 5–6.

[68] Ibid. As the court's (or the prosecutor's?) investigation disclosed, the couple had been married for twelve years and had three children. The husband, a *vydvizhenets* from the working class, had been supported by the wife for five years while he was in school. After the court explained that S had no grounds to ask for a divorce, "S, embarrassed, withdrew his application and apologized to his wife."

were.[69] Legal opinions in 1946–47 were inclined to favor divorce in cases where the marriage had demonstrably and irrietrievably broken down[70] or where a marriage had formally taken place but not led to real marital relations.[71] They did not consider adultery in itself grounds for divorce (though viewing it more seriously if committed by the wife than by the husband), but were inclined to grant divorces if the unfaithful partner had actually set up a new de facto partnership and if a child had been born to it.[72] In a case involving a VIP (both a general and a member of the Academy of Sciences) that was appealed up to the Supreme Court in 1946–47, a lower court refused his divorce petition because his wife opposed it and an (adopted) child was involved, but the Supreme Court reversed this ruling on the grounds that the wife wanted to hold onto the husband's property rather than the marriage itself, no children had been born to the marriage, and the general's new ("happy") relationship had already produced one child, with another on the way.[73]

Things got more complicated in 1949, when the Supreme Court of the USSR decided that lower courts were being too liberal in granting divorces. The divorce rate was indeed rising sharply, though still low by comparison with prewar levels: in 1949, despite the presumed impact of the Supreme Court's decision of July 1949 in the second half of the year, there were 63% more divorces in the city of Moscow than in the previous year.[74] And it appears that the initial postwar drop in the divorce rate was less a product of court refusals than of intimidated citizens deciding not to file.[75] This the Supreme Court set out to change. It was wrong for the courts to assume that "the will of the spouses to end a marriage" is sufficient reason to grant a divorce. Nor should they think that a spouse's establishment of a de facto relationship with another woman was in itself

[69] G. M. Sverdlov (kandidat nauk), "Nekotorye voprosy sudebnogo rastorzhenii braka," *Sovetskoe gosudarstvo i pravo*, 1946 no. 7, pp. 23–26.

[70] For example, in the case of a couple that separated in 1944, dividing their joint property, and agreeing that the two children should stay with the father. *Sudebnaia praktika Verkhovnogo suda SSSR*, 1946–47, vyp. 9, p. 7.

[71] This may mean nonconsummation of marriage: the court concluded that "the actual absence of marital relations" (*fakticheskoe otsutstvie brachnykh otnoshenii*) was grounds for dissolution of the marriage, but the commentary makes no mention of sexual relations, focusing on the fact that the spouses lived in different apartments and discovered "great differences in character." *Sudebnaia praktika Verkhovnogo suda SSSR*, 1946–47, vyp 9, pp. 7–8.

[72] *Sotsialisticheskaia zakonnost'*, 1946 no. 6, p. 29.

[73] *Sudebnaia praktika Verkhovnogo suda SSSR*, 1946–47, vyp 7, pp. 19–20.

[74] TsMAM, f. 2511, op. 1, d. 1. The figures were 4,811 (1948) and 7,581 (1949).

[75] According to Sverdlov's study of 400 1945 cases (cited above, note 69), only 5–6% of petitions were rejected. Even in contested cases—about a third of the whole—the rejection rate was only 23%.

grounds to dissolve a legal marriage. People's courts were not taking the task of reconciliation with which they were charged sufficiently seriously. They should remember that their most important charge was "strengthening the Soviet family and marriage," which in the Supreme Court's current interpretation meant maintaining marriages that already legally existed.[76]

The strict intentions of the All-Union Supreme Court are indicated in its judgement on a case that went through several levels of appeal. The P's marriage of thirty-two years had "ceased" in 1940. During the war, wife P was evacuated while the whereabouts of her husband, who was evidently a senior official, are unclear: probably, given his age, he was not called up but remained in Moscow in the apartment issued him by the government agency for which he worked. By the end of the war, at any rate, P had moved another woman into the apartment, and when his wife, who was by now a first-category invalid, returned from evacuation, P refused to register her or allow her to move back into the apartment, attempting instead to have her placed in a psychiatric hospital. The Supreme Court characterized this behavior as "criminal" and endorsed his wife's right to live in the marital apartment and receive support from her husband.[77]

Judging by the available figures, the Supreme Court's new directive had an impact, but not to the point of reversing the rising trend of divorce (in the city of Moscow, for example, numbers of divorces were up almost 7% in 1950 as compared with 1949, admittedly an improvement on the 63% rise the previous year).[78] In Latvia the republican Supreme Court rejected 39% of the divorce cases that reached it via appeal in the period September-November 1949 (and 61% of cases that were contested).[79]

• • •

Dealing with postwar materials on private life and divorce, one has a feeling of a real "battle of the sexes" going on, with a level of hostility between men and women not seen in the prewar period. While the evidence adduced in this chapter is not sufficient to draw firm conclusions, it seems worth investigating this further. If there was indeed a postwar battle of the sexes, the war surely played an important and complex role here in causing family separations, which often resulted in marital break-

---

[76] Resolution of the plenum of the Supreme Court of the USSR, 16 September 1949, in *Sudebnaia praktika Verkhovnogo suda SSSR*, 1949 no. 11, pp. 1–4.

[77] *Sudebnaia praktika Verkhovnogo suda SSSR*, 1949, vyp 4, p. 3.

[78] TsMAM, f. 2511, op. 1, d. 1. The figures were 7,581 (1949) and 8,091 (1950). The rate of increase stayed in a similar range for the next few years.

[79] LVA SPDN, f. 101, op. 12, d. 84, l. 129.

ups, killing off large numbers of men and thus making men a scarce good for which women—whether they wanted to or not—found themselves competing. Another contributing factor must have been the 1944 family law and the restrictions it placed on divorce.

At this same period, the Party's involvement in the private life of its members increased. (It is not clear whether or not there was any comparably increased involvement of state organs and workplaces in the private lives of non-Communists in the immediate postwar period, though there is certainly evidence for this by the mid 1950s.)[80] One might assume that for men, who were generally the target of criticism, such increased attention was unwelcome, but this does not necessarily hold true for women, who were usually the complainants. Judging by the KPK materials (based on an elite sample, since they dealt only with Communists and their families), many women were eager to have the Party intervene in their personal lives, since they expected its support in their conflicts with absconding husbands and lovers. Such expectations are analogous to those of the women who, in the 1930s, appealed for state and party intervention in their disputes on child support, though there is a change in the character of the appeals (more tending to the humble and supplicatory tone before the war, and to the angry and self-righteous tone after it).

The use of denunciation in marital warfare seems to be mainly an innovation of the postwar period, and to have been characteristically a weapon of women. Clearly, there was an instrumental motive—namely, the new utility of denunciation in preventing unwanted divorces. But it seems likely, as the epigraph to this chapter suggests, that women (unlike men) often responded to the developing paternalism of the party-state in a positive way and regarded themselves as being under its protection, and that their use of denunciations against spouses and lovers reflected these attitudes. The hypothesis that women tended to welcome the post-Stalinist party-state's interventions in "so-called private life," and men to resent them, deserves further investigation.

Women also wrote denunciations of immoral behavior by men in the expectation that they would be well received by the authorities. This was probably not just because of the state's strong pro-family and anti-promiscuity line but also because of increased state encouragement of denunciation in the postwar period, expressed in the 1947 decree making persons

[80] See Deborah A. Field, "Irreconcilable Differences: Divorces and Conceptions of Private Life in the Khrushchev Era," *Russian Review* 57:4 (1998), pp. 599–600, and Brian LaPierre, "Redefining the Hooligan: The Rise of Domestic Hooliganism, 1939–1966," ch. 2 of University of Chicago Ph.D. dissertation in progress, "Defining and Policing Hooliganism in Soviet Russia, 1945–1964."

who knew of crimes but failed to denounce them (*nedonositeli*) criminally responsible along with the perpetrators. The decree (which dealt specifically with crimes of robbery and embezzlement) established a duty to denounce from which family members were not exempt and was characterized by one legal commentator as "a new expression of the social duty (*dolg*) and social morality of Soviet man."[81]

[81] This ruling, contained in the Supreme Soviet's decree of 4 June 1947 "Ob ugolovnom otvetstvennosti za khishchenie gosudarstvennogo i obshchestvennogo imushchestva," is discussed in G. Aleksandrov, " 'Otvetstvennost' nedonositelei po ukazom Verkhovnogo Suda SSSR ot 4 iiunia 1947 g.," *Sotsialisticheskaia zakonnost'*, 1950 no. 7, pp. 26–34, and I. Gorelik, "Otvetstvennost' nedonositelei po ukazom prezidiuma Verkhovnogo Suda SSSR ot 4 iiunia 1947 g.," *Sotsialisticheskaia zakonnost'*, 1950 no. 12, pp. 28–30.

PART V

Impostures

CHAPTER THIRTEEN

The World of Ostap Bender

The trickster has a long history in real life and literature. He is a personage in folklore all over the world.[1] The prime characteristic of a trickster is to play tricks, deceive, and cheat; nevertheless, he is generally a sympathetic figure in folklore, and his tricks are often performed in a spirit of fun, not for personal gain. Folkloric tricksters may be pranksters like Till Eulenspiegel; they may have the ability to turn into animals; they are often subverters of authority and social conventions; they are *bricoleurs*, capable of ingeniously using whatever materials are at hand to get out of trouble; sometimes, like Hermes (Puck in Shakespeare's *Midsummer Night Dream*), they may even be messengers of the gods.[2] The significance of the folkloric trickster has been interpreted in various ways, but most interpretations emphasise the trickster's function as a subverter of norms, one whose jokes (in Mary Douglas's words) make people realize "that an accepted pattern has no necessity" and who carries "the suggestion that any particular ordering of experience may be arbitrary and subjective." As in the world of Bakhtinian carnival,[3] this subversion is neither permanent nor necessarily threatening to the powers that be: the trickster's prank "is frivolous in that it produces no real alternative, only an exhilarating sense of freedom from form in general."[4]

Every society and literature has its own tricksters. In modern times, the confidence man—one who assumes a false persona for the purpose of gain, usually in order to extract money from gullible individuals—is one of the most common variants. In literature—and very likely in real life, too—mid-nineteenth-century America provided the archetypes.[5] It has been said that

---

This chapter is drawn from "The World of Ostap Bender: Soviet Confidence Men in the Stalin Period," *Slavic Review* 61:3 (2002), pp. 535–57.

[1] See William J. Hynes and William G. Doty, *Mythical Trickster Figures: Contours, Contexts, and Criticisms* (Tuscaloosa and London, 1993).

[2] This typology is drawn from Hynes and Doty, *Mythical Trickster Figures*, pp. 32–45.

[3] See Mikhail Bakhtin, *Rabelais and his World*, trans. Helene Izwolsky (Bloomington, Ind., 1984), pp. 94 and passim.

[4] Mary Douglas, "The Social Control of Cognition: Some Factors in Joke Perception," *Man* 3:3 (September 1968), p. 365.

[5] But note that confidence men were also a preoccupation of twentieth-century German literature, notably the Dadaists in the 1920s: see Walter Serner, *Lezte Lockerung: Ein Handbrevier für Hochstapler und solche die es werden wollen* (Munich, 1984; first pub. 1927).

"the American trickster par excellence is the traveling salesman."[6] In fact, nineteenth-century American literature offers a broad assortment of confidence men, including charismatic preachers as well as sellers of snake oil. In Herman Melville's classic exploration of the topic, *The Confidence Man*, written in the 1850s, a Mississippi riverboat provides the setting in which a bewildering array of confidence men using various scams and guises seek to persuade fellow passengers to part with their money.[7]

In Russia, the literary and real-life lineage of the trickster has its his own peculiarities, notably a focus on imposture.[8] Gogol's Khlestakov, the ne'er-do-well en route from St. Petersburg to his father's country estate whom local officials mistake for a visiting government inspector and do their best to bribe so as to prevent an unfavorable report, is often read as the classic literary example.[9] An even older model of the Russian imposter-trickster were *samozvantsy*, impersonators of Tsars like the "false Dmitrii" in the early seventeenth century and Pugachev in the eighteenth.[10] Writing at the end of the nineteenth century, V. G. Korolenko used a derivative of the old term, *samozvanshchina*, to categorize the various types of petty imposter—traveling holy men, self-styled engineers, judges, and officials—whose criminal activities were reported as *faits divers* in the boulevard press of the 1890s.[11]

Writing at the same period about the Kiev criminal world, Aleksandr Kuprin noted the emergence of a new flamboyant type of criminal, the

---

Probably the most famous of all literary studies of confidence men is Thomas Mann's *Confessions of Felix Krull, Confidence Man* (first published in 1954 as *Bekenntnisse des Hockstaplers Felix Krull: Der Memoiren erster Teil*, but set primarily in Europe forty to fifty years earlier).

[6] John Greenway, *Literature among the Primitives* (Hatboro, Penn., 1964), cited in Hynes and Doty, p. 18.

[7] There are a number of scholarly monographs on this literature, starting with Susan Kulmann, *Knave, Fool, and Genius: The Confidence Man as He Appears in Nineteenth-Century American Fiction* (Chapel Hill, 1974). One of the most useful is Gary Lindberg, *The Confidence Man in American Literature* (New York, 1982). On real-life confidence men in America, see David M. Maurer, *The Big Con* (1940) and Jay Robert Nash, *Hustlers and Con Men* (New York, 1976).

[8] The traditional Russian words for trickster and his trickery were *plut* and *plutovstvo*. These had become archaic by the early Soviet period, when the terms most frequently used in the press for real-life tricksters were *moshennik*, *zhulik*, and *aferist*.

[9] Nikolai Gogol, *Revizor* (*The Inspector General*) (1836). In fact, as Catriona Kelly pointed out to me, Gogol insisted (contrary to the popular reading) that Khlestakov had no intention to deceive, and that a better literary example would be Iakov Kniazhnin's *Khvastun* (*The Boaster*), an eighteenth-century play in which a con man passes himself off as a count.

[10] On *samozvantsy*, see Claudio Sergio Ingerflom, "Les representations collectives du pouvoir et l'"imposture' dans la Russia des XVIIIe-XXe siècles," in Alain Boureau and Claudio Sergio Ingerflom, eds., *La royauté sacréee dans le monde chrétien* (Paris, 1992).

[11] V. G. Korolenko, "Sovremennaia samozvanshchina" (1896), in his *Polnoe sobranie sochinenii*, 9 vols., (St. Petersburg, 1914), v. 3, pp. 271–368.

aferist or confidence man. "He buys his clothes at the most fashionable tailors, frequents the best clubs, and bears a sonorous (and, of course, invented) title. He lives in the best hotels and is often distinguished by his elegant manners. His tricks with jewelers and bankers' offices often bear the mark of an inventiveness of near-genius, combined with an extraordinary knowledge of human frailties. He takes on the most varied roles, beginning with messenger and ending with provincial governor, and performs them with a skill that any first-class actor would envy."[12] One of Kuprin's examples was Nikolai Savin, a turn-of-the-century confidence man whose legendary exploits included assuming the persona of "Count Toulouse-Lautrec," obtaining a large loan from Paris bankers for the Bulgarian government, and being awarded the Bulgarian crown by a grateful nation before he was unmasked at the Turkish court by a hairdresser who had known him in Russia.[13]

In Soviet literature, the archetypal conman is Ilf and Petrov's Ostap Bender, protagonist of the humorous novels *The Twelve Chairs* and the *Little Golden Calf*.[14] The formalist critic Viktor Shklovskii traced Bender's descent from the picaresque "trickster" heroes of European and American literature, from Lesage's Gils Blas and Fielding's Tom Jones to Mark Twain's Huckleberry Finn, rather than from any Russian ancestors.[15] But clearly Ilf and Petrov's "smooth operator" (*velikii kombinator*) did have antecedents in both Russian[16] and Yiddish[17] literature, as well as in the real life exploits of turn-of-the-century *samozvantsy* and *aferisty*.

---

[12] A. I. Kuprin, "Kievskie tipy: Vor" (1895), in his *Sobranie sochinenii v deviati tomakh*, vol. 9 (Moscow, 1964), p. 38.

[13] On Savin's career, see Iu. K. Shcheglov, "Kommentarii k romanu 'Zolotoi telenok' " in I. Ilf and E. Petrov, *Zolotoi telenok. Roman* (Moscow, 1995), pp. 447–49. In Ilf and Petrov's *Zolotoi telenok*, Ostap Bender acknowledges Savin as a worthy precursor as a confidence man, though one whose ploys were less suited to Soviet circumstances: "Take *Kornet* Savin, for example. An outstanding confidence man (*aferist*). He would have come to Koreiko disguised as a Bulgarian Tsar, made a scene with the house administrator, and spoilt the whole thing." Ilf and Petrov, *Zolotoi telenok*, p. 107.

[14] Il'ia Il'f and Evgenii Petrov, *Dvenadtsat' stul'ev* (1928) and *Zolotoi telenok* (1931).

[15] V. Shklovskii, " 'Zolotoi telenok' i staryi plutovskii roman," *Literaturnaia gazeta*, 30 April 1934, p. 3.

[16] For example, Ilia Ehrenburg's "Khulio Khurenito" (1922), in I. Erenburg, *Sobranie sochinenii v 9-i tomakh* (1962–67), vol. 1, and V. Kaverin's "Konets khazy" (1924), in his *Sobranie sochinenii v dvukh tomakh*, (Moscow, 1994), v. 2, pp. 5–86. Ilf and Petrov's epithet, "velikii kombinator," recalls Ehrenburg's "velikii provokator" for Julio Jurenito. It has also been suggested that the protagonist of the short novel "Syn Chicherina" by Sven (Ilia Kremlev), published in the satirical journal *Begemot* in 1926, was a prototype for Ostap Bender, but this has been denied by Kremlev himself, who asserts out that he and Ilf and Petrov were simply responding to the same real-life phenomenon of proliferating *samozvanstvo* in the early 1920s: Ilia Kremlev, *V literaturnom stroiu. Vospominaniia* (Moscow, 1968), pp. 189–90.

[17] See Olga Litvak, "The Literary Response to Conscription: Individuality and Authority in the Russian-Jewish Enlightenment," Ph.D. diss., Columbia University, 1999, p. 32.

Bender, like all good confidence men, has the ability to perform a variety of roles with aplomb, switch personae in an instant, and get himself out of trouble by ingeniously improvising a use for whatever raw materials are at hand. He can win the confidence of disgruntled "former people" longing for a return of the old regime (as in *Twelve Chairs*) or merge effortlessly with a group of Soviet writers covering the opening of the Turksib railroad. Yet, for all his dreams of a distant, mythical Rio de Janiero, his great talent is to "speak Bolshevik" with total assurance and fluency, and his most reliable stock in trade—starting with his self-representation as a "son of Lieutenant Schmidt" (a revolutionary hero of 1905)—is to use this linguistic fluency either to convince gullible provincials of his bona fides or to assume the character (and perks) of a Soviet bureaucrat.

The Ostap Bender novels, though not regarded with total approval by the powers-that-be—or, for that matter, the intelligentsia—because of their light-mindedness and lack of a discernable moral stance, achieved instant and lasting popularity with Soviet readers.[18] Though the huge Soviet editions belong to the post–1956 period, the two books, published separately and together, ran through twenty editions before the Second World War.[19] With the possible exception of Nikolai Ostrovskii's inspirational Pavel Korchagin in his quasi-autobiographical novel, *How the Steel was Tempered*,[20] none of the "positive heroes" of socialist realism in the 1930s achieved anything like Ostap Bender's fame and popularity; certainly none was so often quoted or so quickly taken into popular speech.[21]

The Soviet con man is a topic that, with the notable exception of Golfo Alexopoulos's fascinating recent case study of a great con man of the 1930s, Gromov, has scarcely made an appearance in the Soviet historical

---

[18] On the vagaries of Ilf and Petrov's standing with the regime and the intelligentsia, and their high standing with the public, see A. A. Kurdiumov, *V kraiu nepuganykh idiotov: Kniga ob Il'fe i Petrove* (Paris, 1983). For statistics on library borrowing in the early 1930s showing the high demand for Ilf and Petrov's works, see A. Vulis, *I. Il'f, E. Petrov. Ocherk tvorchestva* (Moscow, 1960), 4 (n. 1), citing *Pravda*, 7 June 1934. On the crowds of ordinary people coming to pay their final respects to Ilia Ilf when he died in 1937, see reminiscences of M. Ardov in *Sbornik vospominanii ob I. Il'fe i E. Petrove* (Moscow, 1963).

[19] Excluding publication in periodicals (both *Dvenadtsat' stul'ev* and *Zolotoi telenok* were first published in serial form in the journal *30 dnei*, in 1928 and 1931, respectively). The total number of copies produced in the prewar editions was over 260: Alain Préchac, *Il'f et Petrov. Témoins de leur temps. Stalinisme et littérature*, vol. 3 (Paris, 2000), pp. 751–53. On the postwar fate and publication history of the Bender novels, see below, chapter 14.

[20] N. Ostrovskii, *Kak zakalialas' stal'* (1932).

[21] Even hostile critics of Ilf and Petrov's work remark on the speed with which various of Bender's aphorisms entered popular speech. For examples, see V. P. Beliavin and I. A. Butenko, *Zhivaia rech'. Slovar' razgovornykh vyrazhenii* (Moscow, 1994), pp. 21, 61, 85, 134. (Thanks to Stephen Lovell for bringing these to my attention.)

Figure 10. "Dreaming of Rio de Janiero, and clutching a file that he hopes will make his fortune, Ostap Bender dances a solitary tango." Drawing by K. Rotov from the first publication of *Zolotoi telenok* in the journal *30 dnei*, 1931. Reproduced from I. Ilf and E. Petrov, *Sobranie sochinenii*, vol. 2 (Moscow, 1961), p. 233.

scholarship.[22] This is a pity, since social historians, in particular, have a great deal to learn from it. The con man is in his own way an acute social commentator. A good grasp of contemporary social and bureaucratic practices is as essential to the con man's success as the ability to inspire confidence. The con men described in the following pages are operators

[22] Golfo Alexopoulos, "Portrait of a Con Artist as a Soviet Man," *Slavic Review* 57:4 (1998). The topic of imposture is skirted though not directly broached in J. Arch Getty's *Origins of the Great Purges* (Cambridge and New York, 1985), which emphasizes the Party's concern about fraudulent membership and misuse of Party cards. Among the examples of misues cited by Getty is the criminal in Odessa who used a false party card to rob the State Bank (op. cit., 32). Lacking precise data on the point, Getty speculated that "it would not be surprising . . . to discover that [party] cards commanded a high price" on the black

whose stock-in-trade consists of the skills to steer a course through the Soviet bureaucracy, with its eternal demand for "papers" and credulousness toward anything with an official stamp and letterhead, and to manipulate the Soviet citizenry, endlessly hungry for scarce consumer goods and eager for opportunities to acquire them "on the left." They know how to get at the "soft money" (which also, in the Soviet case, meant "soft" goods) tucked away in the directors' funds of Soviet enterprises; they are connoisseurs of the various ways in which goods travel through the first and second economies via patronage and blat. They know all the special entitlements and statuses that confer preferential access to goods and services and understand how to use common practices like petitioning for private gain.

My objective in this chapter is to examine con man stories, both real and fictional, as a Soviet discourse and use them as a way of exploring social, cultural, and bureaucratic practices. The sources used in this article are primarily reports from central and regional newspapers on con men and confidence tricks, including a few court cases, memoirs, and materials in Russian state and party archives, including one important con man case prominently featured in Stalin's intelligence reports in the postwar period. Literary sources are extensively used as well, for in the 1920s and 1930s there was an unusually intense process of symbiosis between "real life" con men (who are known to us via the stories told about them by journalists and prosecutors, and occasionally through their own narratives) and their fictional counterparts: this means both that the fictional stories are influenced by reported "real life" events and that the telling of the "real life" stories owes a great deal to fiction.[23]

REVOLUTION AND IMPOSTURE

Revolutions are, among other things, identity crises requiring citizens to reinvent themselves.[24] In his memoirs of the Civil War period in the south, the writer Konstantin Paustovskii— like Ilf and Petrov, a native of Odessa—suggests that the line between this reinvention and a confidence trick is a very fine one. In the first chapter, entitled "Ancestors of Ostap Bender," he describes how he himself, as a hungry, aimless, and confused

---

market (ibid., 32). Archival evidence now makes clear that this was indeed the case, and that the black market trade in party cards and other identification documents was huge.

[23] For further discussion of this point, see below, pp. 272–73.

[24] This argument is developed in my article, "Making a Self for the Times: Impersonation and Imposture in Twentieth-Century Russia," *Kritika* 2:3 (2001), pp. 469–87.

young man in Odessa in 1920, became part of an Ostap Bender-like scam
in which a group of journalists without any official authorization constituted themselves the "Information Department" of a newly created Soviet
institution known by the acronym Oprodkomgub.[25] By a mixture of
chutzpah and good luck, the journalists managed to get their "Department" legalized and themselves on the official list of employees receiving
salaries and rations.[26] At the end of the chapter (first published in the
Soviet era), Paustovskii rather awkwardly backs away from his story of
a successful scam, claiming that he and his friends subsequently confessed
all to his new boss, who not only forgave them but also claimed to have
known of the deception all along.[27] This denouement leaves the state looking appropiately omniscient and reclassifies a confidence trick into something completely different—the classic revolutionary trope of "intellectuals coming to work for Soviet power."

Paustovskii's little story is helpful in comprehending both the prevalence of imposture in the postrevolutionary decades and its resonance in
the broader society. It suggests the possibility that for many people in the
revolutionary era, the world of Ostap Bender was not just a world apart,
where tricksters hustled and the law did its best to catch and punish them,
but the world in which they lived themselves—a world in which, to survive, everyone had to become a bit of an operator and impersonator.

Con men and confidence tricks, particularly those involving impersonation of officials and manipulation of the language and mores of Soviet
officialdom, were a familiar part of the Soviet urban landscape in the
interwar period. The 1920s and 1930s (particularly before the general
introduction of internal passports) were a heyday for confidence tricksters
and imposters of all kinds; the characteristic form of the Soviet confidence
trick was a deception by a person posing as an official and expressing
himself with intimidating fluency in a "Soviet" language that many ordinary folk had still to master. The prevalence of this kind of imposture
was known to contemporaries via newspaper reports (which sometimes
identified protagonists as "real-life Ostap Benders"), anecdotes, and everyday life experience. In the 1920s and 1930s, there was a flourishing
black market trade in blank sheets of paper with institutional letterhead,
institutional stamps, and false identity documents of all kinds—party and
Komsomol membership cards, trade union cards, work records, passports, residence permits, *spravki* from local soviets attesting to an individ-

---

[25] According to Paustovskii, this stood for *Osobyi prodovol'stvennyi gubernskii komitet.*
[26] Konstantin Paustovskii, "Povest' o zhizni: Bremia bol'shikh ozhidaniia," in Paustovskii, *Sobranie sochinenii v deviati tomakh* (Moscow, 1981–86), v. 5, pp. 6–23.
[27] Paustovskii, "Predki," pp. 22–23.

ual's identity and social position, and so on. After the introduction of passports in 1933, it became harder and more dangerous to obtain such documents, but certainly not impossible.[28]

Imposture was not a criminal offense in itself, according to the Criminal Code, though it was illegal to "abuse trust or deceive with the aim of obtaining property or the right to use property or other personal advantages (swindling [*moshennichestvo*])" (article 169) or to forge or use false documents (article 170).[29] A great many Soviet frauds were based on three circumstances: the insatiable demand of new Soviet bureaucracies for documents, the credulousness of many officials once documents of any kind were presented, and the comparative ease with which forged or fraudulent documents could be obtained. It was extremely useful for confidence men to have an array of false documents available. One 25-year-old con man apprehended in 1925 was found to be in possession of a party card dating his membership to before the Revolution, a trade union card, membership cards from the Society of Old Bolsheviks and the Society of Former Political Prisoners, and documents attesting to his participation in the 1905 Revolution (!).[30] But confidence men were not the only ones who needed false documents. Many otherwise honest citizens were forced to resort to them, too: for example, to hide the fact that their family had been dekulakized.

One of the traditional forms of Russian *samozvanstvo*—the impersonation of famous men, including Tsars—survived the Revolution, with appropriate adaption to Soviet circumstances. Writers of the 1920s were intrigued by it. Ilf and Petrov commented on "the false grandsons of Karl Marx, the non-existent nephews of Friedrich Engels, the brothers of Lunacharsky, and as a last resort descendants of the famous anarchist prince Kropotkin" who were wandering round the country; Ilia Kremlev wrote a short novel on one such case called "Son of Chicherin"; and Mikhail Bulgakov published a feuilleton entitled "The False Dmitrii" about a man who claimed to be a brother of Lunacharsky, People's Commissar of En-

---

[28] The postwar Harvard Interview Project provides a lot of information on this. See, for example, Russian Research Center, Harvard University, *Project on the Soviet Social System. Interview Records*, "A" Schedule Protocols, #167 (v. 13), 12–13, #358 (v. 19), 18; #432 (v. 21), 19; #87 (v. 30), 3; #338 (v. 33), 3, 19–20, #527 (v. 27), 29. One source gives the going rate for false passports in rural Mordovia in 1935 as 50 to 80 rubles: *Izvestiia*, 15 May 1935, p. 3.

[29] See *Ugolovnyi kodeks RSFSR redaktsii 1926 g. s postateino-sistematizirovannymi materialami*, sost. S. S. Astarkhanov i dr. (Moscow, 1927) and *Ugolovnyi kodeks. S izmeneniiami na 1 iiunia 1937 g.* (Moscow, 1937). Rather surprisingly, even impersonation of an official was not a crime. The only type of impersonation specifically mentioned in the Code was practicing as a medical doctor without the proper qualifications (art. 180).

[30] Kremlev, *V literaturnom stroiu*, pp. 189–90.

lightenment.[31] As Bulgakov tells the story, the false Lunacharsky turned up in a provincial institution and announced that he had been sent from Moscow to be its head, but unfortunately his documents, money, and suitcase had been stolen on the way. This made sense to the local staff because (shades of Gogol's *Inspector General*!) "the head of our institution had just been called to Moscow . . . and we knew that another one would be coming." They generously supplied the impostor with money, clothes, and other necessities and charged 50 rubles to an advance on his salary, after which "Dmitrii Vasilevich vanished to parts unknown."[32] In another similar case, a swindler claiming to be Faizull Khodzhaev, chairman of the Uzbek Central Executive Committee, toured southern cities including Ialta, Novorossiisk, and Poltava and "collected money from the trusting chairmen of the city soviet executive committee."[33]

As these examples suggest, it was more common for samozvantsy of the 1920s to pose as relatives of famous men rather than as the great men themselves. Later, in the Stalin era, the popular practice of petitioning the great generated a variant in which the petitioner represented himself as a long-lost relative and asked for material support on this basis. Klim Voroshilov, longtime Red Army leader and Politburo member, received so many of these letters that they form a special section of his archive.[34]

A variant of the "brother of Lunacharsky" scam was to pose as an Old Bolshevik or hero of the Revolution and Civil War. The gathering of thirty fraudulent "sons of Lieutenant Schmidt" (a hero of the 1905 Revolution)

---

[31] Ilf and Petrov, *Zolotoi telenok. Roman* (Moscow, 1995), p. 20; Kremlev, *V literaturnom stroiu*, p. 189; Bulgakov's "Lzhedmitrii Lunacharskii" cited in Iu. K. Shcheglov, "Kommentarii, k romanu *Zolotoi telenok*" in Ilf and Petrov, *Zolotoi telenok*, p. 352. Of these *samozvantsy* stories, Ilf and Petrov's are presented as fiction, Kremlev's was published as fiction but later described by him as essentially a report from real life, and Bulgakov's feuilleton belongs to a nonfictional genre (though he is now best known as a writer of fiction). In terms of style and content there is very little difference between the three. Almost certainly all three were originally inspired by newspaper reports—but the newspaper reports themselves were written by journalists who were increasingly likely to have read similar stories in satirical fiction.

[32] Shcheglov, "Kommentarii," p. 352.

[33] Shcheglov, "Kommentarii," p. 352, citing a story in *Pravda* by L. Sosnovskii (1926).

[34] Gosudarstvennyi arkhiv Rossiiskoi Federatsii (henceforth, GARF), f. 5446, op., 54, dd. 25, 33, 44, 57, 68, 81, 101, 127 (covering the years 1945–52). Judging by the content of the letters, some were written in the spirit of the confidence trick, but others came from distressed or disturbed people who had lost their families and formed an emotional bond at a distance with a political leader, usually seen as a father figure. Stalin himself received similar letters: see, for example, the one from a sixteen-year-old boy asking permission to take Stalin's name, to which Stalin in 1924 wrote an astonishingly warm reply: "I have no objections to your taking the name of Stalin; on the contrary, I will be very glad, as that circumstance will give me the chance to have a younger brother (I never had any brothers)." *Istochnik*, 1996 no. 2 (21), pp. 156–59.

in Ilf and Petrov's *Little Golden Calf* is a famous example.[35] In real life, this kind of impersonation was often a longterm proposition rather than (as in *Little Golden Calf*) a one-time confidence trick. Old Bolsheviks and revolutionary and Civil War heroes were entitled to a number of privileges like priority in housing, extra rations, and access to closed stores, as well as having a strong claim to personal pensions and good prospects for job advancement. Gromov, the con man of whom Golfo Alexopoulos has written, at one point claimed to be a "partisan"—that is, a fighter on the Soviet side during the Civil War outside the ranks of the Red Army: in Siberia and elsewhere in the 1920s and early '30s "Red partisan" was an official status that entitled the bearer to privileges.[36] A con man called Sergei Meskhi styled himself an "Old Bolshevik," "Hero of the Civil War," and even "the 27th Baku Commissar" when he moved from the Caucasus to Moscow in the early 1920s, and on the strength of this built a successful service career, ending in the mid 1930s as head of the Moscow office of Intourist.[37]

An extraordinary story of repeated and long-term impostures by a man for whom pretense and grandiose storytelling had become a way of life was recently discovered in a Moscow archive by Golfo Alexopoulos. Her impostor, Gromov, began his remarkable career by posing as an engineer and construction manager on new industrial sites. "Gromov . . . walked around in an OGPU uniform and wore the button (*znachok*) of a partisan. Whenever he dealt with any organization, he would say he came on behalf of commissar Mikoian."[38]

Claiming official status was the basis of endless Soviet confidence tricks. One con man "acquired a military greatcoat and began to appear in various institutions under the guise of a Red Army commander,"[39] another represented himself as an investigator for the Procuracy of the USSR.[40] Leonid Inozemtsev, an educated man with a cultured manner, was another master manipulator of the telephone. Posing as a government official, he would call the families of recently deceased middle-level Soviet officials, and tell them that in recognition of their late relative's distinguished ser-

---

[35] Ilf and Petrov, *Zolotoi telenok*, p. 18–29.

[36] Alexopoulos, "Portrait," p. 779. Apparently such benefits were revoked in the mid 1930s, provoking an angry reaction. See report of the deputy head of the West Siberian NKVD, 14 February 1936, in Gosudarstvennyi arkhiv Novosibirskoi oblasti (GANO), f. 47, op. 5, d. 206, ll. 119–21.

[37] On Meskhi's unmasking and trial (primarily for sexual offenses rather than his earlier false claims), see *Izvestiia*, 10 July 1935, p. 4, and 22 July 1935, p. 4.

[38] Alexopoulos, "Portrait," p. 780. Gromov's construction project was a fish cannery, and Anastas Mikoian was People's Commissar for the Food Industry, as well as a member of the Politburo.

[39] *Krasnaia gazeta (Leningrad)*, 6 May 1936, p. 4.

[40] *Izvestiia*, 11 January 1936, p. 6.

vice they had been given the privilege of ordering food and other consumer goods at low prices from a closed store for the elite. (This system of "closed distribution" to persons on special lists, in existence throughout the Stalin period and beyond, became intimately connected with the second economy and lent itself to many forms of abuse.)[41] An order would be placed, and Inozemtsev would arranged to meet at a certain place to deliver the goods. When the relative appeared, he took their money and disappeared.[42]

One Khalfin, a native of Tiflis, specialized in impersonating Soviet officials and their secretaries over the telephone and writing himself fraudulent recommendations.

If Khalfin needs a car, he immediately phones the garage of some People's Commissariat:

"Hallo! Bring out the Commissar's car."

And in a few minutes Khalfin is riding in the car.

In the name of the Moscow Komsomol committee Khalfin recommends himself for work: "The bearer of this is a fine lad. I heartily recommend Komsomol member Khalfin." And after that conversation that same "fine lad" appears in the institution.

These skills enabled Khalfin to get a job in 1931 as a secretary of one of the sectors in the Commissariat of External Trade. When he was asked for documents, he quickly left the job. Using the same telephone approach, he got himself a new job as a consultant at the Commissariat of Justice: "But here they quickly unmasked him, and he ended up with a two-year prison sentence."[43]

Some of the most elaborate confidence tricks involved the invention of entire government institutions, known by impressive acronyms and legitimated by headed paper, official seals and stamps, and other staples of bureaucracy. When A. Leviago lost his job at an engineering institute, he decided to create his own mythical administration, the Central Directorate for Extending Technical Aid and Inculcation of the Newest Achievements in the Field of Construction Industry (TsUNTP) as a moneymaking device. Acting supposedly in the name of his former institutional employer, Leviago opened a current account in the savings bank and ordered a seal and stamp. Then he circularized schools and other educational institutions in the name of TsUNTP recommending that they acquire a poster commemorating the Cheliuskin expedition at the cost of

[41] See E. A. Osokina, *Ierarkhiia potrebleniia. O zhizni liudei v usloviiakh stalinskogo snabzheniia 1928–1935 gg.* (Moscow, 1993), pp. 63–107.

[42] Lev Sheinin, *Zapiski sledovatelia* (Moscow, 1965), pp. 76–80.

[43] *Izvestiia*, 15 March 1035, 4.

21 rubles, payable to TsUNTP's account.[44] In a short time, the account was richer to the tune of 18,000 rubles, though Leviago had not sent out a single poster.[45]

Two journalists reportedly carried out a similar scam in the 1930s—not for profit but to demonstrate the vulnerability of Soviet bureaucracy to imaginative swindlers. Their aim was to establish the legitimacy of a mythical organization and get offers to buy the equally mythical product is proposed to supply. The plotters used a stratagem to acquire an official stamp of the nonexistent All-Union Trust for the Exploitation of Meteoric Metals, printed headed stationery, and then sent letters to number of Soviet industrial concerns offering to supply high-quality metal, which was to be obtained from meteors that (the phony Trust asserted) would fall in Central Asia on certain dates in the near future. Despite the absurdity of this proposition, replies came in from many different economic authorities, including the Automobile Trust, which offered to exchange cars for the metal. These letters were presented to the State Bank, which allocated a large sum of money for expansion of the Trust's operations. Then the plotters asked the Commissariat of Heavy Industry to authorize the building of a plant to process their "special metals"—and there, finally, somebody smelled a rat. To the great disappointment of the journalists, they were forbidden to publish this story because it made so many officials look foolish.[46]

Soviet administration of the provinces in the 1920s and '30s depended heavily on visits from representatives (*upolnomochennye*) of various institutions and political leaders on investigative or troubleshooting missions, another practice that lent itself to abuse. While in the Far East, for example, the con man Gromov would claim to be an emissary of the People's Commissar for Food, Anastas Mikoian.[47] Another con man described himself, more modestly, as "the Moscow representative of Glavprofobr" in carrying out scams in the provinces.[48] This "disciple of Ostap Bender," as *Izvestiia* described him, offered courses in accountancy for a fee of 120 rubles, payable in advance. They were advertised in provincial towns with

[44] The Cheliuskin expedition to the Arctic in 1933–34 and the dramatic rescue of the Cheliuskinites was a topic of enormous public interest: see John McCannon, *Red Arctic: Polar Exploration and the Myth of the North in the Soviet Union, 1932–1939* (New York and Oxford, 1998), pp. 61–68.

[45] *Izvestiia*, 5 February 1936, p. 6.

[46] *An American Engineer in Stalin's Russia: The Memoirs of Zara Witkin, 1932–1934,* ed. Michael Gelb (Berkeley, 1991), pp. 211–12. The journalists were A. N. Garri (identified only as "Garry" in the Witkind book), who wrote for *Izvestiia*, and Bel'skii of the satirical journal *Krokodil*.

[47] Alexopoulos, "Portrait," p. 780.

[48] Glavprofobr was the department of the People's Commissariat of Education in charge of technical education.

due attention to Soviet form (for example, party and Komsomol members were given priority in admission to the courses) and opened with a lecture, "The Place of Accountancy in the World Economic System." After this promising introduction, the con man would vanish with the money he had collected.[49]

One of the oddest confidence tricks involving "representatives" occurred in 1927 in Dzhetysuiskaia province, Kazakhstan, when a Communist named Mukharovskii declared himself the representative of the Party Opposition's "Moscow Center." Mukharovskii, it appears, actually was one of a small group of local supporters of the Opposition (for which he was expelled from the party), as well as a swindler who relieved Kazakh organizations of 9,000 rubles and a new typewriter. But the claim to represent "Moscow Center" seems to have been part of an attempt to blackmail local industrial leaders, since Moscow Center's alleged message to them was that, for tactical reasons, they should hide any Opposition sympathies they may have had but support the cause by giving money to expelled Oppositionists, notably Mukharovskii.[50]

Impersonation of OGPU/NKVD personnel was a flourishing line of fraud. Gromov was known to don an OGPU uniform.[51] There were many reports of thieves gaining entry by posing as secret policemen conducting house searches and "confiscating" valuables.[52] One enterprising con man claiming to be an NKVD official persuaded a number of Moscow commercial stores to allow him to conduct "searches" of their customers under the guise of checking documents.[53] NKVD impersonations were also sometimes perpetrated for other motives, such as prestige in the local community. A peasant from the Central Volga region, claiming to be an NKVD agent, told other kolkhozniks that "if anyone has any complaints, they should pass them on to him and he will set things in motion."[54]

---

[49] *Izvestiia*, 12 January 1936, p. 4. This trick was successfully carried out in Azovo-Chernomor and Tashkent, but led to the con man's apprehension in Iaroslavl.

[50] *6-aia Vsekazakskaia konferentsiia VKP(b) 15–23 noiabria 1927 goda. Stenograficheskii otchet* (Kzyl-Orda, 1927), pp. 57–58. Mukharovskii, who must have been slightly crazy, also at various times claimed to be the son of a German general, the nephew of a police boss in Vienna, and to have worked for the Cheka.

[51] Alexopoulos, "Portrait," p. 780.

[52] See, for example, *Izvestiia*, 28 April 1936, p. 4; *Krasnyi Krym* (Simferopol), 28 August 1937, p. 4. A similar technique was used by a gang in Saratov, except that the thieves claimed to be conducting house searches on behalf of the criminal investigation department and the tax office: *Kommunist* (Saratov), 3 October 1935, p. 4.

[53] *Sovetskaia iustitsiia*, 1937 no. 4, p. 50.

[54] *Krasnyi Krym*, 15 September 1937, p. 2. This particular kind of fraud, like so many others practiced in Soviet times, had its prerevolutionary precursors. Korolenko's turn-of-the-century stories of *samozvantsy* included a rural lad named Smovenko who in 1910 "put on a mask (!) . . . and appeared at twelve o'clock in the village of Razumovka (Chernigov

The fictional Ostap Bender had occasion to pose as a journalist, and real-life confidence men did the same.[55] Another of Bender's tricks that had a real-life analogue reported in the press was the impersonation of a chess Grand Master, through which in *Twelve Chairs* Bender swindles the inhabitants of Vasiuki of 50 rubles.[56] In 1936 *Izvestiia* reported that an ex-convict named Shkriabkov (who, unlike Bender, was a good chess player) wrote himself letters of introduction on the letterhead of a chess journal and, assuming the name of a nationally famous chess players, toured the USSR holding sessions of simultaneous play.[57]

Falsely claiming professional skills in order to gain employment was so common in the 1920s and '30s that it hardly deserves to be classified as a confidence trick; indeed, the prevalence of *praktiki* (uncredentialed engineers) in industry and the practice of promoting workers to learn on the job gave it a kind of borderline legitimacy.[58] Nevertheless, there were real con men among the masses of engineer-*praktiki* in Soviet industry in the 1930s. It was as a self-styled engineer and construction manager on new industrial sites in distant parts of the Soviet Union that Gromov started his con man's career, and after a while, like many others, he felt that he had grown into his role: "If I . . . assumed the title of engineer without having the right to, still, for nearly six years I've acquired experience in the area of construction."[59] This observation reminds us of the many ways that professional confidence men were only a subset in a much larger group of people forced by the exigencies of Revolution to reinvent themselves. Just as Gromov felt himself to have become, more or less, a real engineer, so an ordinary noncriminal citizen hiding undesirable social origins could say that he "began to feel that I was the man I had pretended to be."[60]

In the eyes of the authorities, cross-dressing was also a form of imposture whose purpose (as was assumed in all the reports I have read) was

---

province), announcing that he was a policeman and agent of the investigative department (the mask evidently emphasized his status as a *secret* agent). Demanding to be taken round the village, he conducted a real house search in many homes . . . There were no hints of a desire to profit in Smovenko's actions and the jurors acquitted him." Korolenko, *Polnoe sobranie sochinenii*, v. 3, p. 328.

[55] Ilf and Petrov, *Zolotoi telenok*, pp. 255–69. For a real-life example of a con man posing as a correspondent of *Izvestiia*, see *Izvestiia*, 12 April 1936, p. 4.

[56] See Ilia Ilf and Evgenii Petrov, *Dvenadtsat' stul'ev. Pervyi polnyi variant* (Moscow, 1997), pp. 368–84.

[57] *Izvestiia*, 2 February 1936, p. 4.

[58] On *praktiki* and their importance in Soviet industry, see Kendall E. Bailes, *Technology and Society under Lenin and Stalin: Origins of the Soviet Technical Intelligentsia, 1917–1941* (Princeton, 1978), passim.

[59] Alexopoulos, "Portrait," pp. 783–84.

[60] Cited in Fitzpatrick, *Everyday Stalinism*, p. 132; this issue is further explored in pp. 132–38.

to perpetrate a swindle.[61] In one case, a woman called Zavorykina spent four years in Donbass posing as a man in order (as reported) to marry women and swindle them.

> She 'married' nine times, and each time on the first day she got her 'wives' drunk to the point of unconsciousness, and then disappeared, taking their possessions with her. Legal-medical expertise has established that Zvorykina is a completely normal woman. When she had finished each confidence trick, she stopped wearing men's dress and thus threw the criminal investigators off the trail.[62]

In another case, a woman dressed as a man and calling herself A. Iudushkin, used her job as watchman in a cooperative restaurant to embezzle money from it. The fact that Iudushkin was a woman was discovered only after her arrest and confession. While the reader may wonder just why cross-dressing was necessary to accomplish this scam, an official report had no doubts: "Dressing in a man's suit and even a fictitious 'marriage' to an acquaintance was all done by the con woman so as to successfully win the trust of the ninnies in the cooperative," it concluded.[63]

• • •

Surveying this range of confidence tricks from the 1920s and '30s, several general features deserve comment. In the first place, it should be noted how many of these scams involved the arrival of a con man in a distant provincial city or town—in the Black Sea region, in Central Asia, the Far East, along the Volga, or in one of those anonymous small towns in central Russia in which Bender often operated—followed by perpetration of the scam and then an abrupt departure. As the Bender stories suggest, it was easier to get away with confidence tricks in the provinces, and a swift exit from the site was the easiest strategy for closure. The only disadvantage of the Russian provinces was that they were so poor that even a successful swindle was likely to produce slim pickings.

As to the general lessons that may be learned from exploring the topic of confidence men in the Stalin era, the pervasiveness of the satirical mode in our texts is a discouragement to attempting anything too portentous. It has become a cliché of Soviet studies to say that such and

---

[61] Apparently Imperial authorities viewed it in a similar light. Korolenko reports occasional cases of cross-dressing from the 1890s, including that of a women who dressed as a man who "belonged to a family that was in general inclined to imposture (*samozvanstvo*)"—her brother successively impersonated a military doctor, a professor of Kazan University, and the son of the Emir of Bukhara. Korolenko, op. cit., 348.

[62] *Izvestiia*, 15 December 1935, p. 4.

[63] *Rabochii put'* (Smolensk), 6 July 1937, p. 4.

such social phenomena are incompatible with the totalitarian model; nevertheless, the cliché may bear repeating in this case, since for all Ostap Bender's claim to be an "ideological warrior,"[64] it is difficult to see a society in which con men and imposture flourished to this extent as being under effective totalitarian mobilization and control. The world of Soviet government that the real-life Benders conned was characterized not by totalitarian controls but rather by poor communications, lack of effective accountability, institutional habits of hoarding and "off-budget" distribution, credulous and ill-educated officials, and personalistic practices.

It seems to me that the most remarkable thing about Soviet con men, apart from their shrewdness as observers and manipulators of social practices, is the way people reacted to them. In the 1920s and '30s, the con man seems to have engaged the Soviet imagination with unusual intensity. Not only was Ostap Bender the most popular of all Soviet fictional heroes with the public (though the significance of that should not be underestimated) but the stories of real-life con men attracted great attention, often mixed with a tinge of admiration, from journalists and even officials.[65] The line that should have clearly separated con men from writers, journalists, and other presumably law-abiding Soviet citizens was oddly blurred. The journalist Garri pretended to be a con man; the writer Paustovskii behaved like one. On the other side of the line, Ilf and Petrov not only had Ostap Bender pose as a writer in *Little Golden Calf* but went out of their way to show that he had a better grasp of Soviet journalistic cliché than the professionals,[66] and the real-life con man Gromov ended his career by impersonating (becoming?) a writer and citing this as grounds for clemency.[67] It was as if, in the minds of writers and con men alike, the manipulation of human souls that was the con man's specialty and the engineering of them that was the task of the Soviet writer turned out to be much the same thing.[68]

As this conflation clearly indicates, there was a subversive aspect to the Soviet reading of tricksters, a tendency to overturn accepted hierarchies

[64] Bender described himself as an "ideinyi borets za denezhnye znaki." Ilf and Petrov, *Zolotoi telenok*, p. 135.

[65] The journalistic preoccupation with con men is particularly marked in *Izvestiia* in the mid 1930s under Bukharin's editorship

[66] See Bender's list of indispensable Soviet words and phrases and draft of a leading article and a feuilleton, among other genres, in Ilf and Petrov, *Zolotoi telenok*, pp. 264–67.

[67] While in prison, Gromov wrote a play which he sent to State Prosecutor Vyshinsky, who passed it on to Lev Sheinin (a figure already familiar to us in the trickster connection), who in turn sent it for evaluation to the Union of Soviet Writers. Alexopoulos, "Portrait," pp. 785–88.

[68] See Bender's statement that "I am a neuropathologist, I am a psychiatrist. I study the souls of my patients." Ilf and Petrov, *Zolotoi telenok*, p. 59.

and values and mock official discourses that is characteristic of the genre. But subversion was not the whole story: Soviet con men, as virtuosos of self-invention, had their place in the great revolutionary and Stalinist project of reforging of self and society. In a prescriptive sense, to be sure, Bender was scarcely New Soviet Man—but in a society of Old Pre-Soviet People struggling to reinvent themselves, who was? Bored by the construction of socialism, Bender and his fellow conmen were exemplars of *self-*construction.[69] This makes us look more closely at the building metaphor (*stroitel'stvo sotsializma*) that was at the heart of prewar Stalinism. Was impersonation, the tricksters' specialty, its flip side?

[69] See his statement to this effect, Ilf and Petrov, *Zolotoi telenok*, p. 25.

CHAPTER FOURTEEN

The Con Man as Jew

In the reports of Soviet con men that abounded in the newspapers of the 1930s, ethnicity was not an issue. Sometimes a particular con man had a Russian or Ukrainian name, sometimes a Jewish or Georgian one, but the reports rarely made a point of nationality, and never (in my reading) when the con man's nationality (or recognized ethnicity) was Jewish.[1] However, we cannot assume on this basis that Russian readers made no connection between "conmanship" and Jewishness. A literary tradition of writing about Jewish con men (mainly by Jewish writers) existed from the 1920s. Kaverin's fictional con man, Baraban, for example, was clearly identified by the author as Jewish.[2] There were also some notable real-life Jewish con men, as the story (unpublicized in the contemporary press) of Gromov, né Grinshpan, reminds us. Above all, there was Ostap Bender himself, protagonist of two of the most widely read fictional works of the prewar Soviet period. Bender, identified by Ilf and Petrov only as a "son of a Turkish citizen" has generally been read by Russian readers as a Jew from Odessa and was probably so imagined by his creators.[3]

This chapter is an expanded version of the latter sections of "The World of Ostap Bender. Soviet Confidence Men in the Stalin Period," *Slavic Review* 61:3 (2002), pp. 546–57.

[1] If names were given in the newspaper con man stories of the 1930s (which they often were not), they were rarely Jewish (the exception is Khalfin: see above, p. 275. The same is true of the stories in Sheinin's *Zapiski sledovatelia* (Moscow, 1965), many of which were originally published in newspapers. It is not impossible that in the 1920s and '30s journalists tended to avoid giving identifiably Jewish names in their reports of con men in order not to reinforce anti-Semitic stereotypes.

[2] V. Kaverin, "Konets khazy" (1924), in his *Sobranie sochinenii v dvukh tomakh*, (Moscow, 1994), v. 2, p. 36. On this, see also "Jewish Themes in Soviet Russian Literature," in Lionel Kochan, *The Jews in Soviet Russia since 1917* (London and New York, 1970), p. 196.

[3] On the Turkish connection, M. Odesskii and D. Feldman write in their commentary on Ilia Ilf and Evgenii Petrov, *Dvenadtsat' stul'ev. Pervyi polnyi variant* (Moscow, 1997), p. 467: "the reference to the father's Turkish citizenship would not have been understood by contemporaries as an unambiguous indication of the ethnic identity of the hero. More likely they saw a hint that Bender's father lived in a southern Russian port city, most likely Odessa, where many merchants, usually Jews, took Turkish citizenship so that their children could avoid various forms of legal discrimination associated with their confessional affiliation, and at the same time acquire grounds for release from military conscription." Both the novels' authors came from Odessa, a city notorious as a center both of Jewish culture and Jewish crime, although only Ilf was Jewish (A. A. Kurdiumov, *V kraiu nepuganykh idiotov:*

The Jewishness of Ostap Bender might be little more than an interesting footnote to the story of con men in the Stalin period were it not for the fact that after the war, in the period of rising official and popular anti-Semitism exemplified by the Doctors' Plot, Jewishness became an implicit theme in official reports of con men, particularly in the campaign against "dupes" (*rotozei*) in the Soviet bureaucracy that was launched simultaneously with the Doctors' Plot at the beginning of 1953. The misrepresentation of self that was the stock-in-trade of con men was (the new discourse suggested) characteristic of Jews as well. Jews, like con men, were cleverer than Russians—and it was typically Russians who were the victims of the con man/Jew's duplicity. This chapter will explore the intersection of the Soviet con man story with anti-Semitism in the postwar years.

IMPOSTURE AND CONFIDENCE TRICKS IN THE POSTWAR PERIOD

Given the upheavals associated with the war, it was surely inevitable that all sorts of swindling, confidence tricks, and impostures should flourish in its wake. Many identity documents were lost of destroyed during the war, including whole sets of city records of births, deaths, and marriages. Procuracy and militia archives contain many reports of forged passports and city residence permits, or genuine documents for which the issuing authorities were bribed.[4] Forms of swindling and imposture familiar from the prewar period proliferated in the immediate postwar period, but there were also some apparent shifts of emphasis and new themes. Forgery of educational credentials was reported more frequently than in the prewar period, and scams involving the intertwining of official and unofficial economy also seem to have been on the rise. A new genre of entitlement imposture involved posing as war heroes and war invalids.

The prominence of scams involving false credentials in the postwar period is no doubt related to the sharply increased value placed on expertise of all sorts and the increased prestige associated with a university degree.[5]

Kniga ob Il'fe i Petrove [Paris, 1983], p. 59). Rachel Rubin writes that Bender is "probably a Jew," noting that "some critics refer outright to Bender as a Jew or a half-Jew, and some skirt the issue." Rachel Rubin, *Jewish Gangsters of Modern Literature* (Urbana and Chicago, 2000), pp. 47 and 154, n. 78.

[4] For example, Gosudarstvennyi arkhiv Rossiiskoi Federatsii (GARF), f. 8131, op. 37, d. 4570 (1948); ibid. f. 8131, op. 37, d. 3874 (1947).

[5] In this connection it is interesting to note that a law was drafted in 1945 to establish a badge that university graduates could wear on their chests like a military medal: GARF, f. 7523, op. 65, d. 381, ll. 3–4. This appears to have been approved by the Politburo on 29 August 1945: see *Politbiuro TsK RKP(b-VKP(b). Povestki dnia zasedanii*, vol. 3 (Moscow, 2001), p. 398 (# 227) (thanks to Mark Edele for the latter reference).

Con men regularly passed themselves off as engineers,[6] physicians,[7] and other specialists.[8] Of course, such practices were not unknown in the prewar period, as the Gromov case attests—but before the war, with so many engineer-*praktiki* in industry, it was easy enough to pass oneself off as a engineer, as Gromov did, without bothering to acquire an actual forged diploma.[9] In the postwar period, the forged document comes into prominence, presumably reflecting employers' greater insistence on formal credentials.

Petitioning, both in direct and written form, was a well-established social practice before as well as after the war.[10] In the postwar period, whether by coincidence or not, we find more reports of confidence tricks associated with direct petitioning, where the petitioner comes in person to a government agency to plead his case or appoints a surrogate for this purpose. Deputies to the Supreme Soviet were among those who regularly received citizens' petitions and were expected to take up their constituents' concerns with the relevant bureaucracies. In 1947 an enterprising con man, Z. D. Lavrentev, saw opportunities of turning a profit on this practice. Posing as a Deputy to the Supreme Soviet of the Russian Republic, Lavrentev made known that his services were available—for a price—to help citizens lodge complaints and have grievances redressed by Soviet institutions. He was arrested when he accompanied clients to the reception desk of the deputy prosecutor of Moscow city and, flashing a Deputy's badge (but unable to produce other forms of identification), demanded a reexamination of the criminal charges against his clients.[11]

Blat, the informal system of reciprocal favors through which citizens obtained scarce goods and services, was another prewar Soviet practice that continued to flourish in the postwar period:[12] *Krokodil* wryly celebrated in verse "the irreplaceable" *blatmeister* Anton Fomich who "will pick up the telephone and call / Any supply base / and they will hurry to

---

[6] See, for example, *Izvestiia*, 11 Feb 1953, p. 1 (editorial); ibid., 18 Feb 1953, pp. 2–3; ibid., 25 March 1953, p. 2.

[7] See, for example, *Pravda*, 7 Feb 1953, p. 2.

[8] See *Trud*, 25 Feb 1953, p. 2.

[9] In fact, a diploma is about the only document he apparently did not bother to forge—see Golfo Alexopoulos, "Portrait of a Con Artist as a Soviet Man," *Slavic Review* 57:4 (1998), p. 778.

[10] On the practice of petition writing, see chapter 9.

[11] GARF, f. 8131, op. 37, d. 3874, l. 404. On the growth of bribe-taking during the war and in the postwar period, prevalent even in judicial organs, procuracy, and militia, see the 1946 memo accompanying a new draft law against bribes in GARF, f. 8131, op. 37, d. 2825, ll. 140–44.

[12] On prewar practices, see Sheila Fitzpatrick, "*Blat* in Stalin's Time," in Stephen Lovell, Alena Ledeneva, Andrei Rogachevskii, eds., *Bribery and Blat in Russia: Negotiating Reciprocity from the Middle Ages to the 1990s* (London, 2000), pp. 166–82.

his aid without demur." "A hopeless rogue," says one respectable citizen to another. "Yes, . . . but a *valuable* rogue."[13] But if the Anton Fomiches of the world were smooth operators, they did at least deliver the goods, which con men posing as Anton Fomiches did not. A confidence trick perpetrated in Novosibirsk 1953 rested not only on a false claim to official status but also on the victims' assumption that officials could make personalistic decisions about access to goods under their control and that scarce goods were often available only through outlets closed to the general public. In this scam, an elegantly dressed man claiming to work in a Novosibirsk retail trade authority went round the elite apartments in the region offering to supply fresh fruit. He collected thousands of rubles from credulous academicians, cultural figures, economic managers, and high administrators.[14]

False claims about war service and injuries were ubiquitous, for the simple reason that the status of war veteran (especially with decorations) and war invalid carried special privileges in access to goods and jobs as well as social prestige. A typical case was that of Aleksandr Ivanovich Rybalchenko, who in 1945, aged twenty-two, obtained false documents and uniform and began to impersonate a decorated war hero bearing the title "Hero of the Soviet Union." He made a living by going round the Irkutsk region making speeches about his war exploits at the invitation of local party committees, much encouraged by an enthusiastic local press. He was materially supported by food and other goods issued to him on the basis of his "Hero" status, as well as by contributions from the various women impressed by this status that he met along the way.[15]

Despite this con man's heyday, the great fictional con man, Ostap Bender, was in trouble. The first sign of trouble was in December 1946, when the publishing house "Sovetskii Pisatel'" was asked to "carefully review" works, including those of Ilf and Petrov, slated for republication in the series "Selected works of Soviet literature."[16] A year later, the Central Committee's agitprop department recommended that the same publishing house drop the two Ilf and Petrov novels from the series (though the recommendation was apparently ignored).[17] Then, at the end of 1948, "Sovetskii Pisatel'" was rebuked for publishing a new edition of the two

[13] Vl. Mass and Mikh. Chervinskii, "The irreplaceable," *Krokodil*, 1952 no. 9, p. 3.

[14] *Izvestiia*, 31 January 1953, 1. Like many con men, this one (Zakharkin) was peripatetic. He had earlier successfully carried out the same scam in Kazan and Tomsk.

[15] Rossiiskii gosudarstvennyi arkhiv noveishei istorii (RGANI, formerly TsKhSD),f. 5, op. 15, d. 437, ll. 221–24. For another swindler falsely claiming to be a veteran, see *Izvestiia*, 30 January 1953, p. 2.

[16] Resolution of the Secretariat of the Union of Soviet Writers of the USSR, 15 November 1948," *Istochnik*, 1997 no. 5, p. 90.

[17] Memo of 14 December 1948, signed by D. Shepilov et al., *Istochnik*, 1997 no. 5, p. 92.

Ostap Bender novels in a print run of 75,000. As a result of this censure, it was forbidden to republish Ilf and Petrov's novels, a ban which remained in force until 1956.[18]

While the ban on Ostap Bender no doubt reflected broader sociopolitical trends, including increasing touchiness on the question of Soviet (Russian) dignity and perhaps also rising anti-Semitism, its proximate origins appear to be literary.[19] It followed the scandal about Mikhail Zoshchenko's story "Adventures of a Monkey," condemned for its disrespectful attitude toward Soviet people and Soviet life. Zoshchenko "slanderously represents Soviet people as primitive, uncultured, and stupid, with philistine tastes and morals," the Central Committee pronounced in 1946;[20] and the same body discovered just the same defects in Ilf and Petrov's work two years later: "Ostap Bender . . . is bold, resourceful, witty, and quick-witted; while all the people he meets along the way . . . are shown as stupid, primitive and ridiculous philistines."[21]

THE VAISMAN AFFAIR

The case that exemplified many of the characteristic traits of postwar "conmanship," and moreover came twice to Stalin's personal attention via his weekly intelligence reports in June 1947, was that of Veniamin Borukhovich Vaisman.[22] Vaisman, born in Zhitomir in 1914, was a habitual thief who in 1946 turned to swindling after the amputation of both legs and one hand (a result of frostbite during an unsuccessful escape from labor camp) left him unable to continue his former trade. For 20,000 rubles he obtained an attestation of status as "Hero of the Soviet Union"

---

[18] Kurdiumov, *V kraiu*, 265.

[19] The Union of Soviet Writers' condemnation of Ilf and Petrov was issued in the same month (November 1948) that the Jewish Anti-Fascist Committee was closed down (see below, p. 291).

[20] "Prikliucheniia obez'iany" was condemned in the Orgburo of the Central Committee's resolution "O zhurnalakh 'Zvezda' i 'Leningrada' " (14 August 1946) as "a vulgar lampoon on Soviet everyday life and Soviet people." *"Literaturnyi front." Istorii politicheskoi tsenzury 1932–1946 gg. Sbornik dokumentov*, comp. D. L. Babichenko (Moscow, 1994), p. 221.

[21] Memo from the Central Committee's agitprop Department of December 1948, in *Istochnik*, no. 5 (1997), p. 92. The substance of this critique was reproduced in an article "Ser'eznye oshibki izdatel'stva 'Sovetskii pisatel'," published in *Literaturnaia gazeta*, 9 February 1949.

[22] GARF, f. 9401 ("Osobaia papka I. V. Stalina"), op. 2, d. 170, ll. 65–69, 77–79. Report signed deputy Minister of Internal Affairs S. I. Serov, to Stalin, Molotov, Zhdanov. For another report on the same case, see ibid., f. 8131, op. 37, d. 3874, ll. 60–61. These two reports have recently been published in *Moskva poslevoennaia. 1945–1947: Arkhivnye dokumenty i materialy* (Moscow, 2000), pp. 478–80.

(twice) and decorated his jacket with seven orders and three medals. This made him one of the numerous postwar con men whose scams involved false claims to veteran status. But he also exploited the practice of petitioning (though from a different angle than the case cited earlier) and the existence in all bureaucracies of substantial reserves of "soft" money, not to mention "soft" goods, that was one of the structural underpinning of blat and the second (unofficial) economy.

Vaisman's scam was to visit ministries and other central institutions as a petitioner, representing himself a wounded war hero who had previously worked in their institutions, and asking for money, goods, and other kinds of help. Each visit was carefully researched in advance: as Vaisman explained to security officials after his arrest, his modus operandi was to get a list of provincial enterprise directors under a given Ministry, choose some likely names, and then go out and collect the appropriate attestations (which he dictated to the official in question) testifying to his supposed work in this branch of production before the war. These documents, together with his knowledge of names and enterprises, lent credibility to his claims when he visited the central Ministry.

Vaisman's success was extraordinary. He almost always managed to get in to see the Minister or a deputy Minister, no mean feat in itself, and persuaded them to contribute tens of thousands of rubles and similar values in goods. A total of twenty-seven Ministries succumbed to Vaisman's wiles, and his victims included a whole raft of top Soviet administrators, among them I. T. Tevosian (Minister of Ferrous Metallurgy), V. M. Malyshev (Minister of Transport Machinery), and A. G. Zverev (Finance Minister).[23] Sometimes the officials Vaisman visited gave him cash (up to 3,000 rubles a time), but often he also received gifts in kind—for example, from the Ministry of Forestry, where he claimed to be a driver from a forestry cooperative, 2,500 rubles, plus "a length of Boston cloth, two karakul coats, two women's jackets, two dresses, and other manufactured goods." At the Moscow Party Committee, secretary G. M. Popov instructed that Vaisman be issued two lengths of Boston cloth, one dark blue American suit, three pairs of shoes, 20 meters of cloth and 300 rubles. Manufactured goods to the value of 4,000 rubles were promised by Liubimov (Minister of Trade of USSR)—but at the store where the goods were issued, Vaisman managed to leave with goods worth almost twice that.

Vaisman persuaded a number of highly placed persons to use their blat on his behalf to obtain specific goods and services he wanted. For example, no less a personage than a Central Committee Secretary, N. S. Patolichev,

---

[23] The People's Commissariat of Heavy Machinery evidently deserves credit for seeing through Vaisman, since it was there that he was arrested. (GARF, f. 9401, op. 2, d. 170, l. 65).

instructed the head of the Department of Cadres to help Vaisman obtain an apartment in Kiev; another official of the Central Committee got him the plane ticket. Once in Kiev, Vaisman talked local officials into providing him with furniture for free, as well as 2,500 rubles and "28 sets (*komplekty*) of the American gifts."[24] Members of the Academy of Sciences were no less generous: after a visit from Vaisman, academicians Vavilov and Bardin took him under their protection and signed a letter to Professor Chaklin, director of an artificial limb institute, asking him to take Vaisman as a patient and fit him with the highest-quality artificial limbs.

In Stalin's intelligence report on Vaisman, the Vaisman story is told without strong judgemental overtones (Vaisman is represented not as an "enemy" but just as a criminal, and an ingenious one at that); indeed, the narrative has something of the appreciation of the trickster's skills that was characteristic of prewar newspaper reports, as well as Ilf and Petrov's novels. It is a report (or strictly, speaking, two sequential reports) close to the genre of an extended *anekdot*, an Odessa story. No doubt it reflects Vaisman's own narrative style and assessment of his own achievements, since it is clearly based on the secret police's post-arrest interviews with him; Vaisman, an outsider working against the odds, tends to appear marvelously inventive, while his victims—powerful Communist officials with large discretionary funds and a fondness (bred by the petitioning system) for occasional acts of individual charity—look softheaded as well as softhearted. As Stephen Lovell has written of the Russian *plutovskoi roman*, the protagonist "is spared the social and ethnical responsibilities and scruples of his victims; he comes from outside the various groups with which he comes into contact. And, in fact, he may on occasion seem a good deal more sympathetic than these groups . . ."[25]

Comparing Vaisman's exploits with those of prewar con men, the most striking difference is the high level of the government and political elite at which they occurred. I have not come across any prewar cases of scams involving government ministers and Central Committee secretaries, though, given the fragmentary nature of our sources for the prewar period, this does not mean that there were none. With due regard to the incompleteness of the data, the comparison does at least suggest the possibility that between the mid 1930s (from which most of my prewar data come) to the mid 1940s something changed (more soft money available? more corruption at higher levels of administration?) that made the top

[24] These are not further identified. Presumably they were either goods sent under Lend-lease or donations from some American charitable source, which in the usual manner of Soviet bureaucracy had entered the funds of "soft" money and goods at the disposal of various enterprises and institutions.

[25] Stephen Lovell, "Reciprocity and the Soviet Cultural Revolution: The Literary Perspective," in Lovell et al., *Bribery and Blat*, p. 154.

echelon of Soviet leadership more vulnerable to scams. We know very little about the mores of Soviet government in the immediate postwar period, but it is evident, if only from the generous amounts of soft money that Vaisman managed to tap, that financial accountability was lax and patronage and personalistic practices flourished. With further investigation, the Vaisman affair might turn out to be an early warning of the high-level corruption of politics and government that became evident in the Brezhnev era.

POSTWAR ANTI-SEMITISM

The fact that Vaisman was Jewish was clearly stated in the first sentence of the first intelligence report on him submitted to Stalin, but the report contained no further mention of it.[26] One might speculate, given the atypicality of Stalin receiving two long reports on a single con man's exploits, that Vaisman's Jewishness could have been in some way an issue. But it is also true that the magnitude of his crimes, the vulnerabilities of the Soviet system they demonstrated, and the prominence of his victims (almost all of them personally known to Stalin) were justification enough for the unusual attention.

Nevertheless, this was a period in which both popular and de facto official anti-Semitism were on the rise. The popular anti-Semitism of this period seems to have been exacerbated and to some extent generated by war, evacuation, and occupation, though in ways that are still imperfectly understood. Evacuated Jews were greeted with hostility in Central Asia, in particular (the NKVD reported in 1942) because of their effort "to get jobs in the system of trade, supply, and procurement" in the region.[27] In the West, German occupation was thought by many to have encouraged anti-Semitism by example (though the converse was also sometimes true).[28] But the main incubator of anti-Semitism during the war seems have been the Soviet Army, with demobilized soldiers disseminating the message throughout the Soviet Union after the war. This wartime anti-Semitism focused particularly on Jewish draft-dodging—a long-established part of Jewish stereotypes in Russia, as Ilf and Petrov's "son of a

[26] He was identified as "thief and con man (vor-aferist) Vaisman Veniamin Borukhovich, a.k.a. Trakhtenberg, a.k.a. Rabinovich, a.k.a. Oslon, a.k.a. Zilbershtein, Jewish by nationality, thirty-three years old, born in the city of Zhitomir." GARF, f. 9401, op. 2, d. 170, l. 65.

[27] G. Kostyrchenko, V plenu u krasnogo faraona. Politicheskie presledovaniia evreev v SSSR v poslednee stalinskoe desiatiletie (Moscow, 1994), p. 15.

[28] See the letter to Stalin (October 1945) from a group of Kiev Jews who linked a recent "pogrom" in Kiev with the earlier German occupation of the city, cited in Kostyrchenko, V plenu, p. 53.

Turkish citizen" reminds us—and was part of a larger discourse about Jews' privileged status and lack of patriotism.[29] There were no Jews at the front, wrote an anonymous writer to *Pravda* in 1953; Jews were the first to leave Moscow when it was under direct German attack in 1941 (implying cowardice) and the first to return as Soviet victory was certain (implying an eye for opportunities, including the chance to claim apartments, locate stores of goods, find desirable positions, and so on).[30] "I was in the trenches the whole war," a Kuibyshev worker said, "and saw many nationalities at my side, but there were no Jews. They did not defend our fatherland, they fled to the East, and we Russians went West."[31]

Official anti-Semitism was a more ambiguous phenomenon. On the one hand, the regime's nationalities policy, predicated on equality of ethnic and national groups, forbade discrimination on national and ethnic grounds, including (and often particularly) anti-Semitism. This remained in force in the late Stalin period. In 1946 the party's official ideological organ, *Bolshevik*, denounced anti-Semitism as a "survival of racist chauvinism," citing (without source) Stalin's authority for the remarkable statement that "anti-Semitism, as an extreme form of racial chauvinism, is the most dangerous survival of cannibalism."[32] Indeed, the Party's Control Commission was still reprimanding Communists for blaming Jews as a group for the offenses of individuals at a time (the early 1950s) when official anti-Jewish policies implied that this was just what they *should* be doing.[33] Even during the anti-Semitic upsurge associated with the announcement of the Doctors' Plot in 1953, and thus clearly encouraged by regime actions, local party officials were trying to stop people "confusing a group of traitors with a nation (*narod*)" and reminding them that Soviet nationalities policy was against anti-Semitism.[34]

Official anti-Semitism was always expressed obliquely, never in the form of a statement that Jews were harmful or inferior as a group or that Jewish nationality itself gave grounds for suspicion. On the other hand,

[29] On discourses of Jews and conscription in the Imperial period, see Litvak, "Literary Response to Conscription." On Ostap Bender as "son of a Turkish citizen," see above, pp. 282–83, n. 3.

[30] RGANI, f. 5, op. 15, d. 602, l. 32. For discussion of the "no Jews at the front" myth in the Ukraine, see Amir Weiner, *Making Sense of War: The Second World War and the Fate of the Bolshevik Revolution* (Princeton, 2001), pp. 221–25.

[31] Tsentr khraneniia dokumentatsii noveishei istorii Samarskoi oblast (TsKhDNISO), f. 714, op. 1, d. 1780, l. 39.

[32] B. Kolbanovskii, "O kommunisticheskoi morali," *Bol'shevik*, 1946 no. 15, p. 24.

[33] RGANI, f. 6, op. 6, d. 1574, l. 6. This 1951 censure was not a public document. Thus, unlike condemnations of anti-Semitism in the press of the early 1950s, it cannot be dismissed as a propaganda ploy to confuse foreign critics.

[34] TsKhDNISO, f. 714, op. 1, d. 1780, ll. 25, 55.

the regime's own actions in the past (for example, the deportation of "traitor nations" during the war) had appeared to contradict this principled stance against ethnic discrimination, as a number of policy decisions involving Jews did in the 1940s. In the immediate postwar period, the main targets of official quasi–anti-Semitism were the Jewish Anti-Fascist Committee (JAC), established as a branch of Sovinformbiuro in 1942 and something of an anomaly given the regime's low tolerance since the 1920s of any kind of particularistic association, and various Jewish cultural organizations and groups of Jewish intellectuals. JAC was closed down in November 1948; in February 1949, Jewish writers' organizations were disbanded and Jewish theaters closed.[35] In the spring and summer of 1952, a secret trial of JAC leaders was held, resulting in thirteen death sentences under article 58 of the Criminal Code for crimes against the state.[36]

The climax of official quasi–anti-Semitism in the postwar period was the Doctors' Plot, announced in a TASS communiqué published in all the newspapers on 13 January that disclosed the arrest of a group of Kremlin doctors, almost all bearing Jewish names, as members of a terrorist conspiracy inspired by foreign intelligence agencies against Soviet leaders. "The majority of the participants of the terrorist group—Vovsi, B. Kogan, Feldman, Grinshtein, Etinger and others—were bought by American espionage. They were recruits through a filial of American espionage—the international bourgeois-nationalist organization 'Joint' American Jewish Joint Distribution Committee—and received orders from "the well-known Jewish bourgeois nationalist Mikhoels." In a strange throwback to the class war language of the Cultural Revolution of the late '20s, the editorial castigated those "right opportunists" who believe in "the dying down of class war" and argued, as Stalin had done in the 1930s, that it was the very successes of Soviet power that led that struggle to intensify. "In the USSR the exploiting classes have long been defeated and liquidated, but still remnants of private-ownership psychology and morals still survive—there are still bearers of bourgeois opinions and bourgeois morals, who are hidden enemies of our nation."[37] But now, it was strongly implied, those enemies were Jewish.

What Stalin—who seems to have been the chief instigator of the Doctors' Plot campaign—intended by it, and how far he meant to carry it,

[35] Kostyrchenko, *V plenu*, pp. 124, 154, 162–64.

[36] See *Stalin's Secret Pogrom: The Postwar Inquisition of the Jewish Anti-Fascist Committee*, eds. Joshua Rubenstein and Vladimir P. Naumov, trans. Laura Esther Wolfson (New Haven, 2001, pp. xi, 491–92, and passim.

[37] TASS communiqué, "Podlye shpiony i ubiitsy pod maskoi professorov-vrachei," *Pravda*, 13 January 1953, p. 1. The phrasing of this quotation is very reminiscent of a reported comment by Stalin in 1934: see above, p. 47.

remain a matter of debate.[38] Since Stalin's associates in the leadership ended the campaign and released the accused doctors immediately after his death, we may assume that they thought the whole thing unwise. Indeed, there were many reasons to think it so. Apart from the rising wave of popular anti-Semitism encouraged by the Doctors' Plot communiqué and the immense long-term damage done to the regime's relationship with the Russian/Soviet intelligentsia (a group in which Jews were not only an important presence but an important *Soviet* presence), the regime's green light on anti-Semitism quickly rebounded on itself. In the Ukraine, illegal leaflets called on the population to arm themselves and organize to "destroy the Jews"—but this was also, in effect, a call to arms against the Soviet regime. "Death to the Jews and the Communists," one leaflet proclaimed. "The kikes dominate everywhere. Workers' salaries are being cut. Where are our goods, which the collective farms transfer to the state? Demand higher salaries and goods in the shops."[39] Another leaflet circulated in Kiev oblast called for political action in a legal framework, exhorting "the working class and . . . the working peasantry to unite as one for the elections to local soviets . . . around the single demand: get rid of all Jews . . . from Ukraine, since these people have sold themselves to American imperialism."[40]

In central Russia, too, the state's anti-Semitic campaign produced strong reactions, though they were less violent than in the Ukraine. In the workplace meetings on the TASS communiqué conducted by local party organizations in January-February 1953,[41] deportation of all Jews—to Siberia, to Palestine, to the United States—was suggested again and again, often with reference to the wartime policy of deporting "traitor" nations like Crimean Tatars and Chechens. Some also supported the milder option of expulsion and deportation of all Jews from the major cities (Moscow, Leningrad, Kiev).[42] One of the most prominent themes in the popular discussion was

[38] A recent controversial contribution is Jonathan Brent with Vladimir P. Naumov, *Stalin's Last Crime. The Plot against the Jewish Doctors 1948–1953* (New York, 2003). For a judicious summary, see Yoram Gorlizki and Oleg Khlevniuk, *Cold Peace: Stalin and the Soviet Ruling Circle, 1945–1953* (New York, 2004), pp. 153–59.

[39] Quoted from Ukrainian archival documents published by Mordechai Altshuler, "More about Public Reaction to the Doctors' Plot," *Jews in Eastern Europe* 30 (1996), pp. 28–29.

[40] "More about Public Reaction," p. 45.

[41] In the postwar period, the Central Committee of the Party periodically took soundings of popular opinion on policy shifts like the announcement of the Doctor's Plot in 1953 and Khrushchev's "Secret Speech" in 1956. Local Party committees were required to organize meetings in workplaces and Party cells to discuss these issues, as well as picking up informal comments in the corridors and private conversations, and send detailed reports back to the Center. The document cited is one such report, compiled by the Kuibyshev (Samara) obkom.

[42] The carefully neutral reporting of these discussions by party officials (see, for example, the Kuibyshev oblast reports in TsKhDNISO, f. 714, op. 1, d. 1780, and the reports of the

that Jews were a privileged people in the Soviet Union. According to a summary of letters to Pravda compiled for the party leaders early in 1953, many people "complain that the best apartments in the cities of Odessa, Kiev, Minsk, Riga and other places are occupied by Jews, that many Jews received salaries of 500–700 rubles a month, live luxuriously, have fine dachas, dress well, go every year to Crimean resorts and other places with their whole families." [43] Everywhere Jews were in "cushy top posts,"[44] never doing hard physical work in low-status jobs.[45] They "command the economy," particularly the supply organs, transportation, and the food industry.[46] They were disproportionately represented in higher education[47] and consequently in the professions (medicine and the arts being often specifically mentioned) and in high-paid jobs in government.[48] It was high time, most speakers in the discussions agreed, to purge Jews from the Party and from leading positions in state service and the professions, especially medicine, trade, and culture,[49] as well as restricting their admission to the party[50] and higher education ("let them be educated via labor").[51]

Central Committee's department of Party, trade union, and Komsomol organizations to the Party leaders in RGANI, f. 5, op. 15, d. 407) leave unresolved the vexed question of whether Stalin was in fact planning such a deportation, as has long been rumored, or if this idea actually came from the grassroots and was without official endorsement. As of 19 January 1953, the Kuibyshev gorkom secretary, V. Trusenko, described such popular demands as an "incorrect opinion" (TsKhDNISO, f. 714, op. 1, d. 1780, l. 25), but he may only have been poorly informed about what was correct in the view of the Center. What the tone of the reporting does strongly suggest is that Party officials (particularly Trusenko, who wrote many of the Kuibyshev reports to the Central Committee, but to a lesser extent also the OPPKO TsK officials who reported to their Party leaders) were uncertain what the new policy line was and how far it was meant to go and worried about its anti-Semitic implications and the disruptive enthusiasm of popular response. In OPPKO there is clear evidence of officials hedging bets in the decision (endorsed by CC secretary A. B. Aristov) to include in their summaries of opinion on the TASS communique a strong letter from Party member M. A. Faikin stating that this and the Slansky trial had stimulated anti-Semitism in the population and a clear authoritative statement in the press was needed to stop it (RGANI, f. 5, op. 15, d. 407, l. 33).

[43] RGANI, F. 5, OP. 15, D. 407, L. 104.

[44] From "The Party and Popular Reaction to the 'Doctors' Plot' (Dnepropetrovsk Province, Ukraine)," a publication of archival documents by Mordechai Altshuler and Tatiana Chentsova, *Jews in Eastern Europe* 21 (1993), p. 57.

[45] TsKhDNISO, f. 714, op. 1, d. 1780, l. 27.

[46] "The Party and Popular Reaction," p. 56.

[47] Comment reported from Kiev oblast in "More about Public Reaction," pp. 39–40.

[48] TsKhDNISO, f. 714, op. 1, d. 1780, l. 6.

[49] For a comprehensive but typical list of such demands, see "The Party and Popular Reaction," p. 63.

[50] TsKhDNISO, f. 714, op. 1, d. 1780, l. 31.

[51] "The Party and Popular Reaction," p. 63.

As we have seen above with the Ukrainian leaflets, popular denunciation of Jewish privilege could come uncomfortably close to denunciation of the regime that granted Jews such privileges ("Death to Jews and Communists"). This was not just a mindless repetition of the old "Jewish Bolshevism" myth, though that surely contributed; it was in fact true that in terms of education, high-level professional and administrative jobs, and even party membership, Jews stood markedly higher than any other Soviet nationality including Russians, and that they had achieved this position since and in large part as a result of the Revolution.[52] Small wonder, under these circumstances, if some of Stalin's party colleagues had doubts about the wisdom of the Doctors' Plot campaign on pragmatic grounds, even disregarding the undertone of uneasiness associated with violating a long-standing tenet of party ideology against anti-Semitism.

Another pervasive thread in the discussions drew on a staple of traditional anti-Semitism: dishonesty, deceitfulness, and profiteering of Jews. Jews should be purged from commerce "since they are particularly untrustworthy in measuring and weighing."[53] Jews are "traders (), cunning and always capable of betraying a person."[54] They were "cunning" (a word used over and over again), good at finding patrons and protectors ("This didn't happen without *Kumovstvo*!" exclaimed one indignant letter writer after the release of the Jewish doctors following Stalin's death)[55] and getting things.[56] In Kuibyshev's youth town (said to be "buzzing like a beehive" in response to the TASS communiqué), young people "expressed strong resentment against Jews as people who live cunningly at the expense of Russians."[57] Not often directly articulated but seeming to underlie many of these complaints about Jewish cunning was a sense of built-in unfairness in the relationship of Jews and Russians: in addition to having more education, Jews (it was implied) were just too clever for simple-minded Russians. In the words of one advocate of mass deportation, "let them be exiled to one place, where they can deceive each other";[58] then honest Russians will no longer be their victims and dupes.

[52] For details, see Yuri Slezkine, *The Jewish Century* (Princeton, 2004), pp. 220–26.

[53] "The Party and Popular Reaction," p. 63.

[54] RGANI, f. 5, op. 15, d. 407, l. 45.

[55] RGANI, f, 5, op. 30, d. 5, l. 10. Other comments implying protection include suggestions that Jewish college graduates were more likely to get job assignments in Moscow after graduation (TsKhDNISO, f. 714, op. 1, d. 1780, l. 6).

[56] RGANI, f. 5, op. 15, d. 407, l. 75.

[57] RGANI, f. 5, op. 15, d. 407, l. 40.

[58] RGANI, f. 5, op. 15, d. 407, l. 45.

The Campaign Against *Rotozeistvo* of 1953

The official actions and policies of the late Stalin period that fall under the heading of anti-Semitism focused almost exclusively on elites—Jewish professionals and administrators in various fields, with cultural fields like literature and theater as well as medicine to the fore—and foreign connections.[59] At the beginning of 1953, however, contemporaneously with the announcement of the Doctors' Plot, emerged a new, albeit minor, theme: the Jew as a swindler and con man. The rubric under which this appeared was the short-lived campaign against *rotozeistvo* in the Soviet bureaucracy that was launched in January 1953. This campaign has not been noted, as far as I know, in the extensive literature on postwar anti-Semitism, yet it is clearly a part of that general story, as well as of the particular story of the Jewishing of tricksters that I set out to tell in this chapter.

The term *rotozeistvo*—defined in a 1939 Soviet dictionary published as "extreme absentmindedness, lack of attention"—had made brief appearances in the rhetoric of the Great Purges, when it referred to the carelessness of bureaucrats who failed to notice wreckers and enemies in their midst—that is, to lack of vigilance.[60] It was used in the same sense in *Pravda*'s commentary on the newly announced Doctors' Plot in January 1953, which stated that "Besides these enemies [the "spies and murderers" under indictment], we have still one more enemy—the carelessness (*rotozeistvo*) of our people. Do not doubt but that where there is carelessness among us, there will be wrecking."[61] *Izvestiia* glossed this in a particularly sinister way by inserting a reference to Stalin's famous speech to the February-March 1937 plenum of the Central committee in which he had denounced enemies of the people and summoned his listeners to

---

[59] The intelligentsia focus of postwar anti-Semitism has not been problematized in the literature, though it would surely be worth asking why it was the Jewish intelligentsia rather than the Jewish people a whole that was the target. This question, however, lies beyond the scope of the present chapter.

[60] *Krainiaia rasseiannost', nevnimaltel'nost'. Tolkovyi slovar' russkogo iazyka*, ed. D. N. Ushakov, vol. 3 (Moscow, 1939), "Rotozeistvo." *Rotozeistvo* seems to be primarily a Soviet-era term, though it had not figured particularly prominently in the many earlier antibureaucratic campaigns of the Soviet era. Vladimir Dal, who includes only the verb form, *rotozeit'/rotozeinichat'* (listed under *rot*) defined its meaning as "*zevat', glazet', glazopialit', gliadet' popustu, khlopat' glazami, glupo zasmatrivat'sia na vse vstrechnoe*": Vladimir Dal, *Tolkovyi slovar' zhivogo velikorusskogo iazyka*, vol. 4 (Moscow, 1980; original publication date 1882).

[61] *Pravda*, 13 January 1953, p. 1: "Podlye shpiony i ubiitsy pod maskoi professorov-vrachei . . ."

battle against the "idiotic sickness" of lack of vigilance.[62] This was the beginning of the newspapers' campaign against rotozeistvo. At first, the emphasis of the campaign was on delinquencies such as careless handling of secret documents and loose talk involving state secrets,[63] but within a few weeks the emphasis had shifted from officials' carelessness about secrets to their practice of patronage and protectionism (*pokrovitel'stvo*), including the protection of subordinates who committed crimes.[64]

As the campaign developed, *rotozei* became firmly identified as dupes—people whose unwise habit of patronage and protectionism had allowed unscrupulous persons to carry out all sorts of wrongdoing, particularly economic crimes. The most striking characteristic of this campaign was its strong implicit ethnic component. Dupes—the officials who were exploited by unscrupulous persons—were generally Russian or unidentified by nationality. The protégés and subordinates who duped them were overwhelmingly Jewish.[65]

As in other aspects of the public anti-Semitic campaigns of the late Stalin period, including the Doctors' Plot itself, the rhetoric was not

[62] *Izvestiia*, 15 January 1953, p. 1 (editorial): "Povysit' politicheskuiu bditel'nost'." The newspaper was not fully accurate in its quotation: although Stalin did use the term *rotozeistvo* once in his 1937 speech (deploring the fact that "our leading comrades . . . were . . . so naive and blind that they couldn't discern the real face of the enemies of the people" and recalling the Central Committee's warning to party organization after Kirov's murder against "politicheskaia blagodushie and obyvatel'skoe rotozeistvo" : I. V. Stalin, *Sochineniia*, vol. 1 (14), ed. McNeal, [Stanford 1967], pp. 190–91), the referent of "idiotic sickness" in the passage *Izvestiia* quoted was not actually rotozeistvo but its close relatives: *bespechnost'*, *blagodushie*, and *blizorukost'* (ibid., p. 223).

[63] See editorial "Pokonchit' s rotozeistvom v nashikh riadakh," *Pravda*, 18 January 1953, p. 1, and *Izvestiia* editorial of 15 January cited above. In an internal memo, the Central Committee's department of party organs (OPPKO) dated 19 January used the term in reference to the state security organs' failure to uncover the doctors' treachery earlier. RGANI, f. 5, op. 15, d. 407, l. 99.

[64] See *Pravda*, 1 February 1953, p. 2,: G. Vladimirov and R. Ianson, "Pod kryshkom rotozeev" (reprinted from *Sovetskaia Latviia*). On political patronage and official criticism of the phenomenon, see Fitzpatrick, *Everyday Stalinism*, pp. 109–14 and 195–96.

[65] This generalization is based on a reading of *Pravda*, *Izvestiia*, *Trud*, *Vecherniaia Moskva*, *Krymskaia pravda* (Simferopol), and *Molot* (Rostov on Don) for the first three months of 1953. It should be pointed out, however, that there were exceptions. Not absolutely every "rotozei" article cited an obviously Jewish protagonist, but most did. Central Asians also made appearances as swindlers duping hapless bureaucrats (e.g., in the *Izvestiia* editorial "Watchfully guard and multiply socialist property," 11 February 1953, p. 1, where two of the examples of swindlers cited are Jewish, one Central Asian). While almost all the newspapers I consulted ran their anti-*rotozeistvo* campaign as part of the broader anti-Semitic campaign, *Vecherniaia Moskva* seems to have been an honorable exception (it covered the theme, but without any apparent anti-Semitic overtones). The regional newspaper *Krymskaia pravda* ran a series of virulently anti-Semitic "rotozei" stories—but, interesting enough, these stories appeared during the temporary absence of the regular editor and disappeared once he resumed his post.

straightforwardly anti-Semitic. The TASS communiqué, for example, did not say that *Jewish* doctors were likely to be traitors; it simply gave a list of names of traitor doctors, almost all of which were Jewish. Similarly, it was not alleged in the "dupes" campaign that Jewish employees and clients were particularly likely to swindle their bosses and patrons; it simply happened that the swindlers whose crimes were reported had Jewish names.[66] It was Meyer Shusterl, for example, who carried out "dirty little deals" in an artel in the Crimea; Abram Litman, a warehouse head with a prison record, who swindled his Russian patron; Katsman, a bookkeeper who called himself Kauman, who falsely claimed to be a war veteran; Abram Natanovich Khaitin, who found protectors in the Soviet Latvian beau monde and embezzled money from the Latvian theater society; Leonid Fridman, who managed to get hold of state cars for weddings in Rostov; "a certain E. Gurevich," who duped his patrons in the peat administration and stole 60,000 rubles; "a certain Rozen," a self-styled mechanical engineer, who swindled the railroad machine-building administration of more than a million rubles.[67]

In addition to having Jewish names, several of the swindlers cited had biographies that included evasion of wartime military service, evoking the popular belief that Jews were "Tashkent partisans," that is, draft dodgers.[68] The embezzler Aleksandr Mikhailovich Liubenskii (whose real patronymic turned out to be Moiseevich) was said to have fled from Odessa to Stalingrad at the beginning of the war.[69] L. E. Rofman had allegedly fled from Ukraine to Kirgizia during war and used false documents to get jobs as school inspector and then administrator of local industry; at war's end, he moved to Moscow and worked as chief engineer

[66] As noted above (note 35), not all the newspaper feuilletons against rotozei were dupes of persons clearly identified as Jews, but they may have been read as uniformly anti-Semitic even in the absence of a specific reference—which, of course, would imply a very strong association of Jews and tricksters in Russians' minds. In April 1953, after the release of the doctors, *Pravda* received some very angry letters about its anti-Semitic line earlier in the year, one writer claiming that for fifteen days after the TASS communiqué, "*Pravda* published feuilletons every day whose protagonists were exclusively Jews." In fact, only one of the three feuilletons is (to the uninitiated reader) blatantly anti-Semitic (G. Vladimirov and R. Iansion, "Pod kryshem rotozeev," *Pravda*, 1 February 1953, p. 2, reprinted from a Latvian newspaper). Another (on the *vrach-samozvanets* Kazhdan) could be so construed (M. Burenko and N. Timarenko, "Prostaki i prokhodimets," *Pravda*, 7 Feburary 1953, p. 2), while the third (N. Volkov, "Rotozei," *Pravda*, 24 January 1953, p. 2) is on an *aferistka* with no obvious signs of Jewish ethnicity.

[67] *Krymskaia pravda*, 8 February 1953, p. 2.; ibid., 8 February 1953, p. 2; ibid., 8 Feb 1953, p. 2; *Izvestiia*, 30 January 1953, p. 2; *Pravda*, 1 February 1953, p. 2 (reprinted from *Sovetskaia Latviia*); *Molot* (Rostov on Don), 26 February 1953, p. 3; *Izvestiia* 25 March 1953, p. 2; ibid., 11 February 1953, p. 1.

[68] On "Tashkent partisans," see Weiner, *Making Sense*, pp. 221–22.

[69] *Krymskaia pravda*, 18 February 1953, p. 3.

of a food plant in Nobinsk (using a false diploma from an Odessa engineering institute) before returning to Vinnitsa, where he was arrested in May 1949.[70]

For the most part, the Jewish swindlers featured in the newspaper reports of early 1953 were not accused of being spies or agents of foreign intelligence, or even of having foreign connections.[71] Nonetheless, the tone of affectionate tolerance tinged with admiration that had once characterized treatments of Ostap Bender-like con men was notably absent: in the context of the "dupes" campaign, swindlers' impostures were no longer just criminal but verging on the political.[72] Masking was the pervasive theme, with name changes, forged diplomas, and false claims about war service featuring heavily. These Jewish swindlers were not only practicing deceit but their very identity was false; they were imposters "under the mask" of physicians, accountants, engineers, and so on—enemies "masquerading in the guise of Soviet people."[73]

• • •

The "dupes" campaign of 1953 turned out to be short-lived; after only a few months, it was cut short when the allegations of the Doctors' Plot—and thus, official encouragement of anti-Semitism—were repudiated.[74] It left some traces, however, notably in Khrushchev's notorious campaign against economic crime of the late 1950s and early 1960s. The campaign was directed primarily against currency speculators, but more broadly against the informal "second economy" as a whole; Jews were a major target, to the point of arousing international protests and concern about a revival of anti-Semitism. Arkady Vaksberg concurs that Jews were scapegoated, while noting that "the great majority of 'left' [second economy] businessmen" were in fact Jewish, partly as a result of restriction of legitimate career opportunities for Jews in the postwar period.[75] In 1961

[70] *Izvestiia*, 18 February 1953, pp. 2–3.

[71] This is something of a surprise, since a writer in *Pravda* had warned that foreign spies "use all kind of criminal and degenerate elements as their agents" (N. Kozev, "O revoliutsionnoi bditel'nosti," *Pravda*, 6 February 1953, p. 3), which would appear to be an encouragement to make a more explicit link between the "dupes" campaign and the Doctors' Plot.

[72] On this distinction, see above, pp. 18–21.

[73] *Pravda*, 13 January 1953, p. 1; *Izvestiia*, 15 January 1953, p. 1.

[74] In *Pravda*, 6 April, p. 1, an editorial, "Sovetskaia sotsialisticheskaia zakonnost' neprikosnovenna," stated that wrongdoers within the Ministry of State Security had fabricated the case against the doctors, "honest Soviet people, outstanding figures of Soviet science."

[75] Arkady Vaksberg, *Stalin against the Jews*, trans. Antonina W. Bouis (New York, 1994), p. 285; and see also Evgeniia Evelson, *Sudebnye protsessy po ekonomicheskim delam v SSSR (60-e gody)* (London, 1986), pp. 21–22. Konstantin M. Simis, *USSR: The Corrupt Society. The Secret World of Soviet Capitalism* (New York, 1982) makes no general statement about

the death penalty was brought back for counterfeiting and embezzling,[76] and a series of well-publicized trials of currency speculators in 1961 and 1962 featured Jews prominently among the accused: according to Evelson's figures, 1,676 Jews were defendants in trials for economic crimes in the years 1961–67, and 163 received the death sentence.[77] The campaign put more stress on the defendants' greed and love of foreign lifestyle than in 1953, and less on their cunning and propensity to imposture. In other respects, however, the rhetoric was very similar. Jewish names and patronymics were emphasized to sinister effect, and newspaper coverage of the trials included gratuitous references to defendants with Jewish names who "traveled from city to city bribing their spiritual brethren" and a Vilnius-based network of currency speculators that solved internal dispute by appealing not to Soviet courts but "to the local rabbi."[78]

As for Ostap Bender, he remained loved by readers despite his official condemnation in 1948 and eclipse during the period of the "dupes" campaign, and it did not take long after Stalin's death for him to re-emerge. Andrei Sinyavsky relates an incident during the Thaw of 1953–54 when law students at Moscow University organized a comic mock trial of Ostap Bender, in the course of which one student defender provoked a scandal by his impulsive claim that "Ostap Bender is the favorite hero of Soviet youth!"[79] The prohibition on publication of the Bender novels was lifted in the Khrushchev era and in the 1960s, '70s, and '80s their publication figures were phenomenal: over 2 million copies published in the Soviet Union in the years 1956–65, close to 3 million in the period 1966–79, and

---

the Jewish contribution in the second economy, but his stories imply that both the Jewish and the Georgian contritution were substantial, with Moscow, Odessa, Riga, and Tbilisi being identified as key centers for the second economy (p. 147).

[76] See *Current Digest of the Soviet Press* 13:17 (1959) for the full text of the law, published in *Izvestiia* on 7 May 1959, p. 5.

[77] Evelson, *Sudebnye protessy*, p. 308. These figures, based on a study of 400 court cases, unfortunately do not include information on other ethnic groups, so that it is impossible to tell what proportion of all defendants and those receiving death sentences were Jews. Vaksberg (*Stalin against the Jews*, p. 287) quotes Evelson as saying that 5 death sentences went to non-Jews, as against 163 to Jews, but I have been unable to locate this in her book. From Evelson's description of the trials, it is clear both that many of the accused were Jews and that some were not. One of the early publicized cases, for example, took place in Tbilisi with five principal defendants, all with Georgian names, one of whom received the death sentence (CDSP 13:50 (1961), 28–29, text from *Zaria Vostoka*, 4 December 1961, p. 4, and 12 December 1961, p. 4).

[78] Reported from *Sovetskaia Kirgiziia* and *Trud*, respectively, in *Current Digest of the Soviet Press* 14:2 [(1961), p. 4, and ibid., 14:2 (1959), p. 5.

[79] Andrei Sinyavsky, *Soviet Civilization: A Cultural History*, trans. Joanne Turnbull (New York, 1990), p. 180. The mock court either acquitted Bender or gave him an unacceptably light sentence. In the resulting scandal, one student was expelled from the Komsomol, another from the university.

over 9 million in the 1980s.[80] Copies of each new edition "disappeared instantly" because of the force of popular demand.[81] True, a minority opinion in the literary world continued to hold aloof from Ilf and Petrov and other writers of the "Odessa school," even in the 1960s and '70s.[82] With the turn to a commercial market after 1991, Ilf and Petrov's enormous popularity with the Russian public led publishers from Karelia to Vladivostok to reissue it time and time again, albeit usually in smaller editions than the Soviet ones. In 1994 and 1995 alone, at least twenty-one editions of one or other of the Ostap Bender novels were published in Russia[83]—although, as the humorist Mikhail Zhvanetskii's 1997 tribute suggested, there was actually no need to republish or even reread these works because "we knew [them] by heart."[84]

One assumes that Russians continued to read Bender as a Jew, but this apparently did nothing to hinder his immense popularity with Soviet readers. According to Sinyavsky, Bender was the "old fox" whose survival skills were those of "a Soviet citizen who has imbibed this system body and soul."[85] The Jewish trickster, in short, had become the personification of really existing Soviet Man.

[80] Calculated from Alain Préchac, *Il'f et Petrov. Témoins de leur temps. Stalinisme et littérature*, vol. 3 (Paris, 2000), pp. 754–57.

[81] Kurdiumov, *V kraiu*, p. 33.

[82] See, for example, Oleg Mikhailov, *Vernost': Rodina i literatura* (Moscow, 1974), p. 172 and passim. Kurdiumov (*V kraiu*, pp. 20–21) reads this critique as implictly anti-Semitic.

[83] Calculated from *Knizhnaia letopis'* (Moscow), 1994 and 1995 (some issues are missing from the 1994 set). The most notable new editions of the 1990s were the "first complete editions" of *Dvenatsat' stul'ev* and *Zolotoi telenok*, ed. and with commentary by M. Odesskii and D. Feldman (Moscow, 1997 and 2000), published by "Vagrius," and the "Panorama" editions of the two books with extensive commentaries by Iu. K. Shcheglov (Moscow, 1995). The total number of copies of *Dvenadtsat' stul'ev* and *Zolotoi telenok* published in the Russian Federation in the years 1992–95 was around 2.4 million (Préchac, *Il'f et Petrov*, pp. 758–60).

[84] Mikhail Zhvanetskii, *Sobranie proizvedenii v chetyrekh tomakh*, vol. 4 (Moscow, 2001), "Il'fu—sto let," p. 299.

[85] Sinyavsky, *Soviet Civilization*, pp. 174–80.

Afterword

CHAPTER FIFTEEN

Becoming Post-Soviet

If speaking Bolshevik was something that had to be learned in the revolutionary era, after 1991 it had to be rapidly unlearned. Soviet identities were cast off, new post-Soviet identities invented. This was a self-conscious process—the obverse of learning to speak "Bolshevik" in the 1920s and '30s—in which individuals struggled to empty their consciousness of Soviet morality, purge their language of Sovietisms, and thus fit themselves to be citizens of the new post-Soviet world. As in the earlier Soviet case, the remaking of self was experienced as liberating but also laborious and sometimes painful. It was likely to involve suppressing the memory of one's own past identity as a (more or less) loyal Soviet citizen, perhaps even consigning the whole seventy-four years of Soviet power to a black hole of forgetfulness.

In looking back on the past, post-Soviet Russians sometimes invoked the idea of imposture—of having been forced by the straitjacket of Soviet culture to assume personae that they now perceive as inauthentic. "I feel as if I have lived someone else's life," were the words of an elderly Russian woman in the 1990s.[1] Biographies and antecedents were reinvented to meet the demands of the new age. For example, in his Soviet autobiographies the poet Demian Bednyi (born Efim Pridvorov) was at pains to stress his humble origins (brought up in poor peasant milieu by an abusive mother), though discreditable rumors circulated that he was the by-blow of a Grand Duke. In his grandson's version in the 1990s, the family's aristocratic lineage moved to center stage, displacing not only Bednyi's "man of the people" persona but also the family's other status claim in Soviet times, namely membership in the top Soviet elite.[2]

An earlier version of part of this chapter was published as the concluding section of "Making a Self for the Times: Impersonation and Imposture in Twentieth-Century Russia," *Kritika* 2:3 (Summer 2001), pp. 483–87. Thanks to Katerina Clark, Yuri Slezkine, and Catriona Kelly for helpful suggestions.

[1] Anna Akimovna Dubova interview, in Engel and Posadskaya-Vanderbeck, *A Revolution of Their Own*, p. 46.

[2] For short autobiographies by Demian Bednyi from 1921 and 1942, see Demian Bednyi, *Sobranie sochinenii*, vol. 8 (Moscow, 1965), pp. 253–55; for an unsourced report that he was the illegitimate son of a Grand Duke, see Roberta Reeder, *Anna Akhmatova: Poet and Prophet* (New York, 1994), p. 187. Thanks to Robert Horvath, Melbourne, for drawing this case to my attention and for providing the information about the current generation.

The first half of the 1990s was the heyday of tumultous, chaotic social change and anxious individual reinvention. The comparative brevity of this phase may serve to remind us that, despite the elements of comparability with 1917, 1991 was a revolution only in a rather special sense. It was not a social revolution, bubbling up from below and finally erupting in an unstoppable popular impulse to topple the old regime. Rather, it was a dramatic case of sudden state disintegration; thus, the situation in Russia in the early 1990s could be compared with that of Germany and Japan after 1945, where the old regime collapsed abruptly as a result of defeat in war, as with Russia after 1917. In the case of post–1991 Russia, of course, there was no occupying power; culturally, however, what occurred in Russia after 1991 might be regarded as akin to Western occupation. In Soviet times, the capitalist West was the Other. Now Russia itself had to become this Other: the "normal, civilized life" that was the catchword and object of desire of the 1990s necessarily had Western characteristics because it was Westernism that was the familiar antithesis of Sovietness.

The differences of underlying circumstances in 1917 and 1991 make the similarities of behavioral and psychological responses on the part of individual citizens all the more intriguing. In the new era, no less than the old, impersonation—and surely also imposture—was widely practiced. Former Soviet citizens might now reinvent themselves as *menedzhery*, *brokery*, and *biznesmeny* (feminine: *biznes-ledi*, *biznesmenki*, *biznesmenshi*); practitioners of *konsalting* or *pablik-rileishnz*; *rieltory* and *reketiry*; *programmisty* and *khakery*; *seks-bomby* and *iappi*; *gei* and *biseksualy*—identities whose novelty is conveyed by the exoticness of the newly borrowed terms.[3] The path was open for self-transformation into a *mer*, if the *elektorat* so willed; a *guru* or an *ekstrasens*; or, from the new science of *ufologiia*, a *kontakter* (feminine: *kontaktërsha*: "one who enters into contact with representatives of non-Earth civilizations, receives information from the Cosmos").[4] New identities required new forms of behavior, dress, work habits, time habits, interpersonal relations habits, ways of handling of money, and so on, all of which had to be rapidly mastered and conspicuously displayed—*ipoteki* for the purchase of *kottedzhy*, if there were not enough *baksy*; *akupunktura* and *pitstsa*; repudiation of *seksizm*; mastery of the *internet*; interest in *shou-biznes* and *reitingi*; bodies to be subjected to *sheiping* by a *trener*, *bioritmy* to be observed; the new hobby of *shop-*

[3] For those mystified by these hybrid terms, they refer to managers, brokers, businessmen and women, consulting, public relations, realtors, racketeers, programmers, hackers, sex-bombs, yuppies, gays, and bisexuals.

[4] Words and definitions from *Tolkovyi slovar' russkogo iazyka kontsa XX v. Iazykovye izmeneniia* (St. Petersburg, 1998) and L. P. Krysin, *Tolkovyi slovar' inoiazychnykh slov* (Moscow, 1998). *Mer* = mayor; *ufologiia* is the science of unidentified flying objects.

ping to be practiced.[5] Even in the absence of *shokovaia terapiia*[6] as government economic strategy, *shok* was a condition of life and *shokovyi* the indispensable adjective.

The shock of the early '90s had many different components. Foreign goods flooded in and were sold at first from improvised kiosks and tables in the strees. Wages and salaries collapsed, both because of inflation and because state employers were in chronic arrears in paying them. State industry was privatized, to the immense profit of a very few. Private banks arose and then, in many cases, dramatically fell, taking many citizens' savings with them. Law and order collapsed, as did most state funding of culture. Old restrictions on internal movement, residence, change of employment, and travel abroad were lifted, producing disorientation as well as liberation.[7] Urban apartments were privatized, giving rise to the new commercial realm of "real estate" as well as all sorts of crooked deals that left substantial numbers of former apartment tenants on the street; a new term, *bomzhi* (or persons without fixed abode, *bez opredelennogo mesta zhitel'stva*), came into existence to describe a new large-scale phenomenon.[8] Serious food shortages in the early '90s turned city-dwellers into gardeners, who grew vegetables in small plots on the outskirts of towns. Civil War in the Caucasus created a new class of refugees, in addition to the large numbers of Russians trying to return to central Russia from the non-Russian republics or from the decaying industrial settlements in the north. Rates of alcohol consumption, drug consumption, and suicide rose sharply, as life expectancy for males dropped to a degree unpredented in a developed society in peace time.

The intelligentsia, whose political influence and sense of moral authority had peaked in the heady days of perestroika, found its very existence under threat in post-Soviet Russia as a result of drastic cutbacks in state funding of science and culture. The plummeting prestige of education (that quintessential Soviet value!) contributed to demoralization, as did the brain drain of scientists going abroad. "Stripped of its money, its prestige and its faith," in Masha Gessen's words, it was internally divided

---

[5] *Ipoteki* = mortgages; *kottedzhy* (cottages) is the term often used for New Russian dachas. Other hybrids in this sentence stand for dollars, acapuncture, pizza, sexism, the Internet, show-business, ratings, (body-)shaping, trainer, biorhythms and shopping.

[6] Means shock therapy.

[7] A sociologist reporting on these developments noted that the sudden availability of choice with regard to employment and movement was one of the biggest shocks for citizens used to a life that was minutely regulated: R. V. Ryvkina, "Obraz naseleniia Rossii: sotsial'nye posledstviia reform 90-kh godov," *Sotsiologicheskie issledovaniia*, 2001 no. 4, p. 37.

[8] V. F. Zhuravlev, "Prichiny bezdomnosti skvoz' prizmu biograficheskogo analiza," in *Sotsial'no-ekonomicheskie problemy sovremennogo perioda preobrazovanii v Rossii*, vyp. 7 (Moscow, 1996), pp. 107–21.

"into those who made money and those who did not, those who changed professions and adapted to new conditions and those who proudly eked out a familiar shoestring existence."[9] Some commentators in the capitals found malicious satisfaction that the intelligentsia would finally have to drop its moral pretensions, knuckle down to earning a living like everyone else, and transform itself into a Western-style professional class.[10] Meanwhile, out in the provinces, teachers, doctors, and librarians were facing other problems. "The need to grow vegetables for one's family is probably the biggest single contributor to loss of intelligentsia identity in Zubtsov," reported a British sociologist, citing the sad plaint of a hospital consultant who "would like to consider herself an intelligent . . . if only she could do more reading and less farming."[11]

According to comedian Mikhail Zhvanetskii, "there are no capitalists or communists in Russia. There are people who have adapted and people who haven't."[12] A sociologist identified three stages in the process: first, the shock stage, where the person struggles to survive; second, the "adaptation" stage, where he/she mobilizes adaptive reserves and resources; and finally successful completion of the adaptation process, thriving (*preuspevanie*). She noted extreme variation in the degree of adaptation of the Russian population: while some had gone through all three stages, others "are lost in [the] stage of surviving the 'shock,' unable not only to adapt themselves but even to work out any kind of rational behavior in the circumstances of change of their position in the social hierarchy."[13]

Shok and disorientation extended to all spheres, from the deepest realm of values to the everyday matter of how to greet people. "No matter how you address a stranger in today's Russia, in four out of five cases you risk irritating him," according to a 1993 survey conducted by the All-Russia Center for the Study of Public Opinion.[14] On the issue of how to address groups of unknown people, opinions varied widely: at one end of the spectrum, 20% of those polled found it most natural to use the Soviet-era salutation of "comrades"; at the other, about the same proportion favored the

[9] Masha Gessen, *Dead Again: The Russian Intelligentsia after Communism* (London, 1997), p. 18.

[10] Boris Dubin and Lev Gudkov, *Intelligentsiia: Zametki o literaturno-politicheskikh illuziiakh* (Moscow, 1995), p. 7.

[11] Anne White, "Social Change in Provincial Russia: The Intelligentsia in a Raion Centre," *Europe-Asia Studies* 52:4 (2000), pp. 677–94.

[12] Quoted in Eric Shiraev and Betty Glad, "Generational Adaptations to the Transition," in Glad and Eric Shiraev, eds., *The Russian Transformation: Political, Sociological, and Psychological Aspects* (New York, 1999), p. 172.

[13] L. A. Beliaeva, "Strategii vyzhivaniia, adaptatsii, preuspevaniia," *Sotsiologicheskie issledovaniia*, 2001 no. 6, p. 45.

[14] *Current Digest of the Post-Soviet Press* 45:30 (1993), p. 29, from *Izvestiia*, 24 July 1993, p. 8.

prerevolutionary (and also Western) "ladies and gentlemen" or the Orthodox "brothers and sisters," while the rest of the respondents either preferred more neutral forms of address such as "friends," "citizens," or simply "people," or were at a loss for an answer. Not surprisingly, the over fifty age group tended to prefer "comrades," while those in their early twenties favored "ladies and gentlemen." To add to the confusion, the use of an individual's name and patronymic in polite interactions became much less common, stripping a layer of respect and deference from social life. As *Izvestiia* commented sadly, "purely linguistic shortcomings of the transitional period are having an effect on people's general irritability."[15]

Values had to be revised as well as forms of behavior. In the first years of the transition, starting in the perestroika period, this generally meant repudiation and discrediting of everything Soviet, with a corresponding exaltation of everything that in Soviet times had been condemned. At the beginning of the 1990s, Nancy Ries reported, negation of everything Soviet was omnipresent in the media. "Myths about public order and safety were crushed by constant, explicit reportage about the most gruesome crimes; crime had previously been reported as a plague only of the West. Myths about the Soviet love of motherland were poisoned by exposes about the terrible pollution of Soviet lands. Myths about planning and control were contradicted by disclosures of the most absurd, ludicrous, and wasteful production and distribution practices. And the myth of the Party as the kindly elder brother, the repository of maturity, wisdom, and fairness, was blown apart by a barrage of media bombshells about abuses of power and privilege."[16] Along with this went an inversion of the old "Soviet = good / West = bad" dichotomy, so that "where the Soviet media had regularly exhibited images of the cruelty, unfairness, and contradictions of capitalist systems, in perestroika this practice was inverted, and images of poor people receiving medical care in U.S. clinics were juxtaposed with interviews with Russian mothers who could not obtain medicine or services their children desperately needed."[17] Such inversions often disconcerted Western visitors, who found their Russian friends not only denying, for example, that homelessness was a social problem outside of Russia (where it was an unwelcome novelty) but also going into raptures about the charm and femininity of Nancy Reagan after the Presidential visit of 1988. The inversion imperative was dominant in the "woman question," overpowering another post-Soviet imperative of Westernization. Since women's emancipation through paid employment had been a

---

[15] Ibid.

[16] Nancy Ries, *Russian Talk: Culture and Conversation during Perestroika* (Ithaca, 1997), p. 170.

[17] Ries, *Russian Talk*, p. 174.

Soviet credo, now, by the logic of inversion, it must be discredited. According to the new post-Soviet ethos, women should be encouraged to return to their "natural roles" as homemakers.[18]

"We must become different people" was the refrain Nancy Ries heard again and again in Moscow in 1990.[19] The 1990s was a decade in which individual Russians and other post-Soviet citizens were actively engaged in the project of self-transformation, and at the end of that decade Viktor Pelevin's runaway bestseller *Generation "P"* offered a bemused progress report. In Pelevin's black comedy, *imidzh* is all and identities are not just constructed but "false."[20] Pelevin's hero (whose very name is subject to post-Soviet renegotiation) has reinvented himself as an advertising *kopiraiter* and *krieitor,* but he has no faith in his own invention or anyone else's. All convictions and values are gone; it is just a matter of choosing a persona and projecting it to the world, so that even an apparent anti-Semite in Pelevin's story turns out to have no particular opinions about Jews, but is simply to be trying to impersonate a Russian patriot.[21] "New Post-Soviet Man," in Pelevin's portrayal, can identify himself only in terms of the products he consumes: each of these products carries its own marketing associations with particular character traits and types, and the sum of these produces "the impression of a real self (*lichnost'*)."[22]

For Pelevin's "Generation 'P'," advertising and television were the main guides to self-transformation. Advertising did indeed play a central role, both as a new occupational destination for the young and as a general instructor on mores. For example, a 1991 newspaper advertisement for a bank, illustrated with a photograph of a young man in a hurry, dressed in suit and tie, was captioned "New people." Its text read: "In the office of Sberbank, computers take the place of abacuses. And along with them, the new young generation of service-minded employees, offering advice, reducing the lines, learning to smile . . . They're the **New People . . .**"[23] Sberbank's emphasis on teaching people to smile was no exception. Smiling was part of basic training in the new MacDonald's that opened in Moscow at the beginning of the 1990s,[24] as well as being strongly emphasized in post-Soviet advice and etiquette books.[25]

[18] Ries, *Russian Talk*, p. 178.

[19] Ries, *Russian Talk*, p. 119.

[20] Viktor Pelevin, *Generation "P"* (Moscow: Vagrius, 2000). On its impact on the younger generation after its sensational publication in the summer of 1999, see James Cowley, "Gogol A Go-Go," *New York Times Magazine*, 23 January 2000, pp. 20–23.

[21] Pelevin, *Generation*, p. 122.

[22] Ibid., p. 113.

[23] *Moscow News*, 1991 no. 31, p. 11. (The ellipses and emphasis are in the original text.)

[24] Ries, *Russian Talk*, 118.

[25] Catriona Kelly, *Refining Russia: Advice Literature, Polite Culture, and Gender from Catherine to Yeltsin* (Oxford, 2001), p. 374.

Advice on behavior for the new man was in great demand and generously supplied. A whole series of newly published handbooks provided post-Soviet man with the tools for survival in the new world: dictionaries of marketing, banking, the stock exchange, entrepreneurship, international tourism (as important for the post-Soviet lifestyle as shopping), intellectual property, political parties and associations, civil society, and political science; guides to *kto est' kto* (*Who's Who*) in government, business, and "the scientific elite"; and even *biznes-sleng dlia 'novykh russkikh'* (business slang for "New Russians").[26] Dale Carnegie's *How to Win Friends and Influence People* (first published in the United States in 1937) went through sixty-eight editions in Russian from 1989 to 1997.[27] Norman Vincent Peale's *The Power of Positive Thinking* also had great success in the early 1990s, though Nancy Ries's intellectual acquaintances (who all read it, but maintained a critical distance) "let it be known [by their jokes and sighs] that they thought [Russian] negative thinking was powerful enough to encompass and absorb any instruction in positive thinking that could be offered." All the same, self-help and self-improvement programs mushroomed up in Moscow during perestroika, offering tips on the development of confidence and optimism.[28]

Confidence and optimism were useful attributes for overcoming the shock of transition, but more practical retooling was also necessary. New professions such as advertising, public relations, and real estate came into being. On 27 June 1991, *Izvestiia* reported an "unusual ceremony" in the Russian House of Soviets: "the official presentation of the new profession of social worker. This profession has never before existed in the USSR."[29] Private detectives were licensed as a profession for the first time in a 1992

---

[26] See, for example, *Slovar' delovogo cheloveka* (Moscow, 1992); *Delovoi mir Karelii: spravochnik biznesmena* (Petrozavodsk, 1992); *Marketing: tolkovyi terminologicheskii slovar'-spravochnik* (Moscow, 1991); *Moskovskii bankir: spravochnik* (Moscow, 1994); *Tolkovyi birzhevoi slovar'* (Moscow, 1996); *Tolkovyi slovar' predprinimatelia* (Moscow, 1993); *Kratkii slovar' tekhnologicheskikh terminov mezhdunarodnogo turizma* (Moscow, 1994); *Rossiia: Partii, assotsiatsii, soiuzy, kluby: Spravochnik* (Moscow, 1991); *Intellektual'naia sobstvennost': slovar'-spravochnik* (Moscow, 1995); L. M. Romanenko, *Grazhdanskoe obshchestvo: sotsiologicheskii slovar'-spravochnik* (Moscow, 1995); *Politologicheskii slovar'*, ed. V. F. Khalipov (Moscow, 1995); *Kto est' kto v Rossii* (Moscow, 1998); *Kto est' kto v politicheskoi nauke Rossii: spravochnik* (Moscow, 1996); *Nauchnaia elita: kto est' kto v Rossiiskoi akademii nauk* (Moscow, 1993); V. T. Ponomarev, *Biznes-sleng dlia "novykh russkikh": slovar'-spravochnik* (Donetsk, 1996). Thanks to June Farris, Slavic bibliographer at the University of Chicago, for the very useful "Select Lists of New Reference Titles: East Central and Southeastern Europe and Countries of the Former Soviet Union" that she has been circulating to Slavicists at the University since 1991, on which I have drawn extensively in this section.

[27] Kelly, *Refining Russia*, p. 373.

[28] Ries, *Russian Talk*, pp. 117–18.

[29] *Current Digest of the Post-Soviet Press* 43:26 (1991), p. 22.

law of the Russian Federation "On private detectives and bodyguards."[30] In 1996 Yeltsin issued Presidential Decree No. 1044 mandating the revival and development of psychoanalysis.[31] New professions in turn called for the development of new educational institutions to train them. A Higher Advertising School opened in Moscow in 1995; and in the same year a new Institute of Security Services for Business offered a five-year course training "business security services managers."[32] In addition to learning "basic legal and economic disciplines, English, and information collection and analysis," students would also be instructed on "develop[ing] their physical strength."[33]

For teachers and school principals in elementary and middle schools it was a struggle to revamp curricula so as to give pupils an education appropriate to the post-Soviet world. In fact, it was generally the pupils themselves who led the way in adapting to the new mores. A 1995 report noted that children were no longer playing the equivalent of cowboys and Indians ("Cossacks and bandits") but now preferred to take the roles of "militants and special-forces men." Girls played at beauty contests instead of playing house. "Almost everywhere the innocuous jump rope and hopscotch have given way to more mercantile games. The children play at being racketeers, robbers and shopkeepers—using real money . . ."[34]

Much of the effort of post-Soviet reimagination of self went towards becoming Western and modern—"a normal, civilized person" without the shameful distinguishing marks of a *sovok,* the contemptuous term for a standard-issue Soviet citizen that came into vogue at the beginning of the 1990s.[35] One of the things that characterized a normal civilized person was expertise about sex, a topic whose public discussion had been always been censored in Soviet times on the grounds of morality and good taste. "No sex here! (*U nas seksa net!*)" was the plaintive cry from a Russian audience member at the taping of a television special hosted by Phil Donahue and Vladimir Pozner and touted as a Soviet-American "space bridge" in 1987. As Eliot Borenstein has pointed out, this statement was almost literally

---

[30] *Moscow News*, 1994 no. 1, p. 15.

[31] David Bennett "Guilt as Capital: Psychoanalysis and the New Russians," *Journal for the Psychoanalysis of Culture and Society* 6:1 (2001), p. 123. According to Professor Reshetnikov of the East European Institute for Psychoanalysis in St. Petersburg, Academician D. S. Likhachev was the inspirer of this legislative initiative: *Journal for the Psychoanalysis of Culture and Society* 6:2 (2001), p. 357 (Letter to the Editor).

[32] *Current Digest of the Post-Soviet Press*, 47:16 (1995), pp. 21–22, from *Izvestiia*, 18 April 1995, p. 2.

[33] *Current Digest of the Post-Soviet Press* 47:48 (1995), pp. 20–21.

[34] *Novaia ezhednevnaia gazeta* no. 36, in *Current Digest of the Post-Soviet Press* 47:39 (1995), p. 20.

[35] See entry in V. M. Mokienko and T. G. Nikitina, *Tolkovyi slovar' iazyka Sovdepii* (St. Petersburg, 1998), p. 564.

true of *discourses* about sex, and if, as Foucault suggested in his *History of Sexuality*, modernity is characterized by "a drive to produce more and more discourse about sex," post-Soviet Russia certainly provided a spectacular example of breakneck Foucauldian modernization.[36]

In addition to the translation of Western pornography and sex-instruction classics such as Alex Comfort's *The Joy of Sex*, published in a large format luxury edition with full-page color illustrations in 1991,[37] a number of Russian magazines specifically devoted to the topic appeared. *SPID-Info*,[38] one of the first, started off in 1989 as a publication with the (still quasi-Soviet) purpose of enlightening the public about AIDS and venereal disease, but it soon changed its name (to *SPEED-INFO* in Latin letters) and mutated into "a veritable encyclopedia of sexual life" offering information and consultations with professionals on sex and all its social, economic, and cultural manifestations—a journal that in Borenstein's words "exists not to provoke sexual desire but to provoke the verbalization of desire."[39] Hardcore pornography was available, too, including the journal *Eshche*, which Borenstein reads as addressed specifically to "Soviet" people who now need to adapt to a post-Soviet world: "its erotic adventurers are truck drivers and collective farm workers, and its stories about sexual experimentation in other countries are told from the point of view of the bemused ex-Soviet sex tourist."[40] Other publications celebrated a variety of forms of sexual activity previously regarded as deviant or shameful, recommended the newly discovered gay lifestyle and exhorted readers to enjoy masturbation without guilt.[41]

Nor was the new interest in sex wholly a matter of learning to talk about it. Prostitution (with foreigners, for hard currency) became a boom industry in the big cities in the late 1980s, and Todorovsky's film on the topic, *Inter-devochhka* [1989] (based on a 1988 novel by Vladimir Kunin) provoked enormous discussion.[42] Large numbers of young Russian and Ukrainian women joined the international sex trade in the 1990s, working in many countries of Europe and the Middle East.[43] Economic neces-

---

[36] Eliot Borenstein, "*About That*: Deploying and Deploring Sex in Postsoviet Russia," *Studies in Twentieth Century Literature* 24:1 (2000), p. 53.

[37] Catriona Kelly, *Refining Russia*, pp. 369–70. Komfort, *Radost' seksa*.

[38] SPID is the Russian acronym for AIDS.

[39] Borenstein, "*About That*," p. 60.

[40] Borenstein, "*About That*," pp. 61–62.

[41] Elena Omel'chenko, "New Dimensions of the Sexual Universe: Sexual Discourses in Russian Youth Magazines," in Chris Corrin, ed., *Gender and Identity in Central and Eastern Europe* (London, 1999), pp. 99–133.

[42] For a survey of different interpretations, see Borenstein, "*About That*," pp. 65–66.

[43] See, for example, *New York Times*, 11 January 1998, pp. 1, 6; Igor Nekhames, "Seks-rabyni na vyvoz (Sex Slaves for Export)," *Literaturnaia gazeta*, 2004 no. 15 (14–20 April), p. 5. Lukas Moodysson's 2002 film *Lilya 4-Ever* also deals with this topic.

sity surely played a role in this, and no doubt many of the girls were misled about the nature of the foreign employment that was being offered. But there seems to have been an element of post-Soviet reinvention of self in the eagerness of the young women to take these opportunities. Like advertising and public relations, the international sex trade was one of the new occupational possibilities of the post-Soviet era.

At the other end of the moral spectrum, but almost equally exotic for many former Soviet citizens, was the rediscovery of religion and spirituality. Post-Soviet Russians (re-)embracing Orthodoxy needed help here, too, since few of them knew much about Christianity, Orthodox ritual, church hierarchy and organization, or Old Church Slavonic. Handbooks and guides to Orthodoxy quickly appeared on the market, as well as mass-produced icons, religious medals, inspirational texts, and other artifacts of Orthodox spirituality.[44] Church attendance briefly rose sharply. Reporting on the perestroika period, Ries noted "the widespread abandoning of Communist Party membership, which seemed rampant in 1990, and the simultaneous adoption by many former party members of Orthodox Christian affiliation and practice; it was as if they exchanged, overnight, one badge of legitimacy for another."[45]

The world of popular spirituality blossomed, not to mention the peculiar science of the recovered Russian soul and spiritual mission that goes under the name of *kul'turologiia*.[46] Handbooks on spells and demons appeared,[47] and there was "an explosion of demand for 'alternative' healers: psychics, sorcerers, wizards, 'astrologer-psychoanalysts,' bioenergetic therapists, occultist healers of various kinds—some operating under an Orthodox Church front, using prayers, icons and crosses in rituals promising to heal by 'casting out evil spirits.' " Some ESP experts, astrologers, and self-styled sorcerers (*kolduny*) won a substantial following on national television. Advertisements promised to "Get Rid of the Evil Eye and Wasting Diseases Caused by Spells," and self-taught analysts offered "curbside consultations to shoppers and pedestrians on the streets of Moscow and St. Petersburg."[48]

---

[44] Recent guides include *Khristianstvo: slovar'* (Moscow, 1994), Dmitrii Pokrovskii, *Slovar' tserkovnykh terminov* (Moscow, 1995); *Religioznye ob"edineniia Rossiiskoi Federatsii: spravochnik* (Moscow, 1996); *Utrachennye sviatyni Iaroslavlia: Spravochnik-putevoditel'* (Iaroslavl, 1999); *Pravoslavie: bibliograficheskii ukazatel' knig na russkom i tserkovnoslavianskom iazykakh za 1918–1993 gg.* (Moscow, 1999); and T. S. Oleinikova, *Slovar' tserkovno-slavianskikh slov* (Moscow, 1997).

[45] Ries, *Russian Talk*, p. 177.

[46] *Kul'turologiia: kratkii slovar'*, 2nd ed. (St. Petersburg, 1995).

[47] Elena Grushko and Iurii Medvedev, *Slovar' russkikh sueverii, zaklinanii, primet i poverii* (Nizhnii Novgorod, 1995); *Russkii demonologicheskii slovar'* (St. Petersburg, 1995).

[48] Bennett, "Guilt as Capital," p. 134.

Recovering Russianness was a major preoccupation of the 1990s, coexisting uneasily with the assumption of modern, Western identities. The conflict played itself out dramatically in the realm of language. The influx of foreign words, as well as youth slang and prison argot, into journalistic vocabulary produced strong reaction from defenders of Russian language purity, who spoke of "perversion" and "violation" of the language. "Do our cities not resemble cities subjugated by alien countries, their streets made gaudy by foreign language advertisements and signs, not infrequently appearing in Latin letters?" asked one critic indignantly.[49] Even teenagers sometimes registered the older generation's disorientation in the face of the Western invasion: as one told an interviewer in the early 1990s, "My parents are already in shock that there is no more Russian culture—that's already done and gone with [sic]. Everything is Western, and there is nothing left of our own."[50]

Still, there was an older culture to recover. In 1990 Solzhenitsyn published a remarkable *Russian Dictionary of Language Expansion* listing words that in the Soviet period had disappeared "prematurely" from the language and "still deserve the right to live."[51] Some Russians felt the same nostalgia for the customs of the Russian nobility, and their desire to inform themselves (and, often, claim noble descent) led to a boom in publications on its history, customs, and membership.[52] Those wishing to acquire "the manners of a Russian Gentleman" could consult Olga Muranova's *How the Russian Gentleman was Brought Up*[53] or join the English Club, a renowned Imperial institution, resurrected in Moscow in 1996, which organizes balls, picnics, and banquets in traditional style.[54]

The state shared the problem of individual citizens in establishing a new identity and/or recovering an old. The beginning of the 1990s was a period of wholesale changing of symbols. Statues of Lenin and Dzerzhinsky were demonstratively pulled down; Leningrad recovered its old name of St. Petersburg by popular vote (though it was close); and the state got a new name, a new flag, and a new emblem (with the double-headedeagle and St. George accentuating ties to the Imperial past). To

[49] Michael S. Gorham, "*Natsiia ili snikerizatsiia?* Identity and Perversion in the Language Debates of Late- and Post-Soviet Russia," *Russian Review* 59:4 (2000), pp. 621–22. Quotation from Lev Skvortsov, Rector of Gorky Literary Institute.

[50] Fran Markowitz, *Coming of Age in Post-Soviet Russia* (Urbana and Chicago, 2000), p. 63.

[51] Gorham, "*Natsiia*," p. 626.

[52] See, for example, *Rodnaia starina: slova, terminy, obrazy* (Moscow, 1995), *Dvorianstvo rossiiskoi imperii: Spravochnik* (Moscow, 1995), E. A. Kniazev, *Dvorianskii kalendar': spravochnaia rodoslovnaia kniga rossiiskogo dvorianstva* (St. Petersburg, 1996).

[53] On this 1995 publication, see Kelly, *Refining Russia*, p. 378.

[54] Helena Goscilo, "The New Russians. Introduction: A Label Designed to Libel versus Meimetic Modeling and Parthenogenesis," *Russian Review* 62:1 (2003), p. 5.

be sure, change only went so far: efforts to remove Lenin from his Mausoleum were unsuccessful, and after much debate the Soviet national anthem was retained under Putin, with words revised by their original author, Sergei Mikhalkov.[55]

Yeltsin wanted a new dominant "idea of Russia," and even conducted a public search for one in 1996–97. The winner, Guri Sudakov, stressed the alienness to Russia of materialism and individualism, noting that "Russian national character was not formed on the basis of market activity," which in Western Europe made freedom and law so important; instead, Russia had "society, Motherland, glory and power."[56] But echoes from the past crept in here too, despite the clear indications that the new Russian idea should be quite different from the old Soviet one. Victory in the Great Patriotic War was often cited by contributors to the "Russian idea" search; and the opinion "that Russia, having tackled problems of incalculable difficulty in the previous decades, could surmount any obstacle" surely owed something to Stalin's old dictum that there were no fortresses Bolsheviks could not storm.[57] By 2001 Putin was openly reclaiming elements of the Soviet past: "Is there nothing good to remember about the Soviet period of our country? Was there nothing but Stalin's prison camps and repression? And in that case what are we going to do about Dunaevski, Sholokhov, Shostakovich, Korolev, and our achievements in space? What are we going to do aobut Yuri Gagarin's flight?"[58]

For many Russians, it was hard to recover the sense of being Russian rather than Soviet and even harder to accept the loss of empire that required this. As one teenager put it, "The hardest thing I had to get used to was saying 'Russia.' One of the very first things we learned was where we lived—in the Union of Soviet Socialist Republics, the USSR, the *Soyuz*. And then it was Russia, Russia, Russia."[59] In the words of political scientist Ksenia Mialo, "during the Soviet period, it seemed, we all became so intermingled and denationalized—especially Russians—that we were no longer aware of our own identity and distinctiveness."[60] Admittedly, other observers came up with different conclusions: the anthropologist Dale Pesman, for example, found a powerful and recognizable discourse of the uniqueness of the "Russian soul" out in Irkutsk in the early 1990s.[61] But

---

[55] Robert Service, *Russia: Experiment with a People* (Cambridge, Mass., 2003), pp. 211–12. The whole process of symbolic change is well surveyed in Service, chapter 13 ("Symbols for Russia").

[56] Service, *Russia*, pp. 184–85.

[57] Service, *Russia*, p. 184.

[58] Quoted in Service, *Russia*, p. 195.

[59] Markowitz, *Coming of Age*, p. 145.

[60] *Current Digest of the Post-Soviet Press* 45:17 (1993), p. 12.

[61] Dale Pesman, *Russia and Soul: An Exploration* (Ithaca, 2000).

"the Russian question" of the 1990s had to do with a specific kind of shared identity, one related to the state. According to an opinion survey in 1995, 75% of citizens of Russian Federation regretted the passing of the USSR and saw no merit in having an independent Russian state. A year later, only half the respondents felt themselves to be "citizens of Russia," though the proportion had grown to two-thirds by 2000.[62] To be a citizen of the Soviet Union, after all, had meant belonging to one of the world's two superpowers; to be a citizen of Russia meant nothing so gratifying. It hurt (*obidno*) to see how Russia, "which was formerly such a great state . . . has fallen apart, and . . . become a country of the third world. Well, not really, we're not really third world, things are more or less normal, but we're not the Russian empire."[63] And the ingratitude hurt, both that of the seceding non-Russian republics of the former Soviet Union and that of Eastern Europe ("After all we have done to help them!").[64]

For the millions of ethnic Russians who found themselves living outside the Russian Federation at the time of the break-up of the Soviet Union, the identity problem had a more concrete and acute meaning. They had involuntarily become part of a new ethnic identity group: "Russian-speaking population in the Near Abroad."[65] If they tried to move to Russia, they faced formidable problems or relocation in terms of housing and employment. If they remained, they were likely to face marginalization at best and hostility at worst.

With the old Soviet life retreating into the past, the term *khomo sovetikus* entered popular speech, used ironically.[66] Homo Sovieticus was, almost by definition, somebody other than the speaker, for few would now admit having been sincere in their sometime impersonations of New Soviet Man. In the 1990s it was just as important to purge one's speech of Sovietisms as it had been to master them in the 1920s, and a handy dictionary—the *Tolkovyi slovar' Sovdepii*—appeared to help identify give-away terms and usages.[67] At the same time, there was surely nostalgia

[62] Service, *Russia*, p. 116.

[63] Markowitz, *Coming of Age*, p. 152 (adolescent respondent).

[64] Ries, *Russian Talk*, p. 104.

[65] David D. Laitin, Identity Formation. *The Russian-Speaking Populations in the Near Abroad* (Ithaca, 1998), p. 33 and passim. As of 1989, there were over 25 million Russians living outside the Russian Republic but within the USSR: *Demograficheskie perspektivy Rossii* (Moscow, 1993), p. 38.

[66] From *Tolkovyi slovar' russkogo iazyka kontsa XX v.* Note that in Aleksandr Zinoviev's original use of the term, it was rendered *gomo sovetikus*: see A. Zinoviev, *Gomo sovetikus* (Lausanne, 1982).

[67] V. M. Mokienko and T. G. Nikitina, *Tolkovyi slovar' iazyka Sovdepii* (St. Petersburg, 1998), and see also N. A. Kupina, *Totalitarnyi iazyk: Slovar' i rechevye reaktsii* (Ekaterinburg-Perm, 1995), and *Tolkovyi slovar' russkogo iazyka kontsa XX v.* It is interesting to

in this dictionary of Soviet language, comparable to that fueling the popularity in the mid 1990s of the long-running television show *Staraia kvartira* (The Old Apartment), a celebration of artifacts of Soviet material and popular culture.

At the opposite pole from Homo Soveticus were the "New Russians," the label bestowed on post-Soviet *nouveaux riches*. This group had egregious and closely watched problems of identity and self-fashioning. On the one hand, as nascent capitalists, they could be regarded as the vanguard of Russia's transformation; on the other hand, Sudakov (winner of the "Russian idea" competition) was not alone in thinking that the market values epitomized by the New Russians were inimical to essential Russianness. Popular perceptions of New Russians were mixed—"on the one hand, they are people who have caught the wave of change . . . ; on the other hand, they are corrupt, boorish, and, unforgivably, illicitly rich"— with the negative tending to predominate.[68] New Russians became the butt of endless jokes, rescuing the endangered genre of the *anekdot* after the collapse of its favorite target, the Soviet state. Adding sharpness to the "New Russians" jokes "is the perception that the worst of them are not Russians at all. . . . The frequency of Jewish and Caucasian protagonists . . . indicates that the use of the word 'Russian' in the phrase 'New Russian' is often an ironic reference to the perceived usurpation of Russian wealth by non-Russians."[69]

The New Russians were new, "not only to us . . . [but] to themselves as well."[70] Analysts as well as raconteurs had a field day with them. They were said to turn to the new glossy magazines to learn how to be "true careerists (*nastoiashchie kar'eristy*)"—the term, inverting a discarded Soviet value judgement, used for their businessmen readers by post-Soviet journals like *Kar'era* and *Profil'*.[71] Their self-invention (one anthropologist reports) "necessitates endless performative rituals—from bodily acts (appearance, clothes, gestures, movements, way of walking, manners, voice, style of drinking) to speech acts (types of utterances, genres of

---

compare these projects, the work of professional sociolinguists, with the analyses of postrevolutionary changes in the Russian language that appeared in the 1920s, for example, Selishchev, *Iazyk revolutsionnogo epokhi*. This time round, the linguists' attention focuses not only on the new language (*Tolkovyi slovar' russkogo iazyka kontsa XX v*) but also on the old one (Mokienko and Nikitina; Kupina).

[68] Harley Balzer, "Routinization of the New Russians?" *Russian Review* 62:1 (2003), p. 16.

[69] Ibid., 46–47.

[70] Seth Graham, "The Wages of Syncretism," *Russian Review* 62:1 (2003), p. 38, quoted in a 1995 article by Aleksei Levinson.

[71] Alexei Yurchak, "Entrepreneurial Ethic and the Spirit of 'True Careerism'," *Russian Review* 62:1 (2003), 73.

speech, use of English and of obscenities) . . ."[72] They "ponder the pages of Vogue and feel they should fashion themselves as better than their Western equivalents, because after all they are Russians, and in the vanguard. Hence the importance of styling salons and gyms, where physically new bodies are being pummeled and cosseted into shape."[73] They built—without necessarily occupying—pretentious villas with gables, turrets, and towers whose "thrusting verticality" strikes one observer as "at once ambitious and embattled."[74]

Not surprisingly, our old friend Ostap Bender the trickster made his appearance in jokes and discussion of New Russians.[75] New Russians, the jokes implied, were tricksters because their wealth was illegitimately acquired, because of the cunning that enabled them to seize the opportunities inherent in state collapse. But wait: was it not *Old* Russians who were the tricksters? Was it not a specific quality of *Soviet* life, according to Sinyavsky, to stamp the psyche with the resourcefulness of an "old fox"?[76] And were Ostap Bender's adventures not "*the* prerequisite for understanding Soviet life," according to Dale Pesman's informants in Omsk?[77]

This was not simply a case of "*Plus ça change* . . ." Of all tricksters, Bender was the one whose special talent was to pick up the language and practices of the new order. In a situation where nobody felt like a native, he performed like one. He could pick up New Russian with the same virtuosity that he once learned to speak Bolshevik; in the transition of 1991–92 he illuminated not just Soviet mores but also, remarkably, "our Russian *dusha*."[78] On the road to new post-Soviet identity, the impostor, Janus-faced, was once again in the vanguard.

---

[72] Yurchak, "Entrepreneurial Ethic," p. 80.

[73] Caroline Humphrey, *The Unmaking of Soviet Life* (Ithaca, 2002), p. 181.

[74] Humphrey, *Unmaking*, pp. 200–201.

[75] See Mark Lipovetsky, "New Russians as a Cultural Myth," *Russian Review* 62:1 (2003), pp. 61–67; Graham, "Wages," p. 49.

[76] Andrei Sinyavsky, *Soviet Civilization: A Cultural History*, trans. Joanne Turnbull with the assistance of Nikolai Formozov (New York, 1988), pp. 174–75.

[77] Pesmen, *Russia and Soul*, p. 204.

[78] Pesman, *Russia and Soul*, p. 204 (citing informants).

Suggested Further Reading

Alexopoulos, Golfo. "Portrait of a Con Artist as a Soviet Man." *Slavic Review* 57:4 (1998).

———. *Stalin's Outcasts: Aliens, Citizens, and the Soviet State, 1926–1936.* Ithaca, 2003.

Andrle, V. *Workers in Stalin's Russia: Industrialization and Social Change in a Planned Economy.* New York, 1988.

Ball, Alan M. *Russia's Last Capitalists: The Nepmen, 1921–1929.* Berkeley, 1987.

Bertaux, Daniel, Paul Thompson, and Anna Rotkirch, eds. *On Living through Soviet Russia.* London, 2004.

Boym, Svetlana. *Common Places: Mythologies of Everyday Life in Russia.* Cambridge, Mass., 1994.

Brooks, Jeffrey. "Revolutionary Lives: Public Identities in *Pravda* during the 1920s." In Stephen White, ed., *New Directions in Soviet History.* New York, 1992.

———. *Thank You, Comrade Stalin: Soviet Public Culture from Revolution to Cold War.* Princeton, 2000.

Clark, Katerina. *Petersburg, Crucible of Cultural Revolution.* Cambridge, Mass.: 1995.

———. *The Soviet Novel: History as Ritual.* Chicago, 1981.

Davies, Sarah. *Popular Opinion in Stalin's Russia: Terror, Propaganda, and Dissent, 1934–1941.* Cambridge, 1997.

Durham, Vera S. *In Stalin's Time: Middle-Class Values in Soviet Fiction.* Cambridge, 1976.

Edele, Mark. "Strange Young Men in Stalin's Moscow: The Birth and Life of the Stiliagi, 1945–1953." *Jahrbücher für Geschichte Osteuropas* 50 (2002).

Engel, Barbara A., and Anastasia Posadskaya-Vanderbek, eds. *A Revolution of Their Own: Voices of Women in Soviet History.* Boulder, 1997.

Figes, Orlando, and Boris Kolonitskii. *Interpreting the Russian Revolution: The Language and Symbols of 1917.* New Haven, 1999.

Fitzpatrick, Sheila. *The Cultural Front: Power and Culture in Revolutionary Russia.* Ithaca, 1992.

———. *Everyday Stalinism. Ordinary Life in Extraordinary Times: Soviet Russia in the 1930s.* New York, 1999.

———. *Stalin's Peasants: Resistance and Survival in the Russian Village after Collectivization.* New York, 1994.

Fitzpatrick, Sheila, ed. "Petitions and Denunciations in Russian and Soviet History." Special issue of *Russian History* 24:1–2 (1997).

———. *Stalinism: New Directions.* London, 2000.

Fitzpatrick, Sheila, and Robert Gellately, eds. *Accusatory Practices: Denunciation in Modern European History, 1789–1989.* Chicago, 1997.

Fitzpatrick, Sheila, and Yuri Slezkine, eds. *In the Shadow of Revolution: Life Stories of Russian Women from 1917 to the Second World War.* Princeton, 2000.

Garros, Véronique, Natalia Korenevskaia, and Thomas Lahusen, eds. *Intimacy and Terror: Soviet Diaries of the 1930s.* New York, 1995.

Gerasimova, Katerina. "Public Privacy in the Soviet Communal Apartment." In David Crowley and Susan E. Reid, eds., *Socialist Spaces: Sites of Everyday Life in the Eastern Bloc.* Oxford, 2002.

Gorsuch, Anne E. *Youth in Revolutionary Russia: Enthusiasts, Bohemians, Delinquents.* Bloomington, 2000.

Halfin, Igal. *From Darkness to Light: Class Consciousness and Salvation in Revolutionary Russia.* Pittsburgh, 2000.

———. *Terror in My Soul: Communist Autobiographies on Trial.* Cambridge, Mass., 2003.

Hellbeck, Jochen. "Fashioning the Stalinist Soul: The Diary of Stepan Podlubnyi, 1931–39." In Fitzpatrick, ed., *Stalinism: New Directions.*

———. "Self-Realization in the Stalinist System: Two Soviet Diaries of the 1930s." In David L. Hoffmann and Yanni Kotsonis, eds., *Russian Modernity: Politics, Knowledge, Practices.* Basingstoke, Hants., 2000.

Hessler, Julie. *A Social History of Soviet Trade.* Princeton, 2004.

Hoffman, David L. *Peasant Metropolis: Social Identities in Moscow, 1928–1941.* Ithaca, 1994.

———. *Stalinist Values: The Cultural Norms of Soviet Modernity, 1917–1941.* Ithaca, 2003.

Holmes, Larry. "Part of History: The Oral Record and Moscow's Model School No. 25, 1931–1937." *Slavic Review* 56:2 (1997).

Holquist, Peter. *Making War, Forging Revolution: Russia's Continuum of Crisis, 1914–1921.* Cambridge, Mass., 2002.

Kelly, Catriona. *Refining Russia: Advice Literature, Polite Culture, and Gender from Catherine to Yeltsin.* Oxford, 2001.

Kelly, Catriona, and David Shepherd, eds. *Constructing Russian Culture in the Age of Revolution, 1881–1940.* Oxford, 1998.

———. *Russian Cultural Studies: An Introduction.* Oxford, 1998.

Kharkhordin, Oleg. *The Collective and the Individual in Russia: A Study of Practices.* Berkeley, 1999.

Kimerling, Elise. "Civil Rights and Social Policy in Soviet Russia, 1918–1936." *Russian Review* 41:1 (1982).

Koenker, Diane. "Men against Women on the Shop Floor in Early Soviet Russia: Gender and Class in the Socialist Workplace." *American Historical Review* 100:5 (1995).

———. "Fathers against Sons/Sons against Fathers: The Problem of Generations in the Early Soviet Workplace." *Journal of Modern History* 73:4 (2001).

Kotkin, Stephen. *Magnetic Mountain: Stalinism as a Civilization.* Berkeley: 1995.

Krylova, Anna. "Healers of Wounded Souls: The Crisis of Private Life in Soviet Literature and Society, 1944–1946." *Journal of Modern History* 73:2 (2001).

Lahusen, Thomas. *Life Writes the Book: Real Socialism and Socialist Realism in Stalin's Russia.* Ithaca, 1997.

Lebina, N. B. *Povsednevnaia zhizn' sovetskogo goroda 1920/1930 gody.* St. Petersburg, 1999.

Lebina, N. B., and A. N. Chistikov. *Obyvatel' i reformy: Kartiny posvsednevnoi zhizn gorozhan.* St. Petersburg, 2003.

Lemon, Alaina. *Between Two Fires: Gypsy Performance and Romani Memory from Pushkin to Postsocialism.* Durham, N.C., 2000.

Liljeström, Marianne, Arja Rosenholm, and Irina Savkina, eds. *Models of Self: Russian Women's Autobiographical Texts.* Helsinki, 2000.

Livshin, A. Ia., and I. B. Orlov, compilers. *Pis'ma vo vlast', 1917–1927: Zaiavleniia, zhaloby, donosy, pis'ma v gosudarstvennye struktury i bol'shevistskim vozhdiam.* Moscow, 1998.

Livshin, A. Ia., I. B. Orlov, and O. V. Khlevniuk, compilers. *Pis'ma vo vlast', 1928–1939: Zaiavleniia, zhaloby, donosy, pis'ma v gosudarstvennye struktury i sovetskim vozhdiam.* Moscow, 2002.

Lovell, Stephen. *Summerfolk: A History of the Dacha, 1710–2000.* Ithaca, 2003.

Lovell, Stephen, Alena V. Ledeneva, and Andrei Rogachevskii, eds. *Bribery and Blat in Russia: Negotiating Reciprocity from the Middle Ages to the 1990s.* London, 2000.

Lugovskaya, Nina. *The Diary of a Soviet Schoolgirl, 1932–1937,* trans. by Joanne Turnbull. Moscow, 2003.

Moine, Nathalie. "Passportisation, Statistique des Migrations et Contrôle de l'Identité sociale." *Cahiers du Monde Russe* 38:4 (1997).

Naiman, Eric. *Sex in Public: The Incarnation of Early Soviet Ideology.* Princeton, 1997.

Nérard, François-Xavier. *5% de Vérité: La Dénonciation dans l'URSS de Staline.* Paris, 2004.

Osokina, Elena. *Ierarkhiia potrebleniia: O zhizni liudei v usloviiakh stalinskogo snabzheniia, 1928–1935 gg.* Moscow, 1993.

———. *Our Daily Bread: Socialist Distribution and the Art of Survival in Stalin's Russia, 1927–1941,* ed. and trans. by Kate S.Transchel and Greta Bucher. Armonk, N.Y., 1999.

Pesman, Dale. *Russia and Soul: An Exploration.* Ithaca, 2000.

Ries, Nancy. *Russian Talk: Culture and Conversation during Perestroika.* Ithaca: 1997.

Rossman, Jeffrey. "The Teikovo Cotton Workers' Strike of April 1932: Class, Gender and Identity Politics in Stalin's Russia." *Russian Review* 56:1 (1997).

Siegelbaum, Lewis H. *Stakhanovism and the Politics of Productivity in the USSR, 1935–1941.* Cambridge, 1988.

Siegelbaum, Lewis, and Andrei Sokolov, eds. *Stalinism as a Way of Life: A Narrative in Documents.* New Haven, 2000.

Siegelbaum, Lewis, and Ronald Suny, eds. *Making Workers Soviet: Power, Class and Identity.* Ithaca, 1994.

Slezkine Yuri. *Arctic Mirrors: Russia and the Small Peoples of the North.* Ithaca, 1994.

Steinberg, Mark D. *Proletarian Imagination: Self, Modernity, and the Sacred in Russia, 1910–1925.* Ithaca, 2002.

Studer, Brigitte, Berthold Unfried, and Irène Herrmann, eds. *Parler de Soi Sous Staline: La Construction Identitaire dans le Communisme des Années Trente.* Paris, 2002.

Tikhonov, V. I., V. S. Tiazhel'nikova, and I. F. Iushin. *Lishenie izbiratel'nykh prav v Moskve v 1920–1930-e gody: Novye arkhivnye materialy i metody obrabotki.* Moscow, 1998.

Tomoff, Kiril. " 'Most Respected Comrade . . .': Patrons, Clients, Brokers and Unofficial Networks in the Stalinist Musical World." *Contemporary European History* 11:1 (2002).

Utekhin, Il'ia. *Ocherki kommunal'nogo byta.* Moscow, 1998.

Viola, Lynne. *Peasant Rebels under Stalin: Collectivization and the Culture of Peasant Resistance.* New York, 1996.

Vikhavainen, Timo, ed. *Normy i tsennosti povsednevnoi zhizn: stanovlenie sotsialisticheskogo obraza zhizni v Rossii (1920–1939 gg.)* St. Petersburg, 2000.

Vitukhnovskaia, M., ed. *Na korme vremeni: Interv'iu s leningradtsami 1930-kh godov.* St. Petersburg, 2000.

Weiner, Amir, *Making Sense of War: The Second World War and the Fate of the Bolshevik Revolution.* Princeton, 2001.

Werth, Nicolas, ed. *Être Communiste en URSS sous Staline.* Paris, 1981.

Zubkova, Elena. *Russia after the War: Hopes, Illusions, and Disappointments, 1945–1957,* ed. and trans. by Hugh Ragsdale. Armonk, N.Y., 1998.

Index

abortion, 173, 225, 251
Abramova (KPK official), 247, 248
accountants, 66, 115, 119, 122, 123, 276–77, 298
activists, 48, 116, 119, 129, 135, 140, 147. See also *obshchestvennitsy*
Adamova-Sliozberg, O. L., 132, 133
adoption, 16, 66–67, 108, 111–12, 191, 258
advertising, 308, 310, 312
affirmative action, 5, 7, 39, 134, 143. See also social mobility; *vydvizhenie*
Agranov, Ia. S., 186, 190, 197
agricultural laborers, 37, 77, 103, 109–12
AKhRR (Association of Artists of Revoutionary Russia), 188
Aleksandrov, D. A., 185
Alexopoulos, Golfo, 268, 274
Alianskaia, B. M., 147
aliens, alien elements. See "social aliens"
Andzhievskaia, Anna, 136
Angelina, P. N., 129, 131, 136, 143, 149
ankety, 15, 16, 17(Fig. 2), 44–45, 80–81, 104, 130
"anti-cosmopolitan" campaign, 23
anti-Semitism, 23, 24, 238, 286, 289–99, 308
archives, Soviet, 7–8, 129, 155, 180, 186, 188
Arendt, Hannah, 222
army, Soviet. See Red Army
artisans, 31, 33, 77, 95
autobiographies (*avtobiografii*), 5, 15, 16, 19, 45, 91–92, 104, 130. See also life-stories; memoirs; *testimonios*
Averbakh, L. L., 65n.43, 189, 191

Babel, I. E., 191
Bagritskii, E. G., 191
Bakhtin, M. M., 265
Balashova, A. I., 140, 147
Baltic States, 24. See also Latvia
Bardin, I. P., 288
batrak, batrachka. See agricultural laborers
Bauman, K. Ia., 193

Bazeleva, N. P., 131
Beaverbrook, Lord, 143
Bednyi, Demian, 303
Belskaia, M. K., 126, 131–32, 137, 138, 146–47
Bender, Ostap, 20–21, 23, 267–68, 269(Fig. 10), 270, 271, 276, 278, 279, 281, 282, 283, 285–86, 298, 299–300, 317
besprizornye, 31, 95, 175. See also orphans
bigamy, 253
black market. See "second economy"
blat 161, 183, 184, 200, 236, 270, 284–85, 287; definition of, 284
Bogdan, V, A., 131, 134, 137, 142, 145, 148, 151, 152
Bolshevik Party. See Communist Party of the Soviet Union; Old Bolsheviks
Boltanski, Luc, 237
Bonner, Elena, 137
Borenstein, Eliot, 310, 311
Borkov, G. A., 196
Bourdieu, Pierre, 29
bourgeois, bourgeoisie, 4, 19, 24, 29, 30, 31, 32, 45–46, 57–62, 73, 93, 97, 103, 142, 143, 148, 291
Boym, Svetlana, 167
Brezhnev era, 25, 186, 289
Budagian, Z. S., 141
Bukharin, N. I., 21, 100n.27, 182, 185, 186, 195, 197–98, 211
Bulgakov, M. A., 186, 194, 272–73
bureaucracy, 53n.5, 66, 104, 112(Fig.4), 155, 156, 177, 184, 185, 201–2, 207, 237, 239, 268, 270, 272, 275–76, 287, 288–89. See also file-selves
Burmistrova, Ekaterina, 157–58
Bushueva, A. E., 140
Buskova, M. T., 147
byvshie (formerly privileged people), 34, 46, 57, 58, 60, 161, 171, 199, 268

cartoons, caricatures, 2(Fig.1), 16, 17(Fig.2), 35, 79(Fig.3), 112(Fig.4), 168–69